Information Technology for Retail

GIRDHAR JOSHI

OXFORD
UNIVERSITY PRESS

OXFORD
UNIVERSITY PRESS

YMCA Library Building, Jai Singh Road, New Delhi 110001

Oxford University Press is a department of the University of Oxford.
It furthers the University's objective of excellence in research, scholarship,
and education by publishing worldwide in

Oxford   New York
Auckland   Cape Town   Dar es Salaam   Hong Kong   Karachi
Kuala Lumpur   Madrid   Melbourne   Mexico City   Nairobi
New Delhi   Shanghai   Taipei   Toronto

With offices in
Argentina   Austria   Brazil   Chile   Czech Republic   France   Greece
Guatemala   Hungary   Italy   Japan   Poland   Portugal   Singapore
South Korea   Switzerland   Thailand   Turkey   Ukraine   Vietnam

Oxford is a registered trade mark of Oxford University Press
in the UK and in certain other countries.

Published in India
by Oxford University Press

© Oxford University Press 2009

The moral rights of the author/s have been asserted.

Database right Oxford University Press (maker)

First published 2009

Third-party website addresses mentioned in this book are provided
by Oxford University Press in good faith and for information only.
Oxford University Press disclaims any responsibility for the material contained therein.

ISBN-13: 978-0-19-569796-4
ISBN-10: 0-19-569796-0

Typeset in Baskerville
by Le Studio Graphique, Gurgaon 122001
Printed in India by Chaman Enterprises, Delhi 110002
and published by Oxford University Press
YMCA Library Building, Jai Singh Road, New Delhi 110001

To

my daughter, Srishti
and
son, Hemant

Preface

In 2008, the topmost Fortune 500 company was a retail giant. Worldwide, particularly in developing countries, retail businesses are moving from unorganized and family owned businesses to the organized ones that follow corporate management. With the paradigm shift in retailing in India, a trained and specialized workforce is required to manage retail businesses. Owing to this, retailing is fast emerging as an important area of study in business schools and training institutions. Large retail businesses cannot be run without using information technology (IT) in one form or the other.

Thus, IT has emerged as one of the key subjects for various short- and long-term retail management courses. A study of general IT concepts, systems, and equipment used in various retail operations, payment mechanisms, and enterprise systems required to run desktop and e-commerce applications would help students and retail managers understand the applications of IT to gain competitive advantage. This book fills the need for a comprehensive and all-encompassing text to meet the requirements of various readers.

About the Book

Information Technology for Retail has been written to meet the requirements of retail management students undertaking the courses in information technology or information systems in retail. It provides an in-depth coverage of the concepts, products, and solutions relating to the technology being applied to the contemporary retail business. This book has chapters on automatic identification and data-capture systems, modern electronic payment methods, and specialized electronic point-of-sales (EPOS) hardware, mobile devices based point-of-sales transaction systems, point-of-sales software, and retail-specific enterprise solutions, and so on. Such an exhaustive coverage makes this book a valuable text for the students.

The concepts have been explained with the help of ample examples, caselets, tables, and figures. With its problem-solving approach, the book will also be useful for managers involved in decision-making and implementing solutions for retail businesses.

Pedagogical Features

All the chapters in the book begin with the learning objectives, which summarize what the students are going to learn in the chapter. The text has been interspersed with the images from retail business scenarios to make the subject matter interesting and relevant even to the non-technical readers. Each chapter ends with a summary, wherein all the major points discussed in the chapter have been summarized and the students can recapitulate their learning. Select References have been provided at the end of each chapter for an advanced learner. The important technical terms have been explained in the Glossary at the end of the book.

The chapters are followed by exercises for the students. The concept review questions help the readers fortify their learning. The critical thinking questions have been given to link the concepts with the practical scenarios in today's marketplace, while the project assignments facilitate the experimental learning, information collection, and analysis of the same. The end-chapter case studies accompanied with analytical questions reinforce the understanding of the concepts as well as the practical business scenarios.

The book has the following key features:

- It elaborates on how IT/IS can give retailing a competitive advantage.
- It discusses the practical implementation aspects of IT in retailing.
- It focuses on the technology products and solutions that can be used for decision-making in retailing.
- It includes key topics such as the use of the Internet in the context of e-commerce in retailing, RFID technology, e-tailing, and emerging technologies in retailing.
- It has user-friendly presentation that offers insights even to the non-technical readers.

Coverage and Structure

Efforts have been made to organize the topics in this book in a lucid and comprehensive manner. The entire text has been divided into sixteen chapters.

Chapter 1 gives an overview of basic information technology systems. For the students already aware of basic computer technology, this chapter will function as a recapitulation. For the students who have not studied computers in school, it is necessary to understand complex information systems in organizational perspective. Besides recapturing evolution of computer hardware and software, various technology components are discussed.

Chapter 2 explains information systems and how they are supported by information technology. The information systems have been discussed with reference to their managerial roles, organizational structures, and functional areas. These systems have been expanded keeping in view the retail element. An overview of retail IT components (which include hardware, software, database, networking, automatic identification and data-capture (AIDC) system, and electronic payment systems or electronic fund transfer (EFT) technologies) has been provided. Each of these components has been further discussed in detail in forthcoming chapters.

Chapter 3 on Electronic Point of Sales–Hardware describes the hardware used at retail point of sales. The chapter discusses in detail computer-based point-of-sales systems, electronic cash registers, self-checkout systems, kiosks, and vending machines.

Chapter 4 concentrates on automatic identification and data-capture systems, which include bar code symbologies, bar code printing and scanning, and data-capture equipment. The radio frequency identification (RFID) technology, an emerging automatic identification technology, has been discussed at length.

Chapter 5 deals with database management system. The concept of database management has been illustrated with a fair number of examples. *Chapter 6* is on Networks and Telecommunications. Both these chapters are aimed to help the students understand the basic technology that works behind retail automation and EPOS. Various technical terms related to the database management, networking, and Internet have been explained to give the students a basic understanding.

Chapter 7 delves into the details of EPOS software, concentrating on the core functions and properties of the best-of-breed retail management software. The chapter would help the students grasp the use of EPOS to gain a competitive advantage.

One of the characteristics that makes the retail industry stand out is availability of multiple modes of payment. In *Chapter 8*, various modern electronic payment systems used in retailing have been discussed in detail with respect to credit cards, e-cash, smart cards, etc. Some latest and emerging phenomena in payment system, such as SMS and P2P, have also been discussed. Some of these payment systems discussed are applicable both at the retail POS and in e-commerce, which has been covered later in Chapter 14.

Chapter 9 is devoted to retail servicescape and types of retailers. The chapter discusses at length characteristics and specific trade requirements of various types of retailers. It would help the students understand the nuances and peculiarities of the trade, which will in turn help them understand the technology to manage retailing in a better way as well as to appreciate the technological requirements of the retailers.

Chapters 10 and *11* emphasize advanced learning of software systems. Both these chapters discuss enterprise resource planning (ERP) systems. The basics of ERP, various options available, and implementation methodologies have been discussed in Chapter 10. Chapter 11 discusses the features available in a standard ERP across the world. Various major modules in ERP systems, such as merchandising, distribution, finance, and human resource systems, have been discussed.

Chapter 12 introduces the concept of supply chain management (SCM) and deals with IT tools for managing supply chain. *Chapter 13* focuses on customer relationship management (CRM), which has a pivotal role in modern retail business. Three areas of customer relationship, viz. pre-sales (marketing), in-sales (sales process), and post-sales (service), have been discussed in terms of IT tools and applications.

Chapter 14 discusses e-commerce and e-tailing. The chapter discusses the infrastructural requirements for running a successful e-commerce retail business and throws light on the present Internet scene in India.

Chapter 15 touches upon emerging technologies in retail. It discusses latest technological advancements of mobile commerce, use of global positioning system (GPS) and geographic information system (GIS) in retail, next generation of the Internet (which is being touted as Web 2.0), and software as a service (SaaS). Though the technologies discussed in the chapter have not yet gained full acceptance in Indian retail scenario, they are sure to emerge and change the way business is run today; particularly, mobile computing and its use is going to change retailing in a big way.

Chapter 16 discusses the major IT products used in retail and their suppliers. The chapter would help the students and managers explore further and evaluate the products and their features.

Acknowledgements

Though I have written this book on the basis of my own knowledge and experience of more than twenty-two years and my close interaction with various retail companies while providing them consultancy for designing and implementing solutions, it would not have been possible to write it without consulting various texts, journals, magazines, and online references. I thank all those authors whose works have been referred.

It is not possible to mention the names of all those individuals who directly or indirectly have contributed to the book and inspired me to write it. But I would like to thank my students whose craving for knowledge prompted me to think about writing this book. I am also thankful to my colleagues at BNG Infotech Pvt Ltd for letting me utilize my spare hours in office for writing this book.

I thank the editorial team at Oxford University Press, New Delhi, for encouraging me to write and revise the draft manuscript to make it a comprehensible text. I also thank the reviewers, whose contribution is immense in improving the text.

I would like to pay my gratitude to those people who have contributed to, inspired, and shaped my personality. Foremost among them are my grandparents, Mr Bachi Ram Joshi and Mrs Paruli Devi, and my maternal grandmother, Mrs Jhanpari Devi. I express my indebtedness to Mr Bhola Datt Bhatt for his unconditional help, and Mr C.L. Seth, who always inspired me to think big.

I need to express my special love for *Osho*, who taught me to laugh at odds.

I also acknowledge that logos, trade names, and trademarks referred to in this book belong to their respective owners and have been used with no intention to infringe upon any copyrights.

I will be thankful to the readers for their valuable feedback and suggestions. They may write to me at girdhar_joshi@yahoo.com.

GIRDHAR JOSHI

Contents

1 Introduction to Information Technology

Information technology is much more than just computers. Today, it is the convergence of hardware, software, telecommunication, data, networks, multimedia, images, Internet, applications, and people. These all revolve round one object—computer. But computers were not the same what we see today.

BRIEF HISTORY OF COMPUTERS

Computers have come a long way since Charles Babbage, a mathematician, designed his mechanical device in 1835. He called his machine Analytical Engine. Babbage drew his inspiration from the centuries-old abacus that was used for counting numbers. Babbage's machine could only perform very simple arithmetical calculations. He replaced the abacus beads with mechanical gears, which were similar to the arithmetic logic unit of modern computers. There were lots of developments by scientists world wide. During World War II, there were many developments in the digital arena. The electronic circuits, relays, capacitors, and vacuum tubes replaced the mechanical parts. The architecture designed by John von Neumann was most suitable for digital computing. Even today, most contemporary computers use this architecture. But the most noticeable development and improvement over Charles' machine was the invention of ENIAC (Electronic Numerical Integrator and Computer) in 1945 by John Mauchly and J. Presper at the University of Pennsylvania. It was the first electronic general-purpose machine and was 1000 times faster than other contemporary computers.

Fig. 1.1   Mainframe computer 'baby'

Later EDVAC (Electronic Discrete Variable Automatic Computer) was designed by John von Neumann. With the end of the War, the US Army sold to John Von Neumann the technology that was the basis of modern computers and most mainframes and minicomputers were developed around that architecture. In the real sense of the term, we can call this as the first generation of computers.

The first generation of computers, called the *mainframe,* came out in 1952 (Fig. 1.1). This time, IBM launched its first 'mainframe' IBM701. This machine was huge, weighed around 30 tons, had 18,000 vacuum tubes to operate them, and hardly fitted into a room of 400 square feet. It used the 'machine-level language', which was later known as 'first-generation computer language', and could only understand 0's and 1's as the programming language. (The programming language is an instruction code to the computer that gets translated into the binary numbers, i.e. 0 and 1.) Programming and operating this computer was a strenuous job. It took hundreds and thousands of days to write a small program for simple calculations.

The decade 1960–70 was the period of minicomputers. In 1960, Digital Equipment Corporation developed a computer with keyboard and monitor that was commercially available. Thus came the turn of the second generation of computers, which were called *minicomputers.* These were called so because of their smaller size as compared to the mainframe. In 1969, Data General launched 'Nova', which was the first 16-bit minicomputer (Fig. 1.2). These computers offered relatively more features and were easy to program, use, and maintain.

Fig. 1.2   DG's Nova minicomputer

The programming language had also evolved from the first generation of machine language to the second generation, called 'assembly language', which was converted into machine language by a converter in the computer.

PC—THE PERSONAL COMPUTER

With the invention of a microprocessor by Ted Hoff and F. Foggin at Intel Corporation in the early 1970s, computer technology underwent a sea change. Very large-scale integrated (VLSI) circuits technology was behind this revolution. The third-generation computers came into the picture, which were called *microcomputers,* because they used microprocessors. These computers were extremely small, had much more processing speed, and could store information in magnetic disks called *floppy disks.* Thus, the PC was born. These computers were called personal computers because now any individual person could buy and own one of his/her own. The mainframes and minicomputers were only bought and owned by the government agencies such as defence or large corporations.

In 1971, Intel Corporation released the first microprocessor '4004', which was made for a Japanese calculator company. Later in 1975, Intel 8080 was used to build MITS Altair, the personal computer (Fig. 1.3). This was the first time that Paul Allen and his friend, Bill Gates, developed a BASIC interpreter for Altair and later they formed Microsoft. It was only in August 1981 when IBM released its first PC and used the Intel 8088 microprocessor, which had a speed of 4.77 MHz. This computer was developed on a memory chip that could store 1024 bits of data, which is equal to 1 kilobyte.

Almost at the same time, floppy disks were introduced. These were the first-generation floppy diskettes of 8″ size. IBM (then known as International Business Machines) standardized the configuration of the personal computer (Fig. 1.4). The following components were made compulsory in any PC:

- Central processing unit (having a microprocessor and a memory chip)
- Monitor

Fig 1.3   MITS Altair 8800

Fig. 1.4   IBM's first PC 5150 with two floppy drives

Fig. 1.5 Modern-day personal computer: really personal!

- Keyboard
- Floppy drive
- Speaker

The journey of personal computer started with Intel Corporation introducing the tiny microprocessor or integrated chip (IC) by the code name '8088'. The technology was improved continuously. The size became shorter and the speed and efficiency doubled and quadrupled with every new release (Fig. 1.5). It is said that if the automobile industry had made the progress like the computers did, we would have a car of size of match box with a speed of a jet within forty years. Table 1.1 shows a tentative time of introduction of the chip and its speed.

The fast evolution of microcomputers was because of the invention of the microchip called integrated circuits (ICs). In this technology, the computer logic is 'burnt into' the layers of the microprocessor (Fig. 1.6). A chip of a size of our thumbnail can hold enough logic to run the computer programs we have in our computers. The pace of the evolution of computers was always followed by the development in the field of peripheral devices. Peripheral devices are the various input, output and storage equipment, such as mouse, monitor, printer, and hard disk. Monitors evolved from monochromes to high-resolution coloured to liquid crystal display (LCD) and

Table 1.1 Evolution of microprocessors

Year	Chip	Computers Built around the Chip	Word-length*	Clock Speed*
1981	i8086, i8088	IBM PC	8 bit	8–10 MHz
1983	i8088	IBM PC-XT (Hard disk was added.)	8 bit	8–12 MHz
1983	Motorola-68000	Apple Macintosh, GUI, Mouse Driven	16 bit	
1984	i80286	IBM PC-AT (Advanced Technology)	16 bit	12–16 MHz
1986	i80386	IBM PC-386	32 bit	16–32 MHz
1990	i80484	IBM PC-486	32 bit	32–64 MHz
1996	Pentium I	Pentium	32 bit	64–200 MHz
1998–00	Pentium II-MMX/III	Pentium II/MMX (multimedia extensions)/P-III	32 bit	233–450 MHz
2003	AMD-Athlon	AMD microprocessor based	64 bit	450–1200 MHz
2004	Pentium IV	Pentium IV	64 bit	1200–2800 MHz
2006	Duo Core	Pentium Duo Core	64 bit	2800+ MHz

* We will discuss word-length and clock speed later in this chapter.

Fig. 1.6 Microprocessor—microchip

thin film transistor (TFT). Similarly, introduction of graphic user interface (GUI) based operating system software came along with a mouse. The headache of memorizing DOS commands was gone. Printers evolved from the ubiquitous dot matrix printers to ink-jet and laser jets. In the same way, the hard disks available in 1988 had a 10 MB (megabyte) capacity. Today, we buy a PC with 160 GB (160000 MB) space. This development has been phenomenal by all accounts.

BASIC COMPUTER ARCHITECTURE

In this section, we will discuss the basic components of a computer system.

Input-Process-Output

These devices, made mandatory by IBM, form a complete computer and are ingredients of input, output, and processing system of a computer. Figure 1.7 explains the basic input and output devices. We can add the latest devices in the subsequent diagram.

The central processing unit (CPU) consists of three main components—arithmetic logic unit (ALU), control unit, and primary storage unit.

The *arithmetic logic unit* (ALU) performs all arithmetical and logical calculations in the computer. It can add, subtract, multiply, and divide numbers. Also, it can understand logical calculations and negative numbers. The *control unit* controls and coordinates between various parts and components of a computer. These parts are all input and output devices, storage units, and other internal units of a computer. We will now briefly discuss primary storage system in a computer.

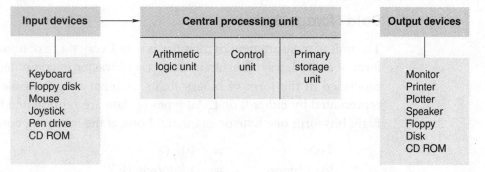

Fig. 1.7 Basic computer architecture and peripheral devices

Primary Storage Unit

Storage of the operating system program during operation and data related to that operation is done in the primary storage area. This is also known as *memory of the computer system*. There are two types of memory systems in a computer—ROM and RAM.

Read-only Memory (ROM)

It is a permanent memory and the retrieval is sequential in nature, i.e. the system can access the second block of memory data only after reading the first block. The data or information in this memory is fused in the chip and stores information about the computer, called BIOS (basic input/output system). You must have noticed some information being displayed on the screen of your computer when your computer boots on. This information comes from the ROM part of the memory.

Random-access Memory (RAM)

It is a temporary memory. This is called 'random' because it can be accessed and retrieved randomly from any location in the memory area. This memory is used to store data or application when the system is working. For example, after starting the computer, it retrieves the operating system files from the hard disk, brings it in the RAM area and executes the commands. In the same way, if you are working on a spreadsheet like Excel, your Excel application, which was stored and dormant in the hard disk, comes in the RAM and you start working on it. The data that you enter in the Excel worksheet remains in this volatile memory until you click the *Save* button and permanently write it on the disk. If you have not saved your work and the computer accidentally switches off, the work done will be lost.

Data Storage System

The unit of measurement of memory is *byte*. Every piece of information in the form of a word, a symbol, an image, or a character in computer is stored and processed in the form of binary digits. A binary digit is called a *bit* and is represented by either 0 or 1. All types of data are represented by 0's and 1's. Eight bits form one byte or character. Look at the following conversion table:

8 bits	=	1 byte
1024 bytes	=	1 kilobyte (KB)
1024 kilobytes	=	1 megabyte (MB)

$$1024 \text{ megabyte} = 1 \text{ gigabyte (GB)}$$
$$1024 \text{ gigabyte} = 1 \text{ terabyte (TB)}$$

Computer Speed

As memory is measured in bits and bytes, computer speed is measured in word-length. It is the number of bits a computer processes at a time. If a computer has a word-length of 16 bits, it can process 16 bits or 2 bytes at a time. As we have seen in Table 1.1, a Pentium computer has a 32-bit word-length, i.e. it can process up to 4 bytes at a time. The chip speed is guided and affected by the 'clock' speed of the computer. This is an internal speed and measured in megahertz (MHz). The megahertz speed is many millions of cycles per second. If a computer has a clock speed of 2600 MHz, it means it can perform 2600 million cycles per second.

COMPUTER HARDWARE

A computer system is built of mainly two major components, hardware and software. We can see, touch, and feel hardware. It is a tangible part of the computer, whereas the software is intangible and stays in coded form either in the hard disk drive, or in the memory of the computer.

Hardware Components

Hardware consists of the following components.

Cabinet   It is a box that houses the main components of the computer such as motherboard, microprocessor, memory chips, hard disk, floppy disk drive, and the CD-ROM drive.

Monitor   It is also known as visual display unit (VDU). Monitors come with cathode-ray tube (CRT) technology, in which a beam of electrons is thrown on the inner surface of the tube to form characters and images. Now, the new-generation monitors are LCD and TFT.

Keyboard   It is an input device. Computer keyboard has all numerals and alphabets of the English language. Besides, it has some special-purpose keys and function keys, which need no elaborate discussion here.

Mouse   It is also an input device and is a must for running Windows (or GUI) applications.

Motherboard   This is the main board inside the computer box that accommodates the main microprocessor, memory chips (RAM and ROM), and input-output unit for connecting with the peripheral devices.

Hard Disk   It is a storage device. It stores data permanently in the computer and the information is retrieved through the software interface, either for system or application (which is discussed in the next section).

Floppy Disk or CD-ROM   Before CD-ROMs were invented, putting a floppy disk was mandatory to load programs and take outputs in the data form. Now, the CD-ROMs have taken this space.

Power Supply   Unit switch mode power supply (SMPS) is the power supply unit in the cabinet box that supplies power to different parts of the computer.

Memory Chips or SIM Cards   These are plugged on the motherboard. One can add memory chips as required and support by the motherboard.

SOFTWARE

Software is a set of instructions to the computer to perform a certain task and that resides in the computer in the coded form as binary digits of 0 and 1. Windows, Word, Excel, SAP, Tally, Unix, Linux, Visual Basic, and Oracle Forms are all examples of software. Software is an important part of a computer system. You can compare software with the blood and life of a person, which makes the person alive. W.S. Jawadekar (2004) defines software as 'a set of instructions to acquire inputs and manipulate them to produce the desired output in terms of functions and performance as determined by the user of the software.' It also includes a set of documents such as the software manual, meant for the users to understand the software system. Today's software comprises the source code, executables, design documents, operations and system manuals, and installation and implementation manuals.

Software can be broadly classified into two categories—system software and application software.

System Software

System software manages computer resources, such as the file system, other hardware peripherals, and communication links. Various operating systems, browsers, utilities, compilers, and device drivers are examples of system software. As the computer technology evolved from mainframes to minicomputers, to microcomputers, software systems also went through major metamorphosis. Initially, the mainframe did not have an operating system at all. Then, Unix was introduced and became a very popular operating system for mainframes and minicomputers.

Operating Systems (OS)

The basic function of operating systems is to mange the computers' internal and external resources, such as files and peripherals devices. It helps in creating directories and folders as well as copying, deleting, and moving files from a physical storage to another. Operating systems offer various utilities to configure the computer as per your environmental settings, such as date formats, numbering system, and memory management. This also helps in adding new programs and removing unwanted programs from the computer. The various devices attached with a computer are linked through drivers, which are commensurate with the computer's operating system.

With the invention of microcomputers, disk operating system was introduced. IBM developed the first disk operating system (DOS) for its personal computers, which was known as PC-DOS. IBM outsourced the development of PC-DOS to Bill Gates and his friend, Paul Allen. Since IBM did not buy the proprietary rights (which is known as the biggest blunder a company ever made in the modern business history), Bill Gates re-launched the DOS under the banner of Microsoft. It was renamed as Microsoft-DOS or MS-DOS as commonly called. IBM sold PC-DOS preloaded in the desktop computers for some time and finally stopped selling it. MS-DOS supports IBM PC standards and is a 16-bit operating system, i.e. it can address data in chunks of 16-bits at a time. The maximum application size it can handle in the memory is 640 KB and it can run only one program at a time (as opposed to multitasking in Windows).

Windows overcame the constraints in DOS. Microsoft launched the second generation of disk operating system in 1995, which was completely based on GUI and was named *Windows 95*. This was a true 32-bit operating system with more capabilities, such as fax, e-mail, scheduling, and Internet browsing. Though Apple Macintosh, which was launched in 1976, already had an operating system that was full GUI, it was popular only with Mac users. Macintosh systems were mainly used for publishing work. Windows family of operating systems, viz. Windows 95, Windows 98, Windows XP, (Fig. 1.8), and Windows 2003, became popular for modern personal computers.

Windows 98, Windows 2000, Windows ME (Millennium Edition), Windows XP (eXPerience), and Windows Vista are the subsequent versions of Windows that were launched with some modifications and improvements from the earlier version. Windows can handle files of sizes more than 640 KB because of its capability to use extended memory. Windows has great functionality to perform multitasking, i.e. it can perform several programs at the same time. You may minimize a program and then run another, and yet another. This functionality is available to users only with Windows (Fig. 1.9).

Fig. 1.8 A typical Windows XP desktop screen

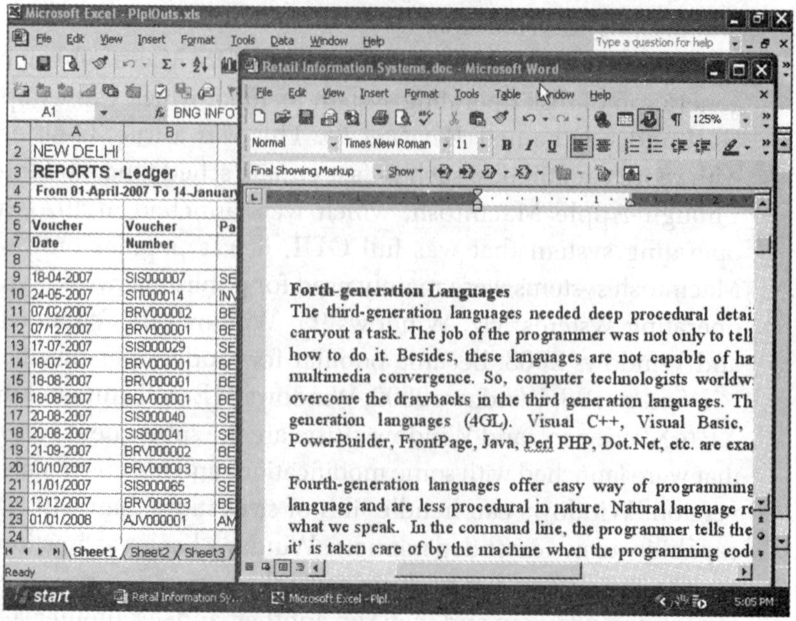

Fig. 1.9 Windows' multitasking capability—working on two documents together

Fig. 1.10   Linux operating system: GUI

Microsoft had a monopoly on the PC operating systems market, until *Linux* was launched at the turn of the century. Linux kernel was developed by Linus Torvalds in 1991. The kernel is the core of the software, around which developers can build tools and utilities. Linux supports open-source technology and is a freeware, that is, nobody legally owns rights over it. Open-source concept propagates non-proprietary rights on the product and allows developments, addition and improvement in the software by any user, mentor, or developer of the system. It can be redistributed along with the improved source code. The source code of Linux is available and one can create additional tools around this OS (Fig. 1.10). One of the many advantages offered by Linux is that it can run on major processors developed by the corporations, such as Intel, Motorola, SPARK, Alpha, and Mips.

Use and development of Linux is supported by Sun Microsystems and IBM, in particular, and Oracle, HP, and other, in general, to champion the cause of open-source technology and also to counter the monopoly of Windows in the market. Initially faced with some hitches, now Linux is gaining acceptance and is quite popular for web-based applications. It is a popular operating system for I Servers. (Also see Case Study at the end of the chapter.)

Network Operating Systems

As Microsoft had a monopoly on the PC disk operating system, Novell Corp had a monopoly on the network operating systems (NOS). *Novell Netware* was a very popular, strong, sturdy, and secure network operating system. It offered capability to network diskless nodes with dedicated Novell servers. Microsoft introduced Windows-NT as the operating system for the networks. Windows NT gave flexibility and an ease of a graphic user interface (mouse compatibility) and was secure enough for local networks. *Windows 2000* integrated capability of Windows NT for secure networking. It can work on PCs, laptops, and servers. As Laudon (2002, p. 177) puts it: 'Windows 2000 can support software written for Windows and it can provide mainframe-like computing power for new applications with massive memory and file managements. It can even support multiprocessing with multiple CPUs.' Like Unix, Linux also supports single machines and multiple servers under networks.

Unix and Xenix were operating systems for mainframes and minicomputers. Unix was developed by Bell Laboratories in 1969 primarily to make it run over network. This was made to offer functionalities like multitasking, interactive, and multi-user. Unix is still regarded as a secure and robust operating system that runs on large networks and high-end servers. But with increase in the popularity and power of personal computers, development on Unix and Xenix stopped in the nineties of the last century.

Application Software

Application software is a program created to perform certain tasks for the end users. Some of these tasks are maintaining a fee register in a school, keeping transaction records of an account-holder in a bank, creating bills at the point-of-sales location, managing inventory in a warehouse, playing a music or movie file, creating a database system allowing users to construct database structure, and developing a programming language that further facilitates creation of software by a programmer.

All kinds of software that are used to manage, run and monitor businesses and process data come under application software category. The word processors, database management software, spreadsheet software, compressing-decompressing software, media players, and software that can play a movie file are all examples of application software. It is assumed that students are aware of the basic office management tools such as word processors, spreadsheets, and Internet browsers. Therefore, detailed study of these applications is not a part of this text. Under application software, we will discuss retail application software in Chapters 7, 10, and 11.

PROGRAMMING LANGUAGES AND TOOLS

As we have discussed earlier, for the first and second generations of computers, programming was done using either machine or assembly languages. These languages were used by scientists and engineers for scientific applications. They themselves were users and creators of the programs. The programs were mainly for numerical calculations using scientific formulae and arithmetical rules and logic. It was a time-consuming and cumbersome job to write programs using these low-level languages. Slowly, the languages evolved to higher levels, popularly known as third-generation (3GL) and fourth-generation languages (4GL).

Third-Generation Languages

In these languages, one can write software for both microcomputers and mainframe computers. The main third-generation languages are C, COBOL, FORTRAN, BASIC, and Pascal, which were developed and became popular in development of the system, database and application programming. *System programming* is the development of tools, compilers, utilities, and operating systems. DOS, Windows, Internet browsers, and Linux are all examples of operating systems. *Database programming* is the development of applications around the database management systems, such as FoxPro, Access, and Oracle. *Application programming* is development of applications to perform a certain task and capture, manipulate and retrieve data from databases. Development of websites and business software packages (such as Tally, RetailPro, SAP, and MS-Office) are examples of application programming. These programming languages are much easier than the assembly languages since these come with a compiler, which converts the normal English-like phrases into binary language that the machines understand.

Fourth-Generation Languages

The third-generation languages needed deep procedural details and step-by-step instruction to carry out a task. The job of the programmer was not only to tell the computer what to do but also how to do it. Besides, these languages are not capable of handling GUI and multimedia convergence. So, computer technologists worldwide developed more languages to overcome the drawbacks of the third-generation languages. These languages were called fourth-generation languages (4GL). Visual, C++, Visual Basic, Oracle Developer Tools, SQL, PowerBuilder, FrontPage, Java, CGI-Perl, PHP, and Dot.Net are examples of 4GL.

```
'-------------------------------------------------------------------
' Procedure : LastDay
' DateTime  : 19-Oct-2006
' Developer : Sunil
' Purpose   : Return Last Date of Month and Year
' Modify History :
' Date    Dr/Cr    Developer    Details
'-------------------------------------------------------------------
Public Function fniLastDay(p_intMonth As Integer, p_intYear As Integer) As
Integer
On Error GoTo ErrorHandler

   Select Case p_intMonth
     Case 1, 3, 5, 7, 8, 10, 12
       LastDay = 31
     Case 2
       If p_intYear Mod 4 = 0 Then
         LastDay = 29
       Else
         LastDay = 28
       End If
     Case 4, 6, 9, 11
       LastDay = 30
   End Select
   Exit Function
ErrorHandler:
   Err.Raise Err.Number, Err.Source, Err.Description
End Function
```

Fig. 1.11 Sample programming in 4GL

Fourth-generation languages offer an easy way of programming (Figures 1.11 and 1.12). They resemble natural English language and are less procedural in nature. (Natural language refers to the language very close to what we speak.) In the command line, the programmer tells the computer what to do. 'How to do it' is taken care of by the machine when the programming codes are compiled and assembled by the specialized tools provided in the language kit.

The reason of 4GLs becoming popular was their ease in writing programs. The lines of codes (LoC) that need to be written to create a function in different languages reduce sharply as the languages evolved.

```
SELECT item_name FROM itemtable WHERE item_name LIKE 'shirt%';

SELECT customer_name FROM transactiontable WHERE amount = 10000 AND
staxamount=500;
```

Fig. 1.12 Query written in a structured query language (4GL)

Table 1.2 Programming languages in descending order of complexities

Assembly	320
C	128
Fortran	105
C++	56
Java	55
Visual Basic	35
Other 4GL	20
Code Generators	15

Source: Jawadekar, W.S. 2005

Table 1.2 shows how lines of codes per function point drop sharply. (The function point is a measure of the complexity of the software.)

MODERN BUSINESSES AND INFORMATION TECHNOLOGY

After understanding the basic computer architecture and terminology, let us discuss information systems and information technology in respect of modern businesses.

Indian society was largely an agrarian society for centuries. After India's independence in 1947, the government tried to establish industries across the country. It was only after 1960 that India started its steps to move from an agricultural to an industrial society. But worldwide, highly industrialized countries, such as the USA, moved from an industrial society to a service society. The emphasis was on services and the service industry is a knowledge-based industry. From the year 1990 onwards, India has ushered in a knowledge society from an agricultural society and a half-baked industrial society. The use of computers is increasing rapidly, especially with availability of the Internet and high-quality telecommunication network. The way information technology has penetrated society, it has become indispensable. Why do information systems play such big roles within the organizations and affect people in all walks of life? The answer is the ever-increasing power and sharply declining costs of computer-technology products. As Laudon (2002) puts: 'Computing power, which has been doubling every 18 months, has improved the performance of microprocessors over 25,000 times since their invention 30 years ago. With powerful, easy-to-use software, the computer can crunch numbers, analyse vast pools of data, or simulate complex physical and logical processes with animated drawings, sound, and even tactile feedback.'

The Internet, which is the network of the networks, has changed the world. It has not only been instrumental in transforming world economies but also has shaken the basic fabric of social interaction. It has changed the way we shop, the way we socialize, the way we study, the way we bank, make payments, the way scholars conduct research. It has also changed the way a father writes a letter to his daughter, and the way we looked at our old family album.

We would not be doing business the way we did a decade back. E-commerce has opened new avenues in business. Organizations cannot ignore the impact. The dot.com burst in 2000 was a necessary shake-up for unprofitable businesses that had built their foundation on faulty revenue models. Now, businesses are taking care of this aspect. E-commerce has emerged as an enabler of the existing business systems and is adding revenues and facilitating business operations on click of a mouse.

Information technology influences every aspect of life and is going to have a big impact on commerce and industry. Therefore, our progress depends on what our system will be able to do. The market share of a company will depend upon what its technology can support. The modern organizations will have to be prepared for it.

SUMMARY

The journey of modern computing started with the invention of the digital computers in 1950s. The microcomputer revolution started in 1980s after the invention of the microprocessor in early 1970. Very large-scale integrated (VLSI) circuits technology was behind this revolution. Computers have the same architecture of input-process-output. Data is entered in computers through various input devices; it is processed in the CPU having an ALU, a control unit, and memory units. The output is sent to devices such as monitor, printer. Computers consist of various hardware components (such as CPU, input and output devices, and peripherals) and software components.

Broadly, software is classified into system software and application software. System software consists of various operating systems, drivers, compilers, assemblers. DOS, Windows, Unix, Linux, and OS/2 are examples of operating systems. The Internet browsers and modem drivers are utilities under the same category. Computer programming languages, database management software, business application packages, and retail EPOS software are examples of application software. With the invention and evolution of new generation of computer hardware, programming languages also evolved. As the programming languages became rich in functionalities and delivery, it became easier for a programmer to write a piece of software using them. Today, languages and tools of fourth generation and beyond are available, with which even a not-so-technical person can try to build programs.

CONCEPT REVIEW QUESTIONS

1. Define the basic architecture of a computer system.
2. What are the core components of a modern personal computer?
3. Write a brief note on evolution of computers.
4. Define 4GL with suitable examples.
5. What are the basic functions of operating systems?
6. What is multitasking?

CRITICAL THINKING QUESTIONS

1. 'It was only personal computer that brought about the computer revolution.' Analyse this statement with practical examples.
2. 'It was not the hardware that forced software development but it was the software that had a catalytic effect on the hardware growth.' Do you agree? Fortify your answer with examples.

PROJECTS

1. Visit a retail store in your neighbourhood and prepare a report on the use of IT at the store.
2. Your organization is implementing retail software. You, as a head of the implementing team, have to decide about the operating system. Your liking is for Linux. Build a business case so that your CEO is convinced.

SELECT REFERENCES

Jawadekar, W.S. 2005, *Software Engineering*, Tata McGraw-Hill, New Delhi.
Laudon, Kenneth and Jane Laudon 2002, *Management Information Systems*, Pearson Education (Singapore).
Linux For You, www.lfymag.com.

CASE STUDY

Haldia Dock Complex: Laying its Own Linux

Linux is gaining ground in almost all spheres of computing, from small desktop configurations to high-end cluster design for mission-critical work environments. And almost every organization that has an implemented Linux swears by its power and stability.

The Company

The Haldia Dock Complex (HDC) has a uniquely designed Linux installation with an active-active cluster set-up, which is considered as one of the best of its kind. This has ensured efficiency and cost-effectiveness. The HDC, situated in the Bay of Bengal, is one of the most active ports in the eastern front of the country. It manages day-to-day operations on Linux for heavy-duty work applications. It is one of the uniquely designed Linux installations and presently one of the best active-active clusters.

Initial Groundwork

The officials at HDC were keen on modernizing their IT and administrative network infrastructure. At the same time, they were studying the cost-effectiveness of implementing a solution to handle the overall load balancing that was required at the complex.

This set-up involved several major players, including (a) IBM, which supplied the machines and its custom DB2 software in addition to other hardware infrastructure, (b) NIC, which was the overall governing council body (unless NIC sanctioned the project, it couldn't take off, and (c) Officials from Haldia complex and Red Hat India, who configured and implemented the active-active cluster.

Unlike earlier organizations that had proprietary systems in their infrastructure, HDC was a fresh set-up. Without much ado, almost every one agreed to go in for Linux from the very beginning.

The project was based on Red Hat Enterprise Linux cluster suite using DB2, a SAN switch (for shared storage), WAS (Web Application Sphere) from IBM, and DRS (Disaster Recovery Site) about 8 km away from the main installed base to provide redundancy, all connected over a fibre-optic channel network.

Active-active clustering

In this type of application environment there are two servers simultaneously accessing data. If one server shut downs, the other picks up the load of running all services. These servers access different partitions. So, in a typical cluster manager environment, the user can simply spread the application services across the two servers in any way that seems appropriate. The applications are processed faster as both the servers share the total load. This is called active-active clustering, since both servers are simultaneously active.

The Fine Art of Cluster Management

Every organization has different needs depending on the work environment. It is up to the system engineers to design and implement robust and scalable solutions taking into account the future needs of the organization. So, when designing a high-availability configuration, the first task is to identify whether the customer's applications will be supported by the planned system. The Haldia complex wanted a Unix-like, sturdy architecture, which ensured stability. At the same time, the system needed to be cost-effective and free of licencing fees. To meet

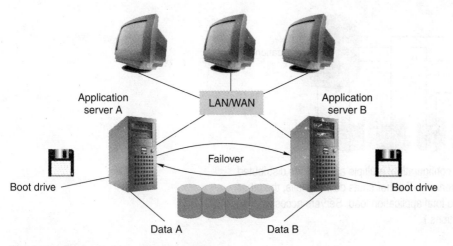

Fig. 1.13 Basic cluster manager operations

these criteria, the experts on the project had to carefully design and implement a smart maintenance and support strategy.

Sandeep Khuperkar, technical specialist, Red Hat India, one of the main architects responsible for the active-active cluster set-up at HDC, agrees, 'we at Red Hat saw the overall design plan and recommended Linux as the de-facto platform for the mission-critical applications. This decision was based on the compatibility and configurability of the OS with other software and hardware such as IBM's DB2 and WAS server applications in sync with the DRS'.

The HDC set-up for the active-active cluster involves one pair of cluster for the database, three servers for WAS and one for the database. The NIC had developed application for the HDC active-active cluster, which is being used by the finance, marine, payroll and human resource departments. At HDC, Red Hat Enterprise Linux forms the basic platform the entire server set-up, with multiple instances running on active-active cluster accessing their own respective DB (database) partitions on external storage (Fig. 1.13).

In the set-up depicted in Fig. 1.14, the cluster manager configuration developed by Red Hat through the SAN switch comprises pair of server connected to an external storage array of devices. The cluster manager software at the HDC is used to control access to storage partitions, so that only one instance of DB2 can access a particular partition at a time. In the event that one of the servers shuts down or fails, the other server will detect the event and will automatically start to run the applications that were previously running on the failed server. This migration of the application from the failed server to the remaining server is called fail-over.

Each server will then operate in the same manner, as if it were a single stand-alone system, running applications and accessing data on its allocated storage partitions. But at the HDC, multiple servers have been used to streamline the steady, demanding flow of data. This typical layout is often referred to as scale-out computing. In addition to their connection to the shared storage array, the two servers are interconnected using a network or serial interface so that

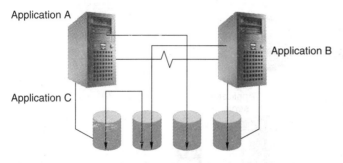

Application A

Application B

Application C

Fig. 1.14 Active-active configuration: multiple applications distributed
across both servers. (If either shuts down or fails, the other
takes over the total application load. Servers access
different partitions.)

they can communicate with each other. So, in this case, there are two nodes: Node 1 and Node 2.

In case a particular application instance fails on Node 1, it is invoked at Node 2, thereby giving continuity of data access to users. As soon as Node 1 is rectified, the application instance that was earlier relocated to Node 2 is relocated back to Node 1.

Sandeep Khuperkar points out, 'this is very important as scalability needs to be enhanced without any breakdown in the service. So the entire application must be designed for fail-over and maintenance.'

Cluster communication

Cluster manager configuration comprises two server systems connected to a shared external storage array. Typically in most environments, the two servers are connected by LAN or RS-232 serial cables. Cluster manager software uses these connections for heart beating between the servers. Each server heart beats with other with regular short messages to check that if it is operating correctly. If the heart beats do not receive an acknowledgement, then the server will use this as an indication that the remote server has failed.

The HDC is a very high-rate active-active cluster and there are various applications being developed and ported on the system. As a result, the design had to consider compatibility with other operating systems and high-end performance. Therefore, it is natural that the cluster must be able to work with the most common database and applications (interconnectivity) and must be easy to deploy and use with custom applications.

On this aspect, Sandeep adds, 'we have tested the cluster successfully and it has worked quite efficiently. Looking at the mission-critical applications required at HDC, the cluster management suite (Red Hat) was configured to use multiple instances of DB2 running on several nodes'.

How does one monitor the network effectively? Sandeep explains, 'the enterprise suite has a very good GUI, which helps the system administrator to check the status and monitor the nodes on the cluster'.

So, what's new?

Ask any expert or user of Linux and opinion will invariably be, 'it's a very strong, stable, robust OS with scope for further enhancements and future requirements'. And what do the people at the site had to say? Abhijit Das, Deputy Secretary, HDC, says, 'we are completely satisfied with the active-active cluster set-up and have found the Red Hat application suite to be perfectly stable for our heavy-duty work'.

Questions:

1. What was the major activity at the Haldia Dock complex?
2. Which activities carried out at HDC were LAN establishing and which ones indicated towards an operating system change?
3. Which part of the operations was most critical and why?

Source: Adapted from Nilesh Kakade, *Linux For You*, December 2003, www.lfymag.com.

2

Basics of Information Systems

Learning Objectives

- To define the concept and scope of information systems
- To review basics of information technology concepts
- To discuss various types of information systems
- To understand information system in the organizational perspective
- To get acquainted with various components of retail information systems

Wal-Mart builds applications for its information systems

"Buy what you can't build, and build what you can't buy" is the proverb. Wal-Mart also shares this view. Wal-Mart has opted for a very centralized development approach. The in-house development supports the ERP solutions it is running across the organization. Instead of buying smaller systems, it prefers to build its own, and it has the monetary power to develop, ahead of its competitors. Wal-Mart's main USP for in-house development is that the company competes on business process expertise. The retail giant considers its IT people merchants first, technologists secondly. The IT persons are supposed to be experts in business processes of retail, merchandizing, and supply chain. This prevents technology for technology's sake.

Wal-Mart, while automating processes, eliminates lethargic processes before automation. In other words, it does not automate bad process. The philosophy is to weed out bad processes and see automation as a re-engineering and change-management tool.

In Chapter 1, we have discussed basics of computer technology, covering mainly computer concepts of hardware, software and memory systems. In this chapter, we will learn how these systems can enable business processes and help in management decision-making. We will understand different processes of management decision-making and what constitutes retail information systems.

The phrase 'information systems' brings to mind the image of computers, people who run those computers, punching of raw data in computers, processing of the data, and finally reports generated by the system for use of the management of the organization. This image may be right from the modern information system organizational point of view. But information systems involve a much wider concept than just the technological aspect. They were there much before the advent of computers. Information systems involved manual processing. The information was processed by various departments of an organization and presented to the management. But introduction of computers has had a big impact on the information systems. Information systems are now full-fledged functions of a modern business organization.

INFORMATION SYSTEMS

It was only with the popularity of computers that information system departments were formalized and known as electronic data processing (EDP) departments. Also called MIS departments, they were centrally coordinated departments manned by computer and management experts. Just as computer systems became hi-tech with the integration of Internet, telecommunication, and multimedia technologies, they evolved into information technology (IT) systems. And the information systems department came to be known as IT departments. Today, IT systems are the backbone of any business. Large businesses have all-powerful IT departments, headed by vice-presidents and directors.

Therefore, a system that enables people to gather, consolidate, and compute data, and present the information in a meaningful and intelligent (that makes sense) format, either with the help of computers or manually, is called information system (IS).

Laudon (2002) maintains that 'an information system can be defined technically as a set of interrelated components that collect (retrieve), process, store, and distribute information to support decision-making, coordination, and control in an organization'. It also helps managers analyse problems and visualize complex subjects and find solutions.

The following are some common and well-received definitions of information systems:

- Information system means an interconnected set of information resources under the same direct management control that shares common functionality. A system normally includes hardware, software, information, data, applications, communications, and people.
- Information system is the organized collection, processing, transmission, and dissemination of information in accordance with defined procedures, whether automated or manual. Information systems include non-financial, financial and mixed systems.

- Information system is a computer system that stores data and supplies information, usually within a business context. Information systems often rely on databases. A system of people, procedures, and equipment, for collecting, manipulating, retrieving, and reporting data.
- Information system is any equipment or interconnected system or subsystems of equipment that is used in the automatic acquisition, storage, manipulation, management, movement, control, display, switching, interchange, transmission, or reception of data and that includes computer software, firmware, and hardware. It also includes computers, word processing systems, networks, or other electronic information handling systems and associated equipment.

Information systems work in similar fashion for individual businesses and large corporations. The only difference will be of volumes and complexities. Let us understand information systems with an example:

Basu Anand, a business owner who deals in gifts and perfumes, has the following sales data for the last three days:

Date	Amount
12/02/2008	12,607
13/02/2008	17,200
14/02/2008	20,225

He enters his bills (input) in a computer system perhaps using Excel (technology).

He calculates (processing) his day's sale for each day (data).

He deduces that on 14th Feb, he made better sales than any other day in the week (information).

It is evident that the sale is increasing (management information system).

Looking at the trend, he buys more goods for selling tomorrow (decision support system).

Look at the words in parentheses. By looking at them, you can easily make out what an information system is all about. Let us understand these terms.

Information

It is the data that can be formed into a shape that is meaningful and useful to the human being. Information is a processed data on which future decisions and actions are based. In the above example, 'sale of a particular day is 20,225' is information, which is useful to the management.

Data

These are the streams of raw facts representing events occurring in the organization and environment before they have been organized and arranged into a meaningful form. In the above example, various figures of sales for different days are just data.

Input

It is collecting or capturing raw data from the environment and/or within the organization. The bills of each day form input documents.

Processing

The conversion, manipulation, and analysis of raw inputs into processed data is called processing. In the above example, each bill's sales value may not have mattered much to the owner of the business. But after computing the total sales, it makes a difference.

Output

It is the distribution of processed information to the people to use it. The processed information is in the form of some value to the manager. This output has helped him make a decision to buy more products for sale on next day or a similar date next year (remember it is a festival day!).

Figure 2.1 combines the above components of information systems and significant components of a modern organization, i.e. technology, management, and organization. We discuss these issues in the following paragraphs.

SIGNIFICANCE OF INFORMATION SYSTEMS IN A MODERN ORGANIZATION

Information systems are built by an organization using information technology. These tools are used by the management to deal with the challenges posed by the internal and external environment. Information technology consists of input, output, and processing systems and devices. The *environment* refers to an organization's suppliers, customers, competitors, stockholders, and the government regulatory authorities. The organization is a combination of people, its policies, procedures, strategies, and culture. Management is a link between all components of technology and organization. It works towards formulating and implementing policies for making the organization viable to operate in the marketplace.

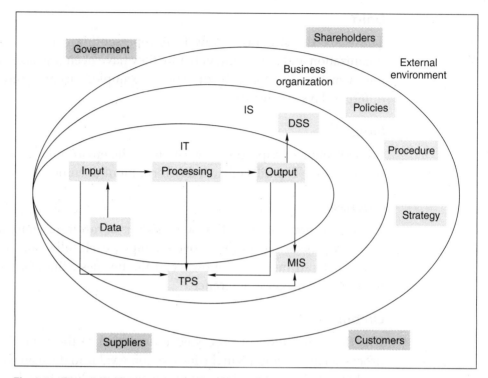

Fig. 2.1   The relationship between IT, IS, organization, and environment

The following are the three dimensions of information systems in a modern business organization (Fig. 2.2):

- Organization
- Management
- Technology

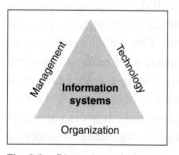

Fig. 2.2   Dimensions of information systems

Organization

In the modern scenario, organizations cannot do without a reliable information system (IS). An organization is made of its people, organizational structure, assets, operating procedures, policies, and culture. People manage, execute, and run systems and implement policies. People are placed in various jobs and tasks as per the organizational structure. They are divided into labour, mangers, experts, etc. Assets are machinery, buildings, stocks, technology, equipment, and knowledge database of the organization. Even if the organization is a pure service organization like a consulting firm, the knowledge that the organization has acquired and built up constitutes its assets. Every organization runs on certain procedures and policies. Standard operating procedures are the rules that have been developed over a period of time for carrying out various tasks. These procedures guide its people while performing their duties. At critical moments, they refer to the procedures that were built over a period of time. Every organization has its business ethics, which are formed as a result of policies and inherent politics within the organization. Most of the time, the ethics represent the values and honesty of the top management. For example, if the top management never evades taxes, the organization builds an honest image of its own, down the years.

Different business functions of an organization are supported by the information system. These functions are supply chain management, sales and marketing, manufacturing and production control, warehousing and inventory management, finance and accounts, and customer relationship and human resources.

Management

The task of organizing, planning, coordinating, and controlling resources is carried out by the managers. They perceive business challenges in the environment and make strategies for responding to these challenges. What are the challenges? Businesses are run under severe constraints, laws, and regulations. There are demand and supply equations. There are also resource constraints, such as men, material, money, markets, and time. The managers have to deliver under tight work and time schedules. They plan their duties and allocate resources—human or financial—to achieve goals and coordinate the work. The ultimate goal of an organization is to make profits and survive the toughest of competition.

Managerial responsibilities and duties vary at different levels of the organization. Top executives and senior managers make long-term plans and strategies. Strategies are tactical manoeuvrings of situations to mould them in the organization's favour. Extending business in a new product line and setting up a plant to produce a sub-product are examples of long-term plans. Middle management carries out the plans and visions of top managers. Their duties are to implement long-term plans and strategic plans. On the other hand, operational managers are responsible for monitoring day-to-day work, which involves carrying out transactions such as sales, purchases, inventory management, marketing, recruiting and retrenching people, collection of outstanding money from the customers, and making payments to the suppliers.

Technology

Information technology consists of hardware, software, data storage, and communication technology. Managers use these technology tools and systems to manage and control changes in the organization, while managing the affairs. We have already discussed these components in general. In the context of retail, we are going to discuss specialized hardware, i.e. electronic point-of-sales (EPOS) systems, software (best of breed retail software and enterprise software system and applications). Data storage consists of both physical storage devices, such as magnetic tapes and magnetic disks, and database management systems. Modern businesses depend heavily on communication technology like networks, the Internet, and intranet for communication of data and sharing of information. Network is interconnecting two or more computer systems. It involves hardware, software, and telecommunication lines. Electronic data interchange (EDI) is now an integral part of data communication and sharing across the globe.

Automatic identification and data-capture (AIDC) systems and electronic fund transfers are additional components of technology and form a part of the information systems in retail businesses. All these technologies represent resources that can be shared throughout the organization.

TYPES OF INFORMATION SYSTEMS

As we have already discussed, managers at different level of the organizations have different roles, responsibilities, and functions. Based on management activity, we can segregate different types of information systems. These systems are supported by information technology and work at different levels of management in an organization. As such, there are four types of management information systems based on four types of management in the hierarchy of an organization. These systems are:

1. Transaction processing systems (TPS)—operation management level
2. Management information system (MIS)—middle management level
3. Knowledge management systems (KMS)—knowledge expertise level
4. Decision support system (DSS)—senior management level

Figure 2.3 illustrates the management hierarchy and how different information systems work to their advantage.

Transaction Processing System (TPS)

The day-to-day operations in an organization are managed by operation people. They create the basic documents, such as bills, purchase orders, material

Fig. 2.3 Management activity—information systems

receipt notes, write cheques, etc. While creating documents by following certain predefined procedures, they gather data and complete the transaction. The predefined procedures are set rules and systems and even format of the document that is generated at the time of carrying out the transaction. For example, every business organization has a system of billing that elucidates steps in perfect ease and the format of bill is same at a given period of time. These systems are called transaction processing systems (Fig. 2.4).

Transaction processing systems are the basic business systems that work at the operational level of the organization. In the modern business environment, a transaction processing system is a computerized system that performs and records the daily routine transactions necessary to run the business. Examples of transaction processing are sales order processing system in a trading organization, hotel reservation systems in a hotel organization, outpatient registration system in a hospital, payroll and financial transactions systems practically in all organizations having workforce and working for profit. At the operational level, tasks are highly structured and well defined. There are well-defined rules for sales, marketing, PPC, accounting, and purchase. The system conforms to these rules and generates primary data, which is further analysed at various levels of the management.

The major transaction processing systems in a retail organization are as follows:

- Purchase and supply management
- Sales and distribution management
- Warehouse and inventory management
- Finance and accounting management
- Production planning and control management
- Human resource management

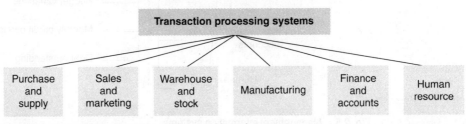

Fig. 2.4 Transaction processing system and its subsystems

Each of these transaction processing systems has dozens of subsystems. We will discuss these systems later in the section on MIS Structure from Functional Perspective.

A transaction processing system has the following basic characteristics:

- Generates primary data that is further made available to other information systems for analysis
- Works on highly structured and predefined procedures
- Is routine and repetitive in nature
- Works at the operation level of the organization

Management Information System (MIS)

Management information systems are for middle-level managers in an organization. The middle-level managers in the organization work on the primary data generated by the transaction processing systems (Fig. 2.5). The primary data is the basic data, such as daily sales figures, cash collected at the selling counter, and credit outstanding. Management information system provides the managers with reports and online access to the organization's

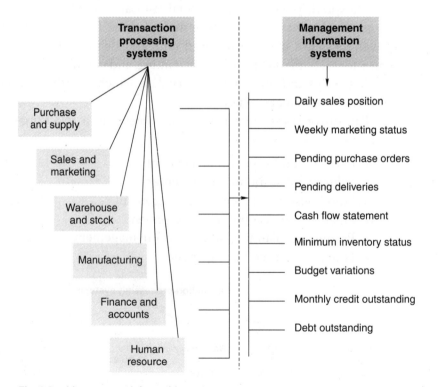

Fig. 2.5 Management information systems

current performance and historical records. It offers routine, periodical, and exception reports. Routine reports are, for example, daily sales report, cash collection report at the point of sales, material receipt report, quality rejection reports etc. Examples of periodical reports are weekly, monthly, and quarterly sales reports, weekly, monthly, and fortnightly stock reports. Examples of exception reports are missing bills, goods sent to a branch but not received by that branch, difference in goods received from supplier and what is accepted by the company's inventory system. These reports are simple and are not analytical in nature.

The orientation of management information systems is internal, i.e. they use the information generated by the transaction processing systems and knowledge work systems. They do not look towards external environment or events. They have been in existence since the last four decades and are still appreciated as the most effective and efficient system for middle managers to carry out their management functions.

The data generated by people through office automation systems, such as word processors and spreadsheets, support MIS. Word processing is the system of creating, editing, printing, publishing, and storing documents. With the advent of e-mail, office communication system has evolved into a very efficient system. Now, a lot of communication is done through e-mail, computer-enabled fax, and videoconferencing. As spreadsheets support advance level of ratio and financial analysis, middle level management uses these systems for decisions-making.

We can summarize the characteristics of management information systems as follows:

- They do not generate any data and work on the data offered by TPS.
- They primarily serve the purpose of planning, controlling, and decision-making at the management level.
- These systems provide managers with routine periodical reports and summaries.
- They work on internal data and do not consider external data.
- They provide fixed reports and hence are not very flexible in nature.
- Office automation systems, such as word processors and spreadsheets, support MIS.

Knowledge Management Systems (KMS)

The term *knowledge* is derived from '*know*'-*ing*. Individuals build their expertise on a subject by knowing it through learning processes, which can be study, interaction with groups, and coming across various situations in day-to-day

Fig. 2.6 Knowledge dissemination systems at work

work. Thus, *knowledge* refers to an individual's accumulation of information and expertise. We can say that knowledge belongs to individuals. Individuals having expertise and knowledge help an organization achieve its goals. But what happens if an individual leaves an organization? Does the knowledge he or she accumulated and created while working with the organization go with him or her? Perhaps yes, but in the fast-changing business scenarios and cut-throat competition, organizations cannot afford to do that. With highly efficient computer systems in place, knowledge management systems have been created.

The two systems of information, viz. TPS and MIS, which have already been discussed, do not cover processes of knowledge discovery, storage, management, and dissemination. Knowledge workers are primarily professionals, such as engineers, chartered accountants, designers, architects, programmers, doctors, and job-specialists, who serve organizations with their knowledge and expertise. As new knowledge is discovered and promoted, it is integrated into the business system. For example, an engineer generates a complex drawing, using his or her knowledge, expertise and inputs from the environment. This drawing enhances data created at the transaction processing system. This drawing is stored by the organization in computers with special references. If a similar drawing is again required, the organization can be said to have knowledge of this. The system can retrieve this knowledge. These activities are knowledge works and the system that promotes, preserves, distributes, and manages these works is known as knowledge management systems (Fig. 2.6).

As in case of management information systems, office systems also support workers at knowledge level. Office-support people use office systems and computer systems, such as word processing, electronic spreadsheet, e-mail, schedulers, and Internet. These systems are designed to increase productivity of support workers, who in turn serve knowledge experts.

Let us summarize the characteristics of knowledge management:

- Knowledge is vested in individuals; so risk of losing critical knowledge is always there.
- Knowledge is an outcome of research and development.
- Knowledge management systems cannot be treated at par with MIS.
- Knowledge is very critical for organizations to promote and accumulate.
- Organizations need to invest on research and development.

Decision Support Systems (DSS)

Strategic and long-term planning decisions are made by the senior and top executive level management. Strategic decisions are unique, non-repetitive, and unplanned and have deep impact on the organization. Decisions to relocate a production unit, venture out in a new line of business, negotiate a tie-up or an amalgamation, and go for a break-up or into liquidation are examples of strategic decisions by the top management. Decision support systems (DSS), also known as executive support systems (ESS), serve the top management with making decisions that are 'unique, rapidly changing and not easily specified in advance'.

Usually, decision support information is presented in the form of graphs and abstract data by processing the internal and external data. The data generated at the transaction processing level is processed to generate reports, graphs, and further analysis. The information presented to the management is highly analytical. It combines data and sophisticated analytical models or data analysis tools to support non-routine decision-making. Decision support systems have more analytical power than other systems. By using tools like OLAP (online analytical processing) and DW (data warehousing), users can derive reports by changing parameters, assumptions, and questions. The OLAP and DW are database analysis tools that work on the huge data in the organization and produce desired reports. The systems also provide sensitivity analysis, i.e. 'what-if' analysis. In 'what-if' analysis, the manager can pose hypothetical questions regarding the future course of business, profitability, and product-market situations, and then get analytical reports through these tools.

Let us take a simple example:

Sunil Mohanty Perfume Corporation has a perfume-manufacturing machine, which the company bought ten years back for Rs 200,000. This machine has started giving problems and needs a maintenance cost of Rs 100,000 every year. The new machine's cost today is Rs 100,000. Obviously, on the new investments, there is 18 per cent annual interest. Sunil, as the CEO of the company, can ask the system: 'What happens if we sell the printing machine and buy a new one at the new price? Will we save money or end up spending more money?' The analysis tools answer these queries.

The DSS/ESS serves at the top or strategic level of the management. The systems at this level are designed to address non-routine decision-making by providing advance graphics and presentations. They work on both the internal and external data and, instead of a specific answer, provide generalized solutions (Fig. 2.7).

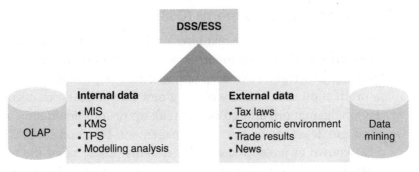

Fig. 2.7 DSS interface with internal and external data

The characteristics of the DSS can be summarized as follows:

- The DSS are meant for the top management of the organization.
- It uses internal financial and revenue data and external data from government agencies and trade results.
- It helps the management with abstract of the data usually in graphical form.
- It uses tools like OLAP, DW, and sensitivity analysis.

INFORMATION SYSTEMS STRUCTURE FROM FUNCTIONAL VIEWPOINT

So far in this chapter, we have discussed information systems from the perspective of management role. We also classify IS by the specific organizational functions, such as sales, marketing, customer relationship, supply chain, warehousing, finance, and manufacturing. Across all these functions lies one set of activities: buy-process-sell goods. The various types of organizational functions are interdependent. An example is discussed below:

You are able to sell goods as a result of good marketing campaign. You invest on a marketing campaign with a plan of selling more goods that you believe are quality products, perhaps manufactured in your own production unit at Noida. You sell more than you can produce; so you buy some ready-made products from your vendors in Chennai, Bangaluru, and Mumbai. You avoid sourcing from Kolkata because of the logistic problem you had last time. Chawla Roadways, the transport company, lost some of the consignments. You buy from different sources, as you cannot rely on just one supplier. Moreover, there are warehousing issues. Due to a municipal ceiling drive in Delhi, your warehouse at Lajpat Nagar was sealed. Now, you do not have much of the space left for storage. The rentals have also gone up and the cost of finance is high. You made a good profit last year, but your revenue seems to

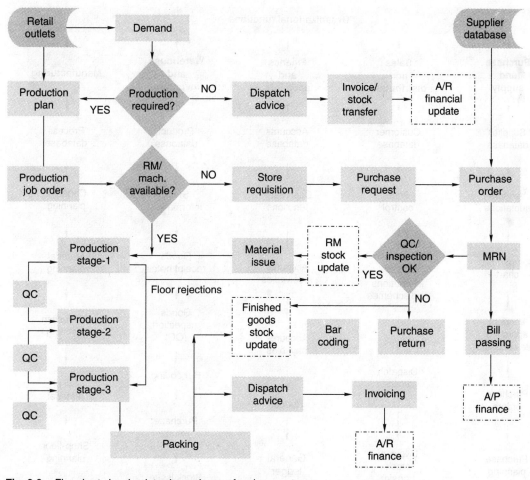

Fig. 2.8 Flowchart showing interdependency of various systems

be dipping this time as a result of all these bottlenecks in trade. You need to realize your outstanding bills receivable just to make a reasonable profit and comfortable cash flow for the next summer season.

Look at Fig. 2.8. What do you find? Are all functional systems interdependent?

The organizational functions are subsystems of transaction processing systems (TPS). They are major producers of the information required by other systems, which in turn produces information for other systems. You can achieve clarity by looking at Fig. 2.9.

These different types of systems are only loosely coupled in most organizations. A small organization may not have a customer relationship department. The marketing coordinator takes care of the customer relationship.

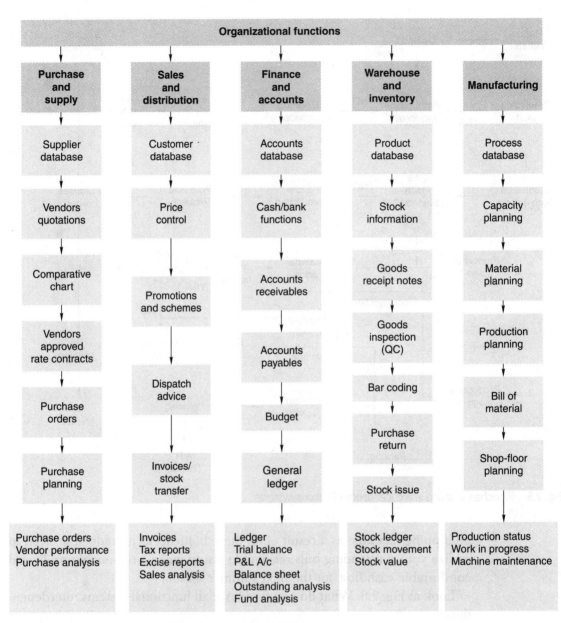

Fig. 2.9 Organizational functions: systems and subsystems

Excise and taxation is taken care by the accounts department, but large corporations have a full-fledged excise department. Similarly, companies do not hire an HR manager, if the employee strength is less than 100. The accounts manager takes care of the human resource functions. Corporations have a dedicated vice-president taking care of its most possessed assets—human beings. Even the names of the functions differ from organization to organization; for example in one organization it may be PPC, which involves all manufacturing activities. In one organization marketing can be a full-fledged department headed by a vice-president, in another organization, marketing can just be a function of sales and marketing clubbed together. Similarly, in some organizations human resource may be known as personnel department.

Various organizational functions are as follows:

- Purchase and supply systems
- Marketing, sales and distribution systems
- Warehouse and inventory systems
- Financial and accounting systems
- Manufacturing and production control systems
- Human resource and payroll systems

Each of the above systems is supported by scores of subsystems. Figure 2.9 illustrates these systems and their subsystems. We will discuss information systems for these functions and their subsystems.

Purchase and Supply Systems

Once Managing Director of Subhiksha, the famous retail chain in India, quipped: 'We make profits by purchasing efficiently rather than selling at a high price.' As he knows well that selling at a high price to the most aware and learned customer of today is not possible. Perhaps this realization makes him sell at low prices and claim (by the customer—in a promotional campaign) in a big way '*bachat mera adhikaar hai* (saving is my birthright)'. Not only for Subhiksha but also for all players in the trade, efficient purchasing is where the profit lies.

Purchase information systems cover activities like vendor identification, evaluation, request for quotation (RFQ), rate contract finalization, price finalization, and issuing purchase orders (Fig. 2.10). Internally, purchase department plans purchases to be made during a particular time period. Purchase planning is based on the sales data of the previous period and it also considers the demands made by various departments and retail stores. The department generates reports on pending supplies, short supplies, vendor-performance analysis, purchase-value estimation, and purchase costing. These information systems bring efficiency in the purchase functions and avoid chances of overstocking.

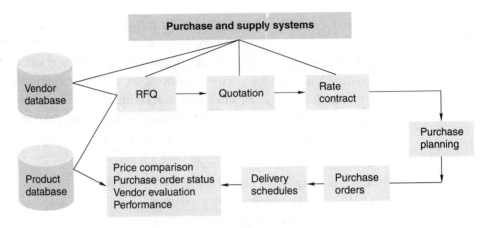

Fig. 2.10 Purchase and supply systems and subsystems

Marketing, Sales, and Distribution Systems

Ninety per cent of the organizational energy is spent on selling, selling, and selling. For the sake of our discussion in this text, we include marketing functions as well. Sales, marketing, and distribution systems support flow of goods from company's warehouse to the end consumer. The marketing functions involve the 4Ps of marketing mix—product, price, promotion, and place—which are supported by the information system. The choice of product is based on the analysis of what sells most at given point of time and place. Price determination is a complex choice of many factors. It is not based on just demand and supply. The system does an analysis of internal factors, such as costs, margins, and quality of the product. The external factors, such as competitors' price for similar product, place, and time considerations of what customer can pay, are important factors for determination of prices. These are the factors that are beyond the control of the organization, such as competitors' moves and government regulations. The systems offer information on all related issues. Similarly, the promotion mix is also decided on the number of factors. Advertising budgets, radio promotions, TV advertisements, offers of spot discounts, and promotional schemes are some of the areas where systems can provide enough material to help the management choose the right promotion mix. Selection of the place is, perhaps, the biggest challenge and strategy in retail business. Even if the organization has all ingredients of a successful recipe, such as quality goods and perfect prices, it does not work at a bad place. Organizations often go through the experience that one of their own retail stores does well while another gives losses. Therefore, analysis of internal and external data is very important for strategic decision by the top management.

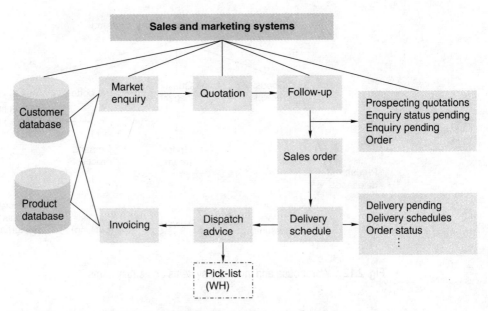

Fig. 2.11   Sales, marketing, and distribution systems and subsystems

Distribution involves order processing. The distribution office receives orders from the customers or demands from various retail locations. The system supports picking and dispatch of the goods to the customer or retail store. In the process, there are subsystems, such as order confirmation, dispatch advice, packing list, invoicing, and physical delivery (Fig. 2.11). Information systems provide sales-analysis tools. At the retail point, sale is captured using EPOS machines. This also creates customer database, which works as a repository for the customer-relationship management tool. As choice of a store location is critical in retail, so is retaining a customer. Retailers use various tactics and techniques to satisfy customer and retain them. There are scores of discount schemes, free gifts, and coupons used as bait to lure the customers and retain them.

Warehouse and Inventory Systems

Warehousing functions in a trading organization involve receipt, storage, and dispatch of goods (Fig. 2.12). Modern business-management techniques talk about 'zero' or 'just-in-time' inventory, but still storage function cannot be done away with. Inventories can be reduced but cannot be completely made to vanish from the warehouse. Systems are needed to size up the inventory value, inventory-carrying costs, and cost of the last-moment procurement in case of stock failure.

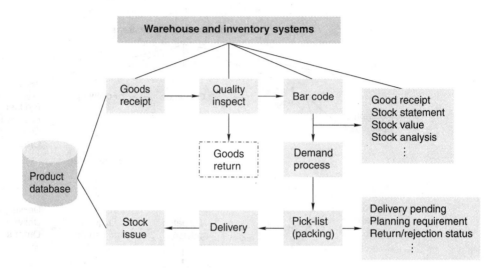

Fig. 2.12 Warehouse and inventory systems and subsystems

Just as goods are received against a purchase order, the goods are inspected physically and tested, if need be, at the warehouse. Stocking of goods in the proper location that is easily approachable and traceable is important. At times, large warehouses use forklifts and radio-frequency tags for automatic identification and locating goods in the warehouse. The systems provide analysis on the space utilization based on the volume of goods.

On receiving a dispatch advice from the logistic or dispatch system, the warehouse system prepares a pick list. Packing and delivery are the last subsystems of the warehouse and inventory functions.

Financial and Accounting Systems

Finance is the central system to all business information systems. The basic function of a financial system is to see if the business is getting a right return on investment. The financial system answers questions like: 'Is the business profitable? Is the business viable in the longer run?' The accounting systems receive data from all other systems, viz. sales, purchases, inventory, and payroll. Sales data of retail stores is posted to financial systems. Enterprise systems do consolidation of data and provide analytical reports. Financial systems have many subsystems, such as general ledger, account receivable, accounts payables, taxation system, and budgeting (Fig. 2.13).

Financial systems produce various reports, such as trial balance, profit and loss accounts, balance sheet, budget analysis, bills receivable analysis, bills payable analysis, ratio analysis, and cost centre analysis.

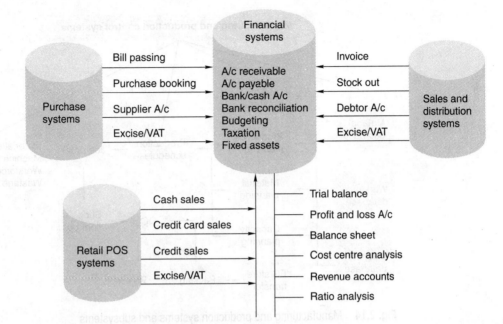

Fig. 2.13 Financial systems and subsystems interface with other systems

Manufacturing and Production Control Systems

The systems that deal with planning, scheduling, and controlling of manufacturing process, are called production control information systems. Planning and scheduling refer to the system of deriving the right amount of goods to be produced within the constraints of manufacturing capacities and material resources. Controlling is the process of monitoring production process so that it is as per the production planning and scheduling. Manufacturing and production control systems provide production schedules, planning, material planning, capacity planning, and shop-floor planning (Fig. 2.14). The systems in planning and scheduling advise the best plan of action for efficient manufacturing of goods. The production schedules are based on the overall production planning for the month or the week.

Human Resource and Payroll Systems

Human resource systems deal with the human factor in the organization. The systems deal with recruitment, retention, and compensation of the workforce. Various subsystems of human resource information systems are payroll, which deals with the monetary part of the compensation, and HR, which deals with the non-monetary aspect of employees (Fig. 2.15). The other subsystems of

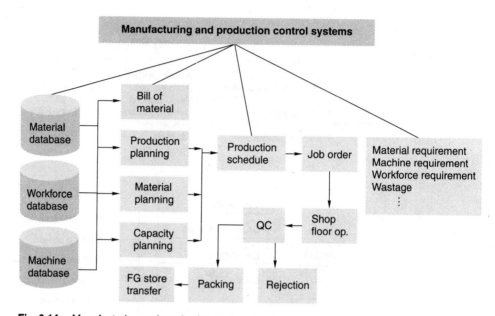

Fig. 2.14 Manufacturing and production systems and subsystems

human resources include recruitment, posting, appraisals, promotions, and transfers. The subsystems of payroll are salary computation, tax computation, provident fund, employees' state insurance, loan processing, and leave module. They produce reports and maintain records of salary, leave, attendance, perks, and taxes.

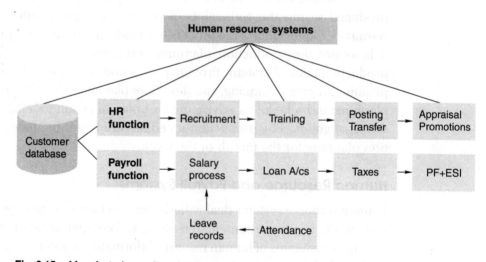

Fig. 2.15 Manufacturing and production systems and subsystems

COMPONENTS OF RETAIL INFORMATION SYSTEMS

Information technology is the backbone of modern retailing. The traditional retailing was easier to manage because of its size, scope, and uncompetitive nature; and usually the shops were managed by the owner-manager. But the modern retail formats, which are superstores and large chains owned by large organizations, are difficult to manage without an efficient and reliable IT system in place. The customer is now 'king' in a real sense of the term and wants value out of the entire shopping experience. The customer is not just satisfied with price and quality of the product but also seeks complete ease, convenience, efficiency, and comfort at point of purchase.

Technology proves beneficial in creating and maintaining customer relationships. Analysis of data collected at the retail point of sales helps understand preferences, buying habits, spending budgets, family needs of an individual customer. Relationships are maintained by utilizing IT for periodical e-mailing, SMSes (short messaging services), greetings, promotional letters, and personal calling.

Therefore, while deciding technology at the retail front, retailer has to look at the two edge benefits. On one hand, it is imperative to provide an efficient point of sales and checkouts, on the other, the systems provide the retailer with an insight into the affairs of the company.

We can classify retail information systems in the following six components (Fig. 2.16):

1. Hardware
2. Software
3. Databases
4. Networks
5. Automatic identification and data-capture systems (AIDC)
6. Electronic payment systems or electronic fund transfers (EFT)

The first four components—hardware, software, databases, and networks—are part of any management information system. Given the peculiarities of retail, we need to study two more specialized components, viz. automatic identification and data-capture (AIDC) systems and electronic payment systems or electronic fund transfers (EFT).

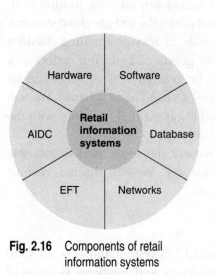

Fig. 2.16 Components of retail information systems

Fig. 2.17   Electronic cash
register .

Hardware

The primary and central component of modern retail information technology is the hardware. Everything else revolves around the machine, tangible and visible to the eye. There are two types of point-of-sales (POS) systems used in modern retail stores: electronic cash register (ECR), which is shown in Fig. 2.17, and computer-based electronic point-of-sales (EPOS) systems. An ECR only has the capability to make and print a bill and accumulate the total sales transaction amounts for the day. It comes with small and limited functionality embedded software to do billing and print the day's sales report on the printer. The software that runs an ECR is embedded into the hardware and offers a very limited application.

On the other hand, a computer-based POS system offers much more extensive features, due to the application software it runs on. The devices in a computer-based POS system typically include monitor, cash drawer, keyboard, mouse, receipt printer, and bar code scanner.

In addition to the computer and its peripherals in an EPOS system, there are other hardware components such as magnetic strip readers, conveyer belts, pole display (also known as customer display or in-counter display), scanner and weighing scales. These additional devices reduce the time spent in serving a customer. Moreover, recent technologies also include devices using biometric identifications and proximity cards in mobile phones. In the near future, the customer will be able to pay for purchases with literally a one touch or swipe.

Self-checkout systems and information kiosks are gaining momentum. Research shows that customers like to shop and prefer the self-checkout systems. The information kiosks can play a major role in service retailing, besides providing information on the availability of goods and placing orders at a good retail store. How comfortable would it be to buy our train ticket and air ticket at a self-service kiosk placed alongside of an ATM at a bank? We will now discuss some core issues related to automation of retail functions with the help of available point-of-sales hardware.

All the hardware devices discussed above are the tools used to increase customers' satisfaction and ensure their loyalty. We will discuss various hardware systems used in retail in Chapter 3.

Software

Compared to the electronic cash register, an EPOS system allows retailers to compute more extensive analysis of sales, product, and customer because of the application software running at the core of it. We have already discussed various software systems, such as, system software, utilities, computer programming languages, and operating systems in Chapter 1. Let us revise what we learnt about systems and application software.

Software is categorized into two broad categories—system software and application software. The software that manages the resources of a computer system, provides utilities to manage files creation, deletion, and storage, and controls various input and output devices, communication links is called system software. Various operating systems, such as DOS, Windows, Linux, UNIX, are examples of such software. Also, various utilities, such as Internet browsers, explorer, compress-decompress programs, are part of the system software. The software created to cater to business requirements and transaction processing is called application software. Supply chain management, production planning, database management software, accounting software, and Web-based air-ticket reservation software are examples of application software.

While discussing retail application software, we classify it broadly into two categories:

1. Best-of-breed, ready-to-use, or stand-alone software
2. Integrated enterprise solutions, commonly known as enterprise resource planning (ERP) systems

Answer to the question 'What to buy?' depends on the individual needs of the retailer. A small retailer, who operates a single store, should go for the first category of software. A stand-alone POS system (Fig. 2.18), which comes under the category of 'best of breed' should be evaluated, including its all core and non-core components. Decision to implement stand-alone best-of-breed software keeps the initial costs low, implementation time short, and employees get onto the work with little or no training. The point to be kept in mind is that these functions and features should satisfy the need of the retailer.

Similarly, for a large retailer who already has retail ERP at the back-office, the solution is again best of breed for the stores. Therefore, when evaluating software, the retailer can bargain for the best and should not pay for what is not needed. The shortcoming in this approach is difficulty in integration of the ready-made retail software with the legacy or ERP system running at the back end. But this difficulty can be overcome by integrating both through a middleware, specifically written to make both the software 'talk' to each other.

We discuss these features in detail in Chapters 7 and 11.

Database Management Systems

Database management systems consist of data and data management tools and systems. We have already defined 'data' as streams of raw facts representing

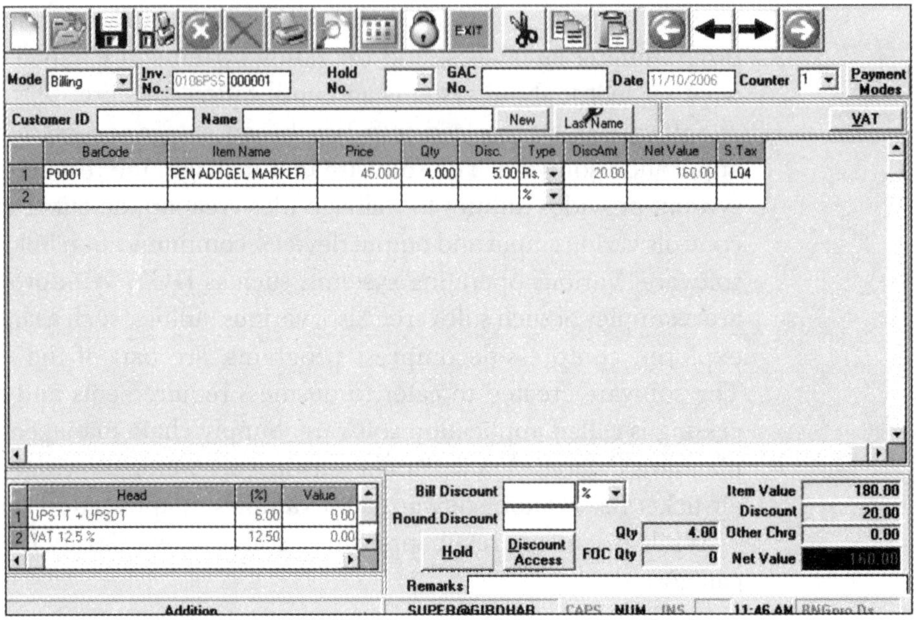

Fig. 2.18 Point-of-sales software

events occurring in the organization and environment before they have been organized and arranged into a meaningful form.

A 'database' is where the data resides. It is a collection of 'related' information stored so that it is available to many users for different purposes. For example, a physical file containing details and marks scored by MBA students in various subjects is a physical database of students. A computer database gives us some form of electronic filing system, which has many ways of cross referencing. Cross referencing is the method of how the database can be approached, referred, and used. This allows users to refer to and retrieve data in multiple ways.

At retail or any business transaction systems, data is collected during transactions, processed, and analysed later for management decision-making. We will discuss various attributes of a database system, database administration, types of database, and some latest trends in database analysis, such as online analytical processing (OLAP), data warehousing (DW), and data mining (DM) concepts.

Networks and Telecommunications

We need to understand networks and communication between computers not just for academic purpose but also to enrich our knowledge and help

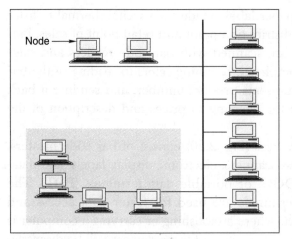

Fig. 2.19 Networks

us make right choice, as managers and decision-makers, when we choose a medium to connect our various offices or retail outlets.

Computer networking is the science and technique of connecting two or more computers together to share files and documents and send messages. Local area network (LAN), wide area network (WAN), virtual private network (VPN), Internet, and intranet are various network systems (Fig. 2.19). A network has a number of nodes. A node can be defined as a computer machine or a connection point on a network. The LAN technology is used to connect computers within an office to share applications, databases, and information. Organizations use multiple applications through the LAN. The WAN is used to connect various offices across the city, country, or globe, using various telecommunication channels. Computers can be connected through a wired medium or a wireless medium of telecommunication. Wi-Fi, RF is a wireless system of connecting networks. Radio frequency (RF) connectivity is gaining popularity because of its ease in erection and maintenance of the network. Using Internet, backbone networks at various offices of the organization are connected. This is known as Intranet. The VPN is established over leased telecommunication lines or an Internet backbone with a high bandwidth. (Bandwidth refers to the capacity of a telecommunication line to transmit volumes of data per unit of time; for example, a 2-Mbps line means that it can transmit 2 megabytes of data per second.)

We will now not only discuss various network technologies but also mull over electronic data interchange (EDI). The EDI is going to be one of the important techniques of interoffice data transmission in the retail organization. The concepts have been discussed in Chapter 6.

Automatic Identification and Data-Capture (AIDC) Systems

The next important component in retail information system is identification of products by some means, either mechanical or electronic. Automatic product identification systems cover tagging, marking, and labelling the product with bar codes, radio frequency identification devices (RFID), or any other technology so that the product is identified with unique code. At the warehouse or the goods-receiving point, products are identified and labelled. Bar codes

Fig. 2.20 A data-capture device

Sources: Percon, geipl.com

are printed on paper labels made for specific thermal-transfer printers. At the distribution point and retail point of sales, bar-coded products are scanned with bar code readers and sales transaction is completed. Scanning refers to reading of the bar codes, which represents product number, and sending it back to the computer for referring to prices and description of the product.

The AIDC devices (Fig. 2.20) consist of bar code printers, scanners, wireless scanners, electronic display labels, and data-capture units (DCU) or portable data terminals (PDT). The portable data terminals are used for faster data access and scanning products where establishing or carrying a computer is not feasible. The various uses of these devices will be discussed in Chapter 4.

Shelf edge labelling refers to an electronic display of products, price, and schemes on the display shelf at the retail outlet. In this kind of display, LCD and other types of display units are used instead of paper or board display.

Electronic Payment Systems

Also known as an electronic fund transfer, electronic payment system is the core of electronic point of sales. A discussion on retail information system would be incomplete if we do not discuss electronic fund transfer (EFT). It refers to making of payments through electronic medium, such as e-cash, e-cheque, credit cards, and smart cards.

As the retail industry has moved from the unorganized to organized retailing, payment systems have also undergone a sea change. While in the old traditional street corner grocery store, cash was the only method of settlement, today plastic currency and electronic transfers have overtaken it. Credit cards, debit cards, and smart cards in the form of store value cards are widely used for payment settlement in retail (Fig. 2.21). Payments can be made by digital token-based currency. E-check and e-cash are managed by digital token. Person-to-person payments as popularized by PayPal have already taken a firm seat in the West, specifically in Web-based transactions. Payments through SMSes using mobile phones are gaining momentum.

Detailed discussions on various popular forms of modern electronic payment systems at retail and e-tailing will be provided in Chapter 8.

Fig. 2.21 Electronic payment technology

SUMMARY

Information system is the organized collection, processing, transmission, and dissemination of information in accordance with defined procedures, whether automated or manual. Information systems involve organization, management, and technology. Technology is used to serve the management to make decisions in order to run businesses and make the organization viable in the marketplace. There are chiefly four types of information systems—transaction processing systems (TPS) at the operation level of the organization, management information systems (MIS) for middle-level managers who take day-to-day decisions, knowledge management systems (KMS) for the specialists and knowledge workers, and decision support systems (DSS) for the top-level managers who make strategic decisions. The MIS work on the internal data collected by the transaction processing systems. The DSS work on internal and external data and present reports in abstract and graphical forms.

Information systems based on various organizational functions are part of management information systems. These functions are broadly classified into six functions of purchase and supply, sales and distribution, warehouse and inventory, finance and accounts, manufacturing and production control, and human resource and payroll. These systems help managers create basic data, which is cohesively linked with other systems. Components of retail information technology have two more components, viz. automatic identification and data capture (AIDC) and electronic fund transfer (EFT). These are in addition to the four components of any information technology, viz. hardware, software, database, and networks.

CONCEPT REVIEW QUESTIONS

1. Define information systems.
2. What are different types of information systems from the management point of view?
3. Write brief notes on data and information.
4. Explain knowledge workers with suitable examples.
5. Define information systems with respect to organizational functions.
6. Briefly explain the various management functions in an organization.
7. What are the different components of an information system? Explain briefly.
8. Explain retail-specific additional components of information systems.

CRITICAL THINKING QUESTIONS

1. How will you establish an IT Department in your retail organization? What will be the basic systems that you will set up?
2. 'Today retailing is very much dependent on information technology.' Discuss this statement.

PROJECT

1. Visit any computerized retail store in your vicinity and prepare a project report covering the following aspects:

   (a) Information technology infrastructure, including computer hardware, EPOS software, operating systems, and product marking systems

   (b) Information systems infrastructure using application software, kinds of reporting systems, and types of the reports they generate, categorizing the reports into TPS, MIS, KMS, and DSS

SELECT REFERENCES

BNG Infotech, www.bng.co.in, last accessed on 02/12/2007.

Laudon, Kenneth and Jane Laudon 2002, *Management Information Systems*, Pearson Education (Singapore).

CASE STUDY

Greeting Customers with Information Systems

Company   Greeting Cards Company

Greeting Cards Company (GCC) was launched by Raman brothers in Chennai in the year 1979 with a modest share capital and infrastructure. With the basic background of printing greeting cards and cine-stars calendar, the company evolved into 'Hallmark' of India. By 2002, the company had strengthened its stable of products by adding multiple products like gifts, perfumes, music cassettes, and photo albums. With a small turnover of Rs 40 crore in 1995, it has achieved a turnover of Rs 104 crore in the year 2006–07. This is despite of the fact that paper greeting cards industry is facing deadly competition from SMS and e-greetings.

In the beginning of year 2002, GCC had 9 divisions, 11 distribution offices, 40 company-owned stores, and around 500 franchisee stores in the country. The company was vertically divided into nine major divisions, viz. 1. Helpage cards division, 2. CRY-cards division, 3. gift division, 4. perfume division 5. photo-album division, 6. paper-flower division, 7. office stationery division, 8. printing division, and 9. egreeting.com (an e-greetings division). All nine divisions run as separate revenue centres. The 11 distribution offices across the country catered to the logistic requirement of 500 odd retail shops.

Keeping pace with the retail boom, the company increased its number of stores to 100 by the year 2007 from 40 stores in 2002. GCC also recognized the importance of the Internet and how it can restructure the businesses. Keeping pace with technology, an e-commerce division www.egreeting.com, was created. The company forayed into retail much before the retail boom happened in this country. Therefore, calling GCC an 'original' Indian retailer will not be an exaggeration.

The various organizational departments for all the divisions at GCC are purchase, production, repacking, distribution, warehousing, accounting, information systems, human resource, payroll, tax, excise, machinery maintenance, and public relations. GCC distributors visit the huge company warehouses, every year before the beginning of season, i.e. *rakshabandhan*. They browse through the new designs, select items they like and confirm the order for the season.

Industry   Retail Chain

Solution Area   Automation of retail stores and warehouses, creation of information systems for various divisions, and corporate managers.

Problem

Managing such a large business is not a simple task. But GCC management was always techno-savvy. Way back in 1989, the company had its inventory on computers. The distribution billing was computerized using legacy software developed in-house. But by the time the company was a 100-plus-stores organization, it could not just rely on the FoxPro-based legacy application. At the stores level, it needed proper electronic point-of-sales systems with user-friendly software packages. The problem was not just billing and stock keeping at the storefront but also gathering of data, analysis of data, valuation of stock, preparation of statutory reports for investors and governments. Keeping a tab on stock movement, analysing the sales graph of each store, etc. were crucial activities that GCC management could not do without. It was felt that to streamline these activities, GCC needed an ERP solution with strong POS interface.

Solution

Now, the search began for the best, Indianized, comprehensive but cost-effective software package. A host of packages were evaluated, keeping in mind the above requirements. The delivery and implementation time was also an important factor. The management zeroed in on one local ERP solution provider by the name of 'BrainSoft'. The software vendor had a good presence in retail but not so good in ERP and a big retail chain organization. By looking at the product features during a series of demonstrations, the senior managers of GCC were convinced of the qualities and felt that it suited their purpose. Since the price was also attractive, there were negligible risks.

The GCC commissioned IBM Servers with dual processors and RAID5 systems having around 200 GB hard disk and 2 GB RAM. Almost 250 systems that were across their nine divisions at the corporate office were connected. Some of the divisions were not cabled and WAN was established using RF (radio frequency) transmission system.

Implementation

The decision of GCC management was not bad. The small vendor-consultant with hardly any big names in its customer list, but with a strong technical know-how and a strong commitment to deliver, made it possible to implement the basic ERP modules within a slender time span of three months. This included system analysis, customization (mostly hardcore that involved modification of the source code), data porting, and training to the staff. There were around 75 major changes and 100 reports that were redone. Even the basic structure of product coding was changed. But the strong will of the EDP team to implement a solution and relentless support of the vendor organization were the key factors behind the success of the project.

Brainsoft customized its ERP 'Revive' to suit GCC's requirements. In the first phase, four information systems were implemented, viz. purchase, distribution, inventory, and accounts. The purchase system took care of purchase order generation and vendor evaluation systems. In distribution processes, handheld data-capture units were used. They scanned each item of their choice. The code of the item was stored in the system and it also reflected the MRP on the screen. Later, this data was downloaded into the computer. Goods were dispatched on the basis of this data. The inventory was streamlined by converting the opening stock data from legacy systems. The product code was 20-digit long, which represented the country code, company code, product code, and batch number. Similarly, finance and accounts were brought into the same system, as they were using Tally for accounts.

Since an ERP implementation involves change management in the organization, the constant support of senior management was a key driver. An ERP Task Force (ETF) was created involving senior EDP and accounts managers of GCC and functional and technical heads of Brainsoft that closely monitored the progress.

Benefits

With implementation of Revive, all the departments and functional areas were brought under one integrated solution. Two IT engineers, who were earlier working on just sending and receiving data from Tally to their old system, were put to better jobs. By automating all the divisions and departments, the huge investment on RF and optical fibre connections for intranet was utilized. The MIS system generated analytical reports on sales and stock of every store. Matrix reports on divisions and products, divisions and segments were available to the top management. Following are some facts based on the quantitative analysis:

- Sales increased from Rs 68m in 2002 to Rs 104m in 2007, which was 53 per cent.
- Investment blocked on inventories decreased by Rs 61.5m in 2007.
- The company was managing 90 stores in Feb 2008 as compared to 38 stores in 2002.
- Employee strength increases 810 in 2002 to 934, just on 15 per cent in spite of a growth of 59 per cent.
- Profits have increased from Rs 753m in 2002 to Rs 1186m in 2007, which was 64 per cent.

Questions:

1. What were the information issues before going for integrated information systems at GCC?
2. From management information systems point of view, analyse present division structure. Suggest if a better structure will benefit the management.
3. Divide the various functions at GCC into TPS, MIS, KMS, and DSS.

Source: Based on interactions with the management and staff of GCC, personal observations during consulting and providing software solutions, and information from the company's promotional material and websites.

3

Electronic Point of Sales—Hardware

Learning Objectives

- To understand various hardware components used at a retail point of sales
- To appreciate the functioning and advantages of electronic cash registers
- To discuss computer-based electronic point-of-sales (EPOS) machines and their advantages
- To choose the right EPOS system
- To understand the role of automated checkout systems and information kiosks in service retailing
- To become familiar with the use and technology of vending machines

Twelve million retail shops in India

As per an international study, the number of retail outlets in India has been estimated as twelve million. This translates into a density of one shop for every 90 people. There was a 30–35 per cent growth rate in organized retail in the year 2006–07. There will be 2.5 million additional jobs in the retail sector by 2010. There were 300 to 600 malls under construction in 2007–08.

The increasing growth of the retail industry has generated a lot of interest in the local and international community of vendors, technology providers, financiers, consultants, students, and other people having a direct or indirect link in retail. There is heavy pressure on the government to allow full foreign direct investment. India appears to be a number one retail destination as per the A.T. Kearney survey conducted in the year 2006.

Is it a $30 billion market for information technology, vendors, and system integrators? Perhaps the market is maturing for thousands of electronic cash registers, electronic point-of-sales machines, and software products.

In Chapter 2, we have learnt information systems and how these systems are helpful in decision-making at the various levels of management in the organization. Use of computers for a fast and accurate billing system brings efficiency at the retail checkout. Efficiency boosts employees' morale and increases customer confidence in the delivery service personnel and in turn in the organization. Moreover, computers help create the database of sales and customer data, on which future actions and decisions of the company would be based.

As per a study conducted by Gartner Inc. in 2007, as more technical devices are brought to bear on retailing, it might be possible to make shoppers more interested in going to the store. (During the first two months of year 2007, Gartner Research, a leading provider of research and analysis about the global information technology industry, partnered with RIS News to conduct a benchmark study about retail technology trends. In conjunction with the RIS News editorial team, Gartner created the survey and posted it online. For details, the readers may refer to http://www.lawson.com/www/resource.nsf/pub/Retail_0907.pdf/$FILE/Retail_0907.pdf.) A Canadian retail technology survey propagates that technology needs to be seen as an investment, not an expense. It is an enabler for strategies that can change the retail paradigm and propel retailers ahead of competition. Retailers should not only invest in enhancing technical capabilities to automate but also train their employees and share the information across the entire organization. Retail point of sales is the first place where automation should be initiated. The creation of huge databases, efficient information systems, and customer satisfaction begins with automating point of sales in retail. This is the first step towards building customer relationship. Database of customer creates a strong foundation for an organization that works towards customer satisfaction. Automating the point-of-sales operations serves two major purposes:

1. Efficiency in service delivery
2. Collection of primary sales and customer data

In this chapter, we are going to discuss the following technologies used at a modern point-of-sales location:

- Electronic cash register
- Electronic point of sales
- Automated checkouts and kiosks
- Vending machines

ELECTRONIC CASH REGISTERS

Electronic cash registers (ECRs) are the basic billing machines that help the grocer in creating bill and printing receipt and basic sales reports. The introduction of ECR interfaced with electronic scales (then also known as automatic checkout stands) occurred in the late 1960s and provided many advantages over mechanical price-computing scales and mechanical cash registers (mechanical computing devices like calculators).

In comparison to manual billing, in an ECR, the total price is automatically calculated by entering a unit price from the ECR product lookup memory (Fig. 3.1). The users can manually enter product code and print a receipt. The

Fig. 3.1 ECR with cash drawer

Source: Absbharat.com

printed receipt or bill from ECR has the capability of providing the customers with more information than the receipts from mechanical cash registers. Manual entries of the total price are no longer required, thus increasing cashier efficiency and decreasing the number of keyboard errors by the cashier.

Electronic cash registers use limited-purpose, limited-functionality software embedded in it for billing and stock reports. *Limited functionality* refers to very little functions offered by the software that is fused in the microprocessor of the ECR. Since ECRs do not have an operating system and cannot hold a third-party database, you cannot load software of your choice. The software is provided by the manufacturer of the ECR. These machines come with various memories to store any number of products.

Components of ECRs

The commonly available ECRs have the following components attached to them.

Electronic Billing Machine

This is the basic machine with full alphabet and numeric keyboard for keying product codes and prices (Fig. 3.2). Usually, it has a two-line LCD display panel on the machine, which displays the product code and price as punched by the cashier at the retail store.

Fig. 3.2 ECR with cash drawer and pole display

Source: Tyche Peripherals/Samsung

Extra-Hot Keys

Some hot keys are available that are pre-programmed by the manufacturer. With these keys, the cashier can perform quick functions, such as saving bills and printing receipts, and as programmed by the engineer.

Embedded Software

Electronic cash registers come with limited-purpose software fused in the processor of the machine, to store product codes and prices. Again, the software is not upgradeable or manageable by a third-party vendor. Only the manufacturer of the ECR can change, upgrade, rectify, or maintain the software.

Integrated Receipt Printer

The ECRs invariably come with a receipt or bill printer. Most of the ECRs have a dot matrix printer (DMP). But if users demand, manufacturer also integrates thermal printers.

Electronic cash registers also come with some advanced tools, such as pole display, cash drawer, bar code scanner, and magnetic card swipe.

Pole Display

This device is an additional attachment to the main ECR. This is also called customer display because the basic purpose of this display is for the customer. It displays the 'net' amount of the bill on the digital screen it offers. It comes with single- or two-line display systems.

Cash Drawer

Some ECRs come with a lockable cash drawer. The drawer opens when a bill is created and automatically gets locked on exit. The basic purpose of cash drawers is that they have different compartments to store currency notes of different denominations and coins. They are secure and reduce pilferage.

Bar Code Scanner

In some of the advanced machines, bar code scanner can be attached for reading bar codes on products. This reduces the chances of keying in error and the bill is created with perfection.

Magnetic Card Swipe

A magnetic card swipe slot is attached with the ECR. On swiping the credit card, the information is read and also printed on the bill. It offers functions of an EFT terminal for swiping credit cards.

Moving up the scale, there are specialist manufacturers who supply advanced ECRs, which are of two basic types—stand-alone and networked. These are not technically EPOS machines but have entry-level software to control stock. Stand-alone machines run independently and are not connected with any other ECR at the store, whereas networked ECRs are connected with each other through a network cable. In both stand-alone and networked ECRs, the vendor will be involved in programming, implementing, and training the employees to use the systems.

Specifications of an Advanced ECR

- A 5 rows × 20 columns LCD operator display
- High backlit customer display
- Built in tiny bar code printer, which supports EAN13, EAN8 bar code printing
- Supports other external devices, such as kitchen printer, weighing scale, customer display, and modem
- Communicates with PC through LAN card
- Supports product lookup
- Provides daily sales report
- Generates top ten quantity reports
- Gives stock report

Advantages and Disadvantages of Using ECR

Advantages

1. Electronic cash registers enable retail outlets to streamline all sales transactions, such as calculating and recording sales and printing receipt for the customer.
2. They reduce errors as price and transaction amount is automatically calculated.
3. They increase accountability by producing correct day reports.
4. Transactions are made quicker as billing is automated through either bar code scanner or product lookup systems.
5. Transaction costs are lowered since electronic processing is faster and less expensive than paper processing.
6. Cash drawer is a secure place where the retailer can keep the cash.
7. They are light, portable, and easy to operate. They are also perfect for start-up businesses and existing businesses with low turnover and temporary sales environment.

Disadvantages

1. The major disadvantage of an ECR is that it cannot provide analysis on the sales data. The limited data is stored for a limited period of time. Computer-based electronic point-of-sales (EPOS) machines fulfil this requirement.
2. The ECR cannot be connected with the outside world like company website or supply chain management.

ELECTRONIC POINT OF SALES

Electronic point of sales (EPOS) is a computer-based billing system that allows greater control over retail business and helps increase customer satisfaction. The EPOS systems are mainly used by businesses that have a large number of regular sales, stock-keeping units (SKU), and customers. One of the important objectives of automating point of sales is to streamline billing operations and increase efficiency. This makes sense only when there are enough sales, products, and customers. A basic EPOS, usually a standard PC with all its accessories, handles payments quickly, updates inventory, and provides instant reports on sales and stocks.

An EPOS system is a computer-based machine (Fig. 3.3) and the software systems it runs are common operating systems and application software products available in the market. We have already discussed various operating systems and computer programming languages in Chapter 1. The application software will be discussed in Chapter 7.

Components of EPOS

Modern EPOS systems are based on Pentium IV or Celeron microprocessor-based computers. Usually, these systems are available with all peripherals of a standard computer. An EPOS system has the following components.

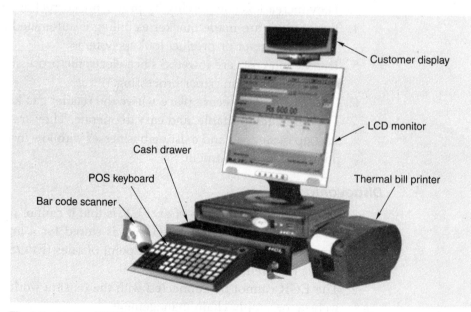

Fig. 3.3 Modern EPOS system with all attachments

Source: HCL Infosystems

Computer with all Hardware Components and an Operating System

It has all the components that we see in a computer. The earlier versions of EPOS came with a small monocolour 9″ monitor. Nowadays, EPOS comes with a TFT and touch-screen monitor (Fig. 3.4). The operating system may be DOS, Windows XP, or Linux, as per the vendor's policy or the user's choice. But one can change the operating system as per the requirements.

Integrated or Disintegrated Keyboard

Fig. 3.4   A touch-screen EPOS system

An integrated keyboard is one that is fixed on the top of the box. But now, because of ease of maintenance, vendors provide keyboards separately.

Integrated Receipt Printer

The EPOS machines invariably come with a receipt or bill printer. Most of these machines have a dot matrix printer (DMP). But if users demand, manufacturers also integrate thermal printers.

Application Software

Application software is the main component that makes EPOS different from ECR. It may or may not be provided by the same vendor, but one can replace it by third-party software.

Pole Display

Pole display is an add-on to an EPOS machine. It is also known as customer display because the basic purpose of the display is for customers. Customer display units display the 'net' amount of the bill on the digital screen it offers. They come with single- or two-line display systems. Separate pole displays are connected through the RS232 or serial port.

Cash Drawer

Cash drawer is also an add-on device. The drawers are automatically lockable on settlement of bills. The drawer opens when a bill is created and automatically gets locked on exit. The functions and operations of a cash drawer in EPOS machines are the same as in ECRs.

Bar Code Scanner

As in ECR, bar code scanner can be attached for reading bar codes on the products. This reduces the chances of keying in error and the bill is created with perfection and accuracy.

Magnetic Card Swipe

Some standard EPOS machines from IBM and NCR come with an attached magnetic card swipe slot. Additionally, external swipe slot can be attached with any computer-based machine. The swipe slot reads the credit card information and also prints the information on the bill. The external card reader can be attached through the keyboard wedge.

Benefits of EPOS

Presence of independent application software over the database and operating system of choice makes an EPOS different from an ECR. These technological tags make all the difference. The system can be connected with ERP systems and supply chain at the back office of the retail organization. (Back office refers to corporate and distribution offices in a retail organization.) Since EPOS systems run specialized software in them, the software can connect with other enterprise software running in the organization's back office. The EPOS can also be connected to websites and e-commerce portals of the organization. The data created at a POS location is the highly valued primary data of customers and sales. Analysis of this data provides a tool for management information and decision support systems of the organization. We summarize the benefits of EPOS systems below.

Database Creation

The EPOS systems create database—the backbone of any information system. Analysis of database helps management to take day-to-day decisions (such as decision to focus on the more profitable lines of business, improve demand forecasting, and minimize inventory) and strategic decisions (such as introducing a new line of products and shutting down loss making product lines) related to the organization.

Flexibility for Software Upgradation

The software can be upgraded whenever required. (Upgrading refers to editing old functions and adding new functions to the application software to meet new business requirements.) An EPOS system allows flexibility in adding new features and functions to the application software. As the requirements of the organization increase, software can be upgraded accordingly. If the user is not satisfied, altogether new application software can be installed.

Connectivity to Back-Office Systems

The EPOS system can be connected to back-office systems. (Back office applications are those that do not directly address the customer, e.g. supply chain management, and enterprise systems. By connecting EPOS to back-office systems, such as ERP, supply chain, and accounting packages, one can increase control over the business and improve profitability. Some EPOS packages export data to popular accounting packages like Sage, Tally, and QuickBooks.

Connectivity to E-Commerce Portals

With popularity of e-tailing, retailers want to update their websites in real time. (E-tailing refers to the e-commerce of retail businesses.) Electronic POS systems are connected with such e-commerce portals and they update data at regular intervals. Such connectivity provides online customers with rapid, up-to-date stock information. If stock runs out, EPOS can update the site to show that it is unavailable and warn potential customers that there will be a delay in delivery or offer an alternative.

Better Customer Relationship

Retaining a customer is more difficult than creating a new customer. Marketing researches propound that making a new customer is sixteen times more expensive than retaining an existing customer. Since application software and database is an important component of EPOS, it helps in analysing the customer data to understand the customer's tastes and preferences through customer insights. The customer data is analysed and the organization remains in touch with the customers through e-mails, messages, and greetings. The customers are also informed about promotional schemes and discount sales. Customer relationship is an important tool to keep the customer happy and satisfied. A satisfied customer is a loyal customer. All this helps in maintaining customer relationship.

Integration of Stock Control System

This allows keeping stock information up-to-date in real-time and streamlines supply chain processes. An EPOS system can automatically determine which products are fast moving and when they need replenishing.

Link to Suppliers' Websites, Extranets, or Back-Office Systems

With the fast-track system of procurement and just-in-time concepts of inventory management, suppliers themselves like to monitor sales of their customers. If EPOS systems are linked to suppliers' extranet, this provides them with access to real-time stock information, allowing them to manage their own purchasing more efficiently.

Information on the Stock Movement

Organizations can monitor stock movement and take required steps in advance. Information can be fed through to the warehouse and purchasing department, thus enabling automated purchasing and restocking. (Automated purchasing is creation of purchase orders based on re-order level of inventory.)

Increased Customer Loyalty and Employee Efficiency

Automated systems at retail counters build customer confidence in company services, which in turn creates loyalty. Fast and accurate billing or checkout systems increase efficiency. Increased efficiency not only increases employee morale but also enhances customer loyalty. It is easier to implement complex promotional schemes, discounting structure, and coupons management through EPOS systems.

Choosing the Right EPOS System

The EPOS systems come with various types, configurations, and specifications. This makes it difficult to decide on a right product for a retail organization. The difficulty is more because of the application and database software used in it, rather than the hardware (Fig. 3.5). For different types of retail applications, solutions offering different features and functions are available in the market. However, the retail organization must choose an EPOS system considering its type of business, volume of sales, and the number of customers it handles in a unit time.

In the following types of EPOS systems, the hardware, more or less, remains the same. But the application software differs from types of usages and volume of business. The difference is more in terms of the number of users in a store and the type of application than the hardware. Retail organizations can invest on different types of EPOS systems, which are discussed next.

Stand-Alone EPOS systems

Stand-alone EPOS terminals come with best-of-breed retail software and standard attachments. These terminals are suitable for a corner-place grocery

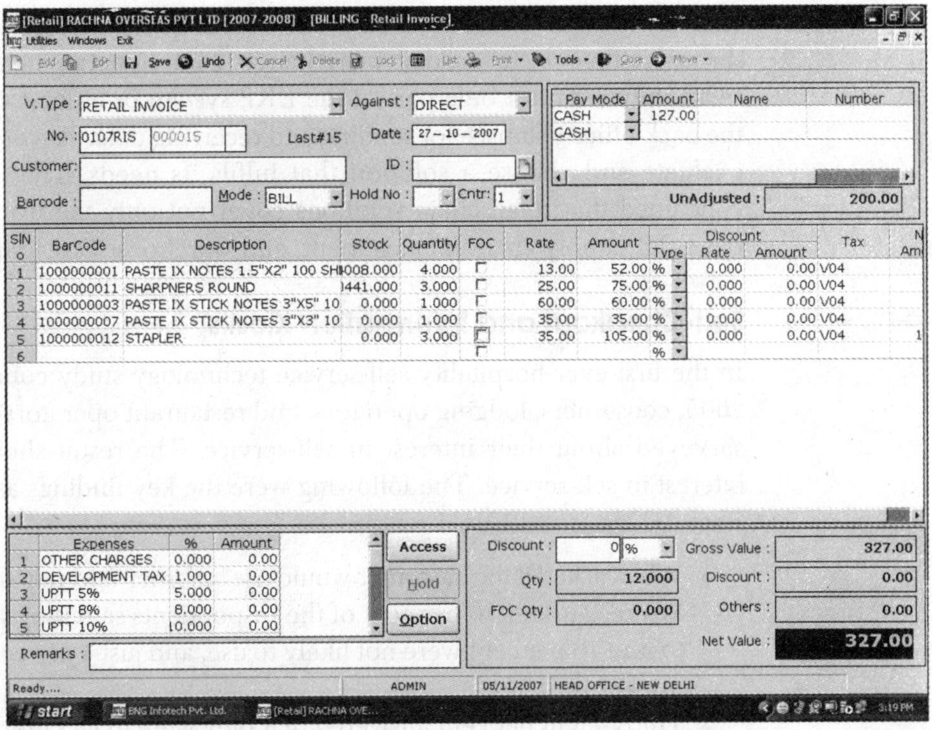

Fig. 3.5 Software used in EPOS

store, a mom-n-pop store, or a company with few retail stores. These machines are not connected to any local area network or back-office computer. The software serves the basic purpose of billing, sales reports, and stock reports.

Multiuser Systems with Accounting Software

If the retail outlet is a department store (which requires multiple billing terminals and systems for recording purchases, bar coding, and accounting), the retailer must go for an EPOS, which provides LAN connectivity with other systems. The software must also be multi-user compatible. Usually, a retailer having a large-format department store would like to use an integrated accounting package. Therefore, one must take care of these functions while deciding on an EPOS system.

Retail Chain Solutions

There is no difference between EPOS for department stores and EPOS for retail chains, except that the software at retail chains will communicate to the back-office systems through some network connectivity. The systems at retail chains will receive and send relevant data to the warehouse and head office through either electronic data interchange (EDI) or data synchronization. The retail software must be a part of the ERP system or at least compatible with the back-office database for sending and receiving data. The organization must evaluate and choose a solution that fulfils its needs. Therefore, it can be concluded that retail chain solutions cover not only the front office EPOS, but ERP, supply chain management, and warehouse distribution systems.

Self-Checkout and Information Kiosks

In the first ever hospitality self-service technology study conducted in April 2005, consumers, lodging operators, and restaurant operators in the US were surveyed about their interest in self-service. The result showed a growing interest in self-service. The following were the key findings as mentioned by Bhat (2005):

- When asked if the customer would use an order-and-pay self-service kiosk at a restaurant, 56 per cent of the respondents said they were very likely to use, 40 per cent were not likely to use, and just 4 per cent said they did not know.
- Thirty-eight per cent answered that they were in fact more likely to go to a restaurant offering self-service check-in and checkout.
- When weighing the potential benefits of hotel self-service check-in kiosks, 61 per cent cited faster service, 59 per cent shorter lines, 58 per cent privacy, 52 per cent accuracy, 50 per cent greater control, and 38 per cent no interaction with the desk clerk, as a reason of using self-service checkouts.
- Just 41 per cent of the respondents indicated that they were more likely to stay at a property that offered a self-service checkout option.

Types of Automated Self-Service Systems

Self-service system can be categorized into two general types of technologies—automated self-checkout systems and interactive kiosks.

Automated Self-Checkout Systems

Automated self-checkout systems are unmanned tools for scanning and billing at a retail point of sales (Fig. 3.6). The billing counter has a regular electronic point-of-sales machine, equipped with bar code scanner and weighing scales. The customer goes to the nearest available checkout gate, scans his or her collection of goods, pays by credit card, collects the goods, and then exits. In

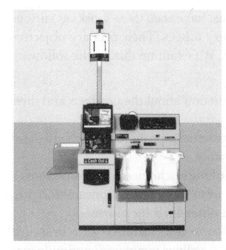

Fig 3.6 NCR Fastlane checkout system

Source: ncr.com

Fig. 3.7 An interactive kiosk–
ncr-easy point 42

Source: ncr.com

this scenario, there is least intervention by a retail employee. The tools used are same as in EPOS system, which have already been discussed.

Interactive Kiosks

Interactive kiosks are computers, preferably with touch-screen monitors, that provide customer information about the store, products, and services. These kiosks are interactive machines based on a normal computer, touch-screen monitor, and application software that is linked with the information database or the transaction processing system of the retail organization (Fig. 3.7). In a service retailing environment like in a restaurant, these kiosks are also used to place an order. With the help of the kiosks, customers can identify and select products without moving around the store or without waiting for the waiters to take order. Interactive kiosks can also guide a customer about the store by publishing a layout chart. Customers spend a lot of time searching for a location. These kiosks can give an indication about the accurate location of a selected merchandise.

According to a report by Summit Research (Sinha and Uniyal 2007), using kiosks to provide product information remains the leading reason to install retail kiosks worldwide. Thirty-three per cent of the retailers said that this was their chief motive for installing kiosks at their retail location. Internationally, there have been instances of using kiosks by large businesses. DaimlerChrysler's dealers, for example, use interactive kiosks that have access to an extended list of vehicle options (including interior or exterior colour selections), standard equipment, and optional features. Similarly, BMW started using interactive kiosks for an online gaming experience, known as BMW X3 Adventure, featuring three different in-car driving experiences and outdoor sporting activities, including mountain biking and snowboarding.

Special businesses, like construction, interior decorators, paint, and tiles dealers, find interactive kiosks very useful, as they can simulate a real-life situation on the kiosks. The customer can experiment with different layouts, colours, and tile designs to find out the best proposed combinations.

Interactive kiosks can be broadly classified into two categories—those providing information and those providing services.

Kiosks providing information   You must have seen these kiosks at various airports, railway stations, and travel-enquiry offices. Their primary objective is to provide information to the customer. We examine this by the following examples:

- Kiosks at a retail shop can give information about the products and their locations, prices, etc.
- They can educate customers about the various promotional schemes and discounting schemes running in the store.
- They can inform the customer about future schemes and promotions.
- They can be used to spread social awareness about consumer rights, ethical marketing, anti-smoking, and other such social issues.
- Kiosks can provide an add-on service to the customers of a brand. If connected with the websites of various airlines companies and railways, they can display schedules of various air-flights and trains in the city.
- Kiosks can also help in language translation for international guests at airports, city travel points, etc.

Kiosks providing services   The business usage of kiosks lies in utilizing the technology for serving customers and generating revenue. The kiosk terminals can be connected to the network and intranet of the organization and can generate transactions. The following are some possible uses of kiosks providing services:

- At a point of sales, kiosks can be used to receive orders from the customer. Orders are received and processed while the customer is surfing the Net or maybe gone for a haircut.
- Imagine a busy office executive dropping in at a large superstore while on her way home; she places her home-delivery order using the interactive kiosk put at the entrance of the superstore. When she reaches home, she finds her order waiting to be delivered.
- You go to the nearest Bikanerwala outlet along with your friends and, to your astonishment, find a long queue at the order window. You punch your order on the touch-screen kiosk, which is equipped with a printer. It generates an order number for you and also prints a kitchen order on the kitchen printer. While you chat and wait at an unoccupied table, your order number is displayed on the order display panel.
- At a hotel reservation, a kiosk can enhance the service that guests expect by providing them the option to quickly check-in, which requires feeding in a lot of information about the guests.

- Kiosks enable large resorts and casinos to manage numerous guests arriving individually or in large groups. Smaller setups do not have much front-office staff to interact with the large gatherings. Frequent guests can utilize kiosks for the same.
- Kiosks connected to biometric locking systems can accept guests' fingerprints at check-in and allow them to open their rooms.
- Large hotels, airline companies, and technology providers can collaborate to help customers and increase their share of the pie in the profit. While checking out of the hotel, customers can print a boarding pass for their travel tickets. NCR has recently launched CheckInHere, a new kiosk solution that provides multi-airline check-in, prints boarding passes, and provides baggage services at off-airport locations like hotels.

Significance of Automated Self-Service

Service is the key differentiator at the point of sales and a cause of great satisfaction for the customer. Automated self-service provides an opportunity to attach quality with the brand. Repetitive tasks, such as ordering a product or service, checking availability of product in the store, enquiring about the prices, and placing order at the retail place, are done more easily through the automated devices. Changes in consumer's attitudes and technology have brought about a general acceptance of self-service in terms of both usability and adoption. Consumers tend to spend less time on the repetitive tasks, which can be easily automated. Self-service kiosks help the industry with cost control, increased revenues, and customer satisfaction by leveraging technology. Improved service is the major driving force towards sustenance and profitability of the organization. For example, self-ordering system at a restaurant increases both speed of service and order accuracy, which leads to satisfaction of both the customer and the employees.

VENDING MACHINES

Electronic cash registers and electronic point-of-sales systems are used for facilitating easy and smooth billing at the checkout. These systems are a replacement of manual bills. Vending machines not only do billing (or a bill is not required at all) but also perform tasks of salesperson, store, and delivery mechanism. Vending machines have been in practice for long for the products that are fast selling and do not require services of a salesperson and meet small day-to-day needs of a customer.

Fig. 3.8 A vending machine

A vending machine (Fig. 3.8) is a machine that dispenses merchandise when a customer deposits sufficient money into a slot or vent to purchase the desired item (as opposed to a shop, where the presence of personnel is required for every purchase). The money (usually coins) is validated by a currency detector.

The first modern coin-operated devices were vending machines that dispensed postcards, introduced in London, England, in the early 1880s. The idea was exported to the US and by 1888, the Thomas Adams Gum Company introduced the first gumball vending machine. This simple idea spawned a whole new type of mechanical devices known as the *trade stimulators*, and the birth of pinball is ultimately rooted in these early devices.

What can be Sold through Vending Machines

In developed countries like United States, vending machines generally serve the purpose of selling snacks and beverages, but are also common in busy locations to sell newspapers. Items sold via vending machine vary with country, for example, some countries sell alcoholic beverages like beer through vending machines, while other countries do not allow this (usually, because of strict laws). Cigarettes were commonly sold in the US through these machines, but this practice is increasingly becoming rare due to concerns about underage buying. Sometimes, a pass has to be inserted in the machine to prove one's age. In some European countries, by contrast, cigarette vending machines remain common.

One major example of a vending machine giving access to all merchandise after paying for one item is a newspaper vending machine (also called vending box). It contains a pile of identical newspapers. After a sale, the door automatically returns to a locked position. But a customer could open the box and make off with all the newspapers, leave all the newspapers outside the box for the benefit of other customers, slowly return the door to an unlatched position, or block the door from fully closing. Thus, the success of such machines is predicted on the assumption that the customer will be honest (hence, the nickname 'honour box'), which is helped by the fact that having more than one newspaper is not often useful.

In Japan, with a high population density, limited space, a preference for shopping on foot or by bicycle, and low rates of vandalism and petty crime, there seems to be no limit to what is sold by vending machines. While the majority of machines in Japan are stocked with drinks, snacks, and cigarettes, one occasionally finds vending machines selling items such as bottles of liquor, cans of beer, and potted plants. Japan has the highest number of vending machines per capita, with about one machine for every 23 people.

The first vending machine in Japan was made of wood and sold postage stamps and postcards. About 80 years ago, there were vending machines that sold sweets called *Guriko*.

Disadvantages of Vending Machines

The main disadvantage of vending machines is its malfunction. Coin acceptors often jam up, especially if a bill or other foreign object is inserted into the coin slot. The product may fall down or hang.

Additional sources of failure can include machines not being supplied with the proper power, damage due to vandalism, and insufficient maintenance or upkeep by the operator. Sometimes, the machine may falsely reject a legal tender bill that happens to be crumpled, ripped, or dirty. This is the reason why most of the machines now accept coins only.

SUMMARY

For a retail organization, automation of point of sales with latest electronic devices is a step towards embracing technology to enhance customer satisfaction, employee morale, and revenues. Point of sales (POS) can be automated by putting a simple electronic cash register (ECR), which is slightly more than just replacement of a mechanical or electronic calculator. Small mom-n-pop stores and street-corner grocers, whose sales and customer traffic are not very high, can opt for ECRs. For the corporate retailers, retail-chain organizations, superstores and hypermarkets, and tech-savvy organizations, electronic POS is the right solution. An EPOS is a computer-based billing machine, with or without a touch-screen display, and equipped with bar code scanner, customer display, magnetic card swipe slot or attachment, and cash drawer. The EPOS system loaded with the operating system, database, and application software gives complete flexibility and comfort of upgradation, change, and replacement. The terminals are the entry points for creation of the primary data related to sales and customers. Analysis of the data by management information systems and decision support systems gives great insight into habits, preferences, buying power, and loyalty of the customer. Sales data is analysed for looking at sales trends and revenue collections. The EPOS helps reduce costs and increase efficiency at the point of sales.

Kiosks are computers with interactive software and touch-screen displays for the customers to use without any assistance. They enable organizations to achieve automation of unmanned checkouts and provide a platform for self-service environment. Kiosks can be used as an add-on service to the customer, providing information related to store locations, products, prices, promotions, etc. They are also used to help in self-service transaction processes. Use of kiosks for order generation, check-in, checkout, etc. is very helpful for both the customer and the organization. They again help in reducing transaction costs and waiting time, increasing customer satisfaction and loyalty, and boosting employees' morale.

Vending machine is a device that dispenses merchandise to the customer when he or she deposits the required amount of money with the machine. Vending machines are storage boxes that are operable with mechanical and electronic devices. These machines are used for selling the products that do not require services of a salesperson. Popular categories of products sold through vending machines are soft drinks, beer, chocolate, tea, coffee, cigarettes, newspapers, condoms, etc.

CONCEPT REVIEW QUESTIONS

1. What are the various components of an ECR?
2. Enumerate advantages of using ECR over manual billing at a point of sales.
3. What are the advantages of using EPOS system?
4. What are the important components of EPOS?
5. 'In an EPOS, software is the major component.' Justify this statement with appropriate examples.
6. What is the concept of self-service system?
7. How can you increase customer satisfaction using an interactive kiosk?
8. What are different types of kiosks and explain their significance?
9. As a manager of retail, for what kind of products would you prefer a vending machine?

CRITICAL THINKING QUESTIONS

1. You own a newly opened retail chain. You have to decide on an EPOS system. What functionalities will you look for in the systems you evaluate?
2. You want to start a travel agency business. Do you find any role of interactive kiosks in this business? Justify your answer with enough examples and case studies.
3. Why are vending machines not so popular in India?

PROJECT

1. Visit a bookshop in your town and prepare a project report covering role and scope of (a) ECRs, (b) EPOS systems, and (c) interactive kiosks.

SELECT REFERENCES

Bhat, Shrihari 2005, 'Tech Zone-POS Strategy', *Retail Biz*.

BNG Infotech, www.bng.co.in, last accessed on 02/12/2007.

Sinha, Piyush Kumar and Dwarika Prasad Uniyal 2007, *Managing Retailing*, Oxford University Press, New Delhi.

CASE STUDY

Retail Cooperatives: Cooperating with Technology

Company Various Cooperative Organizations into Retail

Perhaps Super Bazar Cooperative Stores Ltd, best known as 'Super Bazar', was the oldest cooperative into formal retailing. Created by the Delhi Government (earlier Administration) in the 1960s to meet the challenge of food shortages during wartimes and thwart off mischief by hoarders. But it died before the retail boom appeared in Delhi's horizon. The largest living consumer cooperative society in India, and perhaps the largest cooperative in Asia, is popularly known as Kendriya Bhandar. This cooperative society was set up in 1963 as a welfare project for the benefit of Central Government employees. The basic objective of creation of this cooperative society was to make basic household goods available at a reasonable price during the period of scarcity and shortage. Due to war and famine in 1962, unscrupulous traders resorted to hoarding and overpricing at a later date. To take care of flow of goods and reasonable prices, two cooperatives came into existence in Delhi, viz. Kendriya Bhandar and Super Bazar. Presently, they are functioning under the aegis of Ministry of Personnel, Public Grievances & Pensions, Government of India. Kendriya Bhandar was initially registered with the Registrar of Delhi Cooperative Societies and subsequently registered with the Central Registrar of Cooperative Societies to enable it to work countrywide.

Kendriya Bhandar and Super Bazar are primarily into retailing of grocery, consumer, and household items. They have stationery divisions to handle sale of stationery items, mainly to the government and public sector offices. Both the cooperatives also ventured into sale of medicines and allied items, operating from some of the major hospitals. Today, Kendriya Bhandar can boast of around 115 retail stores across the country, six warehouses to feed them, and one direct-supply store. The sales network was also supported by 15 'shops-on-wheels', which have now been discontinued.

Industry   Retail, Cooperatives

Solution Area   Billing solutions at POS

Problem

At start up, every store had manual billing. But given the number of transactions and heavy rush during the first half of the month, it was a nightmare for the shop employees to write manual bills. Then there was problem of daily computation of sales and stock reports. An additional person had to be deputed at each store to post the sales figures into a separate register. Manual posting was done to maintain the item ledger. Then it took another couple of hours daily to reconcile, compute, and consolidate figures for the head office. Third report was prepared out of the 'registers' for the sake of HO management information system. Whenever a new report was required, one person had to be deployed for the work. So, the objective was to increase efficiency and also get some basic reports on sale, stocks, and profitability, on time.

Solution

Management of Kendriya Bhandar and Super Bazar looked around for a solution. The main objective was to replace the manual billing system and mechanical calculators with some automated system. The core group headed by its top officers evaluated some options. They had two options—ECR and EPOS. It was suggested that electronic cash registers (ECRs) should be used in place of manual billing and mechanical calculators. A few stores were using mechanical calculators for addition of figures and printing of a slip. But that was only for internal calculations of the bill clerk. The slip had no item reference on it.

Suggestion of computer-based EPOS was ruled out, as it required a huge investment in comparison to ECRs, tidy workplace, computer-savvy people, rigorous training, and technology supportive atmosphere. Moreover, the basic requirements of automated billing, auto-pick of prices, and two preliminary reports on sales and stock were possible with ECRs. The ECR is easy to operate and does not need much space at the retail-billing counter. Therefore, the final decision was in favour of the ECR.

Implementation

Keeping in mind the instant benefits, the management of the cooperatives decided to go for ECR. A few vendors and manufacturers were approached. Quotations were called and comparative charts of prices and quality were made. The management decided in favour of

Bradma India Limited. Since at that time, Bradma was one of manufacturer of these machines and also in the panel of suppliers of most of the cooperative stores, to supply to government organizations.

In the first go, Bradma was given orders for 55 ECR machines by Kendriya Bhandar. Training on how to operate was provided to cooperatives' employees at the central place at their respective head offices in New Delhi. These machines were commissioned at fifty-five stores in Delhi.

Later on, other stores were also automated by setting up more ECRs. It was long before the automation with EPOS happened.

Benefits

The results were amazing. Billing time was reduced by half. Employee's satisfaction doubled. The cooperatives' stores were able to serve double the customers within the same time span during the day. Rush hours were now easy to handle. Employees took great interest in implementing these machines and were, in fact, enthusiastic do to so. The level of their enthusiasm can be judged by the fact that most of the employees at the billing counter memorized the 2000 odd product codes. At the time of billing, they did not have to press the lookup key or scan the item list.

Thus, the major cooperative retailers in Delhi, by cooperating with technology, not only increased their sales but also had a lot more satisfied customers and contented employees.

Questions:

1. Do you think that by running profitable retail business and automating them, the cooperatives have drifted from their basic objectives of providing goods at reasonable prices to public?
2. What was the reason that forced the cooperatives to opt for ECRs, not EPOS?
3. Would it have been a better decision if the cooperatives had gone for EPOS?

Source: Based on interactions with management and staff of major cooperatives, personal observations during consulting and providing software solutions, and information from these cooperatives' promotional material and websites.

4

Automatic Identification and Data Capture (AIDC)

Learning Objectives

- To appreciate the importance of marking a product
- To identify various product marking technologies
- To get acquainted with bar code technologies and symbologies
- To know the use of portable data-capture units
- To understand RFID technology and its uses

In the previous chapter, we have discussed the hardware component of retail information systems. The ECR and EPOS are only part of the hardware technology used at a retail point of sales. The other important component is the automatic identification system. Automatic identification systems consist of various product marking and reading devices and systems. In order to understand the functions and utilities of these devices, we need to first understand the concept of product marking.

PRODUCT MARKING

Product marking refers to the system of putting an identification mark on the product, so that it is identified by a person when required. The identification process can be done manually or with the help of a mechanical device or an electronic device. The manual identification process simply involves reading the human-readable number, alphabet, or sign on the product. But the manual identification may lead to errors and mistakes. For the identification by an electronic device, we need a sign or an image on the product that the system understands and displays accurately. For example, a manufacturer of chocolates can put a number, a word, or an image on the wrapper of the chocolate. All the three signs are readable and differentiable by a human being.

But can all people recognize those numbers, alphabets, and signs? Can a manufacturer put a number of different images on the products (like in the above example, how to identify chocolates of different sizes or flavours)? Answers to these questions lead to the following conclusions:

1. The identification mark must be unique so that it does not clash with other products.
2. The mark must be human identifiable and readable for humans to differentiate between two similar products.
3. The mark must be universal, that is, it should transcend the language barrier, to the extent it can.
4. The mark can be supplemented by a machine-readable image or signature. But the supplementary signature should not interfere with the basic uniqueness of the product's mark.
5. As human reading may lead to erroneous identification, machine-readable marks are necessary for the modern businesses.

In order to automate retail operations, certain systems are required to mark the products in a manner that are suitable for machine reading. This facilitates automation of data capturing and its subsequent use in the information systems to help operations, management, and planning.

As the name suggests, automated data capturing involves product-marking systems that are designed to uniquely identify a product at any level.

The following are the various kinds of product-marking systems that we are going to discuss:

- Price labelling
- Magnetic stripe
- Bar code technology
- Radio frequency identification
- Shelf-edge labelling

PRICE LABELS

Price labels are human-readable markings on products. These labels are not auto-identifiable but still are a basic form of product marking. Price labels, or MRP labels as commonly known, are still widely used for product pricing. These are small self-adhesive labels that usually contain product code and maximum retail price on it. These labels are pasted on the product through a mechanical device called applicator or labeller.

Price labels come with single, double, or three lines of band. These are rubber bands (as in a dating stamp) and can be replaced for changes in price or code of the product.

Price labels are only human-readable marking systems. Some price marking guns are shown in Fig. 4.1.

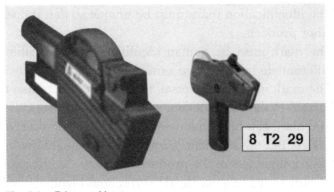

Fig. 4.1 Price marking guns

MAGNETIC STRIPE

Magnetic stripe, as the name suggests, is an identification system based on magnetic technology. Magnetic technology is the oldest in machine-enabled marking and identification system. This uses magnetic ink for writing on the product. The magnetic ink is used in cheques, called the MICR (magnetic ink character recognition) technology. Any products or documents, as in case of cheques, are placed under the reader. The machine reads and sends the signal to the computer.

The magnetic stripes are used in the credit and debit cards. The magnetic stripe is made up of tiny permanent bar magnets. These magnetic particles are polarized to be encoded with the data. There are special purpose machines that write on these magnetic stripes and readers read these stripes. We swipe our bank credit or debit card and get the information on the screen of our computer. Same stripes were used on products. Magnetic stripes are not very popular because of certain disadvantages. Some of them are given below:

1. Magnetic stripes are very costly to be put on products of small values.
2. The life of these stripes is not very long if exposed to open surfaces, magnetic fields, and dust.
3. The normal wear and tear makes scratches on the stripe, which makes it useless for scanning.
4. A magnetic stripe of a size of a credit card cannot be put on smaller products.

BAR CODE TECHNOLOGY

Bar coding is the most widely used technology for product marking and identification system. A bar code consists of a series of bar and spaces of varying

Fig. 4.2 Bar code

width. A bar code is nothing but a graphical representation of human-readable numbers and alphabets. This data is just a reference number. The system looks up into the database for associated records containing descriptive data and other information. The number of characters is represented in a linear inch called the bar code density. This density depends on the bar code symbology. Bar code symbology is the language that bar codes 'speak'. The standards and protocols in language make bar code printers, scanners, and readers from different manufacturers understand the bar code. That is, the bar code density is the number of characters per linear inch. ITF has a bar code density of 17.8 CPI (characters per inch). The resolution of bar code is dependent upon the narrowest element of a bar code (× dimension) and can vary from high nominally < 0.009 in (0.23mm), medium (0.23mm–0.5mm) and low > 0.5mm. There are in excess of 400 different bar code symbologies in use. Some are numeric, others alphanumeric.

A *bar code* is a machine-readable graphical representation of information (Fig. 4.2). The lines or bars are in dark ink on a light background to create high and low reflections, which are converted into 1s and 0s. Bar codes can be read by optical scanners called bar code readers. Bar codes are read by sweeping a small spot of light across the printed bar code symbol. Human eyes only see a thin red line emitted from the laser scanner. But what happens is that the scanner's light source is absorbed by the dark bars and reflected by the light spaces. A device in the scanner takes the reflected light and converts it into an electrical signal. The scanner's laser (light source) starts to read the bar code at a white space (the quiet zone) before the first bar and continues passing by the last bar, ending in the white space that follows it. The height is not significant, but a bar code cannot be read if the sweep wanders outside the symbol area. Therefore, bar heights are kept a little high just to make it easy to keep the sweep within the bar code area. The longer the information to be coded, the longer the bar code needed. As the length increases, so does the height of the bars and spaces to be read.

Bar codes are widely used to implement automatic identification and data-capture (AIDC) systems that improve the speed and accuracy of computer data entry. An advantage over other methods of AIDC is that it is less expensive to implement.

Bar Code Symbologies

Symbology is the language that different types of bar codes 'speak'. Because of the common standards and protocols in creation of bar codes, a variety of scanners built by different manufacturers around the world can read bar codes. The mapping between messages and bar codes is called a symbology. Each symbology has its own way of encoding and decoding single digits and characters of the message. It also incorporates start and stop markers into bars and spaces. Few symbologies require computation of check digit. Symbologies can be mainly categorized under two types:

- Linear
- Stacked

Linear symbologies create straight bars in which one character ending with a space and the next beginning with a bar, or vice versa. Characters in discrete symbologies begin and end with bars; the inter character space is ignored, as long as it is not wide enough to look like a code end. Similarly, another way in linear symbology is how wide and narrow the bars are.

Some linear symbologies use *interleaving*. The first character is encoded using black bars of varying width. The second character is then encoded, by varying the width of the white spaces between these bars. Thus, characters are encoded in pairs over the same section of the bar code. Interleaved 2 of 5 is an example of interleaving.

Stacked symbologies consist of a given linear symbology repeated vertically in multiple. There is a large variety of 2D symbologies. The most common are matrix codes, which feature square or dot-shaped modules arranged on a grid pattern. The 2D symbologies also come in a variety of other visual formats.

Common Symbologies

There are many types of bar codes, but there are some common symbologies that are used worldwide. They conform to either linear or stacked symbology. The most common symbologies are as follows:

- EAN/GS1
- Code 39
- UPC
- Code 128
- Code Bar
- 2-Dimensional Codes or PDF417

EAN (European Article Number)/GS1   Standardized in Europe, this symbology of bar codes is approved and internationally recognized numbering for products. EAN support only numeric bar codes. Global Standard 1 (GS1) is an EAN compatible bar code standard defined and approved in the US.

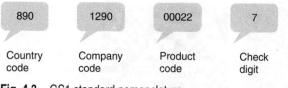

890	1290	00022	7
Country code	Company code	Product code	Check digit

Fig. 4.3 GS1 standard nomenclature

These codes contain 13-digit numbers and first three denote 'country' code, next four denote 'company' code, and the rest cover products of the company.

Figure 4.3 shows how a bar code number '8901290000227' represents different codes.

GS1 India The Government of India has an autonomous body by the name 'GS1 India' under the Ministry of Commerce to regulate and implement GS1 bar code standards in India. By paying a registration fee, one has to apply for the company code. The GS1 organization grants one 4-digit code for the company. Once granted, the company pays an annual subscription fee for using GS1 standards. The organization can start using these codes for its products.

The check digit is automatically generated based on the bar code number, which checks for the uniqueness of bar code number.

Code 39 These symbologies support alphanumeric character sets with full ASCII option. But use of alphabets in bar codes enlarges the length of the bar code, which may not be suitable for printing on smaller articles. Code 39 is the most popular symbology in the non-retail world and is used extensively in manufacturing, military, and health applications. Each Code 39 bar code is framed by a start/stop character represented by an asterisk (*). Code 39 symbology is shown in Fig. 4.4.

UPC Universal Product Code (UPC) is the universally accepted method of bar code technology. The UPC was standardized in the US. This kind of symbology accepts numeric codes and the length of the code is 12 digits. UPC-A is a 12-digit, numeric symbology used in retail applications. The UPC-A symbols consist of 11 data digits and one check digit. UPC-E is a 7-digit code including one check digit.

Fig. 4.4 Code 39

Code 128 Code 128 accepts all alphabets and numeric characters. There is no limit on the length of bar codes. Code 128 is a variable length, high density, alphanumeric symbology. This has 106 different bar and space patterns and each pattern can have one of three different meanings, depending on which of three different character sets is employed. Code 128 also employs a check digit for data security.

Fig. 4.5 Samples of two different 2D bar codes

CodeBar CodeBar is a variable length symbology that allows encoding of the following 20 characters: 0123456789-$:/.+ABCD. This symbology is commonly used in libraries, blood banks, and the air parcel business. CodaBar uses the characters A, B, C, and D only as start and stop characters.

Two-dimensional Bar Codes Two-dimensional symbology, also known as PDF417, is used for encoding large information on one bar code. It has the capacity to encode hundreds of characters at a time. While traditionally bar code encoding schemes represented only numbers, newer symbologies add new characters such as the uppercase alphabet to the complete ASCII character set, and beyond. ASCII (American Standard Code of Information Interchange) is the standardization of all possible characters into numeric forms. The drive to encode more information in combination with the space requirements of simple bar codes led to the development of matrix codes, which do not consist of bars but rather a grid of square cells. A *matrix code*, also known as a *2D bar code*, is a two-dimensional way of representing information. It is similar to a linear (one-dimensional) bar code but has more data-representation capability (Fig. 4.5).

Advantages of Bar codes

Fast and accurate data entry and retrieval is the core of bar code technology. Bar codes are used in retail at the billing counter for checkout automation by using bar code scanners. Bar codes play a major role in retail automation, aiding monitoring of stocks in the entire supply chain (warehouses, distribution, and retail stores). Improved inventory management by reducing inventory in transit and dead stocks is the leading motivation driving the use of bar code in retail industry. Some major benefits of bar codes are listed below.

1. Accurate capture of data ensures proper maintenance of records of transactions. Scanning at the POS and at the goods receiving will eliminate the source of human error. It most definitely reduces

workforce costs and certainly will give management a better control over the operations. It will eliminate the need to have manual pricing and will also reduce the need for manual stocktaking.

2. Bar code technology helps in calculations of the checkout productivity at stock and sales levels.
3. It ensures fast transaction completion at POS and warehouse.
4. It leads to decreased checkout time at the point of sales, thus giving rise to higher customer satisfaction. Again, there will be less cashier errors and customers will automatically get itemized receipt.
5. It will ensure faster customer throughput at high volumes stores. It will automatically generate price and itemized billing. It will help in implementing productivity control.
6. Satisfaction breeds loyalty. Last but not least, it can help in promotion of customer loyalty programmes.
7. The benefits to the management will likewise include provision of faster access to raw data, i.e. on a real-time basis leading to faster management reports and more effective decisions.
8. Management has confidence over the data and hence better operations control, management control, and planning.

Of course, it is not entirely possible to quantitatively access the above benefits in isolation from the overall automation of data capturing and information processing.

Bar Code Tools

Various bar code tools are as follows.

Bar Code Printers

Perhaps the best part of bar codes is that they are created by special-purpose software and printed by special-purpose printers. A human being does not have to draw those thick and thin lines. Bar codes are usually designed on special-purpose software, i.e. the software meant for creating bar codes of different symbologies. They can also be designed using general-purpose software like CorelDraw. There are special packages available that convert the numbers and alphabets into bars of the required symbology. These can be printed on any thermal, dot-matrix, ink-jet, or laser printers. But there come special-purpose printers for bar code printing only (Fig. 4.6). These printers are based on 'thermal transfer technology'.

These printers use a thermal transfer ribbon. The head of the printer heats up and the ink on the wax ribbon is transferred on the labels made of chrome paper.

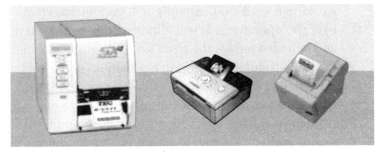

Fig. 4.6 Thermal transfer printers for bar code

Sources: Tec-Toshiba, Samsung, and Epson

Specifications sheet of an entry-level bar code printer is shown in Fig. 4.7.
There are several advantages of using bar code printers. The print quality
on a thermal printer is very good. Whereas, the bar codes printed with a
DMP are not readable after sometime as the ink evaporates or the ribbon
wears out. The density of bar code is very high and the spaces between bars
are fine, so inkjet printers are not suitable, as spraying of ink fills the voids.
Similarly, bar codes printed on a thermal paper (appreciate the difference
between thermal paper and thermal transfer system) evaporate in a very short
time, say fifteen to thirty days.

Bar Code Scanners

Product marking in itself is meaningless unless there is scanning at both the
point of sales and goods receiving end (warehouse) to convert the code into
meaningful data to be used by various information systems in the organization
and reap the benefits of product marking systems in retailing.

Model	408PEL
Print density	203 DPI
Type	Desktop
Head width	4″
Print speed	4″–6″ per second
Memory	2 MB RAM, 1 MB flash memory
Interface	Serial and parallel interface
Options	USB interface optional

Fig. 4.7 Bar code printer specification table

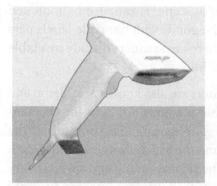

Fig. 4.8 Handheld scanner

Source: www.protocolsolution.com

A *bar code reader* (or bar code scanner) is an electronic device for reading printed bar codes. It consists of a light source, a lens and a photo conductor translating the optical impulses into electrical ones. Additionally, nearly all bar code readers contain decoder circuitry analysing the bar code's image data provided by the photo conductor and sending the bar code's content to the scanner's output port.

The bar code scanners come in various varieties depending upon the application requirements. Bar code scanners or readers can be classified based on their usage and operation and the technology they are built with.

Based on operation point of view, bar code readers are mainly categorized into five types:

1. Handheld
2. Fixed-mount vertical
3. Flat bed
4. Conveyor belt
5. Card-swipe

Handheld Handheld scanners are operated by hand, so they are also called semi-automatic readers (Fig. 4.8). The operator positions the reader near the label, from a distance or almost touching the bar code. Handheld scanners come with or without a trigger. If it is trigger based, the operator presses the trigger. On pressing the trigger, it throws a light of beam on the bar codes and reads the data. A scanner without a trigger can automatically be activated when a bar code label comes in contact with or in line of sight of the scanner. Different scanners read from different distances. The distance can vary from two inches to twenty four inches. Special scanners with a long lead of up to two metres are also available commercially.

These scanners are most widely used. They are favourites with the retailers and are used at point of sales, inventory control, and warehouses.

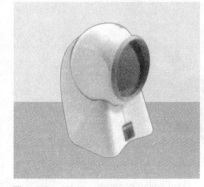

Fig. 4.9 Wall-mountable scanner

Source: www.protocolsolution.com

Fixed-mount Vertical Fixed-mount vertical readers are fixed in place and are vertical in shape. These scanners are used for automatic reading. The reading is performed laterally passing the label over the reader. No operator is required, but the position of the code target must coincide with the imaging capability of the reader. These types of scanners find application in manufacturing and

Fig. 4.10   Tabletop/flat-bed scanner

Source: www.protocolsolution.com

transportation usage. These scanners can also be mounted on a wall (Fig. 4.9) and the goods with bar code labels pass on a conveyor belt. But there are scanners that are available for conveyor belt applications.

Flat Bed   Flat-bed scanners are also known as tabletop and horizontal scanners. These scanners are used for very fast operations in retail and warehousing. The position of the scanner is on a tabletop and the articles with bar code labels pass over it (Fig. 4.10). The scan accuracy and speed is very fast as these scanners emit 18–25 laser beams in omni directions. Therefore, there is hardly any chance that it misses scanning.

These scanners are very fast and robust. They are quite suitable for grocery, departmental stores, pharmaceuticals, etc., where the number of transactions is very high.

Conveyor Belt   Conveyor belt scanners are used for scanning goods moving on a conveyor belt. These scanners are fixed at a place in proximity with the conveyor belts (Fig. 4.11). These types of scanners find applications at airports, warehouses, and assembly production lines.

Card Swipe   Card swipe scanners scan from a very close proximity. The bar code label is put through a slot meant for scanning credit cards (Fig. 4.12). They are in great demand for applications in retail and customer-relationship management. A bar code labelled customer loyalty card is just swiped through these scanners and the information decoded. These kinds of scanners are also available for attendance recording machines.

Fig. 4.11   Conveyor belt scanner

Fig. 4.12   Card-swipe scanner

From the technology point of view, there are three types of scanners:

1. Laser scanners
2. CCD scanners
3. Digital image scanners

Laser Scanners Laser scanners work the same way as pen-type readers except that they use a laser beam as the light source and typically employ either a reciprocating mirror or a rotating prism to scan the laser beam back and forth across the bar code. As with the pen-type reader, a photodiode is used to measure the intensity of the light reflected back from the bar code. In both pen readers and laser scanners, the light emitted by the reader is tuned to a specific frequency, and the photodiode is designed to detect only this modulated light of the same frequency.

CCD Scanners Charged couple device (CCD) scanners use an array of hundreds of tiny light sensors lined up in a row in the head of the reader. Each sensor can be thought of as a single photodiode that measures the intensity of the light immediately in front of it. Each individual light sensor in the CCD reader is extremely small and because there are hundreds of sensors lined up in a row, a voltage pattern identical to the pattern in a bar code is generated in the reader by sequentially measuring the voltages across each sensor in the row. The important difference between a CCD reader and a pen or laser scanner is that the CCD reader is measuring emitted ambient light from the bar code, whereas pen or laser scanners are measuring reflected light of a specific frequency originating from the scanner itself.

CCD wireless scanners CCD linear image scanners are also available from scanning from a distance. These scanners both work on Bluetooth or RF (radio frequency) communication and can work at a frequency of 2.45 GHz. These can work from a distance of 30 meter from the base station.

Digital Image Scanners These are special pen-type readers. Pen-type scanners consist of a light source and a photodiode that are placed next to each other in the tip of a pen or wand. To read a bar code, the tip of the pen moves across the bars in a steady motion. The photodiode measures the intensity of the light reflected back from the light source and generates a waveform that is used to measure the width of the bars and spaces in the bar code. Dark bars in the bar code absorb light and white spaces reflect light so that the voltage waveform generated by the photo diode is a representation of the bar and space pattern in the bar code.

There are also some special-purpose scanners—one such scanner is portable data terminal.

(a)   (b)

Fig. 4.13 Portable data terminals

Source: www.protocolsolution.com

Portable Data Terminals It is a hand-held system that is fitted with a laser scanner module and computer processor module with standard alphanumeric keyboard and 2 to 4 line LCD screen (Fig. 4.13). It can also have the peripheral component for compact data input/output device adaptable to graphical and/or other input/output suitable for different applications. It is programmable and available with a Java or C++ based software development kit (SDK). One can scan and verify data simultaneously. Also, the data can be downloaded on a computer with RS232 or USB interface. The major utility of the portable data-capture units is stocktaking in a warehouse. If attached with a printer, they can also be used as a billing terminal at a remote distance where it is not possible to take the computer and normal scanner for billing.

RADIO FREQUENCY IDENTIFICATION TECHNOLOGY

Radio frequency identification (RFID) technology is the new-generation automatic identification and data-capture technology that uses radio or wireless communication to uniquely identify and transmit data relating to an item, object, or individual (Fig. 4.14). Radio communication works on radio waves or frequencies emitted by one part (tag) of the device and accepted and read by the other part (reader). The radio frequencies are unique in nature so the data transmitted is clearly identifiable. Radio frequency tags can be put on a product or implanted on any living animal.

Fig. 4.14 RFID technology

Invented in 1948 and first used during the Second World War by the US Army for identification of friend or foe (IFF) aircrafts, RF technology gained commercial acceptance during the 1980s and 90s. In an RFID system, the data is carried in suitable transponders, commonly known as RF tags, and is retrieved at the appropriate time and place by means of an antenna and a transceiver/reader, in order to satisfy a particular application need. RFID systems allow for non-contact reading or writing of data and are highly effective in manufacturing and other hostile environments where other bar code labels cannot survive.

The RFID is a technology for collecting information on the following:

- Objects identifiable individually such as products
- Places that these objects pass through
- Time of operations performed on a particular object
- Transactions performed on the object

Let us discuss an example below.

You receive a shipment from one of your suppliers but you do not know which supplier. The product is in an RFID-enabled box. This box has an RFID tag and will be identified at various places during its travel from source to destination by various parties, such as transportation, logistics, and forwarding partners. These parties secure and share this information amongst themselves by using the RFID information network. Before you open the box, depending on the design of the entire system, you can obtain information on the following:

- Contents of the box, ownership, sender details, receiver details, and postal services used
- All cities it has travelled through before reaching you
- The time it was present at all places and the total time taken to reach you
- Details of the agencies and people who handled the shipment

Functioning of an RFID System

The RFID tag is put on an object that needs identification. An RFID reader communicates with the tag using radio waves. The identification code on the tag is read and communicated to the back end system for making useful business decisions.

The RFID tag or transponder consists of a chip and an antenna that helps it to transmit radio waves. The tag is also known as smart or radio tag. The chip consists of mainly three components. It has a processor, a memory and a radio transmitter. The radio transmitter transmits radio waves at a certain frequency. The reader, which is placed at a certain distance, and has its own antenna, receives the signals and sends them to the attached computer (Fig. 4.15). The chips are available in two forms—read-only or read-write. On the read-write chips data can be upgraded regularly.

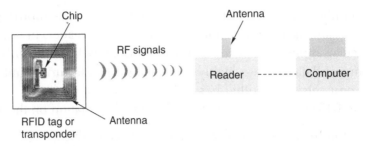

Fig. 4.15 Functioning of an RFID system

Working of an RFID System

The working of an RFID system can be categorized in the following layers (Ranagarajan, Misra, and Talwar 2005):

- The business process analytics
- IT infrastructure
- Middleware
- RFID hardware

The process starts from bottom to top. It starts from layer four, where the RFID hardware interacts and generates event data, that is, the number to identify the object being read. In layer three, this data is picked up from the hardware, filtered, adopted, and logged after which the data becomes usable for processing in the existing enterprise associated system. For example, time and location details associated are added to this data. The existing enterprise system like ERP is one component of an IT infrastructure. Business process analytics is the layer where this data is utilized to meet the objective for which the RFID system has been deployed.

The complete RFID system is being described within these four layers.

RFID Hardware

This is the core and actual RFID layer, which has the following components:

1. RFID tag, programmed to carry unique data
2. RFID reader, for communicating with the tag

Fig. 4.16 RFID tag (band)

Tags RFID tag is a microchip transponder, that is, it acts as a transmitter and responder (Fig. 4.16). It can transmit the data when powered by an electrical source and respond to a call by the reader. It has the following four components:

- A processor for executing instructions
- Memory for storing data

- Source of electricity to charge the circuits
- A transmitter for data communication

The RFID tags are categorized into two types—active and passive.

Active tags are self-powered. They are powered by an internal battery and the tag data can be rewritten or modified. They can be read from a larger communicating distance and have a larger memory size. These types of tags are used in applications that require faster data access from a relatively long distance. Highway toll applications are one area where these tags are useful. But presently such tags are very expensive.

Passive RFID tags do not have their own internal power source and hence require an external power source. They operate without a separate external power source and obtain operating power generated from the reader. The transponder is powered by an electromagnetic signal transmitted by the reader. The signal charges an internal capacitor on the tag. This supplies power to communicate with the reader. The low-frequency passive tags operate at a frequency of 125–134 KHz. The distance they cover ranges from a few centimetres to a few metres. The high-frequncy tags run at a frequency of 13.5 MHz and cover a relatively higher distance. Passive tags are consequently much lighter than active tags, less expensive, and offer virtually an unlimited operational lifetime. As a result, passive RFID tags have shorter read ranges than active tags and require a higher-powered reader. Read-only tags are passive and are programmed with a unique set of data and cannot be modified. The higher performance of high-frequency RFID systems incurs higher system costs.

Reader As the name suggests, it is an electronic device that reads or communicates with the tag. It consists of the following components:

- Antenna for producing radio waves for communication with the tag. (The shape and number depends on the read range and permissible strength of the signal. In case of handheld readers, antennas are integrated with the reader.)
- Signal processors for understanding and communicating with the readers
- Embedded software to process the reads from the tags and communicate with the middleware

The antenna emits radio signals to read and write data to the RF tag. Antennas are the conduits between the tag and the transceiver. Antennas can be built into a door frame to receive tag data from persons or things passing through the door. The electromagnetic field produced by an antenna can be constantly present when multiple tags are expected continually. If constant interrogation is not required, the field can be activated by a sensor device.

The antenna when packaged with the transceiver and decoder becomes a reader (interrogator), which can be configured to either a handheld or a fixed-mount device. The reader emits radio waves, depending on its power output and the radio frequency used. When an RFID tag passes through this radio frequency zone, it detects the reader which decodes the data encoded in the tag's circuit and the data is passed to the host computer for processing.

RFID Middleware

This layer acts as a link between the physical events occurring in the hardware layer and existing IT infrastructure, on which the required business logic is executed. The functions executed in this layer have been divided as follows:

Hardware Interface Hardware comes for different vendors and uses different technologies, architecture, and protocols. The middleware provides a common interface to configure, monitor, deploy, and issue commands to different makes and technology of readers.

Edge Processing The middleware acts like a personal secretary, bringing only the points of interest and filtering out operation details. Low-level details, like multiple reads, will be performed locally to provide filtered contents like content-based routing.

Application Integration An enterprise would like the RFID network to connect to enterprise systems, such as ERP, SCM, CRM, WMS, or any other third party applications. It provides libraries of adapters and APIs (application programming interfaces) for other technologies.

The middleware also helps in the following functions.

Partner Integration One can obtain the maximum return on investment if RFID is used across the value-chain by different players, middleware may also provide B2B integration features like partner profile management.

Process Nanagement and Partner Integration With a disruptive technology like RFID, one needs to rethink the way in which the business is being done. Some middleware also provides tools such as workflow, role management, process automation, and user-interface development.

Managing the Impact on IT Architecture Since the data expands exponentially by adding each RFID node in the network, this leads to excessive processing required by the middleware. Hence, middleware should have automatic load distribution and redundancy for protection against failures.

IT Infrastructure

IT infrastructure is the software and hardware used in an enterprise that is responsible for storage, utilization, processing, or communication of the RFID event-based data.

Software   All event-based data captured by the middleware is passed on to an enterprise product such as ERP so that it can be utilized in the strategic business processes.

Hardware   An enterprise will require WLAN for a seamless transfer of data from a handheld terminal to the IT backbone.

Business Process Analytics

The RFID generates a data stream to bridge the gap between the physical flow of goods and the information flow in the IT systems (Fig. 4.17). This data will be available in an existing ERP or some other layer—enterprise software. The presence of this data presents crucial strategic opportunities that will enhance the performance of the business. This opportunity has to be exploited by an application that 'sits' on top of the layer 2 (IT infrastructure) software. This application can be used for the following purposes.

Closed Loop Systems   The RFID systems where the control is under a single owner or authority as a stand-alone solution, tags return and are recycled. The owner has the mandate for prescribing the format of identification codes.

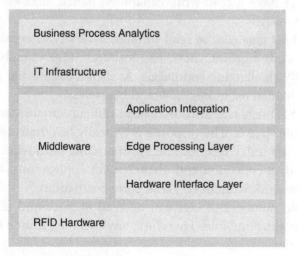

Fig. 4.17   RFID stack

Source: TCS RFID Centre of Excellence

Open Loop Systems These systems have multiple, disparate stakeholders. In other words, they have separate manufacturing, transportation, warehousing, and retail entities utilizing a common system that reads a common tag, which is put at the beginning of the value chain. This enhances the potential tremendously as it would enable companies to track a single case or item throughout the supply chain, instead of relying on input from each touch point. Hence, all companies that are party to such a system require a single universal set of RFID standards and protocols. The electronic product code (EPC) initiative within the supply chain is a good example of an open system.

This application provides an interface to the business user to derive the benefits out of the investments for employing RFID technology in the enterprise. The benefits that can be derived out of an RFID system are discussed below.

Advantages of RFID System

The RFID system offers a lot of advantages over other forms of product marking and identification, viz. bar code technology. The following are the major advantages.

1. The RFID systems are a no-contact, non-line-of-sight technology, i.e. the tag and reader communication will still be established even if they are not facing each other.
2. The data can be read from a distance.
3. The tags have a read-write capability; hence, data can be upgraded continuously.
4. The RFID tags can be read through a variety of substances, such as paint, crusted grime, snow, fog, ice, and other visually and environmentally challenging conditions. At such locations bar codes or other optically read technologies would be useless.
5. The RFID tags can also be read in difficult circumstances and at remarkable speeds. The response is typically less than 100 milliseconds. The RFID today has become indispensable for a wide range of automated data collection and identification applications. It is difficult to imagine work without RFID in certain situations.
6. Multiple numbers of tags can be read at once and in bulk, making mass reading possible. Therefore, any speeding source tag cannot skip the reader.
7. The RFID-based security systems are more effective and reliable than others.

8. Developments in RFID technology continue to yield better results and faster processing.

9. This system can be embedded into any non-metallic surface.

Despite all the advantages, RFID system is, however, a costlier technology (when compared with bar code). It is unlikely that RFID technology will replace bar code in the near future, as this is not as cost-effective as a bar code label.

Applications of RFID Technology in Retail

There are innumerable uses of RFID in all walks of life. In terms of technological advancements, RFID has certainly come a long way from identifying friendly allied planes to tracking fast moving consumer goods in the supply chain management. It is now widely used across a multitude of industry sectors, and applications as varied as access and security control, livestock identification, inventory control, kid identifications at amusement parks, wildlife animal identification, airline baggage tracking, automated vehicle identification and toll collection are providing significant improvements in productivity, efficiency, and convenience to organizations and consumers across the globe. We have identified three major applications of RFID technology in retail:

- Retail Security
- Inventory tracking
- Point-of-sales automated billing

Retail Security

Prevention of theft is the biggest challenge in retail. As per one estimate by Chris E McGoey (2008), $13 billion worth of goods are stolen every year from retail shops. Retail business environment is more prone to theft and pilferage as goods are kept in open displays and racks. Customers and employees have a direct access to them. 'Shop-lifting' is a worldwide phenomenon. Retailers try to find ways of preventing theft and use various technological products to do so. Introduction of RFID holds a great future for theft prevention systems (Fig. 4.18). The systems based on RFID and magnetic-acoustic technology, commonly known as electronic article surveillance (EAS), have come into prominence as an anti-theft measures in retail. The EAS is a technology used to identify items as they come within the range of RFID frequency or pass through a gated area (Fig. 4.19). It is a form of electronic theft protection used by retailers and others. The EAS systems save money for businesses and consumers today.

Fig. 4.18 RFID tags used in garment security

Source: Checkpoint EAS

The EAS is designed to protect individual store items against theft, whilst providing honest customers with the opportunity to browse items and enabling staff to spend more time on customer service.

Technology used in EAS An EAS system has a transmitter sending the signal at a defined frequency to create an electromagnetic field that functions as a surveillance area. This field is then operated usually between two pedestals placed at the exit of a store. The gates are fitted with RFID readers. At the billing counter, the security tags are removed from the product. Upon entering this area, a security tag or label that has not been removed or deactivated creates a signal in the electromagnetic field. This tag is detected by the reader/receiver, which sounds an alarm.

Inventory Tracking

The other major utility of RFID technology is tracking of goods and inventory management in a retail store or warehouse setup. The visibility provided by this technology allows an accurate knowledge on the inventory level by eliminating the discrepancy between inventory record and physical inventory. Each product is fitted with an RFID tag. The tag transmits a signal that is received by the reader. The signal linked with the item code traces the location of the product. If the product is moved from its location, the reader detects the movement and updates the computer database accordingly.

Moreover, RFID technology can be very helpful in physical stocktaking operations. Because of their capability to read in bulk and in one go, stocktaking operations become very easy. Otherwise, it takes days and weeks for organizations to evaluate the physical stock available in the warehouse.

At Point of Sales

The RFID is an emerging technology and its different uses are still being experimented. Point of sales is another area in retail where RFID technology can be used to automate checkouts. It has also been proposed to use RFID for POS store checkout to replace the manual scanning of bar codes by the cashier. There are apprehensions at retail outlets that a retail employee may by mistake or deliberately scan

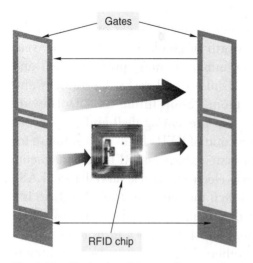

Gates

RFID chip

Fig. 4.19 Electronic article surveillance system

a different item and deliver a different item. By doing this, he or she will be benefiting or cheating the customer. In both the cases, it is unethical and leads to loss inflicting on the retailer. If the product is put with an RFID tag, the system will automatically read the same product.

Challenges in Implementation of RFID

There have been a lot of technological advancements in the field of RFID, but the process of evolution for commercially viable solutions is still continuing. There are regular revisions in the standards for tags, readers, frequency modulation, and data handling. This phenomenon coupled with the lack of relevant RFID expertise in industry, poses a risk to all those organizations seeking to garner benefits offered by the technology. This risk is due to the multiple factors ranging from understating business needs, technological requirement, and the high cost of RFID technology at present. To mitigate these risks, the organization must seek assistance from a technology provider having knowledge of the business process in the vertical, RFID technology, and its limitations as well as having experience in developing custom applications, so that the data generated by RFID infrastructure can be utilized to provide maximum benefits to the organization.

Due to the yet high cost of RFID tags, it is unlikely to replace bar codes at retail billing. Organization may like to invest in inventory tracking solutions for high-value products. This will be possible with significant reduction in the cost of current tags and changes in the operational process around POS. There is some research taking place; however, it will take some years to reach fruition.

ELECTRONIC SHELF SIGNAGES

Electronic shelf signages are electronic display panels on the shelf. These panels display product description or any promotional schemes offered by the retailer. We have discussed earlier in this chapter how scanning offers control over pricing and automation. However, there is still a lack of full automation. The pricing and promotion labels on the shelf still have to be attached manually. This leads to duplicity of data and, therefore, to human errors. We can see that the product pricing in the software and computers can be updated immediately but the shelf edge labels still have to be printed and replaced. In case of a price change within the day, the labels would remain unchanged.

The solution lies in implementation of automated LCD electronic shelf signage. The signage can be connected to the back end computers, update prices on the LCD panel thus, reducing time and human errors.

SUMMARY

Product marking is a system of putting some signs or marks on the product to make them identifiable by humans or technology. Out of four product marking systems, price labelling is a manual system and magnetic tape technology is old and unsuitable for inventory control, or billing at a retail point of sales. Rest of the two technologies, viz. bar codes and RFID are latest, mostly in use and time tested. Bar coding is the system of converting human-readable numbers and alphabets into machine-readable bars, using some common standards and technologies. These technologies are called symbologies. There are various symbologies but EAN, GS1 and two-dimensional symbologies are widely used and most popular. Bar codes are printed on special-purpose thermal transfer printers and read by various electronic devices called bar code scanners. Bar code scanners have mainly two technologies, viz. laser and CCD. From the usage point of view, bar code scanners are classified into handheld, vertical, flat-bed, pen, conveyor-belt, and card-swipe scanners. Portable data-capture units are scanned-enabled terminals that have their own memory to store data and can be programmed as per the business requirements. They come with some customized programs.

The RFID technology is being regarded as one of the high potential technologies on the horizon that holds immense value for various businesses. It is an invisible link between the physical world and the information network. It works when a reader reads an RFID tag on a physical object using radio waves to mark its presence there. This data is then communicated to the business process analytics for better informed business decisions via the middleware and the existing IT infrastructure.

Shelf edge labels are being replaced with electronic shelf signage, which are electronic LCD panels. Connected with back end computers, they offer accurate and on-time updating of the prices.

CONCEPT REVIEW QUESTIONS

1. What are various types of product marking systems and which is the best? Explain.
2. What do you understand by bar code symbologies?
3. For what kind of information you would prefer 2D bar codes?
4. What are the advantages of bar codes?
5. Which are various types of bar code readers from 'placing' point of view?
6. What are technological differences between various bar code scanners?
7. Describe various uses of portable data-capture units.
8. Explain shelf edge labelling.

9. What is RFID technology? Enumerate its advantages.
10. Explain various components of RFID.
11. What applications of RFID are useful in retail? Explain.

CRITICAL THINKING QUESTIONS

1. 'Though bar code technology is most reliable and cost-effective, this technology has limited days on the earth.' Examine this statement in the light of other emerging technologies.
2. 'The RFID is a big technological breakthrough in object identification, but there are hardly any takers for this technology.' Critically examine this statement.

PROJECT

1. Visit a shop selling luxury watches. Construct a project report for implementation of RFID technology, covering the following points:
   (a) Requirements of the organization
   (b) Cost involvement
   (c) Areas covered by RFID technology
   (d) Qualitative benefit to the retailer
   (e) Return on investment

SELECT REFERENCES

McGoey, Chris E. 2008, http://www.crimedoctor.com/shoplifting.htm, July.
Ranagarajan, T.S., Pradeep Misra, and Sumit Talwar 2005, 'The success tag', *Retail Biz*, November.
www.protocol.com.

CASE STUDY

BookWorm: Working on RFID

BookWorm

It is a large book retail shop in Nainital having its store in Mall Road, the busiest street in this picturesque tourist hill station. Though a bookshop is highly unexpected at a tourist place, which is snow clad for six months and full of tourists for three months, a lot of educational institutions and boarding schools make this town a literary place as well. Perhaps, this is the reason why BookWorm is doing well. Although the shop is doing well, it is also facing the problem of plenty. The store is full of all types of books and there are thousands of shelves and racks. But when a customer asks for a particular book, it is not traceable. Either nobody knows if the store has the particular book, or it is at a location that is not easy to locate. When Mr Bhairav Datt Nailwal, the owner-manger of the store, was fighting with this problem, someone suggested that he should implement RFID systems.

Let us look at the following facts about BookWorm:

1. BookWorm has around 20,000 titles by 16,000 authors and 4000 publishers worldwide.
2. The bookshelves are not numbered or identified with some electronic devices.
3. The store uses small point-of-sales software 'BNGpro' provided by a Delhi-based company.
4. This billing application prints bar codes and generates day sales report.
5. BookWorm has not yet entered all the existing stock in the store; so the software is not able to give stock report.
6. There is no search facility by the author name or ISBN of a book.
7. Nainital is highly humid place, almost nine months in a year remains cold and rainy.

Mr Nailwal immediately called a team of experts from New Delhi. The team, after a preliminary study, put up the following questionnaire and recommendation report in front of him.

RFID Implementation Recommendations

We think that RFID is the right technology that can provide an answer to your business problem that has been nagging you. If you also think so, the following is the plan and vision to do so. You can first conduct an RFID pilot. But before preparing budgets for a pilot or a full-scale implementation, the following things need to be analysed.

Evaluating Implementation Partner

Get a right implementation partner or your pilot will fail. RFID is a new evolving technology and bears a number of risks. Selection of a right partner having vast experience is necessary.

Business Requirements

- Since RFID involves substantial investments, do you have clear objectives on what RFID can achieve after implementation?
- Do you have a sound business case that is are you clear on the costs involved/measurable financial benefits that will accrue to your organization?
- RFID will bring in changes in how you do your business. You need to clarify the impact of implementation on your existing business processes.
- RFID implementation may involve suppliers and customers. You need to garner support of your business network partners.
- RFID may have impact on your existing IT infrastructure. Are your ready to invest on more computers, databases, and application software?

Technical Information

- What frequency is best suited for your environment and applications?

- Which technology offers the most optimal performance (benefit per unit cost)?
- What environment would you require for successful RFID reads? Will RFID equipment work in your environment?
- What are the middleware features required? Which middleware suite is best? Is this middleware scalable, reliable, and suitable keeping your future requirements in mind?

Implementation Requirements

- Since RF waves are not best suited for certain material, you need to decide on where and how the tagging will be done.
- Whether the tagging will be done at vendor level or your warehouse? How will the integration be done?

Question:

1. Prepare an implementation blueprint for BookWorm based on the observations of the RFID experts. Ensure how this implementation is going to be a success.

5 Database Management Systems

In Chapters 3 and 4, we have discussed the hardware component of retail information technology. Both point-of-sales machines and automatic identification and data-capture devices constitute hardware. We have studied that data-capture devices read bar code signals and translate them into data that is stored in the computer. The database system deciphers this data into information that makes sense to the user.

In this chapter, we will discuss how this data is created, captured, stored, and managed with the help of software, called database management systems. Before we talk about database management systems, let us understand the concept of data and database.

DATA

Data is defined as some meaningful facts and figures. Let us understand data with an example. Examine the following statement:

'Suman Morning Store makes a sale of Rs 2.10 million in February 2008.'

In this statement, there are two data elements: (a) the sale of Rs 2.10 million and (b) the month, February 2008. Both the data facts put together make complete information.

Traditionally, this type of data is kept in paper or electronic files. Storage of data, in paper or electronic files, for future use, analysis, and retrieval is called *database*. Figure 5.1 displays a database of product prices stored in a spreadsheet file. This is an example of database kept in an Excel worksheet. If such data is stored in paper or electronic files

Table 5.1 Relationship between business decisions, information systems, and databases linkage

Business Decision	Information Processes	Databases
What to buy	Point-of-sales transaction data analysis to find customer's tastes and preferences	Point-of-sales data with product and customer databases
How to buy	Data collection on products, prices, and vendors. Creation of quotations, evaluation, and contract sign up	Supplier database and quotation database
How much to buy	Purchase forecasting, purchase planning, and auto-purchase ordering systems	Sales database and open-to-buy analysis
When to buy	Purchase order generation based on requirement planning and replenishment	Purchase database and stock database

like Excel worksheet, there will be huge number of files containing data within a very short period of time. Large corporations have such data running into millions of pages. Nobody knows what is lying where, and how to get it when required. The problem arises on the methods to manage, retrieve, and analyse this data.

Business decisions, information systems, and databases are cohesively linked. Table 5.1 illustrates the link between these three elements of retail enterprises systems.

CONCEPT OF DATABASE

A database is where the data resides. It is collection of 'related' information stored so that it is available to many users for different purposes. A computer database gives us some form of electronic filing system, which has many ways of cross-referencing. Electronic filing can be of different forms, such as storing in spreadsheets, text formats, application-specific files, or an independent database system. Cross-referencing allows users to refer and retrieve data in multiple ways.

A database has the following implicit properties:

- Data is about place, objects, or things. It is about facts and figures. A database represents some aspect of the real world. A change in the real world is reflected in the data set.
- A database is a logically coherent collection of data. That is, the facts represent some meaning. Unrelated and random collection cannot be

called a database. For example, a data file containing population details of a city will only have data related to the population of that city. It cannot contain data about the eruption of volcano in Japan. These are random and unrelated facts.

- Database has a specific purpose. Data is collected with some objective. Database is designed, built, and managed for some group of users through some application in which users are interested.

The storage of data in physical paper form, electronic text form, or spreadsheet form is difficult to manage and process, involves high costs of maintenance, and is inflexible. Every organization doing any form of transactions creates data. But efficient analysis of data becomes impossible because of poor file management and hence the concept of database management system (DBMS). Database stores the data in a well-structured format and process and retrieves the data in an efficient manner. An analogy of Excel worksheet and database is given in Fig. 5.1.

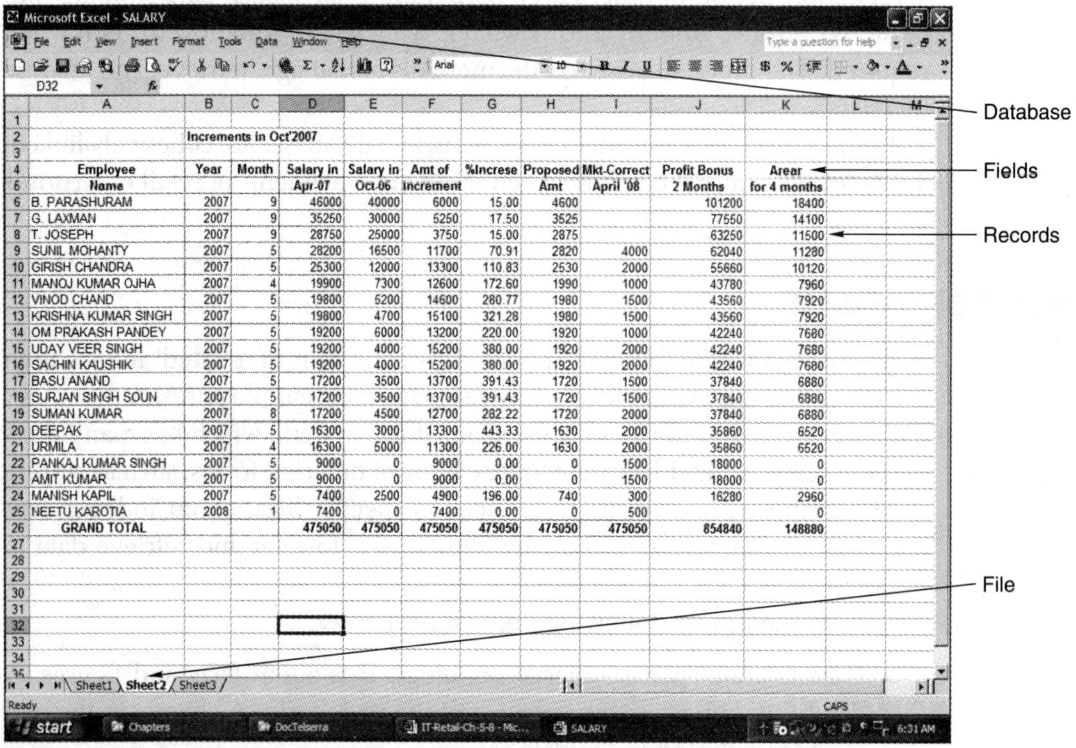

Increments in Oct'2007

Employee Name	Year	Month	Salary in Apr-07	Salary in Oct-06	Amt of Increment	%Increse	Proposed Amt	Mkt-Correct April '08	Profit Bonus 2 Months	Arear for 4 months
B. PARASHURAM	2007	9	46000	40000	6000	15.00	4600		101200	18400
G. LAXMAN	2007	9	35250	30000	5250	17.50	3525		77550	14100
T. JOSEPH	2007	9	28750	25000	3750	15.00	2875		63250	11500
SUNIL MOHANTY	2007	5	28200	16500	11700	70.91	2820	4000	62040	11280
GIRISH CHANDRA	2007	5	25300	12000	13300	110.83	2530	2000	55660	10120
MANOJ KUMAR OJHA	2007	4	19900	7300	12600	172.60	1990	1000	43780	7960
VINOD CHAND	2007	5	19800	5200	14600	280.77	1980	1500	43560	7920
KRISHNA KUMAR SINGH	2007	5	19800	4700	15100	321.28	1980	1500	43560	7920
OM PRAKASH PANDEY	2007	5	19200	6000	13200	220.00	1920	1000	42240	7680
UDAY VEER SINGH	2007	5	19200	4000	15200	380.00	1920	2000	42240	7680
SACHIN KAUSHIK	2007	5	19200	4000	15200	380.00	1920	2000	42240	7680
BASU ANAND	2007	5	17200	3500	13700	391.43	1720	1500	37840	6880
SURJAN SINGH SOUN	2007	5	17200	3500	13700	391.43	1720	1500	37840	6880
SUMAN KUMAR	2007	8	17200	4500	12700	282.22	1720	2000	37840	6880
DEEPAK	2007	5	16300	3000	13300	443.33	1630	2000	35860	6520
URMILA	2007	4	16300	5000	11300	226.00	1630	2000	35860	6520
PANKAJ KUMAR SINGH	2007	5	9000	0	9000	0.00	0	1500	18000	0
AMIT KUMAR	2007	5	9000	0	9000	0.00	0	1500	18000	0
MANISH KAPIL	2007	5	7400	2500	4900	196.00	740	300	16280	2960
NEETU KAROTIA	2008	1	7400	0	7400	0.00	0	500		0
GRAND TOTAL			475050	475050	475050	475050	475050	475050	854840	148880

Fig. 5.1 An analogy between database and spreadsheet

DISADVANTAGES OF TRADITIONAL FILES

Organizations, small or large, accumulate data at every level. Various transaction systems, such as purchases, sales, manufacturing, payroll, and stock movement, create multiple documents and hence data. This data is used by their respective groups of users and the related files are needed by the individual applications. For example, the sales department has hundreds of files related to products, prices, discounts, schemes, customers, taxes, sales persons, enquiries, quotations, customer orders, order terms and conditions, order confirmations, delivery schedules, dispatch advices, invoices, etc. Similarly, purchase department also creates files related to products, prices, vendors, purchase orders, etc. Many of these files are created multiple times. As we see, product and tax files are created by both sales and purchase departments. This leads to duplicity and redundancy of files. We can summarize the major problems in keeping data in the traditional file environment. Laudon (2002) has mentioned five problems with traditional file environment, viz. data redundancy and confusion, program-data dependence, lack of flexibility, poor security, and lack of data sharing and availability.

Duplicity of Data

Duplicity of data refers to maintenance of duplicate data files by various departments or sections across the organizations. This leads to inefficiency as well as storage-related problems. Even in the same file, there can be instances of presence of duplicate data records. Presence of such duplicate records is known as data redundancy.

Lack of Flexibility

Traditional files, like paper-based documents, are not flexible at all, as the data is hardly in a structured format. Locating the data also becomes a problem. But an electronic file system, such as spreadsheets and text, gives only limited flexibility to process and retrieve data. This is only an ad-hoc process, which is most of the times a very costly and ineffective process because the program thus created only caters to that particular sheet or text in the data file.

Poor Security

Traditional file systems are not secure. The paper files can easily get lost and electronic text or spreadsheet can be modified or deleted in spite of being protected by passwords. Moreover, in traditional systems, management does not exercise control over data. The electronic files can be modified without leaving a trace of what was done.

Lack of Data Sharing

Lack of an easy sharing of data forces the departments to create and maintain their own data that in turn leads to duplicity and redundancy. Since the pieces of information are available at different places and different files, it is impossible to share or make the data available to others on a real-time basis.

Program-Data Dependence

Data stored in electronic files can be modified, processed, and retrieved only by programs specifically written for them. The data is not independent. Data existing in an Excel sheet can only be used and retrieved by Excel application. Also, many third-generation languages used for programming like Basic, FORTRAN, and Pascal stored data only in files that are read and modified by the same program. It makes the data and the program cohesively interdependent. You cannot use a third application to manipulate the data. Such manipulation and programming is very costly and time-consuming affair.

DATABASE MANAGEMENT SYSTEMS

The various disadvantages of the traditional file system paved the way for creation of systems that were more flexible and secure and could function independently. Well-managed and carefully arranged files make it easy to obtain data from the data repository. Even a non-programmer can use a data repository and retrieve data by using certain in-built tools in the repository. The system that gives tools to create, store, process, modify, update, and retrieve data from the repository is called database management system (DBMS). The DBMS stores data in it and helps manage data through updation, retrieval, deletion, etc. by providing special tools to do so. It stores data into one location or file instead of multiple files and locations. The single location data serves multiple applications, users, and systems within the organization.

The management of data in a database is done by general-purpose software packages called database management systems. Example of such database management systems are dBase, FoxPro, MS-Access, Oracle, SQL Server, DB2, Ingress, Sybase, MySql, MSDE, SQL-Anywhere, and FireBird.

Database (DB) is an integral part of organization systems. Organizations create, manipulate, and process data and retrieve them in the form of reports and information. Information is stored in the database in data form and the data is stored in the computer in digital form. Employees, vendors, customers, assets, and all transaction processing systems are examples of databases. The data in the databases is created using special-purpose software, commonly known as *application.*

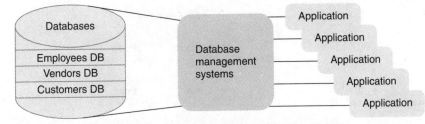

Fig. 5.2   Relationship between DB, DBMS, and applications

The relationship between DB, DBMS, and applications is illustrated in Fig. 5.2.

Database Management Concept

The data in a database can be broken down to the bits level. The computer system organizes data in a hypothetical hierarchy that starts with bits and grows to fields, records, tables, and databases. The bit is the smallest unit of data that the computer recognizes. A group of eight bits, called a byte, represents a single character, alphabet, or digit. Bytes make up a field. As employee name is a field, it contains a name. Multiple fields containing different attributes of the data are arranged in a record, that is different types of data related to one place, person, or thing are called a record. In the Excel worksheet shown in Fig. 5.1, all relevant details accommodated in a single row are called a *record*. A group of multiple records of same type are called a *file* or *table*. For example, employees' information at one place will be called an 'employee table'. There are multiple tables in a database. A human resource database will contain not just the employee table but also dozens, or may be hundreds, of such other tables, such as allowances, perks, leave, loan, taxes, recruitment, training, transfers, appraisal, and promotions. The data hierarchy in a database is illustrated in Fig. 5.3.

Components of Data

Let us explain the above components of a database in simple terms. A data in a database has the following components.

Data Field

Data field is the name of the column that represents data in that field. It is also known as data item. It is a set of characters, used together for representing a particular data element. In Fig. 5.3, P_salary (present salary) of various employees is placed in a single column as follows:

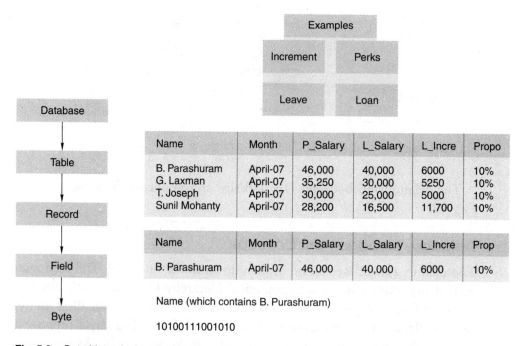

Fig. 5.3 Data hierarchy in a database

B. Parashuram	46,000
G. Laxman	35,250
T. Joseph	30,000
Sunil Mohanty	28,200

We have defined data as similar type of meaningful facts and figures. So, data under a data field represents similar facts. Data is also defined as a representation of facts or concepts that are processed and converted into information.

Record

Record is a collection of related data. One single row in a database table is known as record. A row contains different elements of data. In the example illustrated in Fig. 5.3, all data in the first row belongs to B. Parashuram (also shown below). Therefore, it is related data.

B. Parashuram   April-07   46,000   40,000   6000   10%

B. Parashuram's salary in April 2007 was 46,000, and earlier his salary was 40,000. He received an increment of 6000 and this year his increment is proposed to 10%.

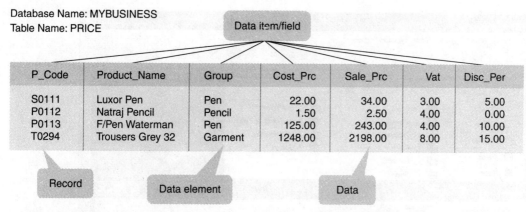

Database Name: MYBUSINESS
Table Name: PRICE

Data item/field

P_Code	Product_Name	Group	Cost_Prc	Sale_Prc	Vat	Disc_Per
S0111	Luxor Pen	Pen	22.00	34.00	3.00	5.00
P0112	Natraj Pencil	Pencil	1.50	2.50	4.00	0.00
P0113	F/Pen Waterman	Pen	125.00	243.00	4.00	10.00
T0294	Trousers Grey 32	Garment	1248.00	2198.00	8.00	15.00

Record   Data element   Data

Fig. 5.4   Records in a price table

Components of Database Management Systems

A database stores data. The data is stored in tables. The database system not only helps manage that data but also stores queries to manipulate and retrieve data, forms for data entry or retrieval, and report files, which are the formats in which the data is placed and presented. Major components of a database are discussed below.

Data Table

Records of the same subjects are placed in a file called data table. Multiple tables are placed under the database. In the example depicted in Fig. 5.4, 'price' is name of the table that contains product price details.

Queries

Queries are created to find and retrieve the data that meet the conditions specified by the user (Figures 5.5 and 5.6). This can also fetch records from multiple tables and update or delete multiple records at the same time and perform predefined tasks or custom calculations on the data. In other words, queries maintain program instructions to retrieve data in desired quantity and quality.

Forms

Forms are the interfaces between the users and the database. They make a bridge that connects the user (data entry or viewer of reports) and the invisible database at the back end. We create the forms to easily enter, view, or modify data. The forms can fetch data from one or more tables and display it on the computer screen in a format as specified by the user (Fig. 5.7). They provide caption, space, and dialogues for data entry or retrieval.

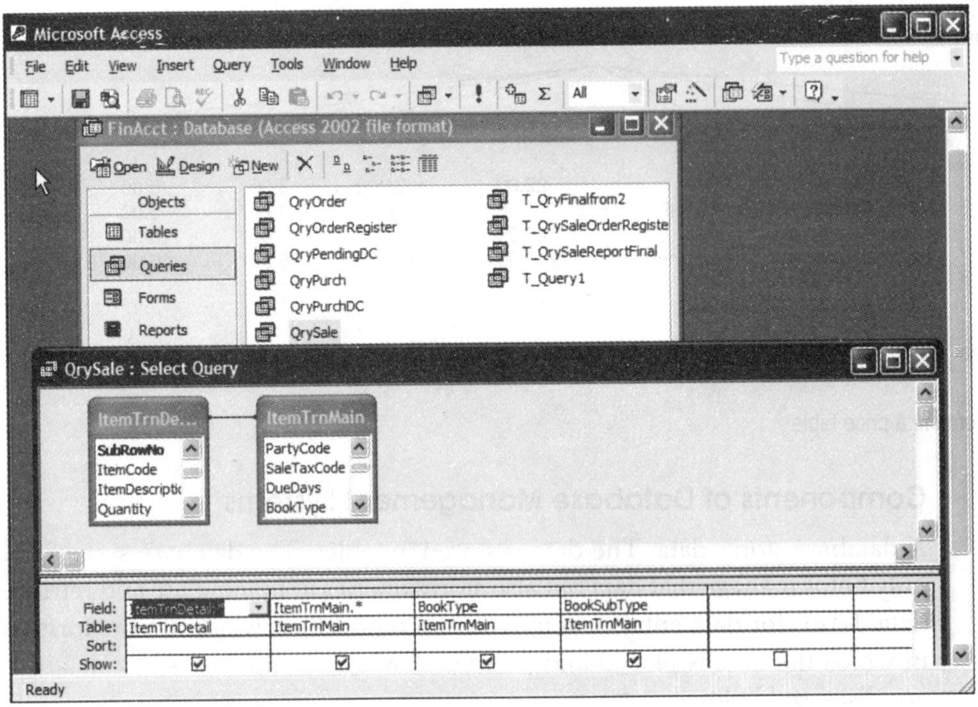

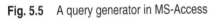

Fig. 5.5 A query generator in MS-Access

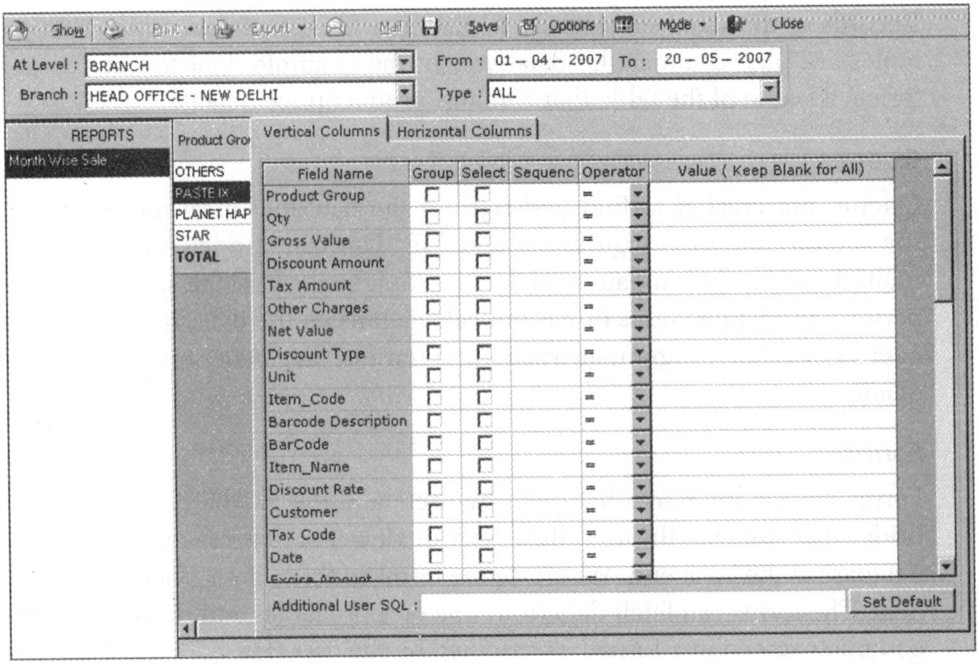

Fig. 5.6 A custom-built query generator

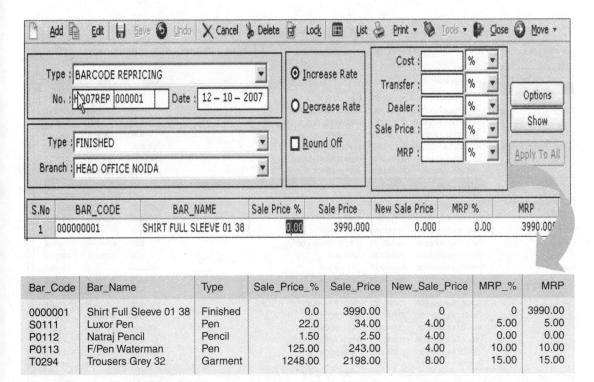

Fig. 5.7 A pricing form and related table relationship: Data displayed on a form retrieved from a database table

Reports

Reports are created to retrieve the desired data from data tables using queries for specific needs. The data is populated either on screen or in a print format. So, report is an effective way to present data in a printed format. It is a formal, presentable, usually a printed document that lists data in a formatted manner (Fig. 5.8).

Advantages of Database Approach

In a traditional file system, where the data is stored in text format, it is possible to easily index the records and retrieve relevant information. Moreover, the same data will be scattered over multiple files. The database approach helps in the following ways:

- It eliminates redundancy (i.e. instances of appearances of the same record multiple times in the database) and duplicity.
- It controls data inconsistency.
- It facilitates sharing of data by many people across the organization or geographical area.

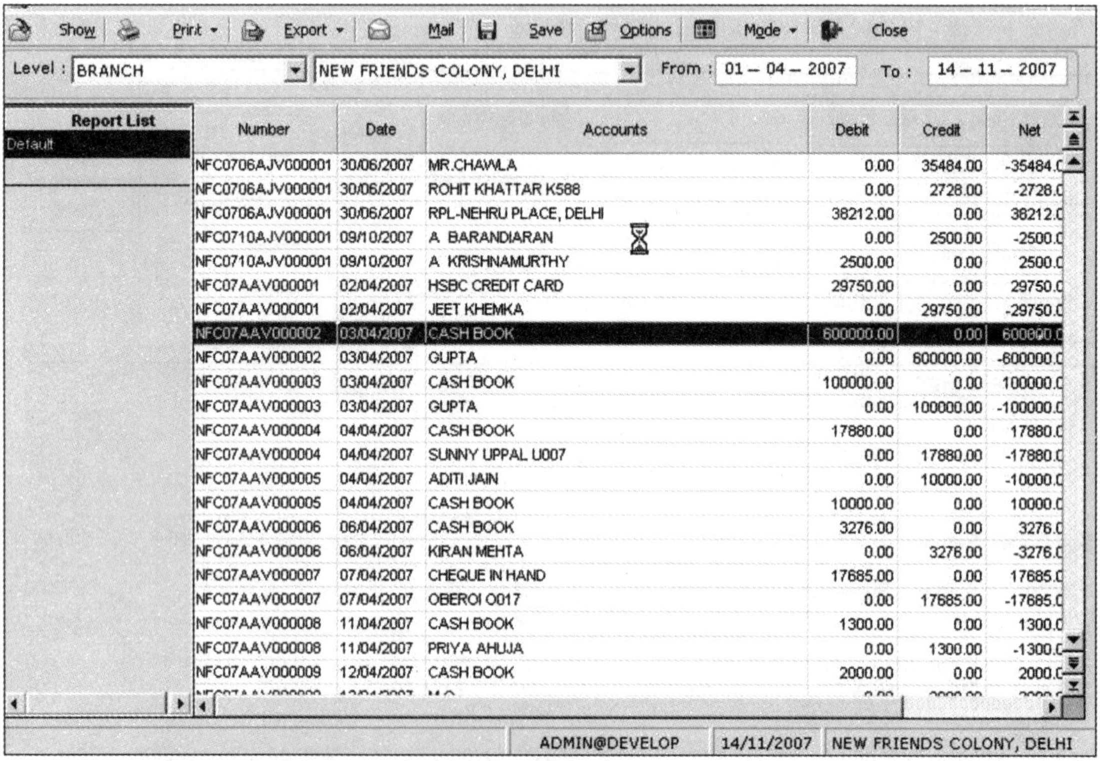

Number	Date	Accounts	Debit	Credit	Net
NFC0706AJV000001	30/06/2007	MR.CHAWLA	0.00	35484.00	-35484.0
NFC0706AJV000001	30/06/2007	ROHIT KHATTAR K588	0.00	2728.00	-2728.0
NFC0706AJV000001	30/06/2007	RPL-NEHRU PLACE, DELHI	38212.00	0.00	38212.0
NFC0710AJV000001	09/10/2007	A BARANDIARAN	0.00	2500.00	-2500.0
NFC0710AJV000001	09/10/2007	A KRISHNAMURTHY	2500.00	0.00	2500.0
NFC07AAV000001	02/04/2007	HSBC CREDIT CARD	29750.00	0.00	29750.0
NFC07AAV000001	02/04/2007	JEET KHEMKA	0.00	29750.00	-29750.0
NFC07AAV000002	03/04/2007	CASH BOOK	600000.00	0.00	600000.0
NFC07AAV000002	03/04/2007	GUPTA	0.00	600000.00	-600000.0
NFC07AAV000003	03/04/2007	CASH BOOK	100000.00	0.00	100000.0
NFC07AAV000003	03/04/2007	GUPTA	0.00	100000.00	-100000.0
NFC07AAV000004	04/04/2007	CASH BOOK	17880.00	0.00	17880.0
NFC07AAV000004	04/04/2007	SUNNY UPPAL U007	0.00	17880.00	-17880.0
NFC07AAV000005	04/04/2007	ADITI JAIN	0.00	10000.00	-10000.0
NFC07AAV000005	04/04/2007	CASH BOOK	10000.00	0.00	10000.0
NFC07AAV000006	06/04/2007	CASH BOOK	3276.00	0.00	3276.0
NFC07AAV000006	06/04/2007	KIRAN MEHTA	0.00	3276.00	-3276.0
NFC07AAV000007	07/04/2007	CHEQUE IN HAND	17685.00	0.00	17685.0
NFC07AAV000007	07/04/2007	OBEROI O017	0.00	17685.00	-17685.0
NFC07AAV000008	11/04/2007	CASH BOOK	1300.00	0.00	1300.0
NFC07AAV000008	11/04/2007	PRIYA AHUJA	0.00	1300.00	-1300.0
NFC07AAV000009	12/04/2007	CASH BOOK	2000.00	0.00	2000.0

Fig. 5.8 Report generated through a query

- This approach enforces standards. The information is stored and retrieved in standard formats.
- It maintains integrity, i.e. two tables containing similar information will not have contradictory records.
- Security restrictions can be applied on a database. Unwanted users cannot perform any action on the database.

DESIGNING A DATABASE

Database designing is a very structured but complex process. When designing a database, one has to keep in mind the purpose of the database, determining the number of tables and structure of tables, identifying unique key, and determining the relationship between various tables. A database system is illustrated in Fig. 5.9.

Various steps in database designing are discussed below.

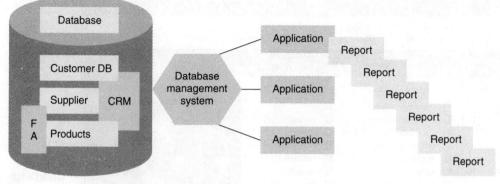

Fig. 5.9   Database system

Defining Purpose of the Database

One must be clear about the purpose for which the database is being created. The subject of the data needs to be identified, which will be stored, processed, and retrieved, once the database is ready. This process makes the designer clearly view the purpose and hence, he designs the objects accordingly. For example, the purpose of a customer database is to hold the primary information about the customer. The database contains customer's code number, name, addresses, communication details, and important dates. The database also holds information about the purchases made by the customer, i.e. sales data of the organization. Data analysis is done on the sales data to find out the tastes and preferences of the customer.

Determining Tables in a Database

Once the purpose is identified, the database designer determines the number of tables required in the database. How to determine the tables in a database? Is one table sufficient to hold all data related to a customer? The answer is based on the purpose of the database. For example, the customer database may have dozens of tables. One master table contains the basic details. The other one can have sales data. Still, the sales data can spread through a number of tables. The bill number, date, and customer ID can be elements in the main sales table, whereas the item break-ups with quantity, price, taxes, and discounts can be stored in another table. This is done for the sake of reducing complexities and making the database tables clean of any duplicate records and fields containing similar data. The criteria of choosing tables are given below:

1. A table should not contain duplicate information, and same information cannot reside in two tables. This is one point where a relational database table differs from a flat-file application like Excel spreadsheet

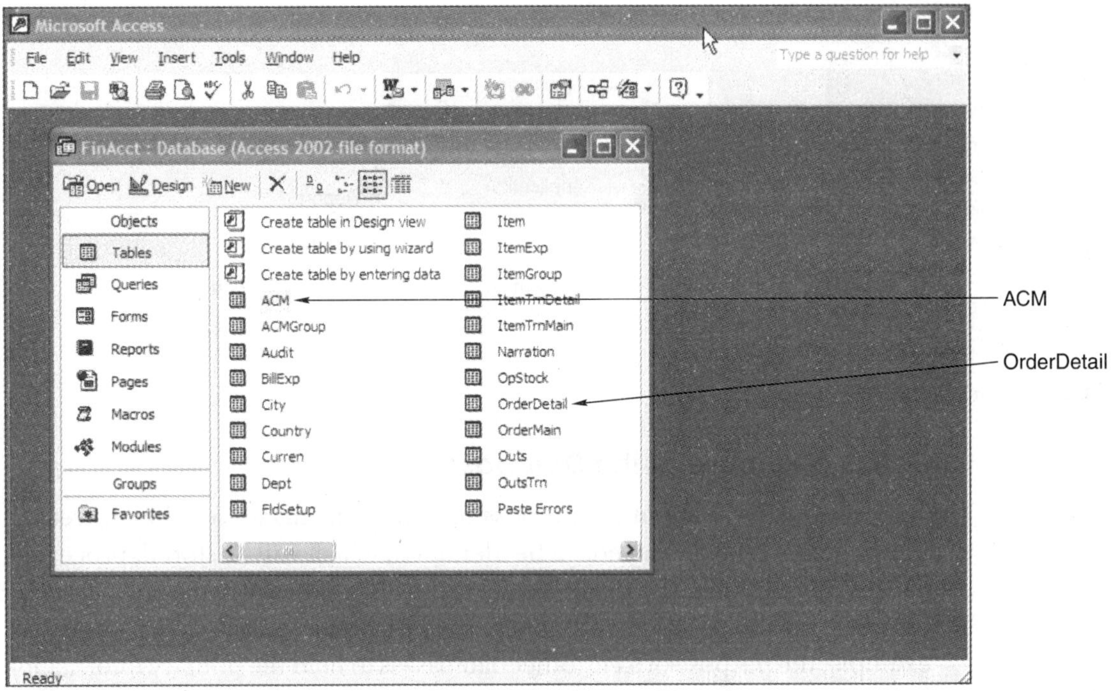

Fig. 5.10   Tables in a database 'FinAcct'

table. It is easier to update and modify a record in one table. It also eliminates the possibility of duplicate entries that contain different information.

2. Each table should contain information about one subject. It is easy to maintain information about one subject independent of other subjects. In Fig. 5.10, the customer's name and address is maintained in the table 'ACM' and the sales order information is stored in another table named 'OrderDetail'.

Deciding the Structure of a Database

As the number of tables has been determined, the next step is to decide the structure of database table. Each table indicates information about the subject and each field in a table contains individual facts about the table's subject. Structure designing is the most crucial and complex job for a database designer. Database architecture affects speed of storing and fetching records, speed of processing of data, and complexities in updating and modifying data. In deciding the database structure, the designer decides the name of the data fields, which must be intelligible, i.e. the system administrators or programmers can make out what it stands for. The database designer has to decide about the other data types, such as text, memo, number, date/time, currency, auto-number, logical type (yes/no), and hyperlinks. While structuring a database table, the following points should be kept in mind:

- Each field should be related directly to the subject of the table.
- All the information required of the subject should be included.
- The fields for information are broken into smallest logical parts, e.g. customer name can be stored in three parts—name, middle name, and surname.
- Good structures do not store the calculated data in a field of the same table.

Identifying Unique Key

Unique key is also called primary key. This is a data field or a set of data fields in every table that is unique. The designated data field contains unique values in each record. The key is used to establish relationship between two or more tables. The main characteristic of primary key is that it cannot be modified, i.e. the data in this field is not changeable. In Fig. 5.11, customer code is the

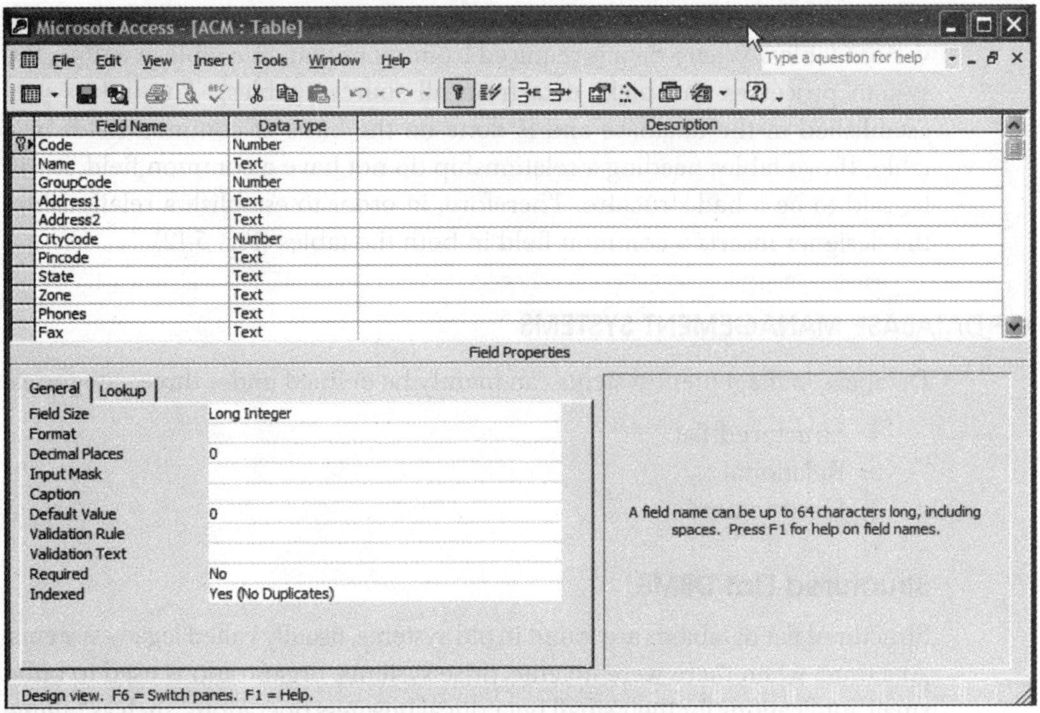

Fig. 5.11 Table design format in MS-Access (The ACM table has a number of data fields.)

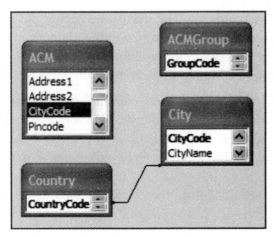

Fig. 5.12 Relationship between tables

primary key. It has also been identified by MS-Access with a key sign (see left-hand top corner).

Determining the Relationship Between Tables

The main attribute of relational database management systems (which will be discussed in the next section) is their capability to establish relationship with various tables. Where data is required from more than one table at a time, the system processes and picks data from all sources (tables). The link is pre-established in the database and is done on the basis of common fields in a table. If two tables needing a relationship do not have a common field, it will be said to be a bad structure. Therefore, in order to establish a relationship, the designer inserts a common field in both the tables (Fig. 5.12).

TYPES OF DATABASE MANAGEMENT SYSTEMS

Database management systems can mainly be defined under three categories:

1. Structured flat
2. Relational
3. Unstructured

Structured Flat DBMS

Structured flat databases are found in old systems, usually called legacy systems. At a time, when there were no enterprise systems, organizations used to build small applications for their small but critical business operations, such as billing, production planning, and logistic management. In these systems, the data elements are organized in pieces of records in each file, usually called a database. To the user, the records look like a spreadsheet row. One type of record having complete information is stored in one database file. The processing and manipulation is carried out in that data file. Some of the older programming languages, such as C, COBOL, and BASIC, supported data only in text files. The data elements are segregated by putting quotes or some special characters.

These types of databases are now considered outdated and are no longer used for building database-driven applications. They are less flexible compared to the modern-day relational DBMS. Their major drawback is difficulty in establishing relationship between two database files containing related records.

Relational Database Management System (RDBMS)

Relational database management system is called so because one table in a database has a relationship with the other tables. It is the most widely used database for applications today and is based on relational calculus. The relational model allows data to be represented in a simple table-like rows and column format. A table is referred to as relation. Each data field is considered to be a column and each record is considered as a row of a table.

In a relational database, data is arranged in files called database files. A database file may contain one or more tables. A table is composed of a number of rows and columns. A row is called a record and a column is called a field. It can relate the data of one table with the data in another table, if both the tables share a common data element. In other words, in RDBMS, each data table has a relationship with others.

Relational database management systems have much more flexibility in processing data for queries, combining information from different sources. These systems allow adding and editing of data without disturbing the old data or any change in the programmed application. Still some of the older system run applications built around these databases. But the Year2000 syndrome caused many companies to shed these applications and they ported their data in new databases.

The database table shown in Fig. 5.4 can be explained in RDBMS terms. To understand the concept, this table is broken into two tables as shown in Fig. 5.13.

Though seemingly independent, these tables do have a relationship between them. The common field, product_code, relates one (or more) record of one table with one (or more) record of the other table (Fig. 5.14).

Product Master

Product_Code	Product_Name	Group
S0111	Luxor Pen	Pen
P0112	Natraj Pencil	Pencil
P0113	F/Pen Waterman	Pen
T0294	Trousers Grey 32	Garment

Price Master

Product_Code	Cost_Prc	Sale_Prc	VAT	Disc_Per
S0111	22.00	34.00	4.00	5.00
P0112	1.50	2.50	4.00	0.00
P0113	125.00	243.00	4.00	10.00
T0294	1248.00	2198.00	8.00	15.00

Fig. 5.13 Database tables

Advantages of RDBMS

The RDBMS is the most popular database system. It offers a lot of advantages over other forms of databases. Almost all the latest developments in application software (such as Oracle, SQL-Server, DB2, Sybase, Ingress, MySql, MSDE, and MS-Access) are being done around RDBMS. The major advantages of this system are discussed below.

Structural Independence   Structural independence means that changes in the database structure do not hamper data access process. Any change in the structure of database does not affect the database's data-access mechanism in any way. The application programs, therefore, do not need any modification even if the structure is modified. Since there is no need of navigational arrangement for the data access, this database offers complete structural independence.

Simplicity of Design and Use   Relational databases run independent of application, data, and structure. They are said to possess data independence and structural independence. Therefore, design and implementation is easier.

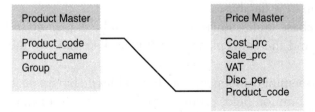

Fig. 5.14 Data table relationship

Advanced Query Capabilities Querying a relational database is very simple, highly efficient, and very powerful. It supports SQL because both have strong foundation of relational algebra and relational calculus.

Unstructured Databases

Traditional and relational database management systems can only store and process fully structured data in the form of text and numbers. They are not capable of storing and manipulating multimedia files, such as HTML text, images, graphics, voice, and full-blown video movies. Now, data is also stored and available in various multimedia forms, as a result of the advent of the Web. Besides the traditional structured form, data also comes in HTML text, images, graphics, and voice, which may need storage and retrieval for various applications. These unstructured databases are handled through the latest breakthrough in database technology, called *object-oriented DBMS* (OODBMS), which is able to store data as objects that can be retrieved and shared. The OODBMS is used to manage various multimedia components in the Web applications.

Though OODBMS can handle large chunk of variety of data, it is not as efficient as RDBMS. Perhaps, that is the reason why RDBMS is still preferred by technologists for storage, processing, and retrieval of large data containing numbers and characters.

DATABASE ADMINISTRATION

One of the main reasons for having a database management system is to have control of both the data and the programs accessing the data. The person having such control over the system is called the *database administrator* (DBA). The relational database management systems are managed and controlled by database administrators. The following are the main functions of a database administrator.

Creation of Schema

The DBA creates the original database schema, which is stored in the data dictionary. *Database schema* refers to the formal language used to define the contents and structure of database. This language defines each data type and its attributes. *Data dictionary* is an electronic file that stores the meaning of each data element and data characteristic.

Creation of Storage Structure and Access Method

The DBA creates the appropriate storage structure and access methods. *Access methods* are the queries written to fetch data from the database. These queries are written using a specialized language that comes with most of the present-day databases and is called *structured query language* (SQL).

Modification of Schema and Physical Organization

Another responsibility of a DBA is to execute commands to modify the original schemas and physical structure.

Granting and Authorization for Data Access

A corporate database is handled, used, and accessed by hundreds of people across the organization. Security of such a database is of prime consideration. Not every user is given rights to play with the data. So, the database is protected by granting permissions to access for specific tasks like editing, deleting, or adding new records. The granting of different types of authorization for data access to the various users of the system is done by the DBA.

Integrity Constraints Specification

Constraints are inbuilt checks in a database that prevent wrong data to be entered or modified in the database. For example, if a particular constraint is applied on *item_name* data field that specifies 'not null', it will not accept any blank entry into the database, or, in other words, a record having no item name cannot be entered by the user. Constraints are integral part of RDBMS. These constraints are kept in a special system structure that is consulted by the database manager whenever required.

LATEST TRENDS IN DATABASE MANAGEMENT

As the organizations grow from single unit, single location business firms to multi-units, multi-products, multi-location, trans-global behemoths; they create and consume large volumes of data. As we know, the basic internal data collection happens at the transaction processing level. At this level, organizations create documents, add data, and analyse it for management information and decision-making purpose. At the same time, external data is also considered for decision support and strategic decision-making. The complex and competitive nature of present day organizations has forced organizations to go beyond simple data analysis of such transaction data. Organizations have progressed from simple data collections in transaction processing systems to online transaction processing (OLTP), online analytical processing (OLAP), data warehousing (DW), and data mining (DM).

Online Analytical Processing

Online analytical processing (OLAP) is a multidimensional data analysis tool to process and filter out data from multiple databases. Multidimensional data analysis refers to viewing the same data in multiple ways. Most of the latest enterprise applications, such as ERP, SCM, and CRM, come with such analytical tools, which can sit on the enterprise database and derive complex reports. These applications provide additional analysis, which is beyond the normal day-to-day descriptive and summarized reports in a business organization. A matrix report showing sales of product per store on one axis and sales figures for each size of the product on other axis is an example of two-dimensional report (Figures 5.15 and 5.16). Similarly, OLAP tools provide capability to present multidimensional reports. The OLAP tools work on various advanced analytical models like quantitative analysis, sensitivity analysis, what-if analysis, transport model analysis, and linear programming tools.

Report List	Product Group	Qty	Net Value	ALEA	ALEXANDER	CHRISTIAN	ERMENEGIL	GOKAN	LAGERFELD	NINA RICC
Default										Ne
Product-brand Sales Matrix	BELT	68.00	371310.00	0.00	150420.00	0.00	0.00	0.00	220890.00	0.0
	BLOUSON	13.00	265590.00	0.00	0.00	0.00	0.00	0.00	265590.00	0.0
	COAT	14.00	351803.00	0.00	0.00	0.00	0.00	0.00	159960.00	0.0
	JACKET	73.00	1475939.40	0.00	0.00	120146.50	0.00	0.00	340528.00	0.0
	JEANS	26.00	226289.00	0.00	0.00	0.00	0.00	0.00	226289.00	0.0
	JUMPER	35.00	163240.00	0.00	0.00	0.00	0.00	0.00	163240.00	0.0
	KNITWEAR	3.00	31254.00	0.00	0.00	0.00	0.00	0.00	0.00	0.0
	LEATHER JKT.	1.00	99990.00	0.00	0.00	0.00	0.00	0.00	99990.00	0.0
	OVERJACKET	5.00	74670.00	0.00	0.00	0.00	0.00	0.00	0.00	0.0
	PANT	20.00	95931.00	0.00	0.00	0.00	0.00	0.00	0.00	0.0
	SHIRT	796.00	4418953.05	463838.75	178164.00	340295.00	0.00	0.00	1144487.00	890095.4
	SUIT	114.00	2947295.30	0.00	0.00	525207.50	0.00	0.00	434804.00	0.0
	SWEATER	43.00	443908.00	0.00	378966.00	0.00	0.00	0.00	0.00	0.0
	SWEATSHIRT	13.00	145388.00	0.00	130094.00	0.00	0.00	0.00	0.00	0.0
	T-SHIRTS	123.00	646775.90	0.00	0.00	278959.90	0.00	0.00	284580.00	83236.0
	TIE	108.00	363527.01	0.00	0.00	0.00	58188.00	65987.54	41004.00	0.0
	TROUSERS	209.00	1722866.30	0.00	303944.00	118164.80	0.00	0.00	0.00	0.0
	TOTAL	1664.00	13844729.96	463838.75	1141588.00	1382773.70	58188.00	65987.54	3381362.00	973331.4

Fig. 5.15 A two-dimensional report provided by BNG-OLAP tool

| | Show | Print ▼ | Export ▼ | Mail | Save | Options | Mode ▼ | Close |

| At Level : | BRANCH ▼ | HEAD OFFICE NOIDA ▼ | From : 01 – 04 – 2007 | To : 26 – 02 – 2008 |

Type : ALL ▼

Report List	Product Group	ALEA		ALEXANDER MCQUEEN		CHRISTIAN LACROIX		ERMENEGILDO ZEGNA		GOKAN
Default		Net Value	Qty	Net Value	Qty	Net Value	Qty	Net Value	Qty	Net Value
Product-brand Sales Matrix	BELT	0.00	0.00	150420.00	18.00	0.00	0.00	0.00	0.00	0.0
	BLOUSON	0.00	0.00	0.00	0.00	0.00	0.00	0.00	0.00	0.0
	COAT	0.00	0.00	0.00	0.00	0.00	0.00	0.00	0.00	0.0
	JACKET	0.00	0.00	0.00	0.00	120146.50	6.00	0.00	0.00	0.0
	JEANS	0.00	0.00	0.00	0.00	0.00	0.00	0.00	0.00	0.0
	JUMPER	0.00	0.00	0.00	0.00	0.00	0.00	0.00	0.00	0.0
	KNITWEAR	0.00	0.00	0.00	0.00	0.00	0.00	0.00	0.00	0.0
	LEATHER JKT.	0.00	0.00	0.00	0.00	0.00	0.00	0.00	0.00	0.0
	OVERJACKET	0.00	0.00	0.00	0.00	0.00	0.00	0.00	0.00	0.0
	PANT	0.00	0.00	0.00	0.00	0.00	0.00	0.00	0.00	0.0
	SHIRT	463838.75	111.00	178164.00	18.00	340295.00	68.00	0.00	0.00	0.0
	SUIT	0.00	0.00	0.00	0.00	525207.50	19.00	0.00	0.00	0.0
	SWEATER	0.00	0.00	378966.00	35.00	0.00	0.00	0.00	0.00	0.0
	SWEATSHIRT	0.00	0.00	130094.00	10.00	0.00	0.00	0.00	0.00	0.0
	T-SHIRTS	0.00	0.00	0.00	0.00	278959.90	57.00	0.00	0.00	0.0
	TIE	0.00	0.00	0.00	0.00	0.00	0.00	58188.00	13.00	65987.5
	TROUSERS	0.00	0.00	303944.00	28.00	118164.80	16.00	0.00	0.00	0.0
	TOTAL	**463838.75**	**111.00**	**1141588.00**	**109.00**	**1382773.70**	**166.00**	**58188.00**	**13.00**	**65987.5**

Fig. 5.16 A three-dimensional report showing the sale of a product by brands in terms of quantity sold and sales value

Data Warehousing

Data warehousing refers to single, centralized, and unified repository of data that works across the enterprise. Such data is collected throughout the lifespan of the organization and is scattered and stored in large but incompatible data repositories. Large organizations are plagued with an increasing amount of data, which is indispensable. The data may be stored in old legacy systems running on COBOL, FoxPro or C applications. The data may also be available in spreadsheets, such as Lotus1-2-3, QuatroPro, MS-Excel, or Lotus Notes. The recent data of the organization may be available in complex RDBMS data files, HTML websites, and XML graphics database. Large corporate bodies with their continuing businesses want to retain that data and undertake analysis of data for looking at their profitability trends, product life cycle, and other general trends in the complex business environments.

The data from these diverse documents and sources is clubbed into one database (Fig. 5.17). Then it is standardized and normalized into one data model. Standardization involves complying with a single system of keeping data. For example, if the date in an old database is written as 'yy/mm/dd' and in another it is written as 'mm/dd/yyyy', in some other database it may be

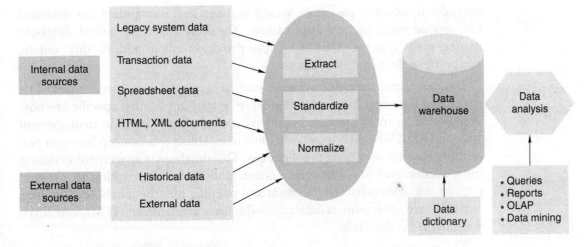

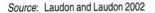

Fig. 5.17 Components of a data warehouse

Source: Laudon and Laudon 2002

written as 'ddmmyyyy'. Therefore the task involved in standardization is applying a single date type for all the data in the data warehouse. Normalization refers to removing all duplicate data that has crept in because of variety of data sources. The duplicate, redundant, and unwanted data is removed. This process is called normalization. Finally, the data is consolidated and made available to different users across the organization.

Data Mining

Data mining is the process of extracting data from data warehouses. As there cannot be a single application or tool to extract required data, data mining involves variety of data-extraction processes. Most of the time, the data extraction is done by running ad-hoc queries. Laudon (2002) puts it as follows: 'Data mining software tools find hidden patterns and relationships in large pools of data and infer rules from them that can be used to predict future behaviours and guide decision-making.'

SUMMARY

Data involves facts and figures about some object or event. Storage of the data in a structured manner, so that it can be retrieved, processed, and presented to those who require it, is called database. Data is stored in the database in the form of tables, records, and data element. This forms the hierarchy of a data system in the database. Large databases of modern nature are managed by specialized software packages, which manage and manipulate the data and are independent of any application. These systems are called database management systems (DBMS). These provide tools to add, modify, delete, and retrieve data in the database.

Database management systems can be grouped into three types. The structured flattened file system that were usually application specific are now outdated. The most used and admired are relational database management systems (RDBMS), which provide tools to establish relationship between two or more data tables within the database. This database management system is most secure and one can apply constraints and authorization to prevent duplication of records and unauthorized peeping into the database. The third and latest are unstructured databases, which are available on HTML and XML documents on the Web.

The need to integrate and process large chunks of data gave birth to the concept of online analytical processing (OLAP), data warehousing (DW), and data mining (DM). The latest trend in database management is the consolidation of various internal and external data in one large repository. The creation of DW involves extracting data from various databases and diverse documents, standardizing the data by applying common rules, normalizing data by removing duplicate records and tables. The consolidated data is then processed and reports generated using various tools, such as OLAP, query generators, and data mining.

CONCEPT REVIEW QUESTIONS

1. What is a database management system?
2. Explain basic characteristics of a database.
3. What are the advantages of a database concept?
4. What is RDBMS?
5. How will you differentiate between DBMS and RDBMS?
6. What steps are involved in designing a database?
7. What do you understand by a DBA?
8. What are the functions of a database administrator?
9. What do you understand by OLAP?
10. Explain data warehousing. Differentiate between data warehousing and data mining.

CRITICAL THINKING QUESTION

1. The best way of maintaining the census survey data is through data warehousing. Critically examine this statement.

━━━━━━━━━━━━━ **PROJECT** ━━━━━━━━━━━━━

1. Design a database structure for employee information of your organization. Consider employee personal details, salary, perks and allowances, deductions and leave records.

SELECT REFERENCES ▬▬▬▬▬▬▬▬▬▬▬

Jaiswal, Mahadeo and Monika Mital 2004, *Management Information Systems*, Oxford University Press, New Delhi.

Laudon, Kenneth and Jane Laudon 2002, *Management Information Systems*, Pearson Education (Singapore).

Turban, Efraim, Jay E. Aronson, and Ting-Peng Liang 2005, *Decision Support Systems and Intelligent Systems*, Pearson Education.

CASE STUDY

Luxor: Writing Retail Success Stories

Company   Luxor Writing Instruments Pvt Ltd

Luxor Group of Companies, headed by Mr D.K. Jain, Chairman of the company, started manufacturing writing instruments in India in the year 1963. Today, Luxor is the brand leader in the Indian writing instrument industry, having a market share of over 20 per cent with an excellent network of dealers and distributors. Luxor was formed in the year 1991. As of today, Luxor is a leading manufacturer and exporter of writing instruments from India with over 15 per cent of export market share. It has four manufacturing facilities in New Delhi and three in Mumbai, employing over 600 people.

Luxor was the first to introduce many new technologies in the Indian market, such as pigment fluorescent highlighters, xylene-free markers, ceramic roller pens, needle point pens, and OHP pens. It is the first company that is recognized by the Government of India as an export house manufacturing and exporting quality writing instruments to over 45 countries all over the world. Luxor also bagged the first coveted ISO-9002 certification for unsurpassed quality of its products. Being a pioneer company, it first took the initiative to transform the unorganized sector of pen manufacturing into an organized one under the able guidance and foresight of Mr D.K. Jain. Luxor tied up with global leaders in the writing instrument industry and brought state-of-the-art technology and world-class brands in the country. It introduced brands like Pilot (1982), Parker (1996), and Papermate in India. It also introduced fibre-tip and large-scale manufacturing of colour pen sets in 1971, roller ball pens in 1978, and Pilot hi-tech needlepoint in 1984. Luxor was also the first company to cross the one million production mark per day of pens in 1999.

Cashing in on the organized retail boom in India, Luxor forayed into retail in 2006 with its *'Signature'* retail identity. Besides retailing its various brands of pens and stationery, the company also sells electronic gadgets like iPODs and digital cameras.

Industry   Retail—Writing Instruments

Solution Area   Database Management

Problem   At the time of launch of *Luxor-Signature*, the company was just the new entrant in the retail business. It did not have any information system to manage retail sales. Although the company was techno-savvy and had started implementation of SAP R/3 for its manufacturing and accounting areas, but it looked for a tested and tried indigenous solution for retail. The benchmarks were set and various products were tested on these benchmarks. Some of the salient tests were related to the solution to conform to Indian taxation laws, from a company providing handholding support, and from a vendor who could provide a few dozen references of its successful implementation. As already stated, Luxor was using SAP R/3 to manage their back-office operations and so the retail software had to be integrated with SAP R/3. Thus, the real problem laid in integration of POS data with the back-office data. One of the most critical tasks involved was data porting.

Solution   Before opening its first retail outlet, Luxor evaluated six nationally reputed vendors of retail software solutions. BNGpro, a retail solution from a New Delhi based company, BNG Infotech Pvt Ltd, was shortlisted and finalized, which met the maximum benchmarks defined by the company. Besides the functionalities in the software, training to the users and support during implementation were critical factors in deciding the vendor. BNGpro's proven track record of successful implementation at various well-known as well as less-known retailers was also a factor in its favour. So, the task with this vendor was to implement the retail solution in various retail outlets opened in the country and provide a data integration middleware with the database of SAP R/3. Luxor uses Oracle 9i as database for its large number of products.

Implementation   BNG Infotech implemented BNGpro, the retail package, which had MSDE, the freeware database from Microsoft. The experienced consultants of the software company felt that the present database management system was not strong and powerful enough to hold large retail data. So, the vendor installed a consolidation-integrated suite for back-office distribution and inventory management, which used Oracle 9i as the relational database management system (RDBMS). The back-office suite was set up on a limited number of computers, since it had to be integrated with SAP R/3 through a custom-built middleware.

BNG's small team, under the supervision of its technical head, implemented the POS at its first store in Shipra Mall in Ghaziabad with an impressive efficiency, completing in a week's time. Similarly, the back-office suite was set up in 15 days. Now, the most critical task that remained was of the conversion of data conforming to SAP format in Oracle 9i to BNGpro format. The data-porting task also involved rearranging product codes in a logical manner. Some of the redundant product codes were dropped. These product codes had to be mapped with multiple States of India, local Governments, VAT rate structures. At Luxor, an IT team—consisting of a system manager to manage IT infrastructure, an application manager to manage various legacy and other application, and a database administrator to manage database—is supervised by a deputy general manager (IT).

Benefits   At the time of automation of the new store, the major focus is on smooth operations of the POS. It takes care of day-to-day activities at the POS, such as unhindered billing, cash collection, credit management, customer database creation, and inventory management at the POS. The data transmission from POS to back office and vice versa takes place smoothly through e-mail or leased lines. The data is seamlessly integrated with the back-office system. The management of Luxor analyses data from the back-office integrated database. Once the basic operations by the software are performed smoothly, only then the company goes into advanced stage of data analysis and reporting. Luxor can now perform online analytical processing of data and derive the required information.

Questions:
1. What is RDBMS implemented by Luxor and why?
2. Luxor is using different applications at retail, warehouses, manufacturing units, and consignees, which are built around different database systems. Is Luxor a fit case of data warehousing implementation? Explain with examples in detail.

Source: This case study is based on interactions with management and staff of Luxor Writing Instruments, personal observations during consulting and providing software solutions, and information from the company's promotional material and websites. Contributions of Mrs Saloni Mohan and Mr C.S. Baddam are appreciated.

6

Networks and Telecommunications

Learning Objectives

- To appreciate the contribution of telecommunications in computing
- To differentiate between various network architectures
- To know various networks in terms of their reach
- To compare various telecommunication media
- To understand communication and Internet protocols
- To understand Internet-based communication

In the previous chapters, we have discussed hardware and databases as important components of retail information technology. Computers, which are central point of IT, hold databases and software to accumulate and manage that data. In a business environment, computers are hardly used as stand-alone systems.

Today, stand-alone computers have been replaced by networks of computers for processing of most corporate tasks. Study of modern computing is incomplete without understanding networks supported by telecommunications, as virtually every computer is a part of a network and networks are yet part of other greater networks. We need to understand networks and communication between computers not just for academic purpose but also to enrich our knowledge and help us make the right choice when we choose a media to connect our various offices or retail outlets (Fig. 6.1). Besides discussing various network technologies, this chapter also ponders over virtual private network (VPN) and electronic data interchange (EDI), which are going to be one of the important techniques of interoffice data transmission between back-office ERP and front-office POS. The concepts have been briefly explained in this chapter.

TELECOM REVOLUTION—CONVERGENCE OF INFORMATION AND COMMUNICATION TECHNOLOGIES

We have seen in previous chapters how computers were invented to help scientists and mathematicians perform

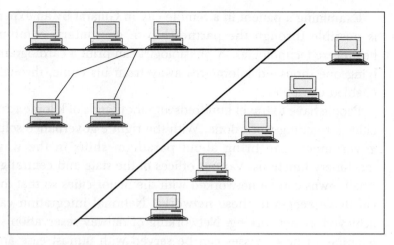

Fig. 6.1 Networks of computers

complex and time-consuming calculations. Computers were not originally meant for what they perform today. They evolved from just computing devices to modern-day panacea for all ills in every walk of life.

Coming together of computers and telephones—information and communication technologies (ICT)—is called *convergence of ICT*. Integration of computers with communication brought about a major revolution in our lifestyles. It has completely changed the way we socialize, entertain, study, and do our business today.

The Internet is an outcome of convergence of information and communication technologies. Online communities have taken place of traditional groups of people belonging to one school of thought. People get in touch with each other through e-mails, chats, bulletin board services, and now blogs. Entertainment through shared systems, free downloads, and music and movies on demand have revolutionized the industry.

Imparting education will not remain the same in future. Distance or classroom education will go where the learners are. Students need not come to the class for a lecture, but the information and communication technology will help them listen to the lecture and browse through the contents in their own time and pace. The Internet is the terminator of time and space. An expert on taxation system need not be present in every city and can speak and deliver his/her lecture from the ease and comfort of his/her home. Learners in various cities can browse the Net or avail of teleconferencing facilities provided by the local telecom operator and listen to the learned speech of the tax advisor. Tutoring a student in California on latest yoga therapies can be done sitting on the banks of the Ganges in Rishikesh.

Examining a patient in a remote city in Gujarat by an expert in New York is possible through the partnership of computers, communication, and healthcare technologies. A physiologist can print a cardiogram of his patient lying one thousand kilometres away from his clinic, through his Internet-enabled computer.

People have to travel hundreds and thousands of kilometres away to major cities for getting work done. With the right e-governance solutions in hand, governments can bring about paradigm shifts in the way government machinery functions. Various offices of the state and central governments in small towns can be networked with the major cities so that the people there can have access to these networks. National integration can be virtually achieved by networking. Networking of railway reservation system is a live example of how masses can be served with utmost ease and just a bit of technology. Properly planned and focused approach in implementation of information and communication technology would help alleviate poverty. India and other Third-World countries can leverage ICT to reach out to the masses and give them information and knowledge at their doorsteps, thus enriching them and leaving with them a bit more money to spend on improving their living standards.

In the 1980s, nobody could imagine if private banks could exist and we would know our bank balance sitting in our homes without meeting the bank clerk. Today, the moment our important courier is delivered or a cheque is debited in our account, we get a message on our mobile. With state-of-the-art technology, private banks function much more efficiently and people have confidence in them.

Conducting business through the Internet using support tools, such as e-mails, messaging, and electronic data interchange, makes things more efficient and profitable. Convergence of information and communication technologies has given birth to an altogether new business model of e-commerce. Selling and buying through the Internet has become very popular. There are thousands of e-commerce stores across the world. Virtual stores are run with virtually nothing in hand—no stocks, shop, catalogues, suppliers, and customers. But the moment a store is created in the Web server, things start happening.

Just a few years back, we could not imagine writing books of accounts of a retail firm in San Jose, while sitting in our cosy office in Gurgaon. Business process outsourcing (BPO) is an industry today and is now taught in the business schools. This has happened only due to marriage of computers and telephones.

NETWORK ARCHITECTURES

Networks are interconnected computers to share data, files, information, and equipment like printers, which are connected through cables and other communication media for transmission of data, graphics, and images. Jaiswal and Mital (2004) define network architecture as 'a framework in which all the components of networks are packaged together into usable network systems that organize functions, data formats, and procedures'. Fundamentally, a telecommunication system consists of the following components:

1. One or more host or server computer, which stores and processes information and provides network resources like network operating system and other communication software.
2. The client computers, which are connected to the server or host computer. They use the network resources but do not provide them.
3. Communication lines through which data and voice is transmitted between the connected computers. These lines are telephone lines, twisted pair, and coaxial or wireless lines.
4. Peripheral equipment to facilitate communication devices, such as modems, multiplexers, and controllers.
5. Communication software, which controls the various input-output processes.

Client-Server Architecture

Client-server networks involve a server (usually a high-end computer) and clients (other computers connected with the server). Clients are also called workstations or nodes. Server is the centralized machine that stores and shares the network resources with the clients. Servers run on various network operating systems (NOS), such as UNIX, Linux, Windows 2000, Windows-XP, and Novell Netware.

Processing based on client-server architecture is called *distributed processing*. Laudon (2002) defines distributed processing as 'the use of multiple computers linked by communication networks for processing'. This is in contrast with centralized processing in which processing is done by one large central computer, usually a minicomputer or mainframe. Client-server computing splits computing between 'client' and 'server'. Both are on the networks and the tasks that are best suited to it are assigned. Servers are usually dedicated server computers, that store and process data and also perform back-end functions not visible to the users, such as managing networks. Clients are normal desktops and laptops and normally process client portion, i.e. user interface of the applications. Figure 6.2 illustrates basic client-server network.

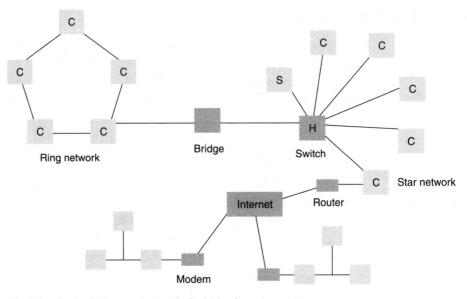

Fig. 6.2 Basic client-server network displaying its components

Networks based on client-server architecture are highly secure. The network resources are centrally managed and provide for efficient functioning. The networks are scalable, i.e. new workstations can be added without disturbing the network architecture.

Peer-to-Peer Networks

Peer-to-peer networks involve two or more computers that are connected through some communication channel. In this type of network, each computer is a host as well as a client. These types of networks are established for simple files and printer sharing, usually in a small network set-up. The number of computers it supports is less than ten. The main advantage of such networks is that they are easy to set-up and cost effective, as no additional resources, such as hardware and software, are required (Fig. 6.3). But the biggest disadvantage is that networks based on peer-to-peer architecture are not secure.

TYPES OF NETWORKS

Networks can be best classified on the basis of their geographical reach, i.e. the distance between various computer resources, connectivity, and the medium of communication they use. We broadly classify them as LAN, WAN, MAN, the Internet, and intranet.

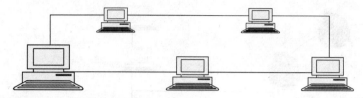

Fig. 6.3 Peer-to-peer network

Local Area Networks

Local area network (LAN) covers networking among the computers located at a limited distance, usually one floor or close floors on the same building. It connects PCs to share printers, data, and applications on a high bandwidth line. The LAN capabilities are defined and managed by network operating systems (NOS), which route and manage communications on the network. Windows NT, Windows 2000 Server, Windows XP, Novell Netware, Linux, and OS2 Warp Servers are examples of network operating systems. The LAN is distinguished from other networks due to its size and transmission technology. Its size is small, usually one room, building, or two adjacent buildings within a campus (Fig. 6.4). It runs on twisted pair or coaxial cables operating at 10 to 100 Mbps speed.

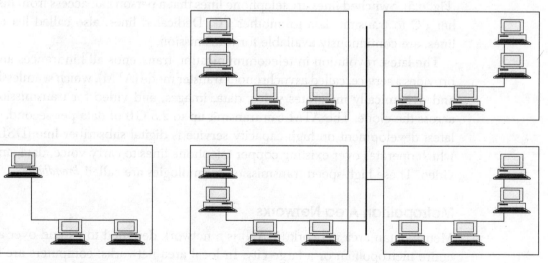

Single-building LAN   Multiple-building LAN

Fig. 6.4 LAN layout

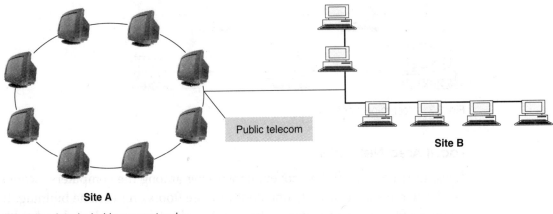

Site A

Fig. 6.5 A typical wide area network

Wide Area Networks

Wide area network (WAN) is spread over broad geographical areas, i.e. city, country, or continental level. It helps in long-distance transmission of data, voice, image, and video. While LAN uses its own resources, WAN connects many LANs and use private and public resources. The major distinction of WANs is that they work over multiple communication channels, such as switched or dedicated lines and microwave or satellite communications (Fig. 6.5). Switched lines are telephone lines that a person can access from his/her PC to transmit data to another PC. Dedicated lines, also called leased lines, are continuously available for transmission.

The latest revolution in telecommunication transcends all hindrances and provides a service, called asynchronous transfer mode (ATM), which seamlessly and dynamically integrates voice, data, images, and video for transmission across the globe. The ATM can transmit up to 2.5 GB of data per second. A latest development on high-capacity service is digital subscriber line (DSL), which operates over existing copper telephone lines to carry voice, data, and video. These high-speed transmission technologies are called *broadband*.

Metropolitan Area Networks

Metropolitan area network (MAN) is a network designed to extend over an entire metropolitan or a large city. In local area networks, computers are in close proximity and connected through privately laid cables, routers, or gateways. But when networks are scattered over a city, it is not possible to lay cables for the individual enterprise. Even if it is possible to lay cables, a cost-effective and better alternative is to use public-utility services provided by a telecommunication company.

The MAN is placed between LAN and WAN. It can use a similar architecture or the telecommunication media as used by WAN. If the distance is high, the network component uses dedicated lines or wireless connectivity like radio frequency, as in case of WAN, even if the network is within the metropolitan city.

Internet

The Internet, also known as the network of the networks, is a self-regulatory and self-managed large network of thousands of smaller networks, in which each computer is a node as well as a server. It works on telecommunication backbone and has global reach. To connect to the Internet, one has to connect to the local Internet service provider (ISP) through telephone lines connected through the modem in the computer. The computer and communication device should agree to certain rules of connectivity and standards of transmissions called transmission control protocol/Internet protocol (TCP/IP).

The Internet is based on client-server architecture. The rules and language of connection is written in the browser we use. The browser helps connect the client with the Web server at a distant location. The Internet is another form of client-server computing, in which client processing and storage capability are very minimal. Most of storage and processing happens at the server end. The client downloads the interface forms, application, and data from the server over the network and completes his/her task.

Intranet

Intranet is a private network owned and managed by a single person or organization. Unlike the Internet, which is a public network encompassing millions of other networks, such as LANs and WANs, intranet is a private network fully protected and secure. An organization needs to share data and information across its offices and so it creates an internal network that provides access to data and information throughout the organization. Intranets are created using the Internet backbone or over other private and public communication channels (Fig. 6.6). These networks are secure with firewalls and specialized software to prevent unwanted elements from peeping into the organization's private networks. The firewall consists of specialized hardware and software placed between the organization network and outside network.

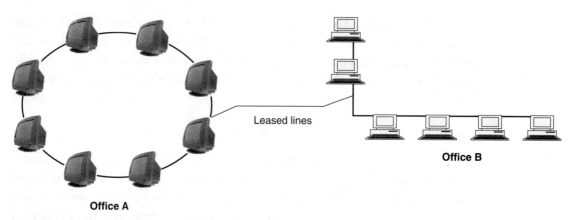

Fig. 6.6 Intranet using private leased lines

COMMUNICATION MEDIA

Computers and other telecommunication devices use electrical signals to represent data. These signals can be transmitted from one device to another in the form of electromagnetic force. These electromagnetic signals need some media through which they can travel. This media can be vacuum, air, or some metal. For our study, we divide the media into 'wired' and 'wireless' media.

Wired Media

Wired media, also known as guided media, is the physical conduit between two or more devices. Twisted pair and coaxial cables use copper wire as conductor for electromagnetic signals in the form of electric current. Optical fibre is made of glass or plastic cables that transport signals in the form of light.

Twisted Pair

Twisted pair cables are a set of two or more insulated copper cables. These are called 'twisted' because the pair of cables is twisted with each other. The normal LAN cable comes in a pair of five twisted pair and called Cat-5 UTP (unshielded twisted pair) cable. Cat-5 refers to category five which is used to transmit data up to 100 Mbps. These cables are connected through a connecter called UTP connecter. Twisted pair is more popular in local area networks.

Coaxial Cable

Coaxial cable is made up of two cables; one is the central solid wire, usually made of copper, which is covered by the other, a mesh or foil of metal. The best example of coaxial cable is the television cables. These cables are connected with bayonet network connector (BNC). In this category of connectors, T-connectors are used to branch off a cable for connection with a computer device. The 'terminators' are used at the last end of the cable. Though coaxial cables can carry signals of higher frequency, they are less in use because of the changing network topologies. A topology defines the layout of computers in a network.

Fibre Optics

While both twisted pair and coaxial cables carry signals in the form of electric current, optic cables carry signals in the form of light. Fibre optic cable contains and directs a beam of light from its source to the target. The one end of the cable is connected with a device emitting light and the other end is fitted with a photosensitive device for receiving and translating the light currents into electromagnetic current to make the cable usable for computers.

Wireless Media

Wireless media is also known as unguided media since the electromagnetic waves are broadcast through air or water. Any device that has a receiving capability can receive and translate the waves into some sort of data. Wireless transmission, which sends signals through air, water, or space without any physical cable, has become an increasingly popular alternative to cabled transmission channels because of its reach and cost-effectiveness. Wireless networks use radio frequencies (RF) media, microwaves, and satellite channels. Today, common technologies for wireless data transmission include microwave transmission, communication satellites, paging, cellular telephones, and mobile data networks. We will briefly discuss radio frequency, microwave, satellites, and cellular telephony.

Radio Frequency

Radio frequencies (RF) are radio waves carrying data. They can travel to any distance and medium and do not require line of sight connectivity. Radio waves travel from very small frequency of 3 kHz to frequencies up to 30 GHz frequencies. The biggest problem today for companies having telecommunication backbone is connectivity at the last mile. (*Last mile* is connectivity between the city offices of the service provider to the clients' office.) Companies use RF-based technology to connect these offices. Inter-city connectivity is done through fibre optical cables.

Microwave

Microwave communication channels require line-of-sight transmission and reception equipment. The towers containing antenna are placed at very high places like hilltops or tall buildings so that the signals can cover a large area. Since microwaves move in one direction at time, two transmitters and receivers are placed to receive and send signals simultaneously. To increase the distance covered by the microwaves, repeaters are installed on each antenna.

Satellite Communication

Satellite communication works like microwave. The satellite orbiting earth functions as a very large antenna and repeater. The signals travel straight in line of sight, but because of the satellite, the reach is increased dramatically. These types of microwaves can cover any corner of the earth and leasing time or frequencies on satellite is a cost-effective way of communication (Fig. 6.7).

Cellular Telephony

Cellular telephony provides stable communication between two moving objects or one mobile and another stationary. The service provider locates and tracks a caller and assigns a channel to the call. Both the instruments sending and receiving calls use this channel for communication. The signal is transferred

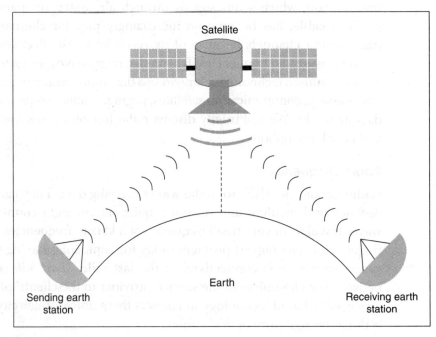

Fig. 6.7 Satellite communication system

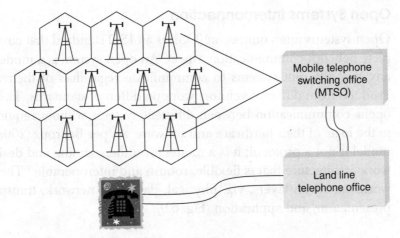

Fig. 6.8   Cellular communication system

from channel to channel if the caller moves from one range to another. To facilitate smooth transmission, the entire range is divided into cells. The mobile tower contains an antenna, which is controlled by a service provider office called *mobile telephone switching office* (MTSO). The MTSO performs tasks of coordinating communications, connecting calls, and recording call information and billing to the subscriber.

The size of a cell is based on the geographical coverage required and the population of the area (Fig. 6.8). The basic range is from 1 to 10 kilometres. But if the population of the area is dense, cell size is reduced to accommodate the traffic.

COMMUNICATION PROTOCOLS

As Behrouz (2003) simplifies protocol 'as a set of rules that govern data communication'. It represents an agreement between the communicating devices. Without a protocol, two devices may be connected but may not communicate. Therefore, we can say that protocols are rules and laws governing communications between two networking devices and systems. In computer systems, different systems come from different manufacturers. One such system may not just receive and accept the communication signal in the same way. Such communications will be incomplete. So, for the communication to be complete, the systems must agree on the protocol.

We will briefly discuss OSI protocols governing networking and TCP/IP protocols governing the Internet.

Open Systems Interconnection

Open systems interconnection (OSI) is an ISO standard that covers the complete network communication aspect. An open system is a model that allows any two different systems to communicate regardless of their architecture. Products from different vendors work on different standards. The OSI model opens communication between different systems without requiring changes in the logic of their hardware and software. As per Behrouz (2003): 'The OSI model is not a protocol; it is a model for understanding and designing a network architecture that is flexible, robust, and interoperable.' The OSI model works on seven layers, viz. physical, data link, network, transport, session, presentation, and application (Fig. 6.9).

Transmission Control Protocol/Internet Protocol

Transmission control protocol/Internet protocol (TCP/IP) is a standard by which computers on the Internet connect with each other. The TCP/IP protocol suite is made of five layers, viz. physical, data link, network, transport, and application.

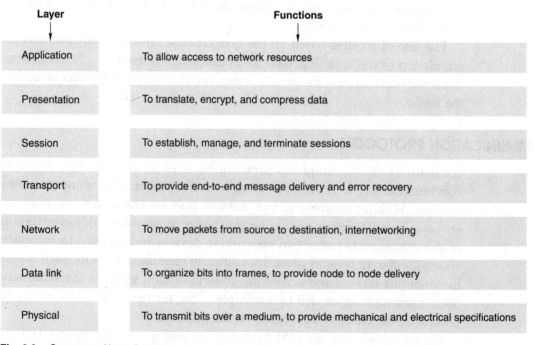

Layer	Functions
Application	To allow access to network resources
Presentation	To translate, encrypt, and compress data
Session	To establish, manage, and terminate sessions
Transport	To provide end-to-end message delivery and error recovery
Network	To move packets from source to destination, internetworking
Data link	To organize bits into frames, to provide node to node delivery
Physical	To transmit bits over a medium, to provide mechanical and electrical specifications

Fig. 6.9 Summary of layer functions

Source: Adapted from Behrouz 2003

The upper level protocol is supported by the lower level protocols. The first layer is 'application', which provides end-users functionality by translating the messages into user software for displaying on their screen. The second layer is 'transport', which offers reliable end-to-end message delivery function. At this layer, TCP/IP defines two protocols—transmission control protocol (TCP) and user datagram protocol (UDP)—breaking application data from the end-user down into TCP packets called *datagrams*. The Internet protocol (IP) receives datagrams from the TCP layer and breaks the packets down further. It contains the header with address information. The fourth layer is network interface that handles addressing issues. The last interface is physical that defines basic electrical transmission characteristics for sending the actual signals.

NETWORKING DEVICES

Connecting many computers over a network is done through hubs and switches. Devices like repeaters and bridges are used to enhance the signals and connected to such networks. They work as bridges between various computers. Similarly, connecting two networks is called *internetworking* and the devices needed to connect them are routers and gateways. We will briefly cover the essential tools used in networking.

Hubs and Switches

Hubs are the oldest devices used to connect computers on a network. With advancement in technology, switches have taken the place of hubs. Their main aim is to provide a junction for data transmission from one direction to another direction.

Repeaters

Repeaters regenerate a weakening signal on the network path. Signal on a network can travel a fixed distance and slow down. A repeater is installed at the designated link, which receives the signal before it becomes too weak or corrupts. The repeater regenerates the original bit pattern and puts the strengthened signal back on the track.

Bridges

Bridges are used to connect two networks using the same protocol. They can divide a large network into smaller manageable segments. Bridges also can keep traffic of each LAN separate. Thus, they play a role of filtering traffic and managing congestion on the network.

Routers

Router is a hardware device or software that acts like a station on the network. They are intelligent devices than the repeaters and bridges. The software in them determines several paths between the addresses and also determines the best path of current data transmission.

Gateways

Gateways are the entrance point for another network in the network path. In the Internet the gateway node work as a link between networks using different protocols. Gateways can accept a packet formatted for one protocol and convert it into a packet formatted for another protocol.

INTERNET COMMUNICATIONS

Virtual private networks (VPN) are close private networks owned and managed by a single organization that use public Internet backbone but are secure and cost-effective. Privacy is the key feature of virtual private networks.

In order to understand VPN, let us explain private networks and hybrid networks. Private networks connect two sites on a LAN cable, or, if the sites are at a distance, on WAN connectivity using dedicated leased telecom lines. These types of networks are highly secure but quite expensive. Hybrid networks use private intranet as well as public Internet for connecting their sites. The internal communication happens through the leased lines, but all external communications are through the Internet. In other words, the sites that are not of critical nature are connected using public Internet backbone.

Virtual private networks use public Internet but are fully secure, so offer complete security. The advantages of intranet are that organizations can run their enterprise applications on these networks while sharing data and information, with a very high-speed and secure network using high bandwidth communication lines.

These networks when established over high-speed dedicated/leased lines are known as intranet.

Electronic Data Interchange (EDI)

The process of communication of data between two computers is known as *electronic data interchange.* Using EDI, trading partners establish computer-to-computer links that enable them to exchange information electronically. International Data Exchange Association, in *EDI Handbook: Trading in the 1990s* defines EDI as follows: 'Electronic data interchange is the electronic transfer from one computer to another of computer processable data using an agreed standard to structure the data.'

The electronic data interchange can be between computers of the same organization (like in case of data transfer from retail POS to head-office servers) or between computers of two different organizations like vendors and customers. In this case, standard transaction documents, such as invoices and purchase orders, are transmitted through a telecommunication network and accepted electronically at the other end. This eliminates the need for printing and paper work. In doing so, the computers at both the ends conform to certain standard formats of data. Presently, there are two most widely used standards:

EDIFACT: International standard for EDI communications
ANSI X12: US standards for EDI communication

Let us not confuse EDI with e-mail. In EDI, the data is transmitted in actual structured format (with distinct homogenous fields) that is received in the same format in the database at the receiving end, whereas e-mail sends data in an unstructured text format like letters.

SUMMARY

Convergence of information and communication technologies has brought about major changes in the working and lifestyle of modern people. It has not only affected the way of social interactions but also changed businesses, banking, investments, governance, education, science, learning, healthcare, entertainment. New styles of businesses in the form of e-commerce and BPO have come up. It has all been possible due to networking technologies.

Network architecture is of two types. Peer-to-peer networking connects two or more computers in a very small set-up. In this type of networking, there is no dedicated server and every computer is a node. Client-server networking connects a large number of computers and involves single server and rest nodes. Most of the modern networking is done on client-sever architecture.

Networks are differentiated on the basis of their reach and size. Different types of networks are LAN, MAN, WAN, intranet, and the Internet. The media used to connect various computers and networks are of two types—one is guided through various types of cables and wires and the other is wireless, which uses radio frequency, microwave, and satellites.

Protocols are rules and laws governing connectivity issues and help to connect two devices and systems from different manufacturers. The commonly used networking protocols are OSI and TCP/IP. The OSI protocols are used for networking and the TCP/IP are used for the Internet. To connect various computers and networks, networking devices, such as repeaters, bridges, hubs, switches, and routers, are used. Data communication between computers and networks is done through creation of virtual private networks, which are the most secure and private networks using public telecom backbone. Electronic data interchange is structured transmission of data from one system to another.

CONCEPT REVIEW QUESTIONS

1. Which are the different fields where computers and communication technologies converged to make an impact?
2. Explain LAN and WAN with suitable examples.
3. What is EDI and how does it function?
4. What are the widely used standards for connecting networks through the Internet?
5. What do you understand by VPN? Is intranet different from VPN in any way?
6. List the seven layers of an OSI model.
7. What is the last mile concept in wireless networks?
8. Explain client-server computing.
9. Differentiate between EDI and e-mail.

CRITICAL THINKING QUESTION

1. Computers would have been just calculators if telecommunications had not collaborated with them to create telecommunication revolution. Explain with suitable examples.

PROJECT

1. Create a network layout for a retail organization having the following organizational structure:
   (a) Head office in Greater Kailash, New Delhi, having five functional departments, 75 employees, and one IT department
   (b) Three warehouses, one in the adjacent building of head office, one each at Mall Road and East Block, R.K. Puram.
   (c) Forty-five retail outlets in New Delhi and 15 retail outlets in other major cities of the country.
   The company wants to connect all the offices and have complete data in the head office.

SELECT REFERENCES

Forouzan, Behrouz A. 2003, *Data Communications and Networking*, Tata McGraw-Hill, New Delhi.

International Data Exchange Association, *The EDI Handbook: Trading in the 1990s*, www.cisco.com.

Laudon, Kenneth and Jane Laudon 2002, *Management Information System*, Pearson Education (Singapore).

CASE STUDY

Thiruvarur, The First E-district: Twenty Years Ahead of Others

Thiruvarur, a district of Tamil Nadu, was declared the pilot e-district by the Government of Tamil Nadu on June 13, 1998. The largely agrarian district, located 350 km from Chennai, had accomplished near-total automation in the field-level government functioning in taluk offices, District Rural Development Agency (DRDA), collectorate, block offices, town panchayat office (local body), and regional transport office. Land record administration, rural development scheme administration, student scholarship administration, public grievances handling, HR administration, social welfare scheme administration (such as National Old Age Pension Scheme, Distress Relief Scheme, Accident Relief Scheme, Marriage Assistance Scheme, and Agriculture Labourers' Insurance Scheme) were migrated to manual register free status, thus removing hurdles in getting citizen service delivery.

For three years, S. Kariyaperumal (65) of Melvidayal village had been frequenting the Valangaiman taluk office for his old age pension (OAP). But on December 15, 2000, at the RDO camp, all he needed was two hours to get his paper work done afresh, and pension sanctioned. Now, in a month's time, he began regularly receiving his pension.

'I had written several times before, but never got a reply. Today, thanks to the computer, I got all done in two hours', said the happily relaxed Kariyaperumal. His is not an experience with just a computer but having a whole governmental transaction (except for revenue inspector's enquiry) done through the computer, including digital signature, which secures for him old age pension under the *Anbupani* (OA) scheme.

Thiruvarur is the pilot e-district in the country and perhaps the first in Asia—inaugurated in 1999 by Tamil Nadu chief minister, M. Karunanidhi, whose home district it is.

Thiruvarur, the youngest district in Tamil Nadu, known to be the birthplace of Tamil savant Thivalluvar is also the rice bowl of the state. The conversion of an absolute agrarian district into a 'computer district' (as the farmers proudly own up) was made possible by Umashankar's zest for software package and Karunanidhi's initiative to accord the district a special status and giving Umashankar almost a free hand in the district's governance.

Today, the revenue department, RTO, PDS, and the whole administration system has been incorporated in the online governance. In a span of one and a half years, 75 to 80 per cent of the district is under e-governance. People are happy, as bribing has been almost eliminated. Fate of each application—be it for OAP or *patta* transfer or any other transaction—is settled within a few hours.

All the seven taluks of Thiruvarur dispatch money orders before the second of every month and acknowledgments start coming in by the fifth or sixth. All records pertaining to every beneficiary are maintained online, enabling the users to monitor implementation status at any point of time. When a beneficiary dies, it is updated online and when new beneficiaries are added, the names automatically get registered in the mailing list. The district today has almost done away with paper-based accounting. The only paper that is retained and filed is the computer printout of each transaction. Umashankar, the 36-year-old collector, monitors the whole district administration from his laptop.

An important aspect is the language interface used in the software—that is, it should speak the language of the user. Therefore, the computerized functioning and the keyboard is bilingual (English–Tamil).

Umashankar's programmers come from both Thiruvarur district and outside; they all have completed MCA and are in the age group of 20–25 years. But the revolutionary aspect of the project is that right from the village administrative officers (VAOs) to all the staff in the district administrative offices, all have undergone computer training and are now quicker in work.

The most impressive of side of the Thiruvarur success is the Taluk Automation Software (TAS). It runs the complicated land record administration online and churns out different certificates overnight after various verifications from the database. It even generates all the village accounts meant for *Jamabanthi* (annual audit of village accounts). Another expertise, designed by Umashankar himself, has been in the evolution of Optical Mark Read (OMR) technology, using scan facility for the civil supply department (PDS) to detect malpractices. The collectorate functions as a corporate office. This maintains the secrecy of operation and a foolproof security system.

The networking was done on LAN, cables and wireless. For the wireless LAN towers and microwave radios, a sum of Rs 4 million was allocated by Nagapattinam, the Member of Parliament. The district could set the trend for the rest of India in using wi-fi technology for high-speed networking during April 2001. Wireless infrastructure is as follows:

50-metre towers at Collectorate	1
45-metre tower at Mannargudi (Police tower)	1
30-metre towers in Tiruthuraipoondi and Muthupet	2
24-metre tower at Valangaiman Taluk	1
18-metre towers at Kodavasal, Needamangalam and Nannilam Taluks	3
6- to 12-metre towers	6

Questions:

1. Is it justified to call Thiruvarur an e-district? Justify your answer.
2. What kind of network infrastructure is required for a district or State to go for such an automation?

Sources: Based on a news item by Swati Das in *The Times of India*, New Delhi, January 6, 2001, and the book by C. Umashankar (IAS), *E-Governance—The Success Story of Tiruvarur, the Road Covered and the Road Ahead*, 2001.

7

Electronic Point-of-Sales Software

Learning Objectives

- To classify different types of POS software
- To appreciate advantages of best-of-breed software
- To understand POS software and its core functions
- To identify salient features available in most of best-of-breed systems
- To understand business functionalities offered by best-of-breed retail software

Tesco prefers 'best-of-breed' software for retail

Tesco is the biggest food retailer of the United Kingdom. It uses a Retek application as one of its core systems but has a number of other package-based products that run around the core 'Retek' application.

Tesco evaluated many ERP systems for its operations. But it found none of them meeting its full requirements. Tesco would have selected an ERP suite vendor if one had delivered at least 80 per cent of the functionality needed. It did not find such a vendor, not even SAP. Tesco says had it gone for SAP, it would not have satisfied point-of-sales (POS) requirements. Tesco believes that a smart approach is to employ ERP as a core and then add systems around it in order to reduce integration issues. Most of the good best-of-breed software products offer seamless integration with well-known ERP systems of this world.

We have discussed in Chapter 2 that retail point-of-sales software is an important component of retail information systems. Software is the top layer of systems in a complex computer technology, over hardware, operating systems, databases, and networks connecting a number of computers. We have already discussed these topics in previous chapters.

In this chapter, we will discuss software used at retail point of sales. Retail software is business application software that is required for help in billing and recording of sales transactions at the checkout point.

POINT-OF-SALES SOFTWARE

Having already discussed the various hardware components of EPOS, now we try to understand the basic types,

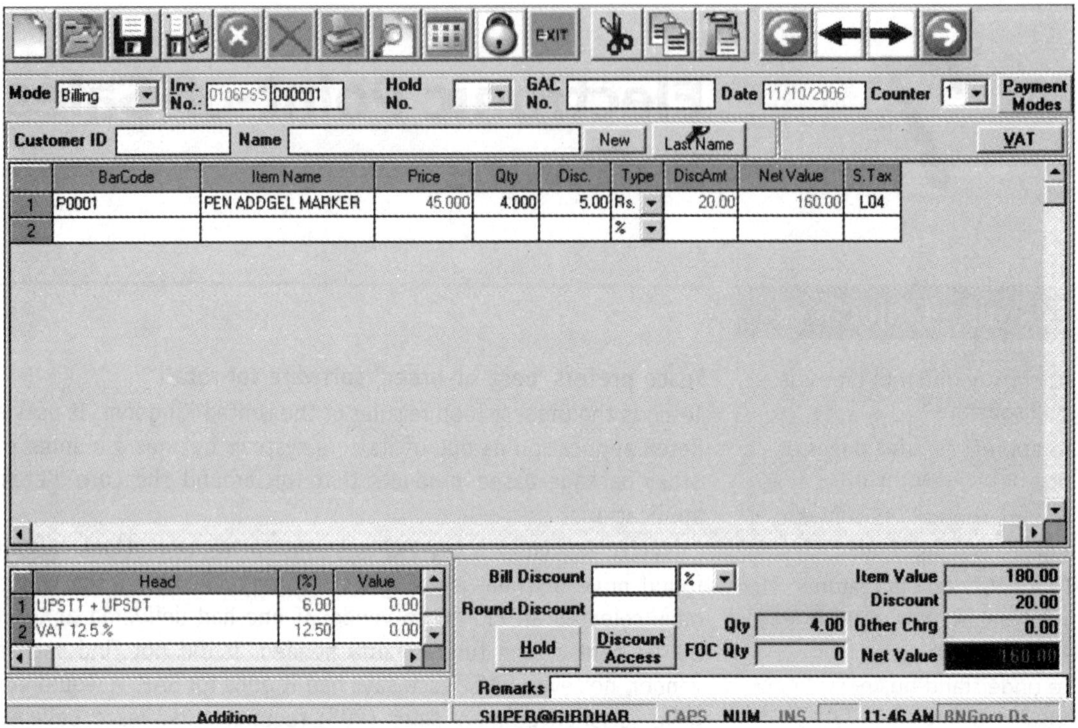

Fig. 7.1 POS billing screen

Source: BNGpro Retail

characteristics, and core functionalities provided by point-of-sales software. Point-of-sales software performs the basic functions of billing at the checkout counter and, at the same time, captures sales and customer data (Fig. 7.1). The software can be run independently without forward or backward links. It can be integrated with back-office enterprise solutions, such as ERP and SCM, or it can be system developed specifically for the organization to meet its own requirements. When evaluating a POS solution, organizations evaluate all these options available with them. All the three options have their own strengths and weaknesses. Retailers choose the systems according to the information technology infrastructure available in the organization.

Based on these characteristics, point-of-sales software can be classified into the following three types:

1. Best-of-breed software
2. Legacy software
3. ERP-integrated software

Best-of-breed software is a software system that runs independently at the retail outlet and has all the basic functions of sales, purchase, stocks, and reporting. These solutions are also known as stand-alone or ready-made software. They usually do not have accounting features. But most of the time they come with an accounting interface that exports relevant data to the existing popular accounting software, such as Sage, QuickBooks, and Tally.

The in-house developed solutions or development by third-party consultants for the specific needs of the organizations is called *legacy systems.* Legacy systems are usually found with organizations that started automation in the early days of computerization, when either good-quality software products were not available or the concept of integrated solutions like ERP was at a nascent stage. Today, developing customized solutions, in-house or outsourced, is a costly and time-taking option. Organizations like to go for readily available and tested solutions at competitive prices.

If the organization goes for an integrated system at the back-office management, it evaluates a product that talks to the back-office system. The *ERP-integrated POS software* can be from the same vendor and available as an ERP-extension. Alternatively, the best-of-breed software may also provide integration with some of the best-known ERPs of the world. For example, SAP and ERP come along with IS Retail, which is standard retail software. IS Retail provides integration with SAP, though both are from different manufacturers but IS Retail is sold by SAP. Microsoft-Dynamic, an ERP, has a tie-up with Singapore-based LS Retail. It is being sold and supported by Navision as a bundled product for the retail segment.

In deciding between a POS system that is stand-alone and one that is not, the organization must first understand the main features that every point-of-sales software product should have. We will now discuss these core functions in detail.

ADVANTAGES OF BEST-OF-BREED SOFTWARE

The ERP-integrated software is meant for retail chains and is definitely superior to any other category of retail POS software. Therefore, the comparison remains between the best-of-breed and legacy software. Though legacy software is created keeping in mind the existing requirements of organizations, it is not cost-effective. It needs continuous developments, refinements, and upgrading, which involves time and huge costs. The best-of-breed software offers certain advantages over legacy systems. These are discussed here.

Selection of Functionally Rich System for each Business Area

Best-of-breed solutions are available in the market as fast-selling solutions. These solutions are created by organizations that have vast knowledge and experience in their domain. Most of these software products come for different verticals in retail. For example, there are software products specifically meant for hospitality business, such as restaurants and fast-food joints. You can find software catering to the requirements of garment trade and department stores. Since each piece of software is meant for a particular line of business in retail, this is functionally very rich and commands mastery over its domain.

Resilience against Single Vendor Failure or Demise

Since there are a number of vendors who offer best-of-breed software, organizations implementing these solutions do not carry a big risk of failure in case a vendor is not able to supply or install the software. The organization can commission another vendor for implementing the software. At times, good software products are sold and supported by multiple vendors and so the organization can take the benefit.

Greater Flexibility in Terms of Substitution of Individual Elements

The creators of best-of-breed solutions evolve through a long period of time. They come up with releases and versions every year or half year. These versions carry new features and functions in the same software. The new features are stored as individual elements in the form of a parameter in the software that can be switched on or off. A functionality not required by an organization can be switched off. Even vendors may charge additional price, based on these parametric functions. Therefore, an organization has flexibility in terms of what it wants and what it does not.

Faster Response from Vendor to Adaptation Needs

Usually, the best-of-breed software solutions are not customized as per individual needs, but when an industry demands a feature in which the vendor specializes, he/she comes up with immediate releases and new versions. This benefits the industry as a whole as well as individual members of the industry who demanded the changes.

More Specialized Vendors

The vendors selling these products are as specialized as the products themselves. Vendors have created niche markets for themselves. For example, in the hospitality industry, there are vendors who supply these solutions only to the pubs and bars. Yet another vendor may implement his/her solution in a restaurant. Therefore, the organization can easily find out what suites it the best.

Lower Risks in Case of Unsuitable System or System Failure

In case the organization finds the software as of inferior quality or unsuitable for their business policies and procedures, what it loses is a small amount spent on the product. The costs of best-of-breeds are much lower than the cost of integrated systems and self-developed software.

Multiple Case References in the Same Industry

The organization can easily check up with competitors and other industry associates about the functioning of the software and the service network of the vendor or manufacturer of the software. There are cases available and the vendors themselves provide the list of their satisfied customers.

Less Time in Setting Up, Implementing, and Training

Best-of-breed software solutions are easy to set up and implement. Most of the software products come along with set-up and user manuals and a little advanced user can do it without any help. Their use is simple and menu driven, with graphic user interface (GUI), which makes the training simple and easy.

CORE AREAS OF POS SOFTWARE

Due to the diversity in retail industry, different POS system features are required for different types of retailers (Fig. 7.2). In assessing these features, the following have emerged as the six best practices, core components or must-have features, regardless of the intended application of the POS system.

Sales Transactions

The sales transaction management function includes all the information required to complete a transaction at the point of sales. The system captures key transaction data, such as sales billing, cancellations, returns, exchanges, refunds, printing and distribution of gift vouchers or certificates, service

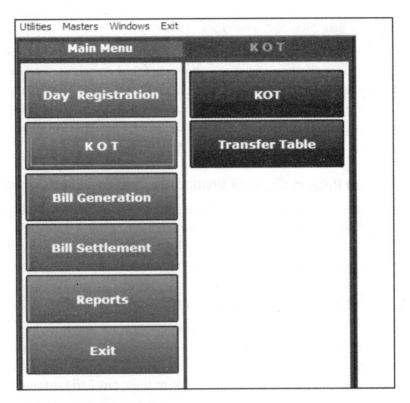

Fig. 7.2   Retail POS software

Source: BNG TouchPOS

transactions, and creation of special orders. The transaction management system validates item information, taxes, and discounts, i.e. it ensures that only right entries are created and stored in the database. The system process payments, which enables the sales executives or counter cashiers to give their full attention to serve the customer, since processing of sale would only require them to scan the bar code on the item and ask the customer only for the method of payment.

Price Management

The prices of the products may need changes from time to time. The price management function allows a retail store employee to manage the retail price of an item. Modification of retail price of a product may be needed for different reasons, such as discounts on damaged items, discounts after negotiations, competitive price matching, and daily price change policy schemes. The price management function keeps track of these retail price changes. It records proper reason, employee code, or the authority carrying out these changes. Price management systems also generate a report for auditing and control purpose.

Day Registration (Day Activity)

The day registration is an integral part of any retail point-of-sales software. The system keeps a record of individual log-ins and log-outs for security reasons. Also, for stores running on shifts, it functions as shift opening and closing procedure. This feature includes processes for counter-opening, day-opening, counter-closing, and day-closing activities. It involves cash-opening, cash-closing, and cash-balancing procedures. It consists of register-opening funds, paid-in and paid-out transactions, currencies, and taxes. Register management should track the cash flow within the business day and should flag any unusual event. This ensures security of data and unwanted peeking by users in the system.

Purchase and Inventory

Purchases and stock management functions include item code creation tools, purchases and goods receipts from suppliers, physical inventory-verification procedures, and inventory adjustments. *Physical inventory verification* refers to counting of stock and matching it with the computer records. For stand-alone department stores, it provides bar code printing and labelling system. For integrated systems, it helps locate and evaluate stock at store or corporate level. By knowing where and how much the inventory is located, the retailers are able to plan their merchandise and sales forecasting. This leads to greater sales and customer satisfactions.

Customer Relationship

Whether stand-alone or integrated software, the point-of-sales system is the first point that generates primary data related to customers. The customer relationship management (CRM) software may further analyse this data and provide interactions history, sales history, contact information, preferences, characteristics, loyalty, etc. of the customer. For a retailer, understanding the customer is of utmost importance and customer purchases are sources of revenue. To make things more challenging, today's customers are more educated, sceptical, and demanding than ever. With the advent of the Internet, price transparency has become a major threat to retailers. Thus, offering a personalized service to the customer is crucial. Having a good CRM module that tracks customer behaviour and preferences will ensure healthy relationships.

Reports and Inquiries

Reports and inquiries enable organizations to analyse the performance of a store, product, or salesperson on daily, weekly, monthly, or yearly basis. You can extract information on inventory, sales, incentives to salesperson, and customers' details. Reports also allow store managers to identify anomalies and take corrective actions. This prevents losses and fuels growth of the organization.

FEATURES OF POS SOFTWARE

Retail software covers front-office activities in retail, commonly known as point of sales (POS). In an ERP environment, the integrated retail management module works on the concept of retail chain business model and distributed technology architecture. The products are defined at the head office and purchases are made at the warehouse, while sales transactions take place at the retail outlet. Therefore, the retail module only allows partial functionality. We are going to discuss the functionalities offered by point-of-sales module. These functions are discussed in the light of business processes carried out at the retail outlet.

The following are major functionalities provided in standard POS software.

Day Registration

Every EPOS system has daily registration of date, users, cash, and currency system. The user has to begin a day, open counter and handover the counter, and close the day in the evening (Fig. 7.3). *Begin day* is a precursor to billing transaction at the retail outlet and is the start of the business day. *Open counter* option activates a counter and allows the user to enter value of currency notes available as opening balance. After opening a counter, our system is ready for billing. *Handover counter* is used to close counter and handover in case the next shift begins. In one day or shift, you can open and close the counter only once. *End day* closes business day and processes data for certain reports and triggers posting into accounts. Once a day has been closed, the POS system does not allow any billing.

Defining Local Settings

The POS module in an ERP system would permit certain master definitions and settings at the POS for individual store setting. These settings are the creation of billing counters, bill sundries, and salesperson database.

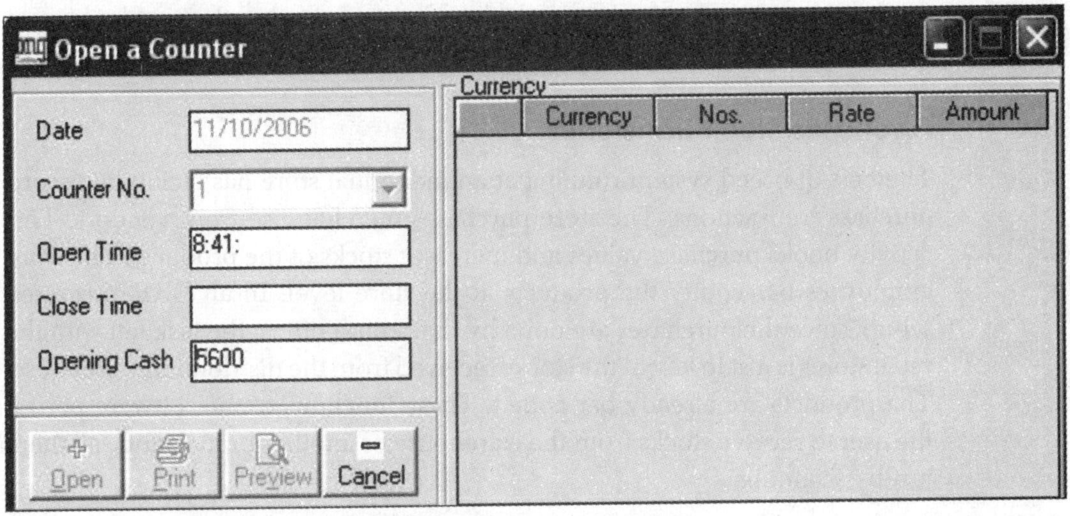

Fig. 7.3 Day registration process in POS software

Billing Counters

In multiple users (LAN) environment, billing is done on multiple billing machines or checkout counters. Each checkout point has an identity number, which is usually printed on the bill for identification.

Bill Sundries

The EPOS system allows each retail outlet to have its own list of levies and incidentals required in billing. Discounts, taxes, freight, and delivery charges are some examples of such levies and incidentals.

Salesperson Database

List of salespersons at each outlet is given. It also defines sales incentives and commission payable to them.

Replenishment

Replenishment is filling up of stocks again at the retail outlet. This is done against the sales made during a particular time period. Intelligent systems are built to notify the stocks at regular intervals. The system prompts with reminders and alerts when the stock of an item falls below the reorder level defined in the system. The system at the retail outlet creates a 'branch indent', 'purchase request' on the head office, or supplying branch. This is a requisition note created by the retail store. The 'requisition' travels to warehouse and the goods are dispatched accordingly. Auto-requisition feature enables the software to send such notes on intervals as and when the stock reaches the reorder level at the retail outlet.

Purchases/Stock Transfer In

The best-of-breed system running at an individual store has facility to record purchase transactions. The store purchases merchandise from vendors. This activity books purchase values and increases stocks of the products. The store employees bar codify the products at the store level. In an ERP-integrated set-up, since the purchases are done by the central office, the task left with the retail stores is just to key in the stocks received from the distribution warehouse. The products are already bar coded. These functions of the software permit the user to receive stocks from the warehouse or another branch and sell them just by scanning.

Returns or Stock Transfer Out

Goods received wrongly or of defective nature are returned to the vendor or the central warehouse. How to dispatch the goods back to the warehouse or any other branch where there is a requirement? The POS software provides the option to make such stock transfers 'out' from the current branch to any other branch/HO along with the dispatch details. Direct dispatch to the vendors are 'returns', whereas returns to own branches or the central warehouse are called 'stock transfers'.

Retail Sales

Retail sales process is the key activity that transfers the ownership and possession of goods to the customer. The sales billing process generates primary data related to sales and customer. The following are some of the key activities performed while completing the sales process.

Billing

The efficiency of sales delivery is denoted by how fast and hassle free is the retail billing system (Fig. 7.4). On scanning a valid bar code on the item, the system automatically populates values on a screen; product name, specifications, quantity, price, discounts, and taxes are various values. A good POS billing system allows *Billing, Exchange,* and *Return* activities seamlessly without jumping over menus. Therefore, POS systems offer hot keys for such crucial activities. *Exchange* mode is used if the customer wants to exchange an item he/she has purchased earlier. The system receives back the sold item, issues a

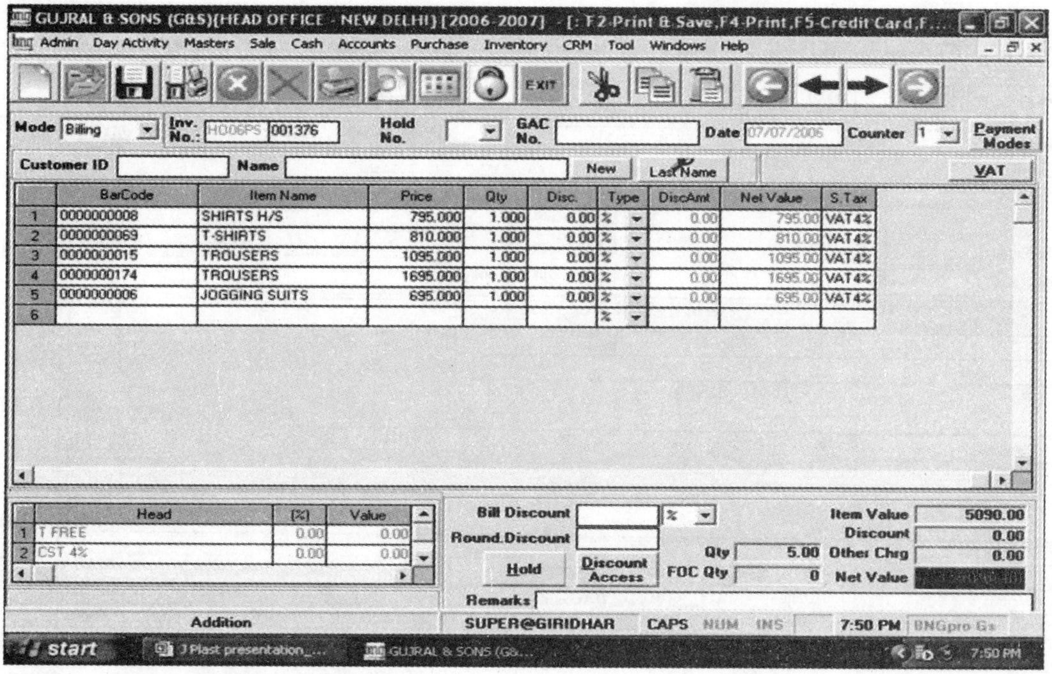

Fig. 7.4 POS billing—capturing sales data

fresh item, and creates a 'difference bill'. *Return* is used if the customer returns an item and does not buy a new product in lieu of the old one.

Credit Note

In case of return of goods by a customer, the retailer has to refund the money. But the trend in retail is to issue a 'credit note' in place of refunding cash. The customer uses it as a refund voucher and can buy goods from the same retailer at a later date. The credit note is a physical voucher that is sealed and signed by the retailer and honoured for future purchases. This ensures that the customer is definitely going to come back for redeeming his/her voucher.

Payment Modes

At the retail point of sales, bill is settled using any payment system—cash or electronic. The system provides options of settlement of bill through various payment modes. Usually, the default payment mode is cash, but paying by credit card, discount coupons, cheques, or foreign currency is also allowed. Bills are also settled through giving outright credit and adjusted against advances received from the customer on any earlier dates. The system usually supports combinations of multiple modes, e.g. partial cash and partial credit cards (Fig. 7.5).

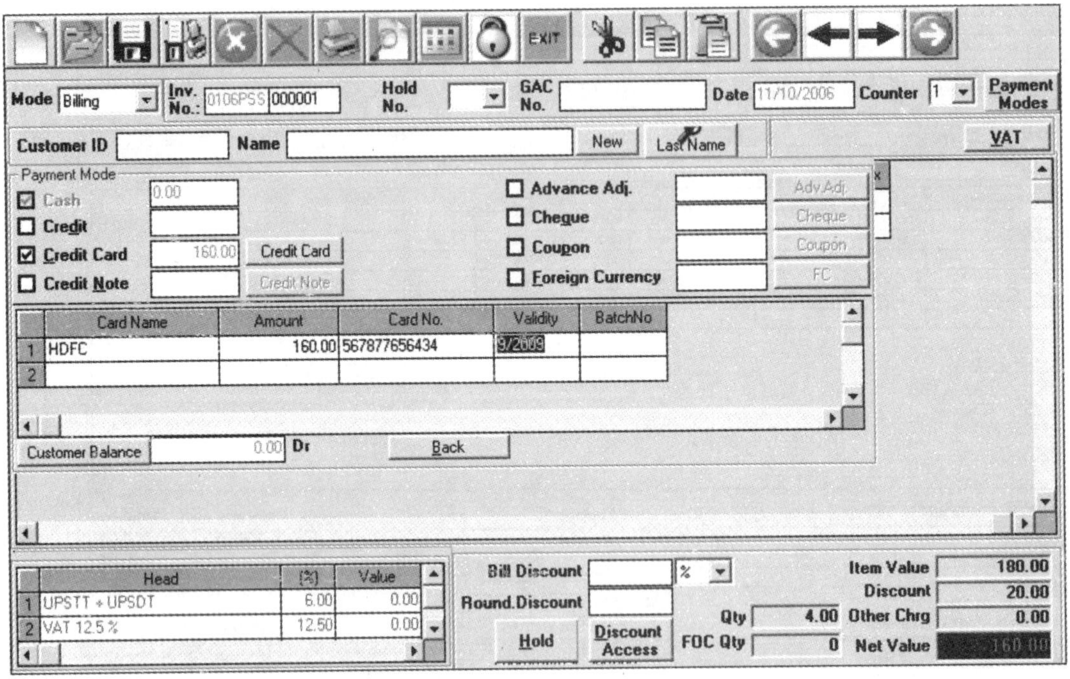

Fig. 7.5 POS billing—multiple payment modes

Bill Hold

In fast-moving and heavy-rush department stores, there comes some instances when the cash clerk may have to stop scanning in the middle of billing. This may happen because the customer goes back on the floor to pick something more. The bill assistant has no choice but to abort this session of billing and restart it when the customer returns. This way a lot of time and efforts are wasted. Therefore, technology providers have come up with solution to this problem—the 'bill hold' function. The cash clerk can press this function putting the incomplete bill on hold and continue with other customers. Just as the customer returns, the bill is retrieved and completed.

Manual Billing

Due to inadvertent situations like power or systems failure, bills are written manually. These bills are entered in the computer to book sales and reduce stocks of the items sold. Since sales and stock records are maintained in computers, so it becomes necessary to enter all manual data in the computer. The system must provide an option through which bills are entered in the system. The manual bill number is different from the system-generated bill sequence.

Coupon Sales and Settlement

Coupon management is a major activity in retail. Some organizations run their own schemes of discount coupons and others entertain coupons issued by other companies and business associates. In the first case, large retail chains create and print series of coupons with sequential numbers. Then they distribute these coupons among retail stores. The retail stores, in turn, either sell these coupons to customers or distribute them free as an incentive to buy from their store. Customers later avail discounts by presenting these coupons. The complete back-office and point-of-sales solutions are involved in creation, distribution, and redemption of coupons.

The other system of coupon management is acceptance of discount coupons issued by third parties. For example, various banks issue coupons to their credit card holders. These coupons are redeemable at various retail outlets. The designated outlets entertain coupons as a mode of payment settlement.

Goods on Approval

'Goods on approval' is rather an Indian phenomenon where local retailers deliver goods to 'known' customers without making a bill. It is an alternative to a 'gate pass' (Fig. 7.6). The customer takes home a few pieces of goods, accepts some, and returns the balance. Later, billing is done only for the goods that the customer has accepted. The 'approval note' updates inventory but no sales is booked. Sometimes, 'goods approval note' is also used for booking orders on phone. Once an order is entered in the system, it is billed on dispatch of goods. In the billing screen, the selected goods approval note is knocked off. Instances of home delivery are also managed through this feature of POS software.

Billing of Items that are not Bar Coded

It is a common incident at retail that goods are placed on the shelf without proper labelling or bar coding. What happens if the bar code of an item is misplaced or the bar code is smudged and not read by the scanner? There is every temptation to sell the product if it is already selected by the customer. But the strategy should be to make the sale and simultaneously not to annoy the customer. The technology providers must find a solution for this.

The solution is to do the billing of the product in a common code, which allows entering product name, price, and tax in the bill entry (presuming that the salesperson knows and suggests the right price of the product). Later, when coding has been done or the product identified, it is regularized through a

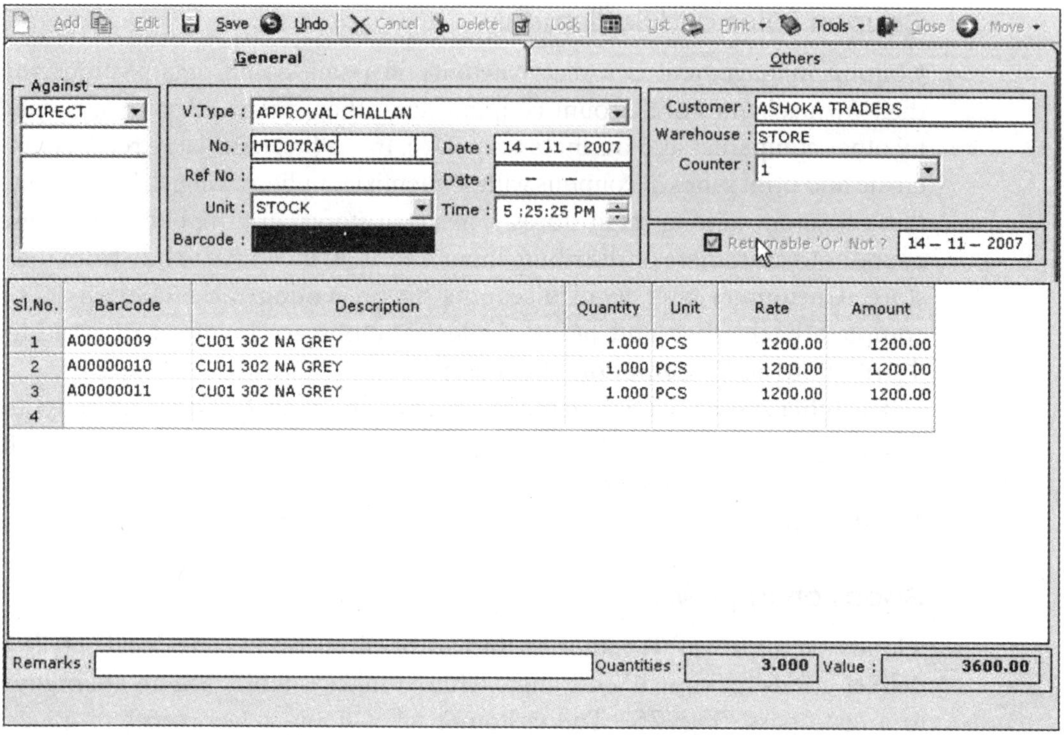

Fig. 7.6 Goods on approval—a gate pass

regularization process. Sales are recorded and inventory is updated for the right code and price.

As an example, let us consider a case when the bar code of a pair of trousers has been lost. The customer has already liked this pair and the retail store has only one pair of this size and colour. The salesperson is eager to sell it and the customer is crazy to buy this. Now, the software has a common code 'Z', which does not have a description but allows new description, price, and taxes in billing. The cashier, on authorization from the salesperson, creates a bill in this code. The bill is made, the product is delivered to the customer, and the payment is received. The sale has been done but the right product code is not updated. Stocks are not correct for this product. Both the sale and the stock are in 'Z' code only. Before the data is sent for financial analysis, a process called '*regularize Z item*' is run. The back-end accountant enters the right code of the product and regularizes the sale. This process posts the amount and quantity in the right head of sales account and inventory.

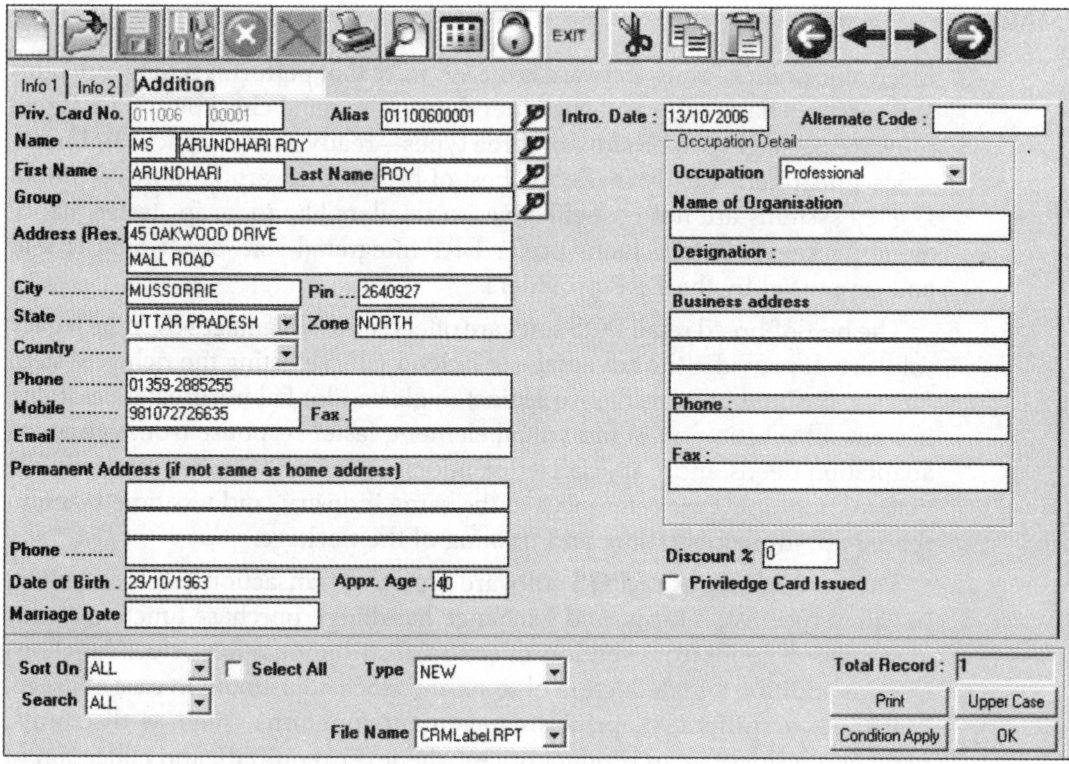

Fig. 7.7   Customer database captured during sales

Source: BNGpro

Creating Customer Data

Capturing and creation of customers' data is an important part of retail environment. At the point-of-sales location, the primary data of the customers is gathered (Fig. 7.7). Analysing customer data helps decision support and management information systems. The customers are grouped, classified, and graded based on their purchase value or income status. Discount structures are defined and discounts are offered to the customers on their purchases.

CRM Data

Retail customers' data is gathered and created at a POS location. The customers' personal details (such as occupation, family members, contact, educational qualification, health, income, date of birth, and children details) are captured during sales and placed in CRM data. Customer relationship management software packages are used to analyse the data that serves management at various levels.

SUMMARY

Electronic point-of-sales software is the software that performs billing functions and captures basic sales and customer data at the retail checkout point. Retail software packages are broadly of three types—ready-made, legacy, and back-office integrated. Ready-made, or best-of-breed, software is most common. Legacy systems are not cost-effective, so retailers like to go for tested stand-alone packages. Retail chains prefer ERP-integrated software, which is sold and supported by the ERP providers.

The best-of-breed retail POS software offers some advantages over the legacy software. It provides the advantage of functionally selecting the richest system for each business area, resilience against single vendor failure, greater flexibility in terms of substitution of individual element, faster response from vendor to adaptation needs, more specialized vendors, lower risks in case of unsuitable systems, multiple case references in the same industry, and less time taken in setting up, implementation, and training of the package.

The core functions of POS software are sales transaction (such as billing, payment receipts, returns, and exchange handling), purchase functions (such as receipts of goods from vendors or central distribution office), stock functions (such as addition and deduction of stock and stock adjustment in case of usage, breakage, or pilferage), price management functions (such as discounts, reduction or increase in product prices whenever required), and collection of customer data for further analysis.

The salient features of retail POS packages are billing and data gathering. Sales features involve bill creation, payment settlement, return, and exchanges. Special features in sales are bill holds, goods on approval, coupon management, and billing of non-labelled products. Other features include purchase or goods receipts from central distribution office. Inventory features are stock receipts and returns, and stock adjustments. Customer data building is a formidable task around which CRM packages run for analysis of customer data and keeping in touch with the customer.

CONCEPT REVIEW QUESTIONS

1. What are the core areas of best-of-breed POS software?
2. What are the advantages of best-of-breed POS software?
3. What are 'must-have' functionalities that you will consider while evaluating retail software?
4. What do you understand by 'auto-replenishment'?
5. How would you do billing of an item that has lost its bar code label?

6. Explain the following terms:
   (i) Bill hold
   (ii) Credit note
   (iii) Multiple payment modes
   (iv) Exchange handling

CRITICAL THINKING QUESTION

1. 'Customer data is invaluable for a retailer.' Explain with examples.

PROJECT

1. Go to a retailer in your vicinity and find out the functions covered by the software it is using. Do you find any extra or missing function that we have not discussed in this chapter?

SELECT REFERENCES

Bhat, Shrihari 2005, 'Tech Zone–POS Strategy', *Retail Biz*.
BNG Infotech, www.bng.co.in, last accessed on 02/12/2007.

CASE STUDY

SAP Comes Up with Solutions for Retail Verticals

Mr Rick Chavie, senior vice president and global head of SAP's retail vertical, explains how the approach of embracing sub-verticals is adopted.

Q: *Will you update our readers on how you will integrate third-party products into SAP's retail products?*

Rick: SAP acquired Triversity (Sept. 2005) and Khimetrics (Nov. 2005), both established solution providers in retail and enterprise segments. This was done to extend its market leadership further in providing an end-to-end solution for the retail industry, interconnecting data of initial consumer interactions at the retail point of sales and enterprise back office and also those in the retail supply chain. To SAP, Triversity brings solution functionality and expertise that enhance the retail solution portfolio of the former. The end result is a better-run business that delivers value to its customers and responds to changing business needs. In November 2005, SAP acquired Khimetrics, a leading US based provider of enterprise software solutions that allows retailers to analyse how to price and position items to boost margins and optimize demand, deliver accurate profitability forecasts and implement long-term sales strategies that promote customer retention.

Q: *How is SAP focusing on retail?*

Rick: Inside SAP, retail is a little different from other industries because we are able to take advantage of the core technology. We have over 500 people dedicated to retail, with 100 per cent of their time devoted to development works and solution management.

Q: *What are the new challenges for retailers?*

Rick: One of the challenges that retailers face today is the chaotic behaviour of customers. People are so acclimated to the latest technology and they move very fast. So, if you have multiple systems, how do you get the right inventory at the right place at the right time to fit the customer demands? Multi-channel shoppers are much more demanding and can be much less forgiving. If customers have had a bad experience online, they might not even come to your store or use your catalogue besides abandoning you online.

Therefore, retailers need to make shopping a seamless experience across channels. So, our challenge, given that SAP has a common platform, is about how do we get on with the retailers and create scenarios that cut across all channels—utilizing common data, MDM, and underlying NetWeaver architecture—to make more or less a seamless experience for customers.

Q: *In which areas, can SAP improve its retail products?*

Rick: One area is where we are working on making it a solution consumable to the business user. Whether a CEO (in terms of the kind of dash-boarding or optimization exploration you want to do), merchandiser, or store person, we want to make it more accessible to everyone (as a much more fundamentally visual, intuitive experience).

Also, SAP wants to be more than a 24/7 organization in the way we serve our customers: to cover all the major markets globally. The result is not only bringing some of the best talents together around the world, but also that talent in those markets can help support growth into those markets.

Q: *What can retailers expect from SAP going forward?*

Rick: We have adopted the approach of really embracing sub-verticals—grocery and apparel. We are going to continue making major investments in the next three years in these areas. We are recognizing that we have to distinguish things for going after sub-verticals. For example, grocery store versus apparel store, all have different nuances. We are taking into account this factor as an element in our development and going forward.

Besides this, we are taking into account the 'industry thought leadership'. Investing more in 'demand insight, intelligent merchandising, supply chain management and customer experience in the store' covering multiple industries are major pushes.

Q: *What do you suggest for the Indian retailers and chains in the present context?*

Rick: India has a large number of medium-sized retailers and retail chains. Unless they adapt to the fast-growing scenario, they will become extinct. Considering that Indian retailers are attempting to do in ten years what it took 25 to 30 years in other major markets of the world to learn through trial and error, flexibility and adapting to market change are critical.

Q: *Why should retailers ask for service from SAP?*

Rick: SAP for retail is an industry-specific solution set that creates value by enabling retailer to become more agile with the proven, future-proof SAP NetWeaver® platform. It also supports customer loyalty and provides real-time business visibility and operational excellence across all core retail processes, while delivering top-line revenue and with cost reduction.

Q: *How does NetWeaver function and help retailers?*

Rick: SAP NetWeaver unifies technology components into a single platform, allowing organizations to reduce IT complexity and obtain more business value from their IT investments. It provides the best way to integrate all systems running SAP or non-SAP software. By delivering pre-configured, industry-oriented business content, SAP NetWeaver solves companies' challenges of integration and reduces the need for extensive custom implementations, making applications simpler to implement, quicker to deploy, less expensive to own and more agile for future business growth and innovation.

Q: *What are the benefits that a retailer can get from SAP?*

Rick: By addressing various needs of retailer segments such as grocery, fashion and hard-lines, SAP for retail helps retailers to achieve the following: Reduced total-cost of ownership through a single end-to-end solution; enhancing customer shopping experience and customer loyalty by meeting unique needs of shoppers in price, promotion and assortment while building a more efficient demand driven supply chain; enhancing efficiency and reducing costs through reduced inventory levels, improved shelf productivity, increased product profitability; better visibility of store operations; more centralized data storage and reduced labour costs; solid transactional backbone, on which retailers can build their business, facilitate data-sharing and effectively manage inventory, promotions, purchasing, sales, sourcing goals, human resources, assets, financials and e-commerce and increased visibility and flexibility and a seamless flow of information across all processes of the retail value chain, from concept to consumer. Access to meaningful data in different systems and real-time visibility into daily business helps retailers make better decisions.

Question:
1. Elaborate on the benefits of using SAP by a large retail chain organization. What could be the disadvantages over an India-made ERP?

Source: Adapted from an interview of Mr Rick Chavie published in *RETAILER* magazine in April–May 2007 issue conducted by S.L. Talwar, Principal Correspondent, along with Lajwant Singh, Editor-in-Chief.

8 Modern Electronic Payment Methods

Learning Objectives

- To understand limitations of traditional payment methods
- To appreciate modern payment methods
- To understand various electronic payment methods, such as digital token based, card-based, and mobile technology based systems
- To understand functioning of e-cash, e-cheques, credit cards, smart cards, proximity cards, biometric, person-to-person payment systems, and SMS-based techniques

Wal-Mart, Costco considering biometric payment systems

Modern retailers are looking for new ways of payment settlement. According to a study conducted by an analyst at the financial firm of Sanford Bernstein, both Wal-Mart and Costco are 'looking closely' at biometric checkout systems, which would allow consumers to pay via finger-scan. To use the system, customers would register at an in-store kiosk, where they would provide credit card information that would be attached to a fingerprint. At the checkout, the customer would place their finger on a scanner, and the appropriate credit info would be pulled up. According to the study, biometric checkouts that are already in use in branches of some supermarket chains, including Albertson's and Piggly Wiggly—could save Wal-Mart as much as 20 per cent in processing costs. But advocates of privacy will be wary of providing their fingerprints to retails. But the general assumption is that, sooner or later, fingerprints are going to play a major role in payment transfers. We are aware that people are also wary of divulging their credit card numbers and handing over the card to the waiter in a restaurant.

Sources: Marc Perton, www.engadget.com, January, 2006, www.biometrics.org, www.stanford.com.

In previous chapters, we have studied various components of retail information technology, viz. hardware, AIDC, databases, networks, and software. But retail information system is incomplete without understanding electronic payment systems. In this chapter, we are going to discuss various modes of payments that are used at the retail POS location.

TRADITIONAL PAYMENT SYSTEMS

In the traditional system of payment at retail, there were only two modes of payments—cash and credit. Cash still is one of the most acceptable and hassle-free systems of settlement at the POS. It is surprising that it is still the most preferred consumer payment instrument even after 40 years of continuous developments in electronic payment systems. Kalakota and Whinston (2002) opine that cash remains the dominant form of payment for the following three reasons:

- Lack of trust in the banking system
- Inefficient clearing and settlement of non-cash transactions
- Negative real interest rates paid on bank deposits

Payments by cash and cheques are not possible in purchases through e-commerce sites, but in face-to-face retail, there are only a few retailers who accept cheques and the numbers of merchant retailers are much more who do not accept credit cards.

Limitations of Traditional Systems

Because of the obvious disadvantage and risk of carrying money, customers have now started appreciating the comfort to pay by plastic currency, i.e. credit, debit, or store value cards.

Non-electronic payment methods, such as cash, cheques, and money orders, are rapidly vanishing from the retail market and they have several limitations in e-commerce. Cash and cheques cannot be used in purchases through e-commerce, as there is no face-to-face contact. Even the customers are wary of disclosing their credit card numbers.

While major issuers of credit cards and payment brands are pressing retailers worldwide to accept cards at their checkout counters, technology creators have come up with newer ways of payment systems. They have invented innovative ways for the consumers to pay, including through swiping, proximity, mobile, and fingers. The USP of these payment modes is that the smart card or biometric methods allow merchants the option of bypassing the established credit and debit card networks and potentially reduce the transaction fees.

Now, we will discuss electronic payment systems with respect to retail sales and e-commerce transactions. An important aspect of e-commerce is prompt and secure payment, clearing, and settlement of credit and debit claims. In the 1970s, the emerging electronic payment technology was known as *electronic fund transfer* (EFT). It is defined as any transfer of funds initiated through an electronic terminal, a telephonic instrument, a computer, or a magnetic tape so as to order, instruct, or authorize a financial institution to debit or credit an account.

The future of payments at a retail counter lies within the following categories:

1. Digital token based
   - e-cash
   - e-cheques
2. Credit cards
3. Smart cards
4. Biometrics
5. Proximity cards
6. Short messaging services (SMSs)
7. People-to-people (P2P) payments

DIGITAL TOKEN BASED SYSTEM

To meet the challenges of growing retail and e-commerce, entirely new forms of financial instruments are being developed. One such instrument is 'e-token' in the form of e-cash and e-cheques (Fig. 8.1). Electronic tokens are equivalent to cash that is backed by a bank.

E-Cash

E-cash is a new concept and used mainly in online payment systems. Since payments cannot be made by cash over the Net, people looking for privacy find e-cash a better option. It combines computerized convenience with security and privacy that improve on paper cash. E-cash focuses on replacing currency cash as major payment mechanism in consumer-oriented retail.

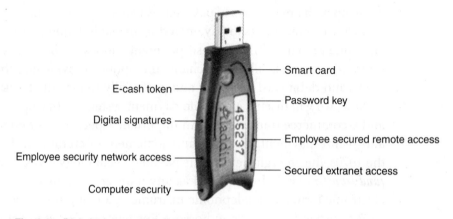

Fig. 8.1 Digital token: multiple functions

Working of E-Cash

E-cash is based on a cryptographic system known as *digital signature.* Digital signatures are being used in a big way for applications other than payments. There are many government documents, such as income tax returns and company registrar returns, that demand digitally signed papers. This method involves a pair of numeric keys that are very large integers. One key is used for locking or encoding, while the other is used for decoding. Signatures encoded with one key can only be decoded with other numeric key. The encoding key is kept private (by the bank) but the decoding key is made public. The bank supplies the public key to its customers for decoding the message and keeps the private key for encoding the message.

Before e-cash can be used for transaction, it has to be bought from the currency server of a bank. It involves the following two steps:

- Opening an account with the bank
- Maintaining sufficient funds in the bank to make the purchases

Some banks may allow the customer to buy e-cash by paying in hard currency. The customer uses a software package (usually supplied by the bank or the token-issuing agency) in his/her computer to generate a random number, which serves as the *note.* (The same process is used while digitally signing a government document.) The customer e-mails this note to the bank. In exchange of the money debited from the customer's account, the bank digitally signs the note for the amount requested and transmits the note back to the customer.

This method of note generation is very secure, as neither the customer nor the vendor can duplicate the digitally signed note. E-cash can be completely anonymous, which ensures that one can spend the money freely on anything, without the risk of disclosing the source or destination.

Okamoto and Ohta (1991) mention that to be successful, e-cash must have the four properties—monetary value, interoperability, retrievability, and security.

Monetary Value   E-cash must have monetary value and must be backed by either currency cash or the credit authorized by a bank.

Interoperability   E-cash must be exchangeable as for other e-cash, paper cash, goods or services, lines of credit, deposits in banking, benefits transfers, etc.

Retrievable   E-cash must be storable and retrievable. Remote storage and retrieval (as through a telephone or mobile) would allow the users to exchange e-cash.

Secure   E-cash should not be easy to copy or tamper with while being exchanged. This includes preventing and detecting duplication and double spending.

E-Cheques

E-cheques are similar to paper cheques in usage and functioning. They are used mostly in wholesale business or B2B transactions. They work in the pretty same manner as regular cheques. The modality of how e-cheques work is given below:

1. The customer has an e-cheque account with the bank, i.e. the bank has the facility to accept and honour e-cheques.
2. The customer makes purchases at any retailer or e-commerce site and then e-mails an encrypted electronic cheque.
3. The merchant then deposits (or e-mails in the same fashion as he/she got it from the customer) the cheque with the bank. The server at the bank verifies the authenticity of the cheque and the signatures on it.
4. Money is debited from the buyer's account and credited to the seller's account.

E-cheques, like the regular cheques, carry signature in digital form, which can be verified. Properly signed and endorsed e-cheques are exchanged between financial institutions through e-clearing system.

Advantages of E-Cheques

E-cheques have the following benefits:

- They work in the same way as traditional paper-based cheques, thus increasing customer acceptance and satisfaction.
- E-cheques are well suited for clearing small amounts of payments. The use of conventional cryptography (the way signatures are imposed on the cheques) makes it much faster and easier than the system based on the public-key cryptography (e-cash).
- They benefit commerce as their use promotes a new line of business. The third-party accounting servers can make money by charging the buyer or seller a transaction fee.
- Financial risk is assumed by the financial server and may result in an easy acceptance.

CREDIT CARDS

Use of credit cards has evolved as the most favoured mode of payments in retail, both in storefront as well as web-based. As per the survey called 'Share of Wallet' conducted by the American Express Bank (Amex), almost 71 per cent of the dinning and 68% of retail purchases in India are settled through credit cards (http://www.rediff.com/money/2003/dec/23cards.htm). This is because credit card is the most convenient way of carrying money without carrying the risks of possessing money. Users of credit cards also get their payments deferred till the credit card statement is received from the bank for payments. In case of requirements, the users can still defer the payments and instead pay an interest for using the money beyond a certain period.

Credit card is a plastic card with a magnetic strip or a smart chip on it, which contains information about the card holder, card number, validity, expiry date, etc. (Fig. 8.2). At a retail outlet, when a customer makes a payment by credit card, the vendor swipes the card through a dial-up modem. This terminal is provided by the bank. The modem connects with the bank server and sends the credit card information to the bank server. If the credit card details are genuine, the server accepts the card and sends an approval number, which is printed on the approval slip on an integrated printer with the modem. The amount is paid to the vendor (merchant organization) by the bank. The bank charges its fee for processing the payment. This amount is collected from the customer that appears in his/her next credit card statement.

A credit card transaction involves the following agencies.

Credit Card Issuer　It is the bank that issues credit cards. Bank's name is printed on the card. The services it provides include transaction authorization and posting, statement generation and printing, and card embossing.

Processors　Processors provide transaction services to banks that issue credit cards and to merchants that accept credit card payments. Services include authorizing, capturing, and settling merchant's credit and debit card

(a)　　　　　　　　　　　　　　　　　　　　　　　(b)

Fig. 8.2　(a) Credit cards and (b) Credit card swipe machines provided by banks

transactions, and handling charge-backs. Charge-backs occur when a consumer disputes a charge. The bank charges it back to the merchant. Processors install credit card readers at the merchant place. These terminals are modems that dial the bank server and get an authorization for the payments.

Merchant Organizations   These are the organizations that accept credit cards for payments by registering with the bank through which the payment is routed.

Users   These are the people who use credit cards for payments.

SMART CARDS

Smart cards are plastic cards in which chips are embedded. These cards, in the form of stored value cards, are fast gaining acceptance as a mode of payment. Smart cards have hundreds of applications besides retail payments. Here, we will confine our discussion to the technology and utility in retail.

Smart card, also called integrated circuit card (ICC), is a pocket-sized card with embedded integrated circuits (Fig. 8.3). There are two broad categories of smart cards—memory cards and microprocessor cards. *Memory cards* contain only non-volatile memory storage components and some specific security logic. (Non-volatile memory is permanent memory in the chip.) *Microprocessor cards* contain both memory and microprocessor components. Microprocessor cards are intelligent cards, since they can do some arithmetical and logical calculations.

The standard perception of a 'smart card' is a microprocessor card of credit card dimensions with various tamper-resistant properties. It possesses secure crypto-processor, secure file system, human-readable data, and is capable of providing security services, for example, confidentiality of information in the memory.

Fig. 8.3   Smart card

The host computer and the card reader actually communicate with the microprocessor. The microprocessor provides access to the data on the card. The host computer reads and writes into the smart card memory.

Brief History of Smart Cards

Roland Moreno actually patented the concept of the memory card in 1974. In 1977, Michel Ugon from Honeywell Bull invented the first microprocessor smart card. In 1978, Bull patented the SPOM (self-programmable one-chip microcomputer) that defines the necessary architecture to auto-program the chip. Three years later, the very first *CP8* based on this patent was produced by Motorola. Today, Bull has 1200 patents related to smart cards. Smart card based electronic purse systems, in which the value is stored on the card chip, were tried throughout Europe from the mid-1990s.

The major boom in smart card use came in the 1990s, with the introduction of the smart card based SIM used in GSM mobile phone equipment. The international payment brands MasterCard, Visa, and Europay agreed in 1993 to work together to develop the specifications for the use of smart cards in payment cards used as either a debit or a credit card.

Smart cards with contactless interfaces are becoming increasingly popular for payment and ticketing applications like mass transit. Visa and MasterCard have agreed to an easy-to-implement version currently being deployed (2004–06) in the US. Across the globe, contactless fare collection systems are being implemented to drive efficiencies in public transit. Smart cards are also being introduced in personal identification and entitlement schemes at regional, national, and international levels. Citizen cards, drivers' licences, and patient card schemes are becoming more prevalent and contactless smart cards are being integrated into passports to enhance security for international travel.

Types of Smart Cards

There are two types of smart cards—contact smart cards and contactless smart cards.

Contact smart cards have a small gold chip about half inch in diameter on the front. When inserted into a reader, the chip makes contact with electrical connectors that can read information from the chip and write information back. The cards do not contain batteries; the energy is supplied by the card reader.

In *contactless smart card*, the chip communicates with the card reader through RFID induction technology. These cards require only close proximity to an antenna to complete transaction. They are often used when transactions must be processed quickly or hands-free, such as on mass transit systems, where smart cards can be used without even removing them from a wallet.

Applications of Smart Card

Smart cards have enormous applications. The applications of smart cards include their use as payment system in retail, debit or ATM cards, SIMs for mobile phones, authorization cards for pay television, high-security identification and access control cards, and public transport payment cards.

In retail, smart cards find utility in payment mechanism. They work as 'stored value cards' and are used as electronic wallets. The smart card chip can be loaded with the funds that can be spent in the marketplace at vending machines or various merchants. Cryptographic protocols protect the exchange of money between the smart card and the accepting machine. A retailer accepting smart card for payment can issue these cards to the customers. These cards are preloaded with some value. The card reader, which also works as a writing device on the smart chip, can update information on the card. On purchase, the value is deducted from the card. The user can recoup the value on payment of the additional amount.

Besides payment systems, smart cards are used for 'customer loyalty programme'. The customers are issued these cards and their purchase reward points are loaded in the smart cards at the EPOS terminal. These reward points are later used for getting discounts and buying new products.

A fast-growing application of smart cards is in digital identification cards. In this application, the cards are used for authentication of identity. The most common example is use of various smart cards by many governments as identification cards for their citizens. When combined with biometrics, smart cards can provide multiple utility in the social sector.

Smart cards ensure privacy as ease of use. By employing contactless smart cards, which can be read without having to remove the card from the wallet or even the garment it is in, one can add even more authentication value to the human carrier of the cards.

Advantages of Smart Cards

1. Smart cards have been identified as suitable for many tasks because they are engineered to be tamper resistant.
2. For large businesses, the failure-management cost can be more than offset by the fraud reduction. That is to say even if the cost of managing the cards is high, the benefits of preventing frauds are much higher.

3. The data present on the magnetic stripe can easily be read, written, deleted, or changed with off-the-shelf equipment. Thus, the magnetic stripe is not the best place to store sensitive information. Also, in case of magnetic stripe cards, it is not possible to easily detect the authenticity of the user and to guard against fraud. But the smart card carries intelligence in its microprocessor, which is there for security.

4. Smart cards are extremely difficult to counterfeit. In addition, they are resistant to x-rays and electrostatic discharge. Magnetic stripe cards are prone to damage because of electric and electro-magnetic interference.

5. Since a smart card has much higher memory, it may be used as a multifunction card, for example as retailer card, leisure card, payment card, and health care card as well as for public services.

6. The services may be split and each service may operate independently and with integrity, confidentiality, and privacy, i.e. the health care terminal cannot access the retailer terminal. Also, the cost of the card may be shared between such service providers.

7. The difference between the magnetic stripe and smart cards is not only in the cost but also in the life of the card itself. A smart card has a much longer life than a magnetic stripe card since there is no wear and tear due to the mechanical motion of the card in the card reader.

8. The smart card read and write units are less costly to maintain since they do not contain any moving parts.

Disadvantages of Smart Cards

1. The major drawback of smart cards is that they are costlier than magnetic stripe cards. Though the cost of smart cards is coming down, it is still much higher compared to that of the conventional magnetic stripe cards.

2. Another problem of smart cards is the failure rate. The plastic card in which the chip is embedded is fairly flexible and the larger the chip, the higher the probability of breaking. Smart cards are often carried in wallets or pockets, which is a fairly harsh environment for the chip.

The application of smart cards is limited only by our imagination. They offer unlimited scope of applications today. The main concern is the economy of scale. The multifunctionality holds the key to cost-effectiveness and acceptance. Imagine carrying one card rather than carrying tens of them for all the different services.

Fig. 8.4 Biometrics in action

Source: www.biometrics.org

BIOMETRICS

Though magnetic stripes and smart cards are widely used payment systems, they are not very secure. If lost, they can be used by proxies. Need for a more secure transaction system has invented biometrics. Use of finger prints for payments and personal identification is going to become common in the years to come. Recent developments in biometrics study have included the methods for uniquely recognizing humans based upon one or more intrinsic physical or behavioural traits, which has found a great application in secure financial transactions.

Biometrics is an automated method of recognizing a person based on his/her physiological or behavioural characteristic, such as face, fingerprints, hand geometry, handwriting, iris, retina, vein, and voice (Fig. 8.4). Biometric technologies are becoming the foundation of an extensive array of highly secure identification and personal verification solutions. As there is always a threat of security breaches and transaction frauds, the need for highly secure identification and personal verification technologies is becoming apparent.

Biometric-based solutions are able to provide for confidential financial transactions and personal data privacy. Biometrics can be used in network security infrastructures, government IDs, secure electronic banking, investing, and other financial transactions, retail sales; as law enforcement and health and social services are already benefiting from these technologies.

Technologies used in Biometrics

Biometrics can be used at retail for payment along with the credit card systems. The following steps are required to complete a transaction:

1. A customer would register at an in-store secure kiosk, where he/she would provide credit card information.
2. The credit card information would be attached to the customer's fingerprint image. If the customer is a loyal customer, this information can be permanently stored in the computer along with his/her identification code, as used in customer loyalty cards issued by the retailer.
3. At checkout, the customer would place his/her finger on a scanner, and the appropriate credit card information would be pulled up.

This saves the customer from disclosing the credit card information again and again. Some studies reveal that biometric checkouts, which are already in use in branches of some supermarket chains, can save the retailer up to 20 per cent of the processing cost.

In banking system, biometrics can be used to encash cheques. To enrol in the system, a person provides identification to the teller at a cheque-cashing bank. The teller then enters the information into the paycheque secure system via a terminal built by BioPay (an American company). After the identification, the information is entered, the teller takes the person's picture and scans his/her finger into the system. The customer enters a ten-digit code that will enable the system to easily find the finger scan for verification. After he/she is enrolled, the customer can cash the cheque simply by scanning the finger and having the cheque scanned by the cashier.

Advantages of Biometrics

Retailers prefer the systems that are less prone to fraud. With biometric systems, individual identity is well established. These systems have the following advantages:

- *Uniqueness* is how well the biometric separates one individual from another.
- *Permanence* measures how well a biometric resists aging.
- *Collectability* is the ease of acquisition for measurement.
- *Performance* is the accuracy, speed, and robustness of the technology used.
- *Acceptability* is the degree of approval of the technology.
- *Circumvention* is the ease of use of a substitute.

PROXIMITY TECHNOLOGY

So far in the chapter, we have discussed various payment technologies that are electronic and need contact with the reader, such as swipe of a credit card and reading of a smart card. This kind of payment processing takes some time at the payment counter, be it retail or high-speed transit exits. There has evolved yet another technology that even reduces this hindrance. We are talking of a technological advancement that is a comprehensive contactless payment system built on near-field communication (NFC) technology, which refers to the system in which the reader equipment reads the signals from a distance.

With proximity technology embedded into it, swiping a mobile phone across a reader may turn it into a transactional tool (Fig. 8.5), whether the transaction is a purchase of a newspaper or a cappuccino, or the debit of a single-journey on the metro. Experiments by Visa International indicate that 89 per cent of the participants who tried phone-based settlement preferred its convenience

Fig. 8.5 Proximity technology embedded in cell phones

Source: www.amonline.com

to alternate payment schemes. MasterCard also supports the cell phone as the next logical progression in proximity payment technology.

Working of a Proximity-Enabled Payment System

This is a technology that enables contactless payments by the wave of a cellular phone or a card having proximity technology embedded in it. The NFC applications allow consumers to store credit card and debit card account information in their cell phones or specially built proximity cards. Then the customer can select a preferred method of payment, from those stored in the e-wallet of the phone, at the time of the transaction.

The application is stored in the contactless chip inside the mobile phone. The phone embedded with a GPRS- or RFID-enabled chip connects with the nearest tower and exchanges information. The payment is made and this completes the transaction.

Let us take an example of payment by a regular traveller of Delhi Metro Rail. Instead of buying tickets on every journey or buying seasonal passes, one can subscribe the proximity payment system. Delhi Metro can have a tie-up with cell phone manufacturers and service providers. A proximity chip, preloaded with a fair value, can be inserted in the mobile phone. At the entrance and exit gates of the Metro station, the reader can just read from the RFID- or

GPRS-enabled phone. The services of the mobile service network provider are needed for downloading the fare chart in the mobile and updating the travel information in the customer account. In the example of Metro, the fair chart can be downloaded in the mobile system using mobile network.

Cell phones with New Capabilities

Technology experts anticipate proximity payments will soon be added to cell phones as they become equipped with near-field communication technology. Instead of carrying credit cards, debit cards, loyalty cards, prepaid cards, hybrid cards, or other settlement media, the cell phone will be used to settle transactions.

Cell phone manufacturers are experimenting with several security options, including hardware modification, such as shell casement and fingerprint authentication, and software add-ons, such as custom shortcuts and voice authentication. Although in its infancy, cell phone settlement technology is expected to become popular as the next-generation consumers, who are already cell phone dependent, dominate the marketplace.

What are the Hindrances

There are still technical and industry hurdles that must be overcome before handset proximity payments become a mass-market reality. While network operators stand to gain the most, they risk ceding control to the handset vendors or even the financial companies, if they do not engage the industry more proactively. Since the proximity application is resident in a handset, it will be difficult for the owner to change the handset frequently. Subscribers moving to a competing operator would be forced to obtain a new set of payment applications. Switching operators would be like losing a wallet and this would have a significant impact on the payment system.

Transmitting payment information via cell phone to a POS terminal is sufficient cause for concern, but the concern is compounded by the possibility of losing the phone. The solution may well be a biometrically controlled cell phone that requires the user's personal attributes to activate settlement.

A real fear associated with the cell phone settlement is the threat of misplacing or losing the handset. Phone absence could also mean a loss of transaction functionality. Security concerns point to a need for better authentication methodologies, including voice and fingerprint authentication built into the phone, so that the lost equipment is rendered unusable (Kasavana 2006).

SHORT MESSAGING SERVICES (SMS)

With mobile telephones being omnipresent, let us examine their capability to be omnipotent. Looking at the hindrances in the way of using proximity-enabled cell phones as a payment tool; we have yet another way of using cell phones for making payment. Technology experts and business enthusiasts have devised how short messaging services (SMS) can be used for making payments.

Bankers, mobile network operators, and retailers have all come together to offer a text message based payment programme to the customers. Unlike the near-field communication, which requires a handset equipped with an NFC short-range radio, this programme will let every cell phone user complete retail transactions from their phones.   (Zeman 2007)

How does it Work

The SMS-based payment mechanism is just taking place. It is a futuristic technology. The way mobile telephony is popular, cheap, and reliable, it is going to stay. Presently, there are two ways in which the systems are supposed to work—bank way and credit card way. As the technology matures, there are going to be more refinements in the system and better services will surface. The two methods are discussed below.

Bank-Way

There are four parties involved in this system of payment—customer, retailer, bank, and mobile operator. The customer and his/her retailer register with the bank for using SMS-based payment system. The customer walks into the shop, selects the items, takes them to the EPOS, and then tells the cashier that he/she wants to pay via SMS. As long as both the customer and the retailer have 'ABC' bank accounts, the customer can proceed. The seller sends a payment request to the buyer with a text message. The buyer then keys in a PIN to approve the sale and responds to the seller's SMS. Once the transaction is complete, both parties receive an SMS receipt. The money is transferred from the customer's account to the retailer's account.

Credit Card Way

In the other method of payment through SMS, there is involvement of a third processor or 'bill-pay company'. The customer needs to register with the bill-pay-company, which can be done through the mobile phone or the website of the company. While registering through the mobile phone, the customer is required to enter his/her 4-digit PIN. This PIN is a confidential password to authenticate all transactions. The mobile number is also registered with the company.

In the second step, the customer needs to register his/her credit card with the company, which goes into the secure (usually) database of the company. This is one-time activity and the customers need not disclose their credit card number with every purchase.

While registering through the website of the company, the customer needs to register his/her mobile number and credit card number. The customer receives an automated PIN number from the bill-pay company on his/her mobile. This is a temporary PIN and can be changed later on for security reasons.

Making the Payment

With the registered mobile, the customer sends an SMS on a particular number (as provided by the company) with the amount of payment. Then the customer authenticates the payment by his/her PIN. The payment is accepted only when it is made through the registered phone and authenticated by the valid PIN. So, it seems secure. The payment thus made comes in the customer's next credit card statement.

Advantages of SMS-based Payments

- It is convenient. The customer can buy an item from the comfort of his/ her home and get it delivered to the doorstep.
- It is useful. All the utility bills can be paid on time, all the time.
- It is safe. Once registered, the customers never have to type their credit card numbers on the Web again.
- Merchants never get to know the customer's credit card number.
- All transactions are controlled by the PIN or password as well as the mobile phone.

What are the Hindrances

The idea of paying through SMS may sound great in concept, but according to trials, the transactions take 18 seconds or longer. At times, it may take more time. As a tool, it is meant to replace cash and is not time-saving. Compared with the 500 milliseconds it takes to complete a RFID or proximity system based transaction, an SMS-based transaction usually takes 18 seconds.

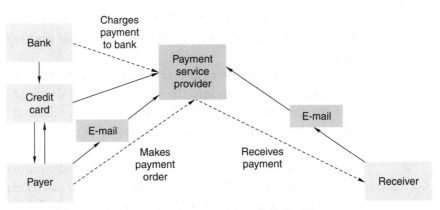

Fig. 8.6 How pay orders and payments are routed in P2P payments

PEOPLE-TO-PEOPLE (P2P) PAYMENT SYSTEM

In people-to-people payment system, one person pays on behalf of the other. Both the payer and the payee must be registered with the middle-person or service provider. The prominent among P2P service providers is 'PayPal'. In this system of payments, a person can make a payment to any other person having an e-mail ID. Both the payer and the receiver should have e-mail IDs and have to register with a service provider like PayPal (Fig. 8.6). The payer need not divulge information of his/her credit card to the vendor or payee. This information of credit card is given only to the PayPal while registering with it.

The selling point in using such P2P service is that it safeguards financial and personal information with high-security systems. It automatically encrypts all sensitive information sent between the user computer and the service provider's servers. When registering or logging in to the server site, the system verifies that the user's Internet browser is running secure sockets layer 3.0 (SSL) or higher. While in transit, the information is protected by SSL with an encryption key length of 128 bits (the highest level commercially available). The servers at the PayPal are highly secure with firewalls.

Benefits of Using P2P Service

1. It is faster than sending cheques or money orders. Payments are instantly debited to credit card account. The customers can fund their purchases directly from any of their bank accounts, instead of credit cards.
2. It is very safe and prevents frauds and helps keep the payer and receiver safe.

3. Financial information is kept private and secure. Not just purchase, funds can be transferred to friends, family, or anyone with an account with the service provider like PayPal.
4. Payments can be made locally or anywhere worldwide. Payments can be sent across the globe through eBay's worldwide marketplace. The payment is automatically converted into the desired currency.
5. Services of a service provider like 'PayPal' are accepted on eBay and other merchant websites.

SUMMARY

Traditionally, cash was the only system of payment for retail purchases. With the development of banking system, cheques were accepted as a valid and dependable means of payments. Whereas carrying cash posed risks for the consumer, acceptance of cheques from unknown customers was even more risky for the retailer. Low risks, comfort of carrying, and high security were prominent reasons that plastic money became widely acceptable means of payment in retail transactions.

With the all-round growth in organized retail, there has been a paradigm shift in the way payment is made at the retail counter. Besides credit card, newer and technologically advanced systems (such as e-cash, e-cheques, biometrics, proximity cards, smart cards, short messaging services, and person-to-person system) were introduced and accepted by both the customers and vendors.

E-cash and e-cheques are both digital token based payment system, wherein the bank authorizes the payment electronically. The electronic document is authenticated by digital signatures using cryptography system. So, there is no physical movement of paper currency.

Credit cards are the most widely used mode of payments at retail. With changes in people's earning, saving, and banking habits, and supported by enthusiastic banks, credit cards are being distributed and promoted to be used as frequently as possible. Still, in a country like India, there is much scope left for credit cards.

Certain disadvantages of using credit cards have led to invention of more secure and comfortable means of payments in the form of smart cards. Smart cards in the form of 'electronic wallet' can carry value and the consumer can buy any thing. This is yet to be seen if the e-wallet is supported by banks. For overall acceptance of the card, the banks need to fill the wallet with money. Otherwise, the use will be restricted to a few retailers.

This is a high-paced era inhabited by high-flying people. Reading and writing on a smart card takes time. Therefore, technologists have come up with proximity cards. Just show it off at the checkout and the transaction is completed. Proximity has right applications at toll bridges and rail travels, where the customer is a frequent visitor and does not have much time to wait and pay.

But what if the e-wallet and proximity-enabled cell phone are stolen and the thief is smarter. The answer lies in biometrics system. Show your fingertip or eye iris, the system is pretty confident that it is you. Lots of frauds were detected using credit card at retail or during Web-based purchases. Payments are routed through third party 'bill-pay service'. Still, we use credit cards but the credit card number is encrypted in the server of the 'bill-pay company'. It need not be given to every retailer or while buying our e-ticket for an air travel. We can be pretty sure that the credit card number is in dependable hands.

CONCEPT REVIEW QUESTIONS

1. What are the limitations of traditional payment system in retail?
2. Enumerate modern electronic payment systems used at POS.
3. Explain modalities in e-cash transactions.
4. What are various types of smart cards?
5. What are the other applications of smart cards besides payment system in retail?
6. What are the advantages and disadvantages of a smart card?
7. Explain functioning of proximity cards.
8. How does payment system through SMS work?
9. Is SMS-based payment system an upgrade on credit cards? If not, why?

CRITICAL THINKING QUESTIONS

1. 'Credit cards are going to remain as the main payment method in retail and e-commerce.' Do you agree? Explain why.
2. Does biometrics overcome the shortcomings of card technology? Explain.

PROJECT

1. Make a project for using proximity card payment system for Delhi Metro Rail. Take care that it is done through a mobile phone, an automatic system that informs the customer about fares, journeys made by the customer, and any changes in the fare structure by the Metro.

SELECT REFERENCES

Card Technology, http://www.cardtechnology. com.

Kalakota, Ravi and Andrew B. Whinston 2002, *Frontiers of Electronic Commerce*, Pearson Education Inc. (Singapore).

Kasavana, Michael L. 2006, *www.amonline.com*, June.

Meagher, Christian 2004, www.insideid.com, June 3.

Okamoto, T. and K. Ohta 1991, 'Universal Electronic Cash', *Advances in Cryptology–Crypto91*, Springer, New York.

Perton, Marc 2006, www.engadget.com, January.

Ray, Joydeep 2003, http://www.rediff.com/money/2003/dec/23cards.htm.

SourceMedia, Inc., http://www.sourcemedia.com.

www.paypal.com, last accessed in September 2008.

Zeman, Eric 2007, *InformationWeek.com*, May.

CASE STUDY

Contactless Cards: Future of Payment Systems

Company   Japan Railways East

Japan's JR East is in full rollout mode. Card Technology puts JR's Mobile Suica through its paces.

Shinjuku station in Tokyo is the busiest in the world, serving more than two million riders a day. More than 11 metro and commuter rail lines feed directly into it. At least five of those lines belong to Japan Railway East, one of the world's largest movers of people and the first transit company in the world to roll out contactless fare collection on mobile phones.

Transit operators elsewhere are watching what JR East does with interest. They see a case to be made for putting their fare-collection applications onto handsets that commuters could use just as they do contactless fare cards the transit operators are rolling out in numerous cities around the world.

Contactless chips and short-range radio antennas also can be embedded inside mobile phones to store a transit application. And unlike cards, the phones are connected to mobile networks—allowing transport agencies to download the fare payment service over the air. This could reduce the number of cards the transit companies must issue. It also gives them another channel through which to communicate with commuters. For example, they could remind them when their monthly passes are due to expire or update them on train or bus delays.

For mobile network operators, the business case is much less clear, but there is interest from some big European operator groups, such as Vodafone and Orange. They could earn revenue from the data traffic when subscribers download the monthly passes and conduct other business with the transit operator. The applications also could help keep subscribers from turning to other operators not offering the mobile-ticketing service.

For Japan's dominant mobile network operator, NTT DoCoMo, putting JR East's Suica fare-collection application on its 'mobile-wallet' phones has always been a priority. In fact, it was JR East that came up with the idea for the contactless mobile wallet five years ago, as it was working on the launch of its contactless 'Suica' fare card. After some hesitation, DoCoMo went for the concept and launched its first contactless wallet phones in July 2004, with such services as the electronic purse and loyalty programmes.

But Mobile Suica was not part of the first mobile-wallet phones. JR East held the application back.

Fifteen Million and Counting

That application has been much anticipated. JR East's Suica card programme has grown to more than 15 million cards issued as of March 2006. And since 2004, JR has also allowed the cardholders to use the Suica card to pay for small purchases at stores in and around its stations. As of December, a reported 3,400 shops, kiosks, restaurants, and vending machines accepted Suica e-money, which cardholders used about 6 million times a month. All told, cardholders used Suica on average nearly 200 million times per month to cover fares and purchases.

But the train operator delayed the move to mobile handsets until late January. It wanted more control over the security of its application. And more importantly, it wanted to make sure the handset-based tickets could handle the waves of travellers that flow through gates at Shinjuku, and the hundreds of other stations accepting Suica. Shinjuku then is an ideal place to put the application through its paces and one that could give transit authorities and mobile operators in Europe and elsewhere an idea of how contactless mobile ticketing could work.

Card Technology tested Mobile Suica in March, a little more than two months after the launch. By then, few commuters were using it, according to JR agents and store clerks we asked. As of the second week of April, only 64,000 customers were using the new mobile service, says a JR's spokesperson. 'We expect that the number of Mobile Suica users will increase because many customers may decide to use it when their commuter pass is expired,' he says.

One Problem is Getting the Application onto the Phone

JR decided that, unlike with its Suica cards, it would also require users of the mobile service to have a 'View' credit card account. JR East's credit card is carried by about 3.5 million consumers. Those consumers would have to register for the mobile fare-collection service. Others would have to apply for a View card. The customers would then be able to load money onto their wallet phones or buy transit passes and JR would charge this to their credit accounts.

The requirement was a disappointment for many who believed Suica could be the service that sparks broad use of the wallet phones. 'First, you have to have a mobile handset that complies with Suica; there are only very new models,' says one observer. 'Plus, you have to have a View card, and a View card will have annual fees. Many Japanese (credit) cards have no annual fees.'

While JR does charge an annual fee for the View card, it's just 500 yen (US$4.22), and the company agrees to waive that fee the first year for Mobile Suica users. Some observers believe JR will eventually open up the service to holders of other credit cards. That's what it did with its Suica card.

Difficult to Download

For the time being, however, JR is forcing would-be users of the mobile service to hold a View card. It takes a week or two to receive the card after applying on JR's website.

As with other mobile-wallet services, much of the Suica applications get downloaded on the phone, but the commuter passes, e-purse and transaction history gets stored on the embedded contactless 'FeliCa' chip made by Japan's Sony Corp.

Once loaded, it's fairly easy to buy monthly transit passes or load value into the Suica purse. Mainly, we entered our special Mobile Suica password, along with customizing the pass. We also loaded 3,000 yen (US$25.40) in e-money from the credit account. We could use it to pay at merchants that accept Suica, including Family Mart convenience stores, kiosks, some restaurants, and a consumer electronics retailer. Most of the stores are within JR's large stations. The e-money purse also covers the cost of rides outside of our monthly pass zone.

When you exit one station beyond Shinjuku, the gate reader neatly deducts the fare from the e-purse. When you stay within the zone, such as exiting at Shinjuku, the reader allows you to pass without an extra charge. In both cases, the transactions are quick, just as fast as with cards, which are less than 200 milliseconds.

Similarly, when one uses the phone to buy snacks at a couple of kiosks in Shinjuku station and at a Family Mart convenience store out in the surrounding commercial and entertainment district. You just have to tap the phone to pay. No scrolling through menus to find a payment application. It's just as if you were using a credit card with remote verification.

Transit Card with Screen

But unlike a card, one could view my balance and e-money transaction history, keep tabs on the status of my monthly pass. The menu offers other features: where to use Suica and updates on train delays. A separate menu item controls buying passes over the network. This saves commuters lots of time queuing in lines.

You can pass through the transit gate or make a purchase with the phone switched off. But the program does require some residual power, with the battery in the phone.

Can it Work in Another Phone?

A key test for Mobile Suica would be whether; transfer of the transit pass and e-money to another phone could be affected. Japanese subscribers change phones often. If they couldn't take the remainder of the pass and e-cash with them, the service wouldn't fly. Unlike the onerous registration process to start the service, we mainly needed to log into the second handset with the e-mail address and password under which we are registered. There were a few other steps, but we were able to move the pass and e-cash over the network from a DoCoMo phone to a handset of the rival KDDI network.

Questions:

1. What were the major problems faced by JR East in implementing proximity system of payments?
2. Prepare a business case of implementing similar services for paying toll tax at a DND Flyover.

Sources: Adapted from www.cardtechnology.com, www.sourcemedia.com, www.smartcard.org, and www.icmrindia.org.

9 Retail Servicescape and Types of Retailers

Learning Objectives

- To understand retail servicescape
- To know how retail is different from other trading businesses
- To identify major types of retail businesses
- To explore complexities of various businesses within retail scenarios
- To understand how technology is modified to serve the purpose

In previous chapters, we have discussed all the components of retail IT, including retail application software and its core functionalities. But as the saying goes 'one size does not fit all', one software application cannot meet requirements of all kinds of retailers. In the myriad world of retailing, different types of products, retailing formats, and government regulations require different functionalities from the EPOS. These functionalities are required out of either the hardware or the application software. In this chapter, we will discuss the unique functionalities required by major types of retailers.

Before we delve more into software technicalities, functions and features, let us appreciate what makes retail different from other trades. The point-of-sales environment offers certain peculiarities in terms of product billing and deliveries. These peculiarities in the trading system of different types of retailers pose serious challenges for the technology providers as a system designed for one type of retail finds it hard to fit into the other. Besides, within the same trade, there are nuances that we need to understand. These complexities of the trade are going to have an impact on how solutions are designed for them. The technology providers, while designing a system, try to either re-engineer the system to suit the technology or mould technology in order to make it suitable for the processes that are stiff and do not allow much scope of flexibility. This chapter discusses the technological requirements at the retail place.

CONCEPT OF RETAIL SERVICESCAPE

Today retailers make an all out effort to satisfy customers and gain their loyalty. Services and environment at the retail point of sales heavily influence customer behaviour and employee satisfaction. From the time a customer enters a retail store and exits from the store after making purchases, the majority of activities happening are services. Retail employees provide these services to the customer to enable sales to happen and for a smooth transition of goods from the retail store to the customer's possession. These services are provided through the welcome of the customer, signage, design, layout, décor, and equipment installed at the store.

Bitner (1992) used the term *servicescape* initially while elaborating on the impact of physical surroundings on the customers and employees at a service delivery point. Servicescape can influence customer choices, expectations, satisfaction, and behaviour. For example, a customer may perceive a store to be selling good quality products and offering good services, if they find an automated self-checkout system installed at the retail store. Similarly, a computerized point of sales may lead to believe that the services must be prompt and satisfactory. This thinking may lead to more purchases from the store and, if satisfied, the customer may come again to the store. As such, the servicescape influences the customer perception and behaviour at the retail outlet.

Zeithaml and Bitner (2006) believe that servicescape can influence customer choices, expectations, satisfaction, and behaviour. Servicescape also improves employee productivity, motivation, and satisfaction. A good servicescape also plays roles of service packaging, service facilitator, socializer, i.e. interaction with bill cashiers at retail and differentiator of services from the organization's competitors.

The concept of retail servicescape encompasses the environment of physical delivery of goods and/or services and the way the service is delivered (Fig. 9.1). It revolves around the customer, the service delivery equipment and the process leading to closing of sales.

TECHNOLOGICAL COMPONENTS OF RETAIL SERVICESCAPE

From a technological point of view, we can group the major attributes of retail servicescape into the following categories:

- Personalized customer service
- Customer insights
- Physical facilities and tangible communications

Fig. 9.1   Retail physical servicescape

- Efficiency in completing sales transactions
- Flexible systems to support customer preferences
- Promotion-driven sales

Personalized Customer Service

The basic attribute of point of sales is walk-in customer—that is, the sales process happens and concludes in the presence of the customer. The selection and de-selection of goods, choice of payment modes, and the delivery mechanism is decided at the retail sales counter. Compare this with the trading sales process where customer is not present at the point of billing. Customer gets personalized services in terms of his proximity with the sales employees, ordering at the store or on phone, home delivery and other personalized services. Modern technology helps the retailers to manage the scale of high customer influx and provide personalized services.

Customer Insights

Customer satisfaction is achieved through keeping in touch with the customer. It may not be possible to understand a customer and know their tastes and preferences if suitable data has not been captured at the retail point of sales. Therefore, one of the primary objectives of automation at the retail counter is building up of customer database and sales database. In the billing process, customer and sales database are created. This data is further analysed to understand the buying patterns, and tastes and preferences of the customer. Technology offers customer loyalty management systems to manage the customer. Retail is a trade that offers direct link with the end-consumer. Retailers want to know more about the customer, their buying patterns, their tastes and preferences, their income levels, and their way of spending. There are ways how retailer should be in touch with the customer. Right technology gives dozens of such tools to manage a customer loyalty programme.

Physical Facility and Tangible Communications

If signage, design, layout, and décor are important ingredients of tangible communication at a retail store, webpage layout and navigational ease are tangible ingredients of virtual stores. Electronic point-of-sales machines, automated self-checkout systems, self-help interactive kiosks, and RFID-enabled electronic article surveillance (anti-theft devices) are important physical facilities at the retail outlet. Customer builds their perception of the store, quality of goods, and services based on these tangible components of retail servicescape. All these tools are technology driven.

Efficiency in Completing Sales Transaction

One of the major headaches for the system designers is to provide a fast checkout system. Customer spends hours in choosing and finalizing products in the retail store but is impatient at the checkout counter. Once the customers have picked their goods, they want to check out as fast as possible. Therefore, a fast billing system with the aid of technology is a boon. Billing and payment settlements happen simultaneously at the point of sales. The sales process is said to be completed only when the payment is offered by the customer and is accepted by the system.

Flexible Systems to Support Customer Preferences

Functionality to support multiple payment modes at the checkout gate is an intangible component. Not only the customer offers hard currency, but there are a variety of payment systems as well. The customers can offer their credit card, debit card, smart card, cheques, and discount coupons received as their rewards points. Shops at places like airports accept payments in foreign currency. The multiple modes of payments and connectivity with the electronic fund transfer systems, such as credit card processing and digital payment systems, are a part of unique retail servicescape. Returns and exchanges are common in retail and handling must be efficient and hassle-free to increase customer satisfaction and building customer loyalty. If the exchange of old is along with the new purchases, the vendor cannot make the system cumbersome by asking the customer to go to multiple billing counters. The trend in retail is that instead of returning money, a 'credit note' is generated, which is redeemed by the customer during any future purchase. Retail billing system provides functions to accommodate multiple payments acceptance and returns handling.

Promotion-Driven Sales

Retail runs on promotional schemes, discounts, and freebies. Retailers invent different, unique, and bizarre ways of selling. *Discounts* can be of various types, such as volume based, value based, and lump sum or a fixed percentage on bill. New trend in discounting is multi-layered, like 50+50 per cent discount. For a naïve customer, it may seem a hundred per cent discount. But in reality, it is 75 per cent discount. *Schemes* are related with offering freebies or discounted goods on purchase of a specified product. Sometimes, schemes are quite bizarre, for example buy one item of a product and get one free, buy three and get two free, buy two pieces of x and get two pieces of y free, buy three pieces of product z, and get 45 per cent on the entire purchases. Retailers also give free *discount coupons* of their own on certain purchases, which are accepted in lieu of currency payments. Retailers also accept free gift coupons issued by other companies to their customers, employees, or shareholders. These coupons are accepted by the designated retailers. Later, the retailer redeems them for payment at an agreed arrangement.

Now, the pertinent question is: Generating all these promotional schemes is easy, but is your POS system flexible enough to accommodate them?

TYPES OF RETAILERS

There are different types of retailers. Retailers can be classified on the basis of the size and stores layouts, such as convenience stores, superstores, department stores, hypermarkets, large format stores, and retail chain stores. Retailers can also be classified based on the type of products they deal in, such as mom-n-pop stores, apparel retail, footwear retail, jewellery retail, restaurants, fast-food joints, service retailing like health spa, and travel ticketing retail.

We are going to confine our discussion to the second types of retailers. Their impact on technology is more from the point of view of the products they deal in—the kind of technology they need to maintain, create product codes, make sales, and manage inventory differences. We need to examine these unique requirements keeping in view the specific demands of the trade and core areas of point-of-sales software, which we have already discussed in the previous section. The core functions of POS software are common for all trades but there are minute nuances of each function and sub-function. We will discuss the peculiarities within a function of that particular business type.

We take up only the critical areas and suggest the best practices to handle the situations through technology. The solution ranges from how a product code is created, bar code is placed, and such sales are handled.

The following types of retailers are discussed here:

1. Grocery/mom-n-pop stores
2. Apparel and footwear
3. Restaurant billing
4. Fast-food retailing
5. Jewellery stores
6. Fabric retailing
7. Loose products like vegetables and meat
8. Pharmacy retail
9. Service retailing

Grocery/Mom-n-Pop Stores

Grocery and mom-n-pop stores use one of the most standard EPOS systems with easy and simple software. Most of the times, their system is designed to do billing and derive just the stock report. The systems use the EAN bar codes pre-printed on the products by the manufacturers. These bar codes are defined in the system along with the product specifications and prices. Some of such retailers also have their own packing of products like rice, lentils, and spices. For such packing, they can go for simple alphanumeric bar codes, such as Code 128, and Code 39 (as discussed in Chapter 4). For own repackaging, they need a system that allows 'repacking'. In this system, the bulk item is broken into multiple pieces of smaller products with separate bar code identities.

For example, a retail store buys sugar in bags of 100 kg. Then it repacks the sugar in smaller bags of 1, 2, and 5 kg (Fig. 9.2). On entering this internal transaction in the system, the inventory is affected accordingly. The bulk bag of 100 kg is reduced by the same unit and each smaller package of 1, 2, and 5 kg are updated (inventory increase) by the new units created. Figure 9.3(a) shows a display at a mom-n-pop store.

Bulk product				Saleable product			
Code	Description	Qty	UOM	Code	Description	Qty	UOM
S100	Sugar	100	kg	S1101	Sugar bag1 kg	20	Each
				S1102	Sugar bag 2 kg	15	Each
				S1103	Sugar bag 5 kg	10	Each

Fig. 9.2 Repacking system for mom-n-pop stores

(a)   (b)

Fig. 9.3 Display at (a) mom-n-pop and (b) apparel stores

Technological Requirements

Mom-n-pop stores need the following systems:

1. A normal electronic point-of-sales system with POS software, barcode scanner, and bill printer.
2. Thermal transfer printer for additional bar code printing for retailer's own goods.
3. Functionality within the POS software, which allows the retailer to 'repack' goods and maintain stock of both bulk and repacked units.

Apparel and Footwear

The peculiarity in fashion trades comes due to 'style', 'size', and 'colour' attributes of the products. Figure 9.3(b) shows an apparel store. The products are purchased by sizes, sold by sizes, and stored (inventoried) by sizes and colours (Fig. 9.4) Most of the sales analysis and material planning is based on what size and colour sell most. Analysis is required on what was the best selling style in the previous season (Fig. 9.5).

Another peculiarity of the trade is that no style repeats itself. Even weaving of the same fabric the next time gives differentiating constructions. So, products built next time with similar fabric, size, and colour shall be given a new code. This way, within a few years, there will be millions of product codes in the database, and most of the codes will be redundant and unusable. Once sales

Item Master

Item Code	SUA029
Name	SUIT AZURE

Unit

Stock	PCS	**Purchase**	PCS
PCS	= 1 PCS	**Sales Tax**	T4

Vendor

Name	AZURE
Item Code	

Excise

☐ Exciseable

ED Rate : 0.00

Discount

☑ Discountable

Discount : 0.00 % ▼

Group

Group	SUIT
Label	AZURE
Sub Group	
Dept	
Location	GROUND FLOOR
Section	
Classification	

Size ->	36	42	Export	GENERA
Applicable ->	☐	☐	☐	☑

	Stock Point	Min.	Max.	Re-Order
1	GYANS - KB	0.00	0.00	0.00

Stop Cursor in Billing At

NONE

☐ Expirable Item
☑ Clear Screen

Add	Modify	Save	Save&Print	Delete	Print	Preview	List View	Close

Fig. 9.4 Product master in an apparel-specific EPOS

happen and stock figures are zero, these codes are not utilized for any thing. The database becomes larger, slower, and sluggish, which takes up a lot of computer resources and time in analytical processing.

Now, how to solve this problem? Solution experts have devised ways to tackle this problem. This can be done by adopting two different types of bar code patterns:

Fig. 9.5 Apparel store: choosing the best selling style

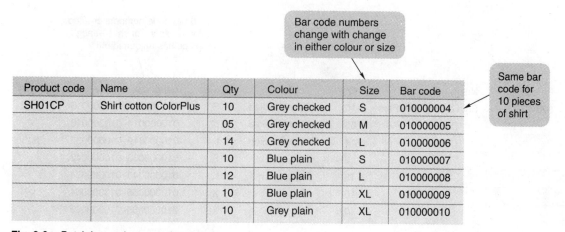

Fig. 9.6 Batch bar code generation system

- Batch bar code systems
- Unique bar code systems

Batch Bar Code Patterns

As the name suggests, in this system, bar codes are generated in batches. In batch pattern, there are two codes for the same product. One is 'product code' and the other is 'bar code'. Every time a product is created or purchased, a new bar code number is assigned to the product. The three important attributes, size, colour, and styles, are linked with the bar code. The bar code is put on the product through the bar code label. This batch number is scanned and the product is moved or sold. All the analysis is done on product code and style code, which are different and have unique identities. The steps along with examples are given in Fig. 9.6.

Unique Bar Code Patterns

These are sequential numbers generated for each product. As in batch bar code system, in unique bar code, dual coding pattern (one for the product code and other for sequential number) is followed. The only difference is that in batch bar code, one number is generated for all products of the same attributes purchased at a time; whereas in unique bar code system, all the quantities of the same products purchased at a time, are given different numbers, usually sequential numbers. As an example, you can find out how many shirts you have bought since last one year and which shirt of a particular bar code number is lying at which store (Fig. 9.7).

10 bar code numbers created for 10 pieces of shirt—each piece has unique identity

Product code	Name	Qty	Colour	Size	Bar code
SH01CP	Shirt cotton ColorPlus	10	Grey checked	S	010000004–010000013
		05	Grey checked	M	010000014–010000018
		14	Grey checked	L	010000019–010000032
		10	Blue plain	S	010000033–010000042
		12	Blue plain	L	010000043–010000054
		10	Blue plain	XL	010000055–010000064
		10	Grey plain	XL	010000065–010000073

Fig. 9.7   Unique bar code patterns

Codification of Apparel

The 'Style' master is different from the item bar code. Style master is created by using some aliases of attributes. It is based on the process of auto-style code creation. Besides automatic code generation, manual codes by user can be done (Fig. 9.8).

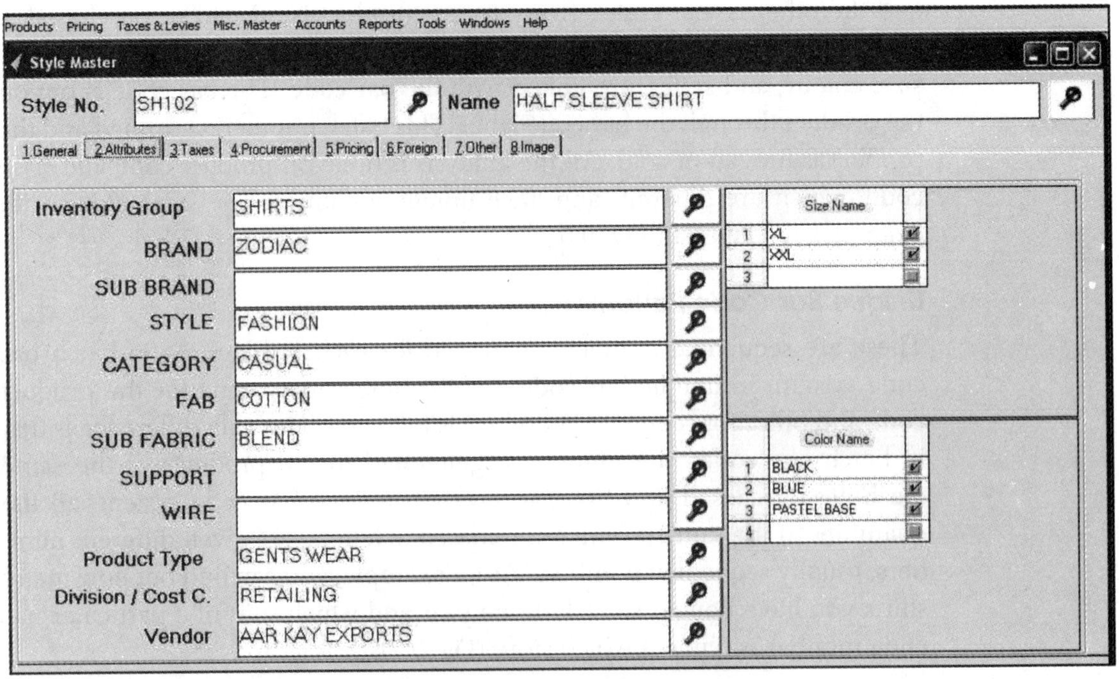

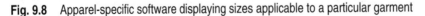

Fig. 9.8   Apparel-specific software displaying sizes applicable to a particular garment

As an example, a garment can have the following attributes:

(a) Type of garment—like shirts (SH) and trousers (TR)
(b) Fabric—like cotton (c) and polyester (P)
(c) print type/number—three-character code or number (777)
(d) Gender/age—ladies (L), gents (G), kids (K)
(e) Year/season—2005 (05)
(f) Three characters are left for the sequence numbers.

Thus, a typical style code may be like SHC777L05001.

These style codes are generated on item creation. Now size and colour codes are added to make 'bar codes' for it. All transactions are done on bar codes but sales and stock analysis reports are available on 'style code'.

Colour and size codes are added in bar code table. Some examples are given below:

(a) Black—BK, Blue—BL, Green—GN, Grey—GR
(b) S, L, M, XL, XXL, or 34, 36, 38, 40, 42, 44

Using these aliases, a typical bar code looks like SHC777L05001BLXL and TRP123G05002BK40, or a sequential number like 0000123, 800000001, and 800000002.

Purchase Orders for Finished Products

Assuming that the retailers outsource their products in ready-to-sell condition, a different PO format is used (Fig. 9.9).

Suppose the shirt code is SH01CP, GCC and BLP are codes for Grey Checked and Blue Plain colours respectively, and S, M, L, Xl, XXL are common size codes. The retailer gives its vendor the break-up of styles/colour/sizes in the format shown in Fig. 9.10.

Bar code labels are printed and sent along with the PO to the vendor. The vendor sends the goods pre-labelled (or source-labelled).

Receiving Material

At the time of receiving goods from a vendor, a document, called *material receipt note* (MRN) or *goods receipt note* (GRN), is generated. The MRN and GRN are used interchangeably in this text. Material is received against the PO issued to vendors. It is inspected and sent to stores.

But the MRN is created by scanning the bar codes on the products, which is tallied with the purchase orders. The format shown in Fig. 9.11 is used.

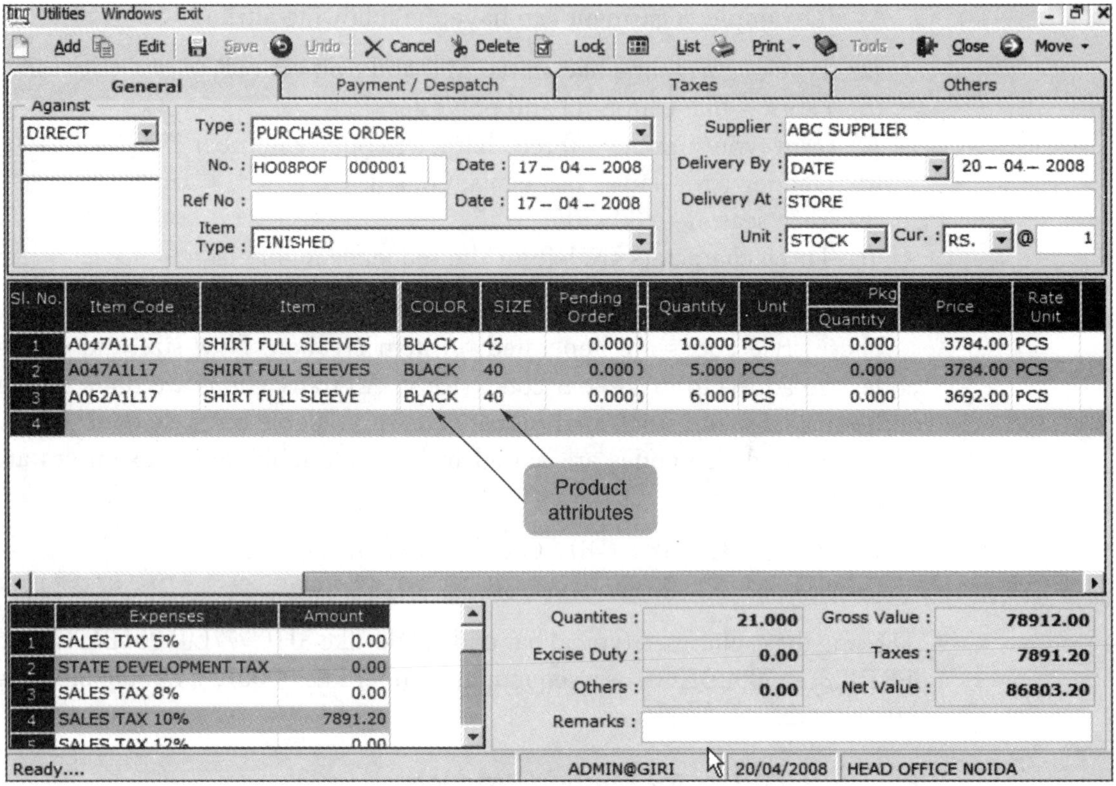

Fig. 9.9 Purchase order in a software application giving break-up of colours and sizes

Technological Requirements

Apparel and footwear retail requires the following systems:

1. An electronic point-of-sales system with billing software and scanner
2. Thermal or dot matrix printer for bill printing
3. Purchase order system attached with bar code label printer
4. Colour and size bifurcation in purchase orders and goods receipt notes
5. Scanning possibility at the time of material receipts
6. Back-office inventory management and stock analysis

Style code	Colour code	Size	Size2	Size3	Size4	...	Total	Rate	VAT	Net
		S	M	L	XL					
SH01CP	GCC	10	5	14	0		29	780.00	4.00	9999.99
SH01CP	BLP	10	0	12	10		32	770.00	4.00	9999.99

Fig. 9.10 Purchase order system giving break-up of colour and sizes

Bar code: | 010000010

Style code	Colour code	Size S	Size2 M	Size3 L	Size4 XL	...	Total	Rate	VAT	Net
SH01CP	BLP	2	0	0	10		12	...	...	...

The data is updated on scanning.

Fig. 9.11 Scanning pre-labelled products at the time of material receipts

Restaurant Billing

Products in a restaurant cannot be bar coded and restaurants provide a product-cum-service environment. Besides the products and service combination, restaurant retail involves two additional components to be taken care of. One is *Table*, where the service is provided and the other is *KOT* (kitchen order ticket), which is the customer's order to waiters. The waiter takes the order from customer and creates a KOT and mentions table number on it. The KOT is printed on the kitchen printer. Figure 9.12 shows how the two situations are handled in the EPOS.

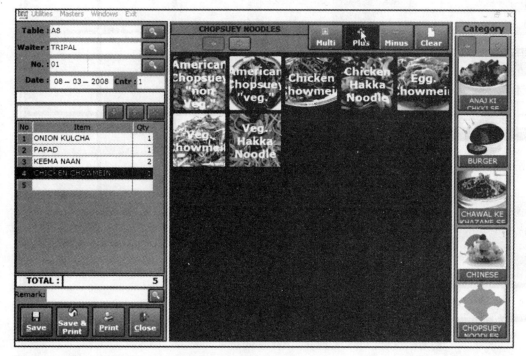

Fig. 9.12 Billing and KOT generation at a restaurant

KOT

The KOT forms part of restaurant billing. Your EPOS system permits to generate a KOT. It is created in duplicate usually with table number. One copy goes to the kitchen and other remains with the counter. If a kitchen printer is networked, printing is directly done on the kitchen printer or the bar printer, whatever the case. There could be multiple KOTs for the same customer or table that is served by a single waiter. With the mobile wireless computing in place, now mobile handheld terminals with an integrated printer can be used by the waiter to enter the order. The technology can provide GPRS connectivity and the order is transmitted to the server. The server then fires the KOT to the kitchen printer and prints a KOT at the kitchen.

Billing against KOT

The EPOS software has options to bill against previously raised KOTs. The system allows the user to pick multiple KOTs for billing (Fig. 9.13). Once a KOT is knocked off, it is not available for further billing.

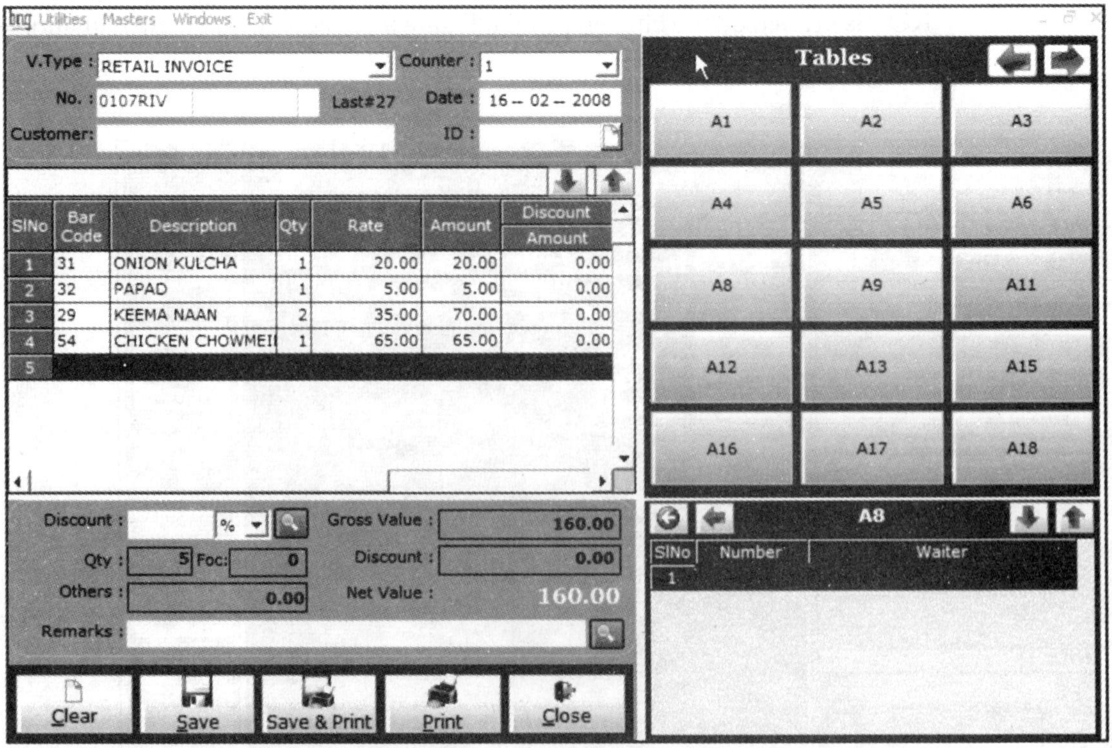

Fig. 9.13 Billing against KOT

Technological Requirements

Restaurant billing requires the following systems:

1. An electronic point-of-sales system with touch-screen or mouse-compatible software at the front office to generate KOT
2. Thermal or dot matrix printers in networks to print KOTs at various kitchens
3. Table views with seating arrangement. Display of occupied or free tables at any time
4. Bill split or consolidation feature in POS software
5. Settlement of bills in multiple currencies
6. Back-office inventory management and recipe creation

Fast-Food Retailing

Fast-food retailing needs yet another feature in the technology. Most of the fast-food joints have a very limited product list. The list contains between 15 and 100 products. The products are also well classified, based on the type of food or drink. These joints are usually kiosks and run at small spaces, which are manned by one or two service persons. There are three main characteristics of fast-food retailing:

1. We cannot put a code or bar code label on the product.
2. People serving at fast-food joints are hardly computer savvy.
3. Since fast-food joints are usually run from places like kiosks, vans, and subway outlets, there are space constraints.

In this scenario, what is the best method for billing and tallying cash?

Touch-screen EPOS is the answer, in touch screen, the layout of the billing screen is user-friendly (Fig. 9.14). The characters are bigger and one touch leads to another. The bill clerk need not remember codes and prices. The organization of item is hierarchical. Usually, a two-layer structure serves the purpose.

Example: SOFT DRINK->>COKE CANE,
PIZZA->>VEG PIZZA 8',

Technological Requirements

Fast-food billing requires the following features in the EPOS:

1. An electronic point-of-sales system with touch-screen monitor
2. Compatible software to generate bills
3. Multiple currency payment settlement

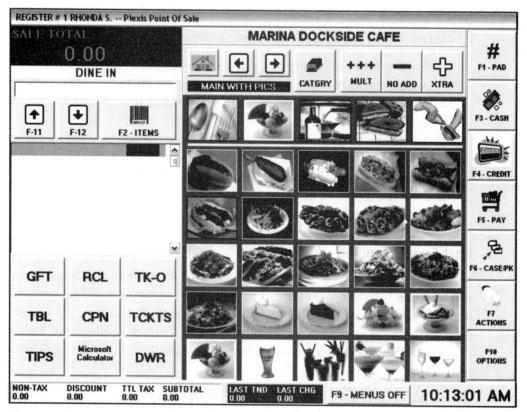

Fig. 9.14 Touch-screen software for fast-food retail

Jewellery Stores

The requirements at jewellery stores are different from those at other kind of retail shops, because the prices of the articles change every day. The change in prices is due to fluctuation in the gold prices. The pricing of the articles is not based on design or any other product attributes but weight of the substance. Along with the SKU numbers, the bar code on the product also represents 'weight' of the product. Therefore, the system offers the following flexibility to accommodate jewellery trade (Fig. 9.15).

- Daily gold rate change system
- Weight of article as the 'quantity' component
- Picking daily gold prices as 'product prices' instead of article prices

Technological requirements

Jewellery stores require the following features in the EPOS:

    1. An electronic point-of-sales system with normal monitor and scanner

Billing			
Date: 01/03/08			
Code	Wt.	Price	Amt
R01234	10.00	1110.0	11100.0

Daily Gold Prices	
Date	Price/gm
01/03/08	1110.00
02/03/08	1099.00
03/03/08	1035.00
04/03/08	1089.00

Billing			
Date: 04/03/08			
Code	Wt.	Price	Amt
R01234	10.00	1089.0	10880.0

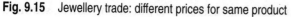

Fig. 9.15 Jewellery trade: different prices for same product

2. Compatible software to generate bills
3. Software having features to enter daily gold rates
4. Multiple currency payment settlement

Fabric Retailing

Retailing of fabric poses another problem for the technology implementers since the fabric comes in large sizes in bales or *thana*, but sells in small pieces. You cannot pre-cut the large pieces and paste bar code labels in advance. Secondly, a single bar code label on a large roll of one hundred metre will not suffice, it will have enormous wear and tear, and may not be readable by the scanner, or it maybe misplaced altogether. The other reason of complicacy is that after cutting a number of pieces, the last cut piece is not traceable. It is also a problem to keep an inventory for each bale. The fabric retailer may ask: 'Can my system tell me how many metres of cloth are available from each bale?' To provide the best solution and answer the retailer's questions, technology providers have designed the following solution.

In the retail system, a batch bar code system is maintained (Fig. 9.16). At the time of purchases, each bale number along with the length in metre is

| (a) | (b) |

Fig. 9.16 (a) Bar code labels for a bale of fabric and (b) fabric bales at display

provided in the system. The system generates a unique number for each bale (sequential number) and an equal number of bar code labels are printed. For example, you buy 2 rolls of fabric. Roll number 1 has 98 metre and roll number 2 has 104 metre. Both the rolls will be issued separate bar code numbers and quantities in the stocks will be taken as 98 and 104 respectively. The system allows 98 or less stickers and 104 or less to print each time. These stickers are pasted on a detachable paper (so that it can be put on the piece of fabric at the time of sales). Alternatively, the labels can also be put on a polybag attached with each bale (roll). At the time of sales, each label is put on the fabric, scanned and billing is done for the product. This selling process, as usual, reduces the stock from the particular bar code and books sales.

Retailing of Loose Products

Selling loose products like vegetables and meat that are not packaged and do not sell in fixed quantity are treated differently at the point of sales. Examples of such products are vegetables and raw meat. One way of selling such products is to pre-pack them in fixed quantity of 1 kg or 500 gm packs. But this may not always be feasible. The trend in the market is of tying the sales of loose products with a bar code enabled weighing machine (Fig. 9.17). Whatever the customer buys, a bar code of that quantity is printed. At the billing counter, this bar code is scanned for quantity and the product is billed. This method gives the following advantages:

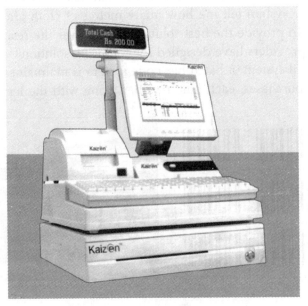

Fig. 9.17   Weighing scale enabled EPOS

- The customer has flexibility to pick what is needed.
- Bar code enabled weighting machine prints bar code for the exact quantity of goods; it reduces the chances of error.
- Same bar code is scanned at the billing counter, which again speeds up the work and eliminates the errors.

Technological Requirements

For billing of loose products, the following technology is required:

1. An electronic point-of-sales system with POS software
2. Weighing scale with bar code printing on labels
3. Scanning facility at POS

Pharmacy Retail

The manufacturing and sale of pharmacy products are regulated all over the world. These products expire after a certain period. Therefore, mentioning batch number and expiry date on the document of sales and purchase is a legal requirement. The batch numbers are linked with expiry date of the product. Ethically and legally, it is unacceptable to sell expired items. Therefore, it becomes imperative for the retailer to keep inventories of only valid products and sell them before the expiry date. Not only this, in certain cases the sale report also goes to the local government. Every medicine comes with a batch and expiry date. At the time of purchase, both these elements are entered in the system. So movement of these items always carries batch identity with them. At the retail, when a product is sold, the billing screen provides two additional columns of 'Batch' and 'Expiry' in it. On scanning or entering code number of the product, the system either automatically picks or asks the user to enter batch number and expiry date. The user either manually enters this information or can scan a bar code if it is already put on the product packing.

The system must provide the following things:

1. Stock reports for such products
2. Stock reports for already expired products
3. Stock of expiring products within next 'n weeks' or 'm days'

Service Retailing

There is not much difference between product and service retailing (Fig. 9.18), as far as technology is concerned. But retail servicescape provides a different service scenario than product sales. Let us first examine service scenarios:

Fig. 9.18 Custom tailoring section: servicing in retail

Courtesy: Blues Clothing Co, New Delhi

- Services are provided by the service employees, which are inseparable from the services.
- Most of the services are provided at the service place, i.e. the retail outlet, for examples the services like haircut, massage, and beauty care.
- Service pricing is not very standardized and structured. Some services may be priced on duration, i.e. hourly price and others may be priced on quality of service. Pricing of services is also done on the basis of the expert who provides it, like services of a doctor or an advocate.
- Services involve service tax, in place of VAT.
- Services are intangible, consumed while they are created. Hence, no stock keeping is required.

The EPOS system for managing, recording, and billing services takes into consideration the above elements. A normal or touch-screen EPOS is suitable for billing and salespersons can easily maintain the service delivery point. The system provides flexibility regarding whether to bill service on the basis of the time duration or the number of times the service was taken, for example, price of services of a massager can be based on the time taken in hours or minutes, but for pedicure it can be the number of times the pedicure was done.

SUMMARY

Understanding retail servicescape is important from the point of understanding the technology that helps in service delivery. Retail servicescape refers to the tangible and intangible environment and forces that lead to closure of sales at the retail POS. These forces are loosely divided into six categories. Personal attention to the walk-in customer, multiple payment settlement, and proximity with sales experts are some components of personalized customer service. Building and managing customer loyalty programmes, and creating database are customer insights. Physical facilities are tangible objects like EPOS, self-checkout systems, anti-theft systems, and web page layouts. Use of these tools to speedily conclude sales denotes efficiency at the retail POS. Returns and exchanges are parts of retail and form flexible systems as a component of the retail servicescape. Promotions and schemes are indispensable parts of retail and hence constitute an element of retail servicescapes.

Retailers can be classified into many categories. Based on the nature of their business or the products they deal, nine categories have been identified. Grocery/mom-n-pop stores, apparel and footwear stores, restaurant billing, fast-food retailing, jewellery stores, fabric retailing, loose products (such as vegetables and meat), pharmacy retail, and service retailing are the major groups. These categories pose different nuances and peculiarities. They demand a change in process of product or service delivery at the retail POS, which, in turn, warrants change in the technology implementation.

CONCEPT REVIEW QUESTIONS

1. What do you understand by retail servicescape?
2. How is apparel retailing different from other types of retailing?
3. What technological difference you need to look at while setting up computer systems for a fast-food retail chain?
4. What features you will need for a restaurant billing EPOS?
5. 'Simple POS software cannot work in a jewellery store.' Do you agree with this statement? Justify your answer.
6. What component of retail technology poses a problem while implementing software for a large fabric store?
7. What extra equipment you will need to computerize a vegetable shop?
8. 'Putting bar codes on each apple at my shop would be the best solution.' Do you agree? Why or why not?
9. What additional functionality would be required for selling medicines?
10. What functionality you will seek from your EPOS, while implementing it at your massage parlour?

1. 'Different retailing businesses have different nuances.' Explain this statement in the light of three types of retailers.

1. Go to your nearest computerized apparel or footwear store and find out the system it uses to bar code and bill its products. Make a detailed study report.

SELECT REFERENCES

Bitner, Mary Jo 1992, 'The Impact of Physical Surrounding on Customers and Employees', *The Journal of Marketing*.

Zeithaml, Valarie A. and Mary Jo Bitner 2006, *Services Marketing, Integrating Customer Focus Across the Firm*, Tata McGraw-Hill, New Delhi.

CASE STUDY

Studio Apparels: Garments Fitting All

Company   Studio Apparels Pvt Ltd

Studio Apparels was launched by Mr Manu Mehra, after completing his study of fashion designing. His father was already running a men's boutique on Ajmal Khan Road in Karol Bagh, New Delhi, since his early days. Senior Mehra used to make high-quality clothes for men. He had a tailor sitting in the makeshift mezzanine floor for stitching clothes for his regular customers who were very loyal to his brand of clothes. His clientele increased .tremendously from friends and acquaintances to high-flying business executives to fat belly politicians. Mr Manu Mehra closely watched his father moderately progressing in his business, but it aroused an interest in him. He pursued studies in fashion just as soon as his schooling was over. Manu observed the business for two years, understood nuances of running a fashion business, and also tried to understand the changing tastes and preferences of his customers.

Manu drew a blueprint for his success. The organized retail boom was just taking shape in India. He visualized opening a few master stores of his own in and around Delhi. These retail outlets were supposed to act as quality centres for their brand of clothing. The next stage was creating a large pool of franchisee business. He targeted sub-metropolitan cities, State capitals and tier two and tier three cities in the country for reaching out to people through the franchisee model of business.

On the format of organized retailing, Manu created his company 'Studio Apparels Pvt Ltd', in which he had an equity of 90 per cent, 8 per cent was owned by his father, and 2 per cent by his fiancée, who later graduated to become his wife. Along with creation of the company, Manu launched his brand ' *Studio99'*. He opened seven retail outlets owned by his company and planned for 199 stores on a franchisee business model. By December 2005, his seven stores were up and running and generating enough revenue to sustain long-term growth.

In January 2007, Manu started work on his franchisee business model. He put up advertising in local newspapers in each State and rushed his team members to finalize the franchisee agreements with prospective resellers. Between January and March, fifty franchisees were finalized and agreements signed. He had already created a vast production capacity at his Gurgaon-based manufacturing unit. It could produce more than Manu could sell through his seven stores. He planned to utilize his spare production to meet the requirement of the franchisee. The logistics were upgraded and so was the production capacity, keeping in view immediate supplies to fifty odd retailers and future retailers that were to sign agreement with him. The opening of franchisee outlets was finalized on April 13, 2007. The dates of opening were decided and circulated to the concerned groups and managers. The schedule was fantastic and ambitious! Fifty stores in 99 days! And 199 stores by September 9, 2009.

Industry   Garments Retail Chain

Solution Area   Automation of retail stores and warehouses

The Requirement

The plan was quite ambitious but interesting. The next important job was to handle the sales at franchisee level, goods dispatches, warehouse inventory management, and revenue reporting and collection on a regular basis. To achieve this, proper automation of franchisee point of sales, bar coding, stock maintenance at a central distribution warehouse, data receiving and sending through various online or offline media, consolidation of data, and reporting were the top-most priorities. Just dispatch of goods and believing on sales figures reported by individual retailers was not enough. Studio Apparel required the most robust and secure but highly flexible and easy applications to run at both franchisee and central offices.

The Solution

Manu looked for a right piece of EPOS software for franchisees and enterprise solution for his central office and distribution warehouse. He received technical and financial bids from a dozen odd national and international solution providers. The international ERPs was costly in terms of product price, licensing, and implementation costs, but the domestic players were not so trust-worthy as far as quality of the software and number of installations were concerned. He had to work on a trade off between high costs of foreign ERPs and the risk of buying faulty software. But risks of failures are attached with both the software.

Manu zeroed in on a local solution provider BNG Infotech. BNG has a reasonably small set-up but a proven track record of implementing its EPOS and ERP solutions at various garment retailers. The negotiated price was also quite low and could in no way burn a hole in Manu's pocket. Studio Apparels signed an agreement with BNG Infotech for fifty EPOS licences, warehouse management, and corporate office ERP. The POS software was to be installed at each retailer's outlet and two days' training at the site was a part of the contract. (The agreement with franchisees provided that the EPOS infrastructure would be offered by Studio Apparels against the security deposits of the franchisees.)

BNF Infotech was given a schedule of opening of stores in each city. BNG received the schedule on March 25. The company had just only half a month to do all its preparation and chalk out the schedule of implementation, changes, workforce arrangement, and deployment.

Implementation

The first and foremost task for BNG technocrats was to look at the coding structure of product, deciding on product classification, deciding on bar code types and symbologies, connectivity medium between HO, warehouse and franchisees, electronic data interchange standards, troubleshooting, and support mechanism for stores at interiors and remote areas.

The coding pattern was redesigned. The basic code of product was reduced to a ten-digit code incorporating product, major group, design and fabric used. It also had season and year of introduction on it. Dual coding pattern of item code plus bar code was introduced. Earlier, the company was creating bar codes for the products that were being dispatched to stores. There was no accounting of inventory at the warehouse. Bar code labelling was started at the originating point. The moment goods entered the warehouse from the manufacturing plant, they were bar coded. This system streamlined the dispatch processes. On receipt of dispatch advice, the store employees scanned each individual item and created delivery notes.

Most of the functions at Studio Apparel were supported by the BNG Retail ERP, but still some functions were modified to suit the requirements and initial data conversion. One such utility was created to accommodate the pre-existing fourteen-digit product code numbers. The utility facilitated automatic capturing of item groups, classification, and attributes on entering the product code in the code field. This utility saved a lot of time in filling up the item creation form, which needed data entry in approximately thirty to forty columns.

The second important activity after bar coding was implementation at franchisee stores. BNG deployed three engineers for outstation installation, set-up, and training. One or two days before the opening were enough. The remote support was provided through a utility like PC-anywhere.

Fifty stores were opened and installation completed within the targeted time of ninety days. There now remained the complex task of data transmission from stores to HO, which was required for consolidation and management information reporting. Initially, this was done through offline method where the data was created by the franchisee manually through a utility within the POS software and sent to principal company HO as an e-mail attachment. Later, it was found that some of the franchisees were reluctant to send their sales data. And, there were variations between actual sales and reported sales over the telephone. To solve this problem, a web interface was created. In the new system, the franchisees' POS created the EDI file on day's close and synchronized the data on the web server. The HO server, connected with the web server downloaded the data on predefined intervals.

Questions:

1. What changes were required to make the already-available apparel system compatible with the Studio Apparels' requirements?
2. Do you see any discrepancy in the product coding system already used by Studio Apparels for its stores?

Source: Based on the author's experience while implementing retail automation systems with various organizations and interaction with retail and management experts.

10 Enterprise Resource Planning (ERP)

Learning Objectives

- To get acquainted with enterprise systems
- To understand various advantages and disadvantages of ERP systems
- To appreciate challenges of ERP systems
- To identify core areas of ERP systems
- To define implementation processes, strategies, and methodologies

ERP keeps Coop in good health

Switzerland's second largest retailer, Coop, believes in 'big solutions, better solutions' approach. Coop plans to implement SAP on a Sun Microsystems platform over an Oracle database. The retail giant compares SAP to a Swiss Army knife, with many useful and compact features built into one. For Coop, the best-of-breed approach is more like a tradesman's toolbox—very heavy but unsure of availability of the right tool.

Coop manages its supply chain, inventory, and customers with SAP applications. Coop warns against deploying solutions from multiple vendors. It is because of 'passing the buck' syndrome. When problems occur, time is often lost when interdependent partners pass the problem between them in order to apportion blame and cost, without actually resolving the issue. Thus, the ultimate sufferer is the retailer.

In the previous chapter, we have learned the nuances of retail trade and how the unique requirements are met with technological advancements. Besides solutions for the retail point of sales, larger solutions are required to meet the needs of entire organization. The integrated solutions used across large organizations are called enterprise solutions. In this chapter, we will understand enterprise solutions and learn how these solutions are implemented across the enterprise.

When the organizations are small, they use general applications for keeping records and maintaining documents in word processors, spreadsheets. But with growing needs, they build mission-critical applications for individual process or department, such as billing, stock control, and excise department. The time comes when these segregated applications do not serve the complete purpose. Therefore, larger and integrated systems are built to cover the organizational needs.

ENTERPRISE SYSTEMS

Large organizations usually have a number of software applications for different functional areas of business because as the organization grows, it keeps adding various information systems. Since all these applications are developed over a period of time and in piece-meal manner, they do not 'talk' to each other. This leads to duplicity of data and inconsistency in reports. To solve this problem, organizations build *enterprise systems* to provide companywide integration. The enterprise systems are based on a single platform, compatible databases, and computer systems. Supply chain management (SCM) and enterprise resource planning (ERP) are examples of enterprise systems. Laudon and Laudon (2002) defines ERP as 'firm wide information system that integrates key business processes so that information can flow freely between different parts of the firm'. The information that was previously fragmented in different systems can seamlessly flow throughout the organization such that it can be shared by business processes in procurement, manufacturing, sales, distribution, accounting, and human resource.

Thus, ERP involves the following activities:

- It integrates various processes in the organization and provides consistency throughout the value chain.
- It provides opportunity to implemented processes that are the best practices in the industry.
- It works on consistent and unified data model for the entire enterprise. Unified data model is a single database or set of databases that are communicating with each other in terms of data exchange.
- It integrates key business processes into single application software, for example, the distribution module takes care of customer order processing, dispatches, and billing and delivery management that are critical business processes.

ADVANTAGES AND CHALLENGES OF ERP SYSTEMS

While ERP systems (Fig. 10.1) integrate diverse business processes and provide consistent reporting, they are also difficult to implement and as such pose challenges.

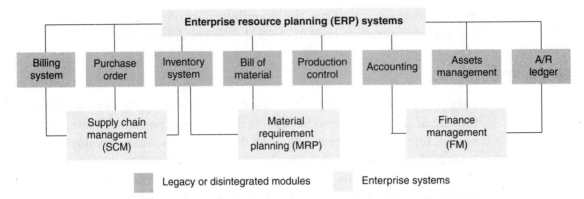

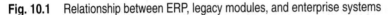

Fig. 10.1 Relationship between ERP, legacy modules, and enterprise systems

Advantages of ERP Systems

Advantages of ERP systems are enormous. ERP not only places the whole of information system on a single compatible platform, but also brings in efficiency and effectiveness in the management of the organization. This helps in changing and re-engineering age-old rotten systems.

Uniform Organizational Structure

The ERP systems help in creating and maintaining uniform organizational structures, systems, and procedures throughout the geographical area. Uniform organizational culture refers to type of system in which everyone uses similar processes and informatics, for example, Samsung uses similar systems, procedures, and documents for purchases throughout the world. Similarly, Coca-Cola uses similar distribution processes throughout the globe.

Unified Single Platform and Information Architecture

The ERP systems are built and operated on a single platform. As the organization upgrades itself, it shuns multiple platforms, for example, Marks and Spencer use the same application on Windows platform in all of their offices. ERP systems work around a single unified architecture, which helps organizations to form common and standardized definitions and formats that are accepted by the whole organization. They work on a single integrated repository or database for key business processes.

Change Agent

At times, organizations want to get rid of old, lethargic, paper-friendly systems and introduce newer and more efficient systems that go with the times. But they find it very difficult to introduce such modern systems. ERP systems work as catalysts to re-engineer the work processes within the organization. Implementation of ERP systems work as a change agent and bring in more efficient systems and operations.

Improved Management Reporting and Decision-making

The ERP systems not only automate key transaction processes like purchases, sales, marketing, and production but also improve management reporting and decision-making. Critical reports are structured around cross-functional business processes. *Cross-functional business processes* are organizational functions that are scattered over more than one business process, for example, supply chain involves purchase systems on one hand and inventory and distribution on the other. If management wants to analyse report which covers the entire supply-chain, it refers to such reporting system. Systems also generate periodical reports for quick decision-making.

Efficient Operations

The ERP systems help create customer-driven and vendor-oriented work culture. Modern organizations work on customers' demands. Since ERP systems are built around the best business practices, they help organizations to adapt to such changes. By integrating discrete business processes, such as sales, finance, production, and logistics, the entire organization can efficiently respond to customer requests for production. Modern management concepts, such as zero inventory, just-in-time inventory, and zero budgeting, are introduced to make the organization efficient.

Link with the Outside World

The ERP systems not only smoothen and streamline internal operations but also connect with the outside world, such as customers and vendors, which may have access to the relevant part of the system. The system may be designed to create an automatic purchase order on a vendor. The vendor receives the orders instantly as the stock goes below the reorder level at the warehouse and proactively processes the dispatches. The customer (retailer) knows in advance what is on the way.

Challenges of Using ERP Systems

Although enterprise systems improve organizational coordination, efficiency, and decision-making, they prove to be very difficult to build. They require not only large investment on technologies, but force fundamental changes in the way the business operates. The ERP systems require complex software and large investments of time, money, and expertise.

Daunting Implementation

Implementation is the toughest part of ERP systems. This not only requires changes in the current system but a deep understanding and analysis of the existing business processes of the company. Failure to understand a critical business process may lead to faulty implementation and hence, the organization is not able to reap the benefits of its investments. While a smaller organization can implement an ERP system in twelve to eighteen months, it may take a large corporate from three to five years to implement it fully. If the company loses confidence and patience, it will not be able to achieve a higher level of functional and business process integration.

High Upfront Costs

Enterprise systems are very costly. There are large upfront costs that are highly visible. (Upfront costs are direct costs paid to the vendor for licences and implementation.) The costs are not just in terms of price of application software but also towards database management systems, operating systems, third party tools, high-end servers, and networking equipment. Sometimes it is difficult to justify the investments as the benefits are not quantifiable in the beginning.

No Immediate Benefits

The ERP system takes a long time in implementation and the benefits start coming even longer after that. Initially, due to process changes and introduction of new processes, the disadvantages are more prominent than the advantages. Once the system stabilizes and there is wide acceptance of the new processes and procedures, the benefits (qualitative as well as quantitative) start surfacing.

Resistance to Change

'Resistance to change' is a rule rather than an exception. This is more so because of dramatic changes in the processes or introduction of new processes. This resistance is not only from employees but could also be from customers and suppliers as well, who may have to go through additional processes or documentation. For instance, a customer may not like a mandatory process of 'order confirmation', which involves filling in another form of sales.

Inflexibility

The ERP systems are complex because of the thousands of business rules and the logic defined therein. It is difficult to master ERP in all systems and modules. Since the business rules and logic pertaining to different functional modules are intertwined, a change in one place will affect logic at other places. There is a possibility of rewriting the whole system again for a major change. ERP systems are complex to modify as compared to a legacy system in which a particular piece of software can be changed easily by the creator. This is precisely the reason why technologists pay more attention to understanding system and analysis.

CORE AREAS OF ERP

We have determined the core components of POS software that are essential, whether it is a one-off store or chain of stores. We discuss the following functions as core components of ERP, which are not essential for a single store but are required in a retail chain set-up.

Merchandising

Purchase orders, request for quotation, vendor evaluation, goods receipt, and product planning are parts of merchandise management system (MMS). A purchase order feature enables merchandisers to communicate to vendors for supply of goods. An MMS requires the ability to order and receive goods. The best-of-breed system at POS, which is integrated with back-office MMS, needs an ability to receive goods against the orders generated by the merchandising system. The PO module in an MMS offers various functionalities, such as different types of POs, automatic POs, and multiple discount features.

Pricing

The price change feature is used to manage the retail (selling) price of goods. This feature can offer tools for lowering or raising the retail price. A POS price change component allows permanent or temporary markdowns and mark-ups. The price change module included in retail offers multiple pricing capabilities, markdown and mark-up, price change at location, department, class, and vendor levels. Due to the awareness among customers, prices on products must be equitable, they cannot be higher than the competitor but cannot be lower than the cost. However, markdowns are allowed for products that are less in use. The pricing feature keeps a track of price changes and can provide management an insight into the price fluctuations and their impact on the sales.

Distribution

Distribution refers to dispatch of goods from central warehouse to various retail outlets for sales. The logistics of goods received at the central warehouse of a retail chain is managed through distribution module provided by the ERP. This covers acknowledgement of requirements of various stores, consolidation of purchase requisitions and dispatch of material as demanded by each store. Advanced features include automatic sales forecasting and planning. The system enables management to see through data as what to dispatch to the stores.

Finance

The financial component is not considered a core element of stand-alone POS system. However, the POS software should have the means to communicate with third-party standards. Also, popular financial systems (such as Sage, QuickBooks, and Tally POS software) must also communicate with back-office ERP systems (such as SAP, Oracle Financial, and Baan). Finance management is an integral part of ERP systems used for retail chains. This component includes general ledger, cash management, accounts receivables, payables, budgeting, costing, profit and loss, balance sheet reports, fixed assets, and reporting tools. Taxation and VAT reporting are also parts of finance system. The module at the centre or corporate office has the ability to manage taxation at various levels of sale. Usually, VAT varies from regional, state, or country level, depending on various government regulatory authorities. The systems should provide flexibility to create and manage different tax rates for some of different products.

Data Analysis

The central module of ERP is capable of receiving from and dispensing data to various retail outlets and warehouses and provides facilities to consolidate data pertaining to the outlets. Various data analysis tools, such as online analytical processing (OLAP), online transaction processing tools, and data warehousing (already discussed in Chapter 4), are used to further consolidate and analyse the data of retail transactions.

Besides these core functions, ERP systems can also have modules like human resource, payroll, and customer relationship building. But here we have discussed only the core functions related to retail ERP (Fig. 10.2). The ERP systems do come with dozens of other function modules in manufacturing set-up.

IMPLEMENTING ERP SYSTEMS

Implementation of ERP systems involves evaluating various options and products, deciding on various strategies, defining objectives, setting targets

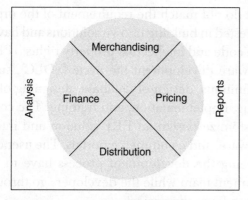

Fig. 10.2 Core areas of retail ERP

and benchmarks, and choosing right implementation methodology. As we have discussed earlier, implementing ERP is a daunting task and involves risks of failure and, therefore, utmost care should be taken in deciding course of action.

Evaluating Options

What are the various options available with an organization?

As a student of information system or a manager deciding on implementing solutions for an organization, you may think of either getting a system developed by commissioning a consultant or setting up your own IT department for in-house development. You can also think of going for a rental model, i.e. a third vendor (known as ASP), that lends you a system through the Net. You pay as per your usage. Yet another option that is available with you is to go for a tried, tested, and trusted ERP, which is being used by a host of companies, including your competitors. It will be a difficult task to decide on the right strategy. It is imperative to choose the best out of various options available. The budget, scope of usage, and availability of in-house skills will dictate your choice. We discuss here the following three options with their advantages and disadvantages in brief:

- Custom-built development
- ASP model
- Standard ERP solution suites

Custom-built Development

Custom-built or bespoke development refers to constructing a software solution from scratch. Custom-built development is done if the existing software solutions in the market do not match the requirement of the organization, or the organization is interested in building its own solutions and having complete control over the source code and intellectual property rights (IPR). It involves all the stages of a software development life cycle (SDLC), such as system study, requirement definitions, design of database, designing of graphic user interface, coding, testing, implementation, and training. The consultants and software specialists customize/design an ERP solution and integrate it with existing hardware, software, and e-commerce portals. The user organization's representatives overseeing the development process have to be closely in touch with the development team while the developers go through all SDLC processes and finally handover the project.

The advantage of custom-built development is that the systems are designed and developed as per the requirements of the company. There is less resistance to change, as the employees are involved from the beginning of the project. The transfer of knowledge is smooth, as employees are aware of their internal business processes. There is complete control over the software package thus built by the organization. But the costs are enormous because of high cost of development staff, such as programmers, system analysts, front-end designers, database designers, trainers, and others. Besides the costs, custom-built development carries risks of failure because of exit of key employees in the development team. The in-house development provides the solutions that are not functionally rich, as they cater to only the immediate requirements of the company. They hardly see beyond a certain horizon.

ASP Model

The ASP in the context of ERP refers to application service provider. An ASP is a third-party specialist who owns and manages applications and application servers and 'rents' the specialized software package and also provides a secure, Internet-based link to your system. They provide consultancy and manage the entire show from the back end. The application and the database reside in ASP server; the organization gets functions and reports as required and paid for. With the invention, popularity, and viability of Internet, ASP is only becoming available and getting acceptance worldwide. The ASP can host and integrate EDI system and deal with any technical problems. The organization seeking ASP services only need to run the system in its hardware network (probably through a browser like Internet Explorer) and a broadband connection between the ASP server and the organization's network.

The ASP model saves on hiring costly experts to manage the system and small upfront costs, as it is paid on per use basis. The biggest advantages are lower initial investments and flexibility to discontinue if the system does not seem to meet the requirements. This incurs only small losses to the organization.

But the million-dollar question is: Are you willing to trust valuable data to a third party such as an ASP? How will you determine quality of service levels?

Standard ERP Solution Suites

Standard ERP solution suites are 'tested', 'tried', and 'trusted' solutions available in the market. Let us call them 3T ERP solutions. Looking the disadvantages of the two options discussed earlier, ready-made ERP solutions are the best bet. Insufficient Internet bandwidth availability and poor security aspects over the Net make the ASP choice infeasible. High costs of development, high risks of a bad and incomplete solution, high maintenance costs, make the choice of going for custom-built development, non-workable. Though implementing international ERPs is a daunting task, yet a high degree of assurance of successful implementation and conforming to best business practices of the industry make obvious choice in favour of this option. There are scores of good-quality international and domestic ERPs available. SAP, Oracle Apps, Baan, JDA, Retek, Dynamic, JD Adwards, PeopleSoft, FNS, and Sage Accpac are some of the best international enterprise solutions. Figure 10.3 shows ERP modules in SAP. We do have hundreds of ERP solutions grown and matured in the domestic market, but only some of them have a pan-India presence. Some of the Indian ERP systems are Ramco, Finnacle (banking), MakESS, eBizFrame, SifyForum, Genesis, Vishesh, Revive, BNG Business Suites, and Nuton.

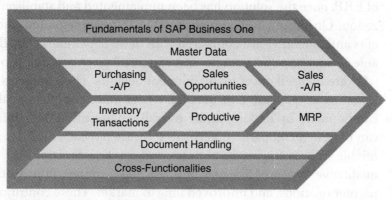

Fig. 10.3 Modules of ERP in SAP

Source: SAP Training Slides

Notwithstanding the type or name of the ERP, the methodology of implementation is the same for all. Henceforth, we will be discussing only the ready-made products and how they can be implemented successfully.

DEFINING STRATEGIES

Implementation strategies involve preparing the organization to take up the task, budgeting and resource development, setting objectives and benchmarks, deciding on the path (where to start from), and so on. All these tasks are interwoven with implementation stages throughout the life cycle of implementation process.

Setting Objectives

The ERP implementation is always preceded by setting up of clear objectives about the organization's aims and targets. In the first place, broader objectives are decided, which are further divided into smaller and measurable objectives. Some objectives are given below:

- Improve stock control
- Integrate sales information with your other business processes
- Aggregate sales from a bricks and mortar store with an online Web store
- Capture and analyse more sales data
- Work more closely with partners

Defining Key Performance Indicators

Key performance indicators (KPI) are the benchmarks for testing the success of ERP, once the solution has been implemented and stabilized in the organization. On successful completion of ERP implementation, the accrued benefits and outcomes are compared with these benchmarks. By doing so, one is able to measure the volume and extent of success of the project. The ERP software by itself offers many inherent benefits. These benefits can be further classified as qualitative or quantitative. A more complete analysis of returns can be made by looking at the overall payback that the enterprise software can offer to a company. Enterprise software payback includes not only quantifiable improvements in bottom- and top-line functionality but also more qualitative measures like new business opportunities, improved customer and partner relations, and improved time to market. These contribute significantly to the success of a company's enterprise software implementation and use.

Quantifying Key Performance Indicators

The benefits in quantity terms are easy to measure and monitor. Therefore, quantify (to the extent possible) the benefits of more efficient transaction processing and unified data model. The KPI objective datasheet should have information as given in the sample data below:

1. Increase turnover from Rs _____ million to Rs _____ million.
2. Reduce inventory from Rs _____ thousand to Rs _____ thousand.
3. Reduce inventory-carrying cost from Rs _____ thousand to Rs _____ thousand.
4. Reduce order delivery average time from _____ days to _____ days.
5. Reduce rejections at shop floor from _____ to _____ pieces per month.
6. Increase efficiency in billing. Reduce average time taken by one POS to make a bill presently _____ seconds to proposed _____ seconds.
7. Reduce complaint handling time from _____ hours per complaint to _____ per complaint.
8. Reduce employees' absenteeism from _____ person-days per week to _____ person-days per week.

The ERP, other than the day-to-day business transaction, is also aligned to perform and measure these initiatives to give the necessary feedback to the business.

Mustering Support for ERP Implementation

Create a politically conducive environment. The ERP implementation endeavour must be supported by the key employees and stakeholders in the organization. It needs to be understood that ERP is not a driver but is an enabler to business. All expected benefits cannot be achieved unless business owners are committed to it. The KPIs must be identified and the targets must be decided and agreed upon by all process owners. Necessary business initiatives must be in place to achieve these targets.

Committing Resources

All things said and done, nothing moves without enough money and power. These organizational resources are budgets for buying new systems, hardware, software, and databases. Resources in terms of critical time of key personnel, time of data creators, and testers in the organization is very important. As per one estimate, 40 per cent of the projects fail because of insufficient system study. The consultants cannot understand organizational processes if they are not given enough time by internal people. Thus, the gap between the facts and the analysts' perception of the processes leads to faulty solution delivery. The implementation process has to be closely monitored and guided by the taskforce created for the purpose. The task force should have representatives from all groups of stakeholders.

ERP IMPLEMENTATION: METHODOLOGIES AND APPROACHES

Methodologies

Deciding on a right methodology (a tried-and-tested road map to perform a task) for ERP implementation is crucial. Knowing what to do at each step is important; even more important is what follows so that it can be planned. A methodology usually makes the difference between success and failure. It chalks out implementation sequence that best fits an organization and helps in creating a project plan, tracking project progress, monitoring deliverables, and estimating resource requirements.

Most methodologies come with a set of tools that make the implementation easier, such as tools for project planning, documentation, and status reporting. Recent methodologies use 'templates' and sample deliverables field-tested at other implementation site in the same industry sector. These methods cut down a lot of implementation time and cost.

A methodology divides the entire implementation project into smaller and more manageable groups of activities. The best methodology encompasses all the components that go on to provide a complete business solution, rather than merely implementing a software package. It incorporates the following five tracks, which run throughout the implementation life cycle:

- Business process analysis
- Change management
- Infrastructure development
- Customization and localization
- Project management

Approaches

While creating a blueprint for ERP implementation, strategies and approaches are decided well in advance. Implementation approach encompasses the sequence in which the ERP package is implemented and rolled out to various business units. The following are the most popular choices an organization can make.

Big Bang Approach

Big bang approach believes in 'do everything in one shot'. In this approach, all modules of ERP software are implemented at one go across all functional departments and business units of the company. This kind of approach has its own positives and negatives. The plus point is that it offers an integrated platform for all departments and all the holes are plugged at once. But taking up all the departments in one go requires a lot of coordination, human resources, and will. It is very risky, as failure in one department may lead to failure in another, or at least the stakeholders may loose confidence.

Pilot Approach

To overcome the negatives of the big bang approach, organizations tread with caution. A pilot approach is one in which all modules are implemented across some key department or business unit. Once the implementation is successful, it is rolled out in the entire organization. It saves on specialized resources, as the organization can use this expertise in further implementation.

Phased Approach

Phased approach is followed when the implementation is done in phases. This is done as per the modules of the package. One module is taken up at a time. For example, marketing module is followed by sales and distribution module. The modular approach is more helpful as it covers both pilot and big bang approach. It takes up one module at a time and takes the entire chain of users who are involved in this process. For instance, while implementing marketing module, it will involve the front salespeople, the customer relationship people, and the managers up on the hierarchy.

Business Model Approach

This is a rather recent trend and is a combination of big bang and pilot approaches. In this system of implementation, a global prototype is developed, followed by a geographical rollout across all business units. In this implementation strategy, one business unit is taken up first. Usually, strategists take up the unit that is relatively easy, forthcoming and where the business processes are relatively systematic. Easy and simple units offer less resistance, lower risks, and costs, thus ensuring ERP acceptance and success. The first successful project gives confidence to both the implementers and the organization.

IMPLEMENTATION STAGES

Before we discuss implementation stages, it must be made clear that an ERP software package comes with standardized functionality. The term *customization* in ERP parlance refers to configuration of the system. The basic source code is not modified. The implementing organization is expected to configure the package to suit its business processes. Configuration is done with the help of consultants or the implementing team. The team achieves this by entering and defining parameters in the relevant forms provided by the ERP systems. Thus, the implementation is confined to understanding users requirements, analysing them and mapping them against the functionalities available in the ERP, making those changes in the configuration file and finally training the users.

Chakraborty (1998) divides entire implementation life cycle into four sections of activities (Fig. 10.4):

- Analysis
- Design
- Construction
- Implementation

Analysis

Analysis involves study, identification, and documentation of business requirements and chalking out project work plan. It aligns the project with the long-term strategic goals of the enterprise. The aim of this exercise is to arrive at a set of critical success factors. The existing business process of the organization is studied and documented. Simultaneously, an evaluation of the existing technical infrastructure of the company is carried out.

Analysis is done by the most experienced team members, who possess vast functional knowledge of the business processes. This is followed by 'gap

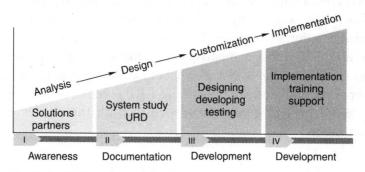

Fig. 10.4 ERP Implementation life cycles

analyses', which involves mapping of the existing business processes with the software functionality and the best practices in the industry. The aim is to devise an optimum process that supports the software and at the same time conforms to the best business practices. At this juncture, the functional team should also map the envisioned processes to the package features and come out with gaps, special reports, forms, or interfaces with the existing system. While deciding on these changes, it must be kept in mind that you cannot change the basic way in which the package is structured. Customization of code, i.e. changing the source code as per the customer requirements, is not possible. Indiscriminate customization can lead to system failure or at least a system that is impossible to upgrade and maintain.

Design

Design stage starts off with the functional team developing the organizational structure. The design team develops the tree structures, such as organization's business units, offices, warehouses, and retail outlets. The ERP package is later configured through parameter setting to accommodate the organizational structure and gaps or to-be-built findings. Once the gap analysis is complete, the development team works on designing the modules that will enhance the functionalities in the package.

The gaps should be as minimal as possible; too many gaps identified at later stages are not doable and hence spoil the game. Instead of incorporating heavy structural changes, custom code design ideally should focus on the following objects:

- Custom reports to meet client-specific requirements
- Interfaces to existing legacy system that need to exchange data with the ERP system
- Data conversion routines to load historic data

Construction

In the construction phase, the programming team works on customization within the scope of the gap analysis. The team refers to the study documents created during the system study and design documents created by the design experts. Program development and testing are two important aspects of construction phase. Various types of tests are carried out. Functional, logical, load, and speed tests are carried out. The functionalities thus created are tested logically and in the light of user requirements. On-site tests are carried out on live data and changes made as per the requirements.

Implementation

Implementation mainly involves installation of application and training to end-users. The implementation stage performs the last few critical activities necessary for system live processing. This also involves on-site testing and basic training. It is imperative for the functional team to start conducting end-user training on live data. The training should be process driven, i.e. the persons should be trained only on their related parts of the ERP that figure in their daily lists of tasks. Subsequent to this, the system should be put through a detailed test on a simulated environment resembling the production environment. This shows the integration of the prototyped system and the custom-developed objects.

Finally, it involves setting up the ERP applications on individual workstations, configuring printers, and testing the connectivity. This also involves data porting, data migration, and finally signing off. *Data porting* is importing of data from other systems like legacy software to the ERP. *Data migration* refers to change of database because of change in database management software; for example, earlier the system may be using SQL database but now the new ERP system works on Oracle database.

SUMMARY

Enterprise systems are integrated systems built on single platform and unified databases. They provide integration across the divisions, units, and functions of a company. Enterprise resource planning (ERP) systems, supply chain management systems, and material requirement planning are examples of enterprise solutions. The ERP systems offer advantages like uniform organizational structures, single platform, and single architecture, change agent, improved management reporting, better decision-making, efficient operations, and they provide links with outside world like customers, suppliers, or government. Notwithstanding the advantages, there are challenges in implementing ERP systems. These challenges are daunting and the implementation process involves high upfront costs, no immediate benefits, and resistance to change and inflexibility.

The core functions of an ERP system are merchandise management, price management, distribution, finance, and advanced data analysis. The advanced data analysis is also done through analysis tools like data warehousing and online analytical data processing.

Implementing ERP involves a very structured approach. The organization has to evaluate various options available with it, such as whether to go for a custom-built (bespoke) development or an ASP model (rent-a-software), or simply buy standard ERP software. The organization decides based on its requirements and budgetary provisions. Great organizational preparedness is required for implementing ERP. This involves setting up objectives and defining benchmarks in terms of key performance indicators (KPIs), which need to be defined in quantitative terms that are easily measurable after the system has started giving results. Notwithstanding the benefits and budgets, the ERP implementation fails if there is no internal and external support to it. Sufficient resource commitment, in terms of money, workforce, and time, is necessary to make ERP implementation a success. Also, the organization should follow a well-defined and well-structured implementation methodology. Various approaches of implementation are big bang, pilot, phased, and business model. Again, what is chosen by the organization depends on the individual needs of the organization.

The entire implementation process is divided into four stages, viz. analysis, design, construction, and implementation. The analysis involves understanding the needs of the organization. The design refers to creating organizational structure, data structures, and process designs based on analysis. The construction involves customization of application as per the gap analysis findings and design documents as well as testing. Finally, the implementation is installation of applications on servers and workstations, live testing, and training to end-users.

CONCEPT REVIEW QUESTIONS

1. What do you understand by ERP?
2. What are the advantages of enterprise solutions?
3. Are there any challenges involved in implementing enterprise solutions?
4. You want to automate your large retail chain. What are the various options available with you?
5. What kind of organizational preparedness is required while implementing ERP systems?
6. Discuss various ERP implementation strategies.
7. Explain important ERP implementation approaches.
8. What strategies will you use while implementing ERP systems?
9. What are the four stages of ERP implementation?
10. What does 'analysis' mean while preparing for ERP implementation?

CRITICAL THINKING QUESTION

1. What do you think of most Indian retail chains, whether they may like to go for custom-built development, ASP model, or standard ERP system? Justify your answer with suitable reasons, facts, and figures.

PROJECT

1. Search for a retail chain in your city that has already implemented an ERP and find out the processes this organization used. Do you find any deviation from what you studied and the actual practice adopted by the organization?

SELECT REFERENCES

Chakraborty, Partha 1998, *ERP Demystified*, DataQuest, December.

Kalakota, Ravi and Andrew B. 1996, Whinston *Frontiers of Electronic Commerce*, Pearson Education.

Laudon, Ken and Mary Laudon 2002, *Management Information System*, Pearson Education (Singapore).

Reynolds, Jonathan, Christine Cuthbertson, and Richard Bell 2004, *Retail Strategy: The View from the Bridge*, Elsevier Butterworth-Heinemann.

Training Slides, www.sap.com, last accessed in December 2007.

CASE STUDY

ERP Success Stories: Making ROI Happen

Information technology systems are enabler of business processes. A perfect synergy between IT systems and business processes is considered the ideal technology investment. Any investment in technology can only be justified if the user company gains significant benefits from its overall business. After all, what is the purpose of IT investment if it fails to bring in improvement and desired results? Investment levels on ERP systems are high when compared to legacy systems and best-of-breed POS software. While deciding on an ERP, one needs to consider various aspects and plan for a 'return on investment' on the ERP to happen as planned.

When an enterprise invests a huge sum in a piece of infrastructure, it expects to recover the investment within a finite period. And in these cases, the return on investment (ROI) matter is discussed right in the beginning, when the management is approached for funds. Since ERP software is also considered an infrastructure investment, it is natural to expect financial returns.

How ROI Comes

There are no tested figures on the period of return on investments. The period varies from company to company. But a period of five to ten years is a normal period in which the company gets ROI. 'ROI does not come from ERP. ROI comes from what you do using ERP. ERP is a tool and it all depends on how well you use this tool. There are organizations that have got substantial benefits, which are many times their investment. And there are organizations that have not got the desired benefits,' said sources at Enterprise Solutions, Baan Info Systems India.

Tata Refractories had to literally start from scratch. The situation was such that the company's employees were not very familiar with the use of sophisticated IT systems. But the company wanted to stay ahead of competitors, which was impossible without the use of IT. Its managers were plagued with questions like 'will training initiatives be fruitful and will we be able to justify the investments made in IT?'. All this because the ROI could be assessed only after a certain point of time, while qualitative benefits would be experienced as soon as the company went live with the new system.

Eastern Software Systems (ESS) suggests that implementation of vertical-proven ERP can bring in fast ROI. While the horizontal solutions may fit 60–70 per cent to your business, the same percentage can be as high as 85 per cent with vertical solutions. But it will be impossible to achieve a 100 per cent fit even with vertical solutions. So, some customizations/workarounds are unavoidable even when you chose a vertical solution. The vendor's experience in a specific or related vertical is always an advantage, as the vendor would have acquired some domain knowledge and vertical processes as a part of the implementation.

How to Measure ROI

Although many people say it is difficult to measure ROI, there are tools, models, and methodologies for actually doing this. When a company seeks capital, it approves and justifies it through some means, tools, and audits. The finance department has to go back and do an audit to justify an investment. Similar benchmarks can be created and compared. Once the ERP has been implemented, there is a stabilization phase, which typically lasts between six months and a year. After that, the organization will try to calculate ROI in definite terms. But many are not able to quantify ROI on ERP for certain reasons. It is very difficult to measure the returns, given that these are not visible immediately.

One reason why organizations are not able to quantify their ROI in ERP implementation is that at the beginning of the project the KPIs (key performance indicators) and measurement criteria were not defined. Companies fail to measure the ROI as they think about it only after implementing ERP.

Companies implementing ERPs should think about improving these metrics right at the beginning. For instance if outstanding were X number of days, we planned to reduce it by 50 per cent within two years. This can be done with ERP. ERP implementation changes the existing business processes in favour of ones that are streamlined to the best ones followed in the industry. It changes the way business is done. The work profile at the end user level also changes. The productivity gains resulting from both improved processes and integration of financial, business, and transaction data are huge.

'The best thing to do is to identify the objective or purpose of ERP before implementation, and then compare the achieved benefits to those desired,' says an expert at Baan Info Systems, India. To help measure ROI, JD Edwards offers a value assessment process for setting the benchmarks and then monitoring the implementation, to work towards achieving those benchmarks and measuring them.

Apart from achieving a complete turnaround in internal processes, Tata Refractories (TR) benefited in other ways from its ERP implementation. From an organization where the use of computers was confined to a few key people, TR emerged as an organization where the entire business was driven by the use of IT. Some excellent training, change-management initiatives, and the advantage of not having to deal with legacy systems eased the whole process.

Eastern Software Systems (ESS) says that ROI from an ERP implementation is mostly qualitative in terms of a better response time to the market, improved funds and cash flows, reduced inventory levels, and more efficient utilization of existing staff. 'Quantitative measures are possible if the implementing organization has adequate historical data about the above parameters, which can be later compared to the post-ERP scenario.'

The ERP provides both qualitative and quantitative benefits. But quantitative benefits are easy to measure. The issue that people tend to think about more is on recovering the investment. The question is how does one measure the returns in rupee terms.

This is due to the fact that most ROI models are focused on quantifiable measures of return. While this is a useful and often necessary function, the focus on purely quantifiable measures leaves little room for a discussion on more qualitative success factors that are often difficult to fit into a fixed economic model. The ROI models do not necessarily apply to a large extent because a lot of these are not necessarily quantifiable.

Actual Benefits

Most of the user companies believe more about process improvements rather than financial returns. Controlling costs and speeding up order fulfilment (customer delivery) is the main focus. The key to doing this is keeping inventory levels within control and maintaining accurate information (about aspects like orders and raw materials) at all times. Here are some examples of how companies are enjoying certain tangible and intangible benefits.

Oracle India maintains that ERP has helped Kirloskar Oil Engine bring down the order registration time from 15 days to one day. At Indian Aluminium Company (INDAL), the customer resolution time was brought down by 65 days. At BOSCO, the budgeting used to take 110 days, and the company brought it down to 30 days. In the same company, the sales lead time was brought down from 60 to 15 days. The delivery time was brought down from 30 to 7 days.

In Pidilite Industries, ERP has improved customer service, reduced working capital, standardized processes, reduced inventory, and provided a centralized set up from the previous distributed model. After implementing ERP, TEI Electronics have got better control over inventory and is able to meet customer expectations. The errors in the manual system have been eliminated and the duplication of accounting has been avoided.

At Escorts Agri Machinery, because of ERP, service levels have improved tremendously across the organization. There is visibility of online data, so top management, middle managements and senior executives can all access the data. Previously this was performed in batch mode and getting updated information used to take a lot of time, and MIS reports used to be created a month late. Now you can take on-the-spot decisions. There is much better working capital management in the organization now. This was due to better visibility on the inventory, creditors, and debtors, which enabled the company to better manage cash flows.

The experience in implementing ERP at Goodlass Nerolac Paints, says that they have not really got down to calculating ROI in financial terms, but are happy to note other benefits that ERP has brought in. With ERP they can drill down to any level of detail. This helps us in setting better policies and improvement plans for the organization. We can remove inefficiencies in the organization. Due to all these changes, we were able to implement a balance scorecard. A balance scorecard is a performance benchmark used to track corporate performance.

At Tata Refractories, there was reduction in communication costs (by Rs 20 lakh per annum) since the output data relating to customers and suppliers is hosted on the Internet.

Questions:

1. 'Measurable benchmarks are key issues in success of ERP implementation.' Evaluate this statement in the light of this case study.
2. What are the key factors indicating sufficient 'return on investment' by an organization.

Sources: Brian Pereira, *Network Magazine*, Oct. 2003; case histories at www.Baan.com (Tata Refractories); e-bizframe at www.essindia.com; www.Oracle.com.

11

Retail ERP: Functions and Features

Learning Objectives

- To identify various ERP modules and enterprise systems
- To understand ERP module deployment architecture in a retail scenario
- To get acquainted with salient features of ERP systems from IT perspective
- To evaluate functions of finance and accounting management
- To comprehend functions of human resource management
- To define roles and functions of IT departments

In Chapter 10, we have learnt various types of enterprise solutions and strategies for their implementation. We have also learnt benefits of using them and the challenges in implementing these solutions. In this chapter, we will discuss various functions of an enterprise resource planning (ERP) system that caters to retail chain businesses. An integrated ERP system covers the back-office transaction systems, data analysis, and management reporting systems as well as the point-of-sales (POS) functions. The POS module is, however, connected with the back office through the database. We have already discussed the functionalities offered by any POS software in Chapter 7.

The ERP systems encompass the entire business processes and come up with any conceivable functional module. But certain processes and modules are grouped together to form enterprise systems, such as supply chain management (SCM), material requirements planning (MRP), and customer relationship management (CRM). We will study SCM and CRM separately in chapters 12 and 13 respectively. Material requirements planning (MRP), which consists of order processing, inventory, bill of material, and production planning, is a consolidated module for manufacturing processes. In the context of retail, MRP is beyond the scope of this text. The ERP modules of purchase, inventory, and distribution will be discussed along with e-procurement in the next chapter on Information Systems for Supply Chain Management.

Figure 11.1 depicts ERP and its various modules.

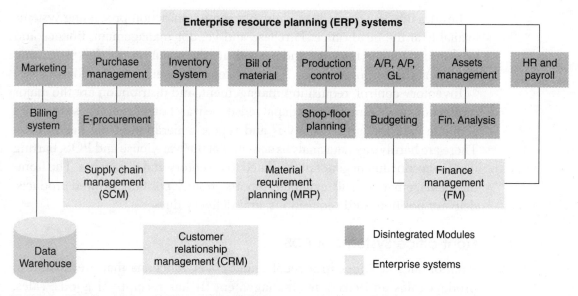

Fig. 11.1   Various modules of ERP and their contributions in building enterprise systems

ERP DEPLOYMENT ARCHITECTURE

Figure 11.2 illustrates how ERP module is deployed across the retail organization. This can be called a 'three-tier-deployment' architecture. All functional modules are deployed at the corporate office for viewing, analysing, and storing data. The main database server is placed at the head office, which is primarily used for data analysis through OLAP and data warehousing tools.

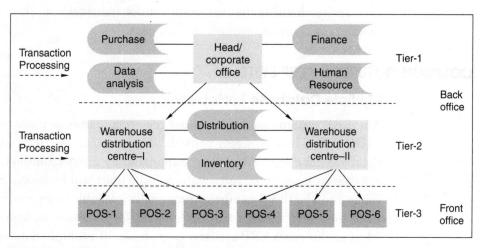

Fig. 11.2   ERP module deployment architecture

Besides the data depository, there are some transaction processing systems available at the head office. Purchase and vendor management, finance and accounting, human resource and payroll, are the major transaction processing systems at the corporate office. These systems also generate data for analysis.

Inventory control, requisition management, and distribution are the major transaction processing systems deployed at the warehouse level. These modules generate data for further analysis and report generation at the head office. There are hardly any data analysis activities at the warehouse and POS, barring day-to-day document generation related to inventory and dispatches. The front-line management usually generates reports on stock position, expired products, delivery positions and requisitions, and delivery dues.

Front-office Systems or POS

Point-of-sales activities in a retail outlet cover functions that are related to product sales and customer management. It has receipts of goods, sales, inventory, and customer relationship management. We have already discussed these functions in Chapter 7.

Back-office Systems

Back-office functions in large retail chain organizations are those that are not directly related to the customers. These functions are related to the creation and management of various transaction processing systems and reporting systems at the back office, i.e. the physical space, such as head office and warehouse of the company. Back-office system covers functional modules, such as merchandise management, vendor management, price management, distribution, human resource, and finance.

COMMON FEATURES OF ERP SYSTEMS

Multiple Database Portability

The ERP systems are built around relational database management systems (RDBMS). These systems provide the most robust, flexible, and reliable database handling and support exponentially greater transactions. They are suitable for large companies with multiple units and locations. Since there are many good RDBM systems commercially available in the market, individuals have their own choices and preferences for database management systems. Most of the good ERP systems give choice of multiple database portability. For instance, they give a choice of running your ERP system either on Oracle or on an SQL server.

Client-Server Network Architecture

The ERP systems are built on client-server technology. The solutions are designed to work both online and offline. The online versions work on any virtual private networks (VPN) created over dedicated broadband lines or public Internet. The offline systems work independently on local area network and use EDI tools for data transmission.

Electronic Data Interchange (EDI) Compatibility

The ERP systems accept major EDI protocols, send, and receive data from customers, suppliers, and other branches of the organization. In retail, EDI tools for data transmission from HO to warehouses and POS and vice versa transmit data. With this process, the day's data is converted into an encrypted structured flat file, which is e-mailed to other locations. A simple utility at the other location imports the data. The data transmission system through EDI is smooth and time-tested, and used by large number of organizations that do not wish to invest on costly networks.

Data Consolidation and Analytical Reporting

Data consolidation and analytical reporting using various tools, such as OLAP, are core features of any ERP. The system provides facility of consolidating data from various branches or POS location. The user can derive cube and matrix reports of multiple stores with multiple products in relation to sales and stocks. Sales cubes and sales matrix are multidimensional reports on sales data. Most of the ERP systems come with an extra reporting tool. The tool gives flexibility to filter data on user-defined conditions, add and remove columns from the report, and edit captions or report heading. The report writer also provides matrix reports wherever applicable.

Business Process Flow Support

Different organizations function differently, for example, some organizations may follow a centralized procurement policy. They purchase goods at a central warehouse, bar code them and then distribute to their retail outlets. Another company may allow their retail outlets to procure material locally and sell at a predefined margin. ERP systems are built to support the business flow of centralized or decentralized procurement and distribution. There can be numerous such situations that are handled by parametric setting in the ERP.

Completely Secure System

One of the major features of ERP systems is their impregnable security system. They provide multiple levels of security. The database itself is password protected and does not allow undesired opening of data tables. At the second level, databases provide constraints that do not allow bad data and duplicate data into the database. The front-end GUI also provides strong security systems. First, the package cannot be run without having a valid password. Further, the data entry and report forms are protected through button level security. Users may be restricted or given privileges to add, modify, delete, view records. They also provide company, module and menu level security. No unauthorized access to the system is possible as it is password protected.

Controllable through System Administration

System administration modules of ERP systems allow a system manager to configure and control the entire package. One can configure various modules and define business processes, manage users and security, define documents and layouts. These modules allow the system manager to create and maintain financial year, companies, and branch database creation. System administrator permits transfer of balances from one financial year to another, takes periodical backups and restoration of data, facilitates security through locking of account heads, company for specific periods for disallowing transactions. ERP systems maintain a track of changes done in the data, which is called an audit trail. Audit trail is maintained with date and time details of addition and modification of a record by the user. It allows a user to create other users and assign them passwords, rights, and privileges. Business process rules are defined in each module, allowing users flexibility and adaptability as per the business needs. System administration can define rules for data validation to ensure accuracy of data at entry level.

Transactions Authorization System

What makes ERP systems more secure, robust, and desirable is 'authorization' of transactions. The user can enter transactions in all types of transaction processing systems discussed earlier in the chapter. The ERP systems facilitate checking of data through a vouching process call 'authorization'. In general, 'authorization system' has the following characteristics:

(a) The document remains at a temporary state until it is authorized.
(b) The data is not posted to the main database server (read the database that affects the head of account).

Fig. 11.3   Probable ERP modules in a retail set-up

(c) The document is not printed unless authorized.

(d) Once authorized the data is posted to the subsequent heads of accounts.

(e) The data is available for further processing, analysis, and reporting only after the authorization.

(f) Once authorized, the document is not modifiable or editable.

In financial systems, the process of authorization pulls data and posts it into various ledgers and sub-ledgers.

Some probable ERP modules in a retail set-up are shown in Fig. 11.3. We will now discuss them in detail.

FINANCE AND ACCOUNTS (FA)

Finance is a crucial part of ERP and plays a pivotal role in any ERP system. It takes care of money (finance), men (human resource), and machines (assets) in the organization. This helps not only in management decision-making based on analysis of internal transactional data but also in strategic decision-making, which is the result of external and internal data analysis. Information systems for finance offer measurable benefits in terms of cost reductions, profit maximization, and revenue realization. The information provided by finance functions helps the management to have better control over the affairs that offer better competitive advantage and long-term business sustenance. Finance is expected to be more responsive in budgeting and forecasting, mitigating

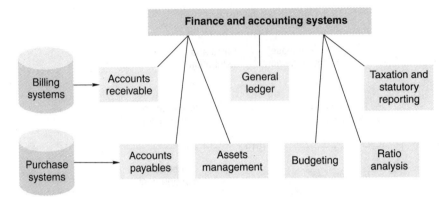

Fig. 11.4 Finance module functions in ERP

risks by managing risks and be effective by supporting the value chain. With the organizations metamorphosing from single location-single unit businesses to huge global giants, keeping track of the workforce and managing the assets is becoming a critical aspect of finance information systems.

Finance systems cover the following modules and subsystems (Fig. 11.4):

- General ledger
- Accounts payables
- Accounts receivables
- Budgeting and allocations
- Taxation and statutory reporting
- Ratio analysis
- Assets management

General Ledger

General ledger (GL) is central to the accounting system. It provides a platform for transaction entry, processing, consolidation of data pulled from various subsystems, and consolidation of data. Various reporting systems, such as ledgers, trial balance, balance sheet, and analytical reports, are generated. General ledger encompasses creation of chart of accounts, entry systems for cash, bank and journal transactions, allocations of transactions into various cost centres, and bank reconciliation. Some of the important reports and documents are ledger accounts, trial balance, profit and loss accounts, balance sheet, cost centre analysis, and expense analysis.

Chart of Accounts

Worldwide, the modern accounting systems culminate to balance sheet, which is the net result of an organization's affairs at any particular point of time in a

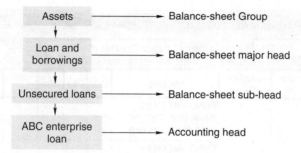

Fig. 11.5 Hierarchy in chart of accounts

year. Balance sheet heads are grouped under two major categories of assets and liabilities. At any point of time, the total assets of an organization are equal to the total liabilities. There are several heads under each of these categories. All expenses, revenues, payables, and receivables heads are maintained. Accounting modules in ERP systems provide flexibility to create heads as per the organizational needs and traditions. Figure 11.5 illustrates an example of hierarchy of such accounting heads.

Transaction Systems for General Ledger

The information system covering finance should have very comprehensive system of data capture through its transaction entry systems. Transactions related to cash, bank, and journal are primary data creators. Data for bills receivables and bills payables are pulled from the sale and purchase subsystems. This is done through an appropriately provided layout using graphic user interface in the modern ERP systems. Cash receipts, cash payments, bank receipts, bank payments, and journal forms are used to create transaction data through the system called 'vouchers', for example, cheque received from a customer on account of his outstanding bills, is entered in 'bank receipts' form. This transaction performs a series of actions in the system. It increases bank balance, reduces outstanding balance, knocks off unpaid bills, and updates various databases that help in data analysis (Fig. 11.6).

Debit and Credit Notes

These are subsidiary transactions created to support or effect a change in the main transaction. The debit and credit notes are created for respectively debiting or crediting an account (for example, a supplier, a customer, or an expense account) for a value. If, for example, the customer has returned the goods, a credit note is created for the value of goods. This process effects sales returned and customer account with the appropriate value. Similarly, changes

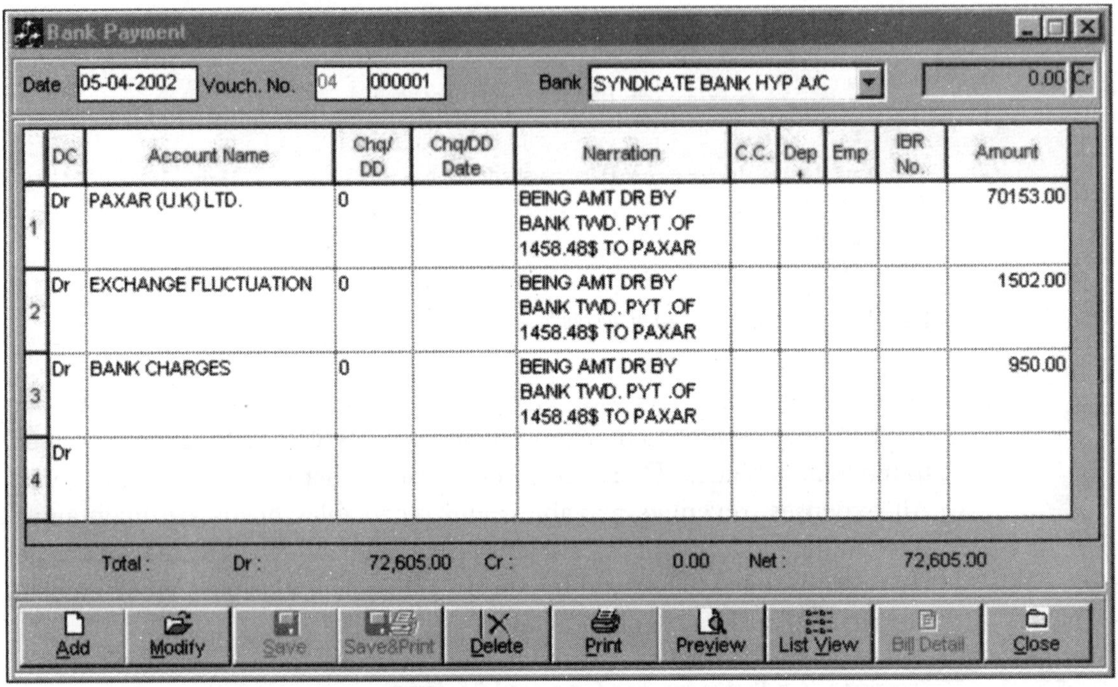

Fig. 11.6 Transaction system for bank payment

in main transaction due to rate difference, shortages, excesses, and changes in taxes by the government are effected through debit and credit notes.

Take the example of a sudden change in sales tax structure. When you signed the purchase order with your vendor, the VAT on shirts was four per cent. But suddenly the tax authorities increased the VAT on shirts from four per cent to six per cent, applicable from midnight. Your supplier abides by the law and dispatches hundred shirts applying the new six per cent VAT on the goods. The supplier's bill does not match your PO in value terms and increases by two per cent on the whole. Your ERP rules do not allow you to modify the material receipt to make it differ from the purchase order. The purchases are booked for the original purchase order value, but there is difference in your account and supplier's account. Later, the accounts system allows for creation of a credit note in favour of the supplier. In the credit note, the supplier's bill is increased by the new additional value and, at the same time, the purchase or VAT value is increased by the same amount (as per the universal accounting law, debit is always equal to credit). Figure 11.7 shows transaction system for credit note generation.

The ERP systems provide bank reconciliation features. *Bank reconciliation* refers to a system in which the bank balances are tallied with balances of the

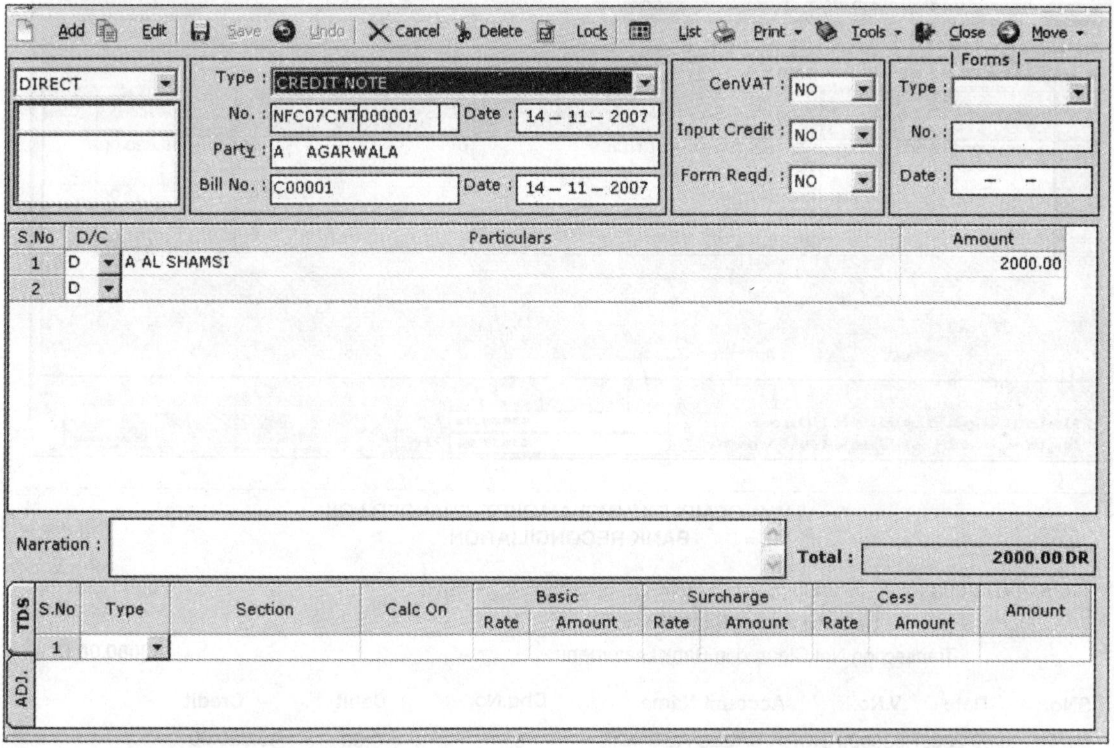

Fig. 11.7 Transaction system for credit note generation

bank in company's books of accounts. Banking is a continuous process, where cheques are deposited and amounts withdrawn by writing cheques in favour of other parties. At any point of time, there may be number of cheques that were deposited or issued but have not gone through the 'clearance' process. Clearance refers to the phenomenon of cheques deposited by value not transferred in the account wherein the cheques are deposited. Similarly, cheques may be issued which reduce our bank balance in our books of accounts but actual balance is reduced from the bank when the cheque is presented by the other party for clearance. In the bank transaction book, such transactions are called unreconciled entries. The reporting system should show true picture of affairs of the organization. For making the balances represent true picture, reconciliation report is generated by knocking off the 'cleared' cheques (Fig. 11.8).

As a control measure, ERP provides automatic reconciliation feature, wherein the user has to just enter the date of clearance for the cleared entry. If the ERP is linked with the bank's database, it can also reconcile entries and present a reconciliation report. The system helps generate a number of reports

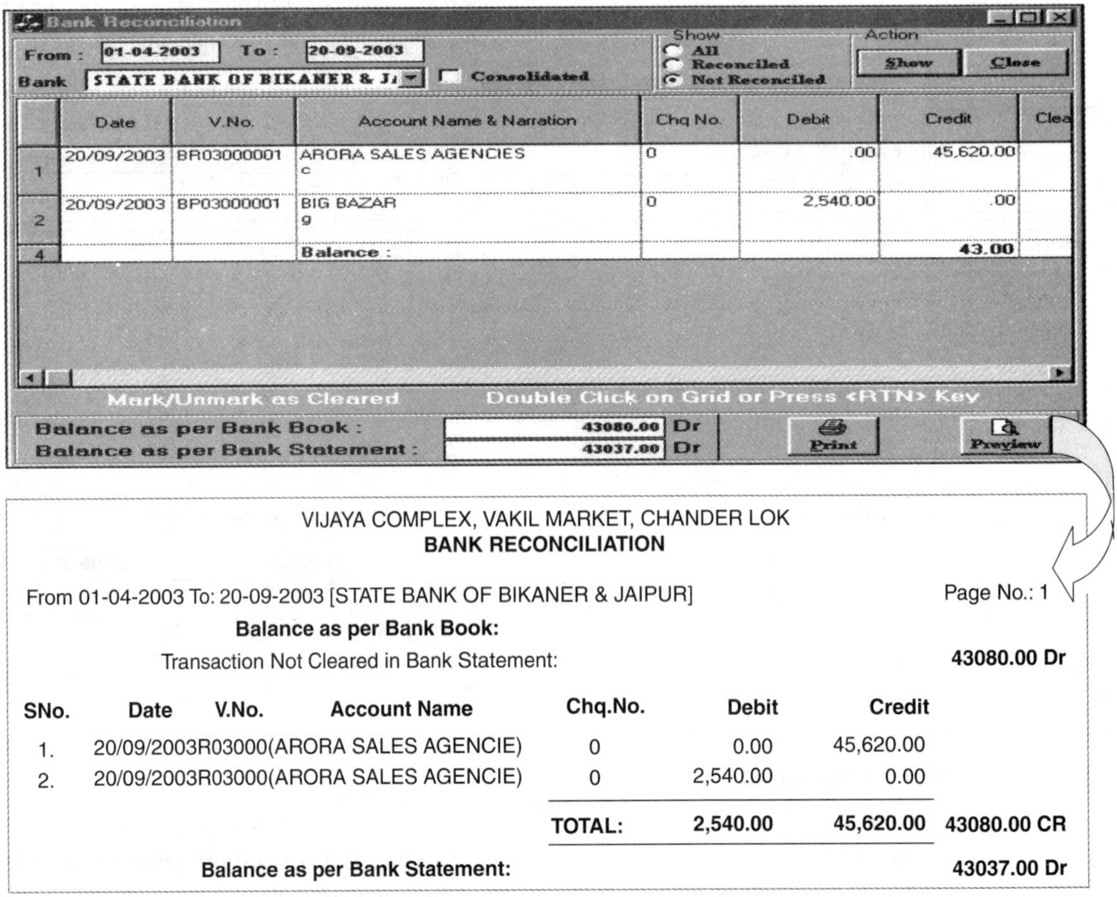

Fig. 11.8 Bank reconciliation system in ERP

related with cash and bank transactions. Accounts ledger as on any date is produced by the system. Analysis on cash and fund position of the company is created. The module creates final accounting statements, such as trial balance, profit and loss account, and balance sheet.

Pulling Data from Various Subsystem

The interface between finance module and other transactions module of ERP is provided through data integration. Most of the ERP packages follow 'push', 'pull', or combinations of both the systems of data integration. In the 'data push' system, the data is pushed into the financial system automatically at the time of creation of a transaction or through a specially designed procedure that is activated on a press of the mouse button.

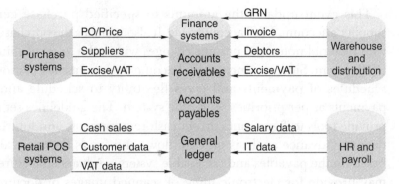

Fig. 11.9   Pulling data from various other systems

For example, when a bill is created, it updates sales database, customer database, and other heads like taxes. The activity itself pushes data into bills receivables. The data is now available to 'bills receivables' module for further processing, monitoring, and control. Therefore, no extra key is pressed or procedure is run to receive data in financial systems of bills receivables.

Most of the times, finance people in the organization want to scrutinize the data before it is posted to financial systems. For such systems, ERP provides 'data pull' procedures (Fig. 11.9). In financial systems, a process is available, which shows all the documents required to be scrutinized and the data pulled. Just on checking the data, the person can put his/her electronic seal and authorize the transaction.

Let us take an example of purchase transaction. At a warehouse, the store manager receives goods from the supplier. He checks the supplier's bill and matches it with the purchase order generated. He creates a document called material received note (MRN) or goods received note (GRN). At the warehouse, the goods have been added to stock, but no financial entries affected. The data is not posted to either suppliers account or bills payable ledger. The next step in this process is to pull the data for account system.

Accounts Payables

Recording of expenditures and obligations of payments to vendors are done in accounts payable module. Systems like 'bill passing' or 'bills approval' are given in the finance module that perform the task of pulling of data from the material module. These options in finance show material receipt notes, which are pending for data pull. Finance persons do the checking of material receipt note from an accounting perspective and authorize the supplier's bill for posting into accounts payable module.

This event updates the amounts to specified purchase general ledger, supplier's account, VAT accounts, etc. It also matches the purchase order values with material notes and permits changes within the tolerance limits set in the ERP system. Since payments also become due and a click of mouse generates schedules of payments and gives flexibility to schedule and re-schedule payments as per priorities set by the system. The guidelines set in the system provide tools to figure out current cash requirements and future expenditure outlays. Advance analysis on cash flows and funds flows are also generated based on the payables and receivable systems. Advanced features in the ERP may provide for electronic filing of scanned images of documents, such as supplier's bill, and material receipt note, and linking it with the purchase accounting document thus generated. This really paves the way for a paperless office.

Accounts payable systems involve complete processing of suppliers' bills, generation of payment schedules, pending payments to individual customers, and aging of their bills in flexible classification of days.

Accounts Receivables

Accounts receivables refer to payments pending from customers. The goods are sold to them on their unwritten promise to pay the money later. If the payment is not charged in cash or kind (like cheque or credit card) at the time of bill settlement in retail, the bill is posted as a credit bill. This money is later realized from the customer. The ERP system can work on any of the two ways, as discussed above, of data assimilation. Whatever the system, the process posts all relevant data to financial database, updating information on customer receivables, VAT, etc.

The accounts receivable systems involve complete processing of customers bills, generation of recovery plan, pending payments from individual customers, and aging of debts up to the last minute details. This helps in cash flow management of the organization that is crucial for efficiency, effectiveness, and long-term sustenance of the organization. A financially sound organization can have a competitive edge and work towards satisfying its customers and employees.

The bills outstanding are assets of the organization in the hands of customers. Accounts receivable systems help finance managers to formulate plans for the recovery of these assets and plan cash flows. The aging and recovery plan reports generated by the system help managers plan expenditures in advance (Fig. 11.10).

Particulars	0 - 30 Days Amount	31 - 45 Days Amount	46 - 60 Days Amount	61 - 90 Days Amount	91 & Above Days Amount
AMEERA	0.00 Cr	54250.00 Cr	0.00 Cr	0.00 Cr	0.00 Cr
ANAND GENERAL STORE	0.00 Cr	0.00 Cr	0.00 Cr	0.00 Cr	376.00 Cr
ASH & CO	0.00 Cr	2000.00 Cr	5618.00 Dr	0.00 Cr	1.00 Cr
BONJOUR DEPARTMENTAL STORE	0.00 Cr	0.00 Cr	0.00 Cr	0.00 Cr	1483.00 Dr
BRITE LIGHT	0.00 Cr	0.00 Cr	8000.00 Dr	0.00 Cr	0.00 Cr
D.B. ENGINEERING PRIVATE LIMITED	0.00 Cr	0.00 Cr	0.00 Cr	0.00 Cr	150000.00 Cr
DELUX FREIGHT CARRIER	0.00 Cr	0.00 Cr	0.00 Cr	0.00 Cr	1.00 Dr
DEMA DESINGS	25000.00 Cr	0.00 Cr	0.00 Cr	0.00 Cr	0.00 Cr
DIWAN SAHEB FASHIONS PVT LTD	0.00 Cr	0.00 Cr	0.00 Cr	0.00 Cr	75000.00 Dr
GREAT EASTERN IMPEX PVT LTD	0.00 Cr	0.00 Cr	0.00 Cr	0.00 Cr	3.00 Dr
GREENWAYS	15000.00 Cr	0.00 Cr	0.00 Cr	0.00 Cr	0.00 Cr
GYANS MESTROS PVT. LTD.	0.00 Cr	0.00 Cr	75000.00 Dr	0.00 Cr	15000.00 Cr
HANDLOOM EMPORIUM	1.00 Dr	0.00 Cr	0.00 Cr	0.00 Cr	0.00 Cr
IMAGES PEARL RETAIL SOLUTIONS PVT LTD	4200.00 Dr	0.00 Cr	0.00 Cr	0.00 Cr	10500.00 Dr
KADS FASHION	0.00 Cr	0.00 Cr	0.00 Cr	0.00 Cr	269473.40 Dr
KENDRIYA BHANDAR	0.00 Cr	22472.00 Dr	0.00 Cr	0.00 Cr	1142.20 Dr
KIRAN ROADWAYS	20000.00 Cr	0.00 Cr	0.00 Cr	0.00 Cr	0.00 Cr
LIBAAS	0.00 Cr	54250.00 Cr	0.00 Cr	0.00 Cr	0.00 Cr
LUXOR WRITING INSTRUMENTS PVT LTD	20000.00 Dr	0.00 Cr	0.00 Cr	0.00 Cr	0.00 Cr

Fig. 11.10   Aging of accounts receivables

Budgeting and Cost Centre Allocations

Budgets and cost centre allocations are an important part of advance financial management. The ERP systems comprehensively offer budgeting and analysis on cost centres. Budgets are permitted outlays on individual heads of expenditures. Organizations plan in advance on how much to spend on what. The figures are either set for each month and added up for the whole year or set for a year and then further broken down for each month. The budgets are set on the basis of past experience and future probable planned and unplanned expenditures. Budgeting modules help organizations to set budget and compare the actual expenditure on periodical basis. Variance analysis is provided by the module. This helps maintain expenditures within the permitted level and take remedial actions if the budgets overshoot. The reason is that if more money is spent on one type of expenditure, there will be hardly any money left for the other. The organization will not achieve its goals in the desired manner. Figure 11.11 illustrates cost centre analysis.

Cost centres are categories of expenses other than the head of account. Expenditure on one head of account can be further divided into subcategories. Cost centre can be a general classification, a department, or an employee.

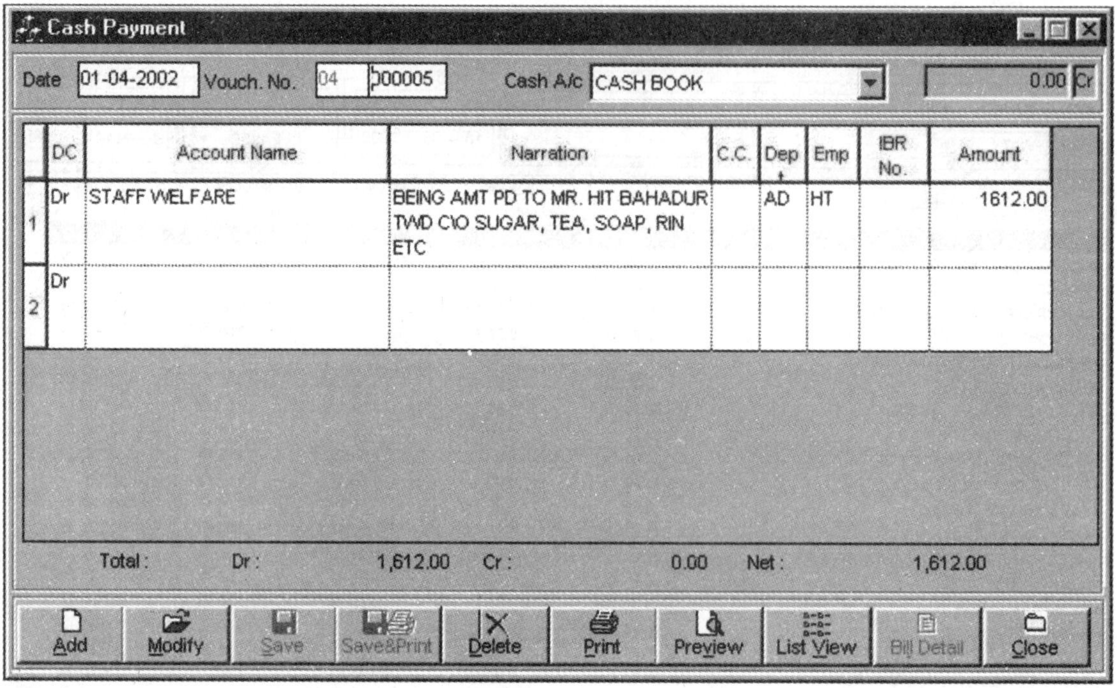

Fig. 11.11   Cost centre analysis transaction is classified on cost centre basis

Let us understand this with an example. One makes a payment of Rs 20,000 to a person Rajesh for his salary for previous month. Rajesh is a marketing manager and posted at New Delhi. This payment comes under the accounting head 'salaries'. But we can have three classifications of this payment for the sake of budgeting and profitability analysis. The general cost centre (GCC) is 'New Delhi', the department cost centre (DCC) is 'marketing', and the employee cost centre (ECC) is 'Rajesh'. The finance manager can find out the answers to these questions: How much total salary has been paid to Rajesh? What is the total cost incurred by the 'marketing' department as salaries? How much salaries have been paid to the staff in 'New Delhi'?

Account Head	GCC	DCC	ECC	Amount (Rs)
Salaries	New Delhi	Marketing	Harry	20,000

You can see from the example that Rs 20,000 was paid to Rajesh (employee cost centre), a marketing person (department) on account of salary (account head), for New Delhi office (general cost centre).

As in case of annual budgets, cost centres are compared on monthly or annual basis.

Taxation and Statutory Reporting

Taxation is an indispensable part of the accounting systems. The government tax systems are very complex and tend to change frequently, at least once in a year. There are local, state, and central taxes. There is proper accounting of all these taxes and periodical information in the form of 'returns' is sent to the government. These taxes are in the form and name of excise duty (ED) on manufactured goods, sales tax, value added tax (VAT) on traded goods, service tax on services rendered to the customer, and tax deducted at source (TDS) on payments made to service providers and suppliers of services (like vendors supplying embroidery service).

A product carries *excise duty* at the manufacturing point. The suppliers levy excise duty in their bills, which is paid by the retailer. The retailer can take credit for the excise duty paid against the excise duty levied on goods or service tax levied on services. This is called MODVAT (modified value added tax). There are a few records that are essentially maintained in predefined and government-approved formats and around two dozen standard reports, such as RG-1 and RG-32, sent to the government on periodical basis. Large organizations maintain dedicated excise departments, whose primary task is to accurately maintain these records and generate reports. Excise departments minutely examine each purchase and sales bills to ensure that proper taxes have been levied. This is also done to pull or push excise data into the financial system.

Value added tax (VAT) is a State tax levied on many classified products. Each product has a category of tax and different States have different categories and types of taxes for the same product. In a retail scenario, where the product is sold in many States in the country, it is very complex to maintain accurate taxes and reports. Even the reports and returns vary from State to State. The VAT tax envisages that the trader pays tax on the value addition he/she does for the product. For example, let us assume that a retailer buys a product at Rs 100 and sells it at Rs 120. The retailer pays a sales tax (VAT) of Rs 10 (if it is 10 per cent VAT on the product). Also, the retailer collects a sales tax of Rs 12 on the same product. The value addition is Rs 20. Therefore, the retailer has to deposit a tax of Rs 2 to the government as the difference between the tax collected and the tax paid on the same product. There are a number of reports that are sent to the government and the mandatory records are maintained and shown to the tax assessing authority on demand.

The new *service tax* rules cover hundreds of services. Service tax is paid to the Central government and is handled by the excise department. This tax is levied on the services provided by a service vendor. For instance in retail, health care and beauty care services may come under service tax rules. The retailer will have to levy service tax on the services provided to a customer. The service tax collected during a month is deposited to the government treasury before the fifth day of the next month. Service tax is guided by certain common rules.

Note: The actual rates of taxes and date of returns must be checked from the latest Government circulars on the issues.

Firstly, service tax is calculated on a receipt basis. That is, if a credit bill is raised in the previous month, the service tax does not become due as payable this month. If the payment of the bill is received in this month, the service tax is due for payment to the government before fifth day of the next month. Secondly, service tax is paid on prorata basis. Service tax is deposited on the realized amount of bill. For example, if as a retailer you made a credit bill of Rs 10,000 plus 12.36 per cent service tax, on 25 January. Out of this money, the customer paid only Rs 7000 on 20 February. Therefore, the service tax that becomes due for depositing with the government is only on Rs 7000 (12.36 per cent of Rs 7000). Thirdly, the service provider can take benefit of service tax credit, as in case of MODVAT. If the service provider has paid service tax on certain service consumed and has levied service tax on certain services provided to the customers, he/she needs to deposit with the government only the difference of such amount as collected and paid.

To make this point clear, let us take an example. Laxmi Nath is a hairdresser. She charges her customers a service tax of 12.36 per cent. During the month of March, she made a sale of Rs 10, 000 and collected a service tax of Rs 1236. During the same month, she got her phone bills on which she paid a service tax of Rs 396. She can take credit of service tax she has already paid. So, she needs to deposit only Rs 840.

This is a fairly complicated calculation and one needs to keep records and proof of such transactions. Taxation modules of ERP systems take care of it. The modules not only maintain records but also generate reports and prepare returns to be submitted to the Government.

Tax deducted at source (TDS) is another area that needs intense record building and comprehensive reporting. Indian taxation system makes it mandatory for companies to deduct tax when payment is made against services provided by a vendor, an individual or an organization. All kinds of services that come under TDS purview are classified under five categories, viz., contract, consultancy, advertising, rent, and interest paid. The rates of taxes vary from two per cent to twenty per cent. The tax becomes due for deposition with the government at either the time of making a payment or booking the expenditure in the books of accounts, whichever comes first. Payments up to Rs 20, 000 in a financial year are exempt from deduction under this Law. Certain payments are also exempt from deductions. Figure 11.12 illustrates how TDS transaction is done by an ERP system.

The TDS modules in ERP systems provide comprehensive reporting tools. The cohesively integrated module provides interface of deduction of tax at the time of booking of expenditure or making the payment to the party. The database of transactions is built and reports are processed on monthly basis.

Ratio Analysis

Most of the strategic decisions related to an organization are based on and influenced by the financial position of the company. The financial health of the company is presented by analytical reporting in the form of various financial funds flows and ratio analysis. Financial ratio analysis is the most widely used method for determining an organization's strengths and weaknesses, which are dependent on the investment, financing, and dividend areas. Since the functional areas of business are interrelated, financial ratios can signal strengths or weaknesses in management, production, research and development, marketing or computer information systems activities.

An organization's income statement and balance sheet are used to compute the financial ratios. Computing financial ratios helps in reflecting the position of a business at just one point of time. Two key financial ratios that indicate whether or not a firm's financial decisions have been effective are the debt-to-equity ratio and the debt-to-total-assets ratio.

The financial ratios are grouped under some common ratio types like, liquidity ratios, leverage ratios, activity ratios, and profitability ratios. Some of the most commonly used types of ratio analyses are shown in Fig. 11.13. An accounting analysis in ERP systems is shown in Fig. 11.14.

Assets Management

Organizations accumulate large number of assets during their lifetime. Assets are used, depreciated, transferred from to one location to another. Keeping track of the assets becomes a nightmare especially, if the organization is large, multi-location, and multi-unit. Assets management module takes care of such complexities. The module maintains a history of assets since purchase of the same. It links all expenses incurred on repair and maintenance of the asset. Annual depreciations are calculated as per the laws and rules. Systems also provide advanced analytical reports on replacement costs and realization values of assets.

(a)

FORM No. 16 A

[See rule 31 (1) (b)]

Certificate No : 0107194C000003

Certificate of deduction of tax at source under section 203 of the Income-tax Act, 1961

[For interest on securities; dividends; interest other than 'interest on securities'; winnings from lottery or crossword puzzle; winnings from horse race; payments to contractors and sub-contractors; insurance commission; payments to non-resident sportsmen / sports associations; payments in respect of deposits under National Savings Scheme; payments on account of repurchase of units by Mutual Fund or Unit Trust of India; commission, remuneration or prize on sale of lottery tickets;commission or brokerage; rent; fees for professional or technical services;royalty and any sum under section 28(va); income in respect of units;payment of compensation on acquisition of certain immovable property; other sums under section 195; income in respect of units of non-residents referred to in section 196A; income from units referred to in section 196B;income from foreign currency bonds or shares of an Indian company referred to in section 196 income of Foreign Institutional Investors from securities referred to in Section 196D

Name and address of the person deducting tax	Acknowledgement Nos. of all Quarterly Statements of TDS under sub-section (3) of section 200 as provided by TIN Facilitation Centre or NSDL web-site.		Name & address of the person to whom payment made or in whose account it is credited
BNG INFOTECH PRIVATE LIMITED	Quarter	Acknowledgement No.	**RETAILORS**
	Q1	Q126Q11111	
	Q2	Not Available-Statement not yet filed.	
A-42X, NARAINA INDUSTRIAL AREA, NEW DELHI 110 028	Q3	1111	
	Q4	060930200143466	

TAX DEDUCTION A/C NO. OF THE DEDUCTOR **DELB09480C**	NATURE OF PAYMENT	PAN NO. OF THE PAYEE **AAACF7431R**
PAN NO. OF THE DEDUCTOR **AACCB6543L**	**PAYMENT TO CONTRACTOR - ADVERTISING**	FOR THE PERIOD 01/04/2007 TO 31/03/2008

DETAILS OF PAYMENT, TAX DEDUCTION AND DEPOSIT OF TAX INTO CENTRAL GOVERNMENT ACCOUNT

(The deductor is to provide transaction-wise details of tax deducted and deposited)

Sr No	Amount paid/credited (Rs.)	Date of Payment / Credit	TDS (Rs.)	Surcharge (Rs.)	Education Cess (Rs.)	Total Tax Deposited	Cheque/ DD No (if any)	BSR Code on Bank Branch	Date on which Tax Deposited	Transfer Voucher / Challan Identification No.
1	8,000.00	20/09/2007	240.00	24.00	8.00	272.00	111	033145	10/10/2007	7
2	8,000.00	26/02/2008	272.00	0.00	0.00	272.00	834737	033145	10/03/2008	6
	16,000.00		512.00	24.00	8.00	544.00				

Certified that a sum of INR Five Hundred Forty Four Only

has been deducted at source and paid to the credit of the Central Government as per details given above.

For **BNG INFOTECH PRIVATE LIMITED**

Signature of person responsible for deduction of tax

Place	NEW DELHI	Full Name : GHANA NAND JOSHI
Date		Designation : DIRECTOR

(b)

Fig. 11.12 (a) generation of TDS certificate using ERP system and (b) a sample TDS certificate

Ratio	How it is Calculated	What it Signifies
Liquidity ratios		
Current ratio	Current assets/current liabilities	The extent to which the organization can meet its short-term obligations.
Quick ratio	(Current assets – inventory)/ current liabilities	The extent to which the organization can meet its short-term obligations. Without relying upon sale of its inventories
Leverage ratios		
Debt-to-assets ratio	Total debts/total assets	The percentage of total assets provided by creditors
Debt-to-equity ratio	Total debts/total share equity	Percentage of total funds provided by creditors versus owners
Activity ratio		
Inventory turnover ratio	Sales/inventory of finished goods	Whether the firm holds excessive stocks of inventories
Fixed assets turnover	Sales/fixed assets	Sales productivity of plants and assets
Account receivable turnover	Annual credit sales/accounts receivables	The average time taken to collect debts or accounts receivables
Profitability ratio		
Gross profit margins	(Sales – cost of goods sold)/ sales	The total margins available to cover operating expenses
Net profit margin	Net income/sales	Profit per unit rupees of sales
Earning per share	Net income/number of shares in equity shares	Earning available to the owners of equity stocks

Fig. 11.13 Various types of ratio analyses supported by ERP systems

HUMAN RESOURCE MANAGEMENT

Herb Kelleher, co-founder and former CEO, Southwest Airlines, once said:

We are not an airline with great customer service. We are a great customer service organization that happens to be in the airline business. The company believes that *employees come first.* When the systems, structures, policies, procedures, and practices of an organization are designed and lived out so that employees genuinely feel that they come first, trust is the result. Southwest employees trust the company and love its leadership, so they are not skeptical or apprehensive when management says 'do whatever you think is right'.

(Kevin and Freiberg 1996)

Employees come first. The satisfied employee is going to serve the customer better. This modern concept of human management coupled with informa-tion technology as a tool and enabler of systems brings HR management on the centre stage of the organization. IT is playing a key role in people

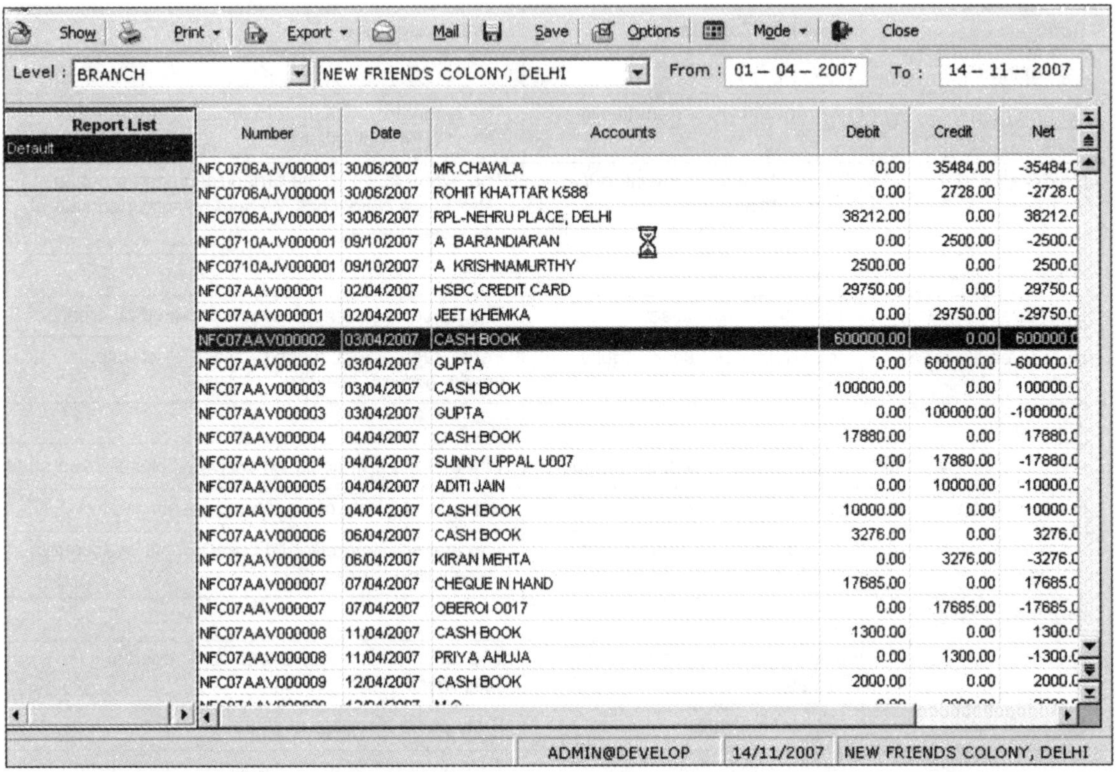

Number	Date	Accounts	Debit	Credit	Net
NFC0706AJV000001	30/06/2007	MR.CHAWLA	0.00	35484.00	-35484.0
NFC0706AJV000001	30/06/2007	ROHIT KHATTAR K588	0.00	2728.00	-2728.0
NFC0706AJV000001	30/06/2007	RPL-NEHRU PLACE, DELHI	38212.00	0.00	38212.0
NFC0710AJV000001	09/10/2007	A BARANDIARAN	0.00	2500.00	-2500.0
NFC0710AJV000001	09/10/2007	A KRISHNAMURTHY	2500.00	0.00	2500.0
NFC07AAV000001	02/04/2007	HSBC CREDIT CARD	29750.00	0.00	29750.0
NFC07AAV000001	02/04/2007	JEET KHEMKA	0.00	29750.00	-29750.0
NFC07AAV000002	03/04/2007	CASH BOOK	600000.00	0.00	600000.0
NFC07AAV000002	03/04/2007	GUPTA	0.00	600000.00	-600000.0
NFC07AAV000003	03/04/2007	CASH BOOK	100000.00	0.00	100000.0
NFC07AAV000003	03/04/2007	GUPTA	0.00	100000.00	-100000.0
NFC07AAV000004	04/04/2007	CASH BOOK	17880.00	0.00	17880.0
NFC07AAV000004	04/04/2007	SUNNY UPPAL U007	0.00	17880.00	-17880.0
NFC07AAV000005	04/04/2007	ADITI JAIN	0.00	10000.00	-10000.0
NFC07AAV000005	04/04/2007	CASH BOOK	10000.00	0.00	10000.0
NFC07AAV000006	06/04/2007	CASH BOOK	3276.00	0.00	3276.0
NFC07AAV000006	06/04/2007	KIRAN MEHTA	0.00	3276.00	-3276.0
NFC07AAV000007	07/04/2007	CHEQUE IN HAND	17685.00	0.00	17685.0
NFC07AAV000007	07/04/2007	OBEROI 0017	0.00	17685.00	-17685.0
NFC07AAV000008	11/04/2007	CASH BOOK	1300.00	0.00	1300.0
NFC07AAV000008	11/04/2007	PRIYA AHUJA	0.00	1300.00	-1300.0
NFC07AAV000009	12/04/2007	CASH BOOK	2000.00	0.00	2000.0

ADMIN@DEVELOP | 14/11/2007 | NEW FRIENDS COLONY, DELHI

Fig. 11.14 Accounting analysis in ERP systems

management and human resource departments are discarding the costly, time-consuming rotten processes and adapting IT-enabled HR systems.

Human resource information systems are used for the following purposes:

- Integration for various human resource applications
- Collection of data at various points in the HR functions
- Integrating intranet based application for streamlining processes, coordination, and workflow management
- Integrating web based solutions related to employee management and welfare

Human resource activities in an organization can be divided in two parts—human resource functions and payroll functions. Human resource functions cover the non-financial activities related with employees' recruitment, training, placement, appraisal, and promotions. Payroll activities are related with the financial part, such as remuneration, perks, provident fund, employee state insurance, and income tax computation and deductions.

Human Resource Management Systems (HRMS)

HR System makes all the raw data of an organization and moulds it into a management tool. It enables managers to better understand what exactly is required as workforce, given the fact that managers have less time to analyse organizational data. The tool reduces costs, improves recruitment of skilled staff, streamlines union grievances, improves workforce morale, and reduces time spent on generating statutory forms to the Government.

The HR functions cover the following activities.

Creating Employee Profile

Employee profile is created giving joining information, probation, confirmation details, present position and family details, local address, contact person details, emergency address and contact person details, medical history, accident information, awards given to employee, club membership profile, assets given to employee and other social activities in which the employee takes part (Fig. 11.15).

Recruiting New Employees

Recruitment process involves creation of a candidate profile bank, handling of requisitions from departments, matching of candidate profile against the requirement of the requisition. Candidates, who come through employee references as well as placement agencies, can be invited for the interview. Interview schedules are finalized and the selection is done. The HR modules help create an offer letter. The selected candidate's profile is transferred to employee profile.

Training is provided to the selected candidates. The HR module helps in creating schedules for training, assigning employee to the schedule, identifying employees and departments for such training, taking training feedback and history, and taking instructor details. Posting, transfers, and promotions are handled by HR systems. Leave records are also maintained by them.

Employee Appraisal

It is an important part of any HR system. Appraisal consists of questions that are answered by the employee himself/herself and his/her senior. A good HR system offers multiple types of questions that can form a good appraisal chart. Marks are assigned and stored. Retirement, gratuity, and related issues are also handled perfectly with the proper module of HR in place.

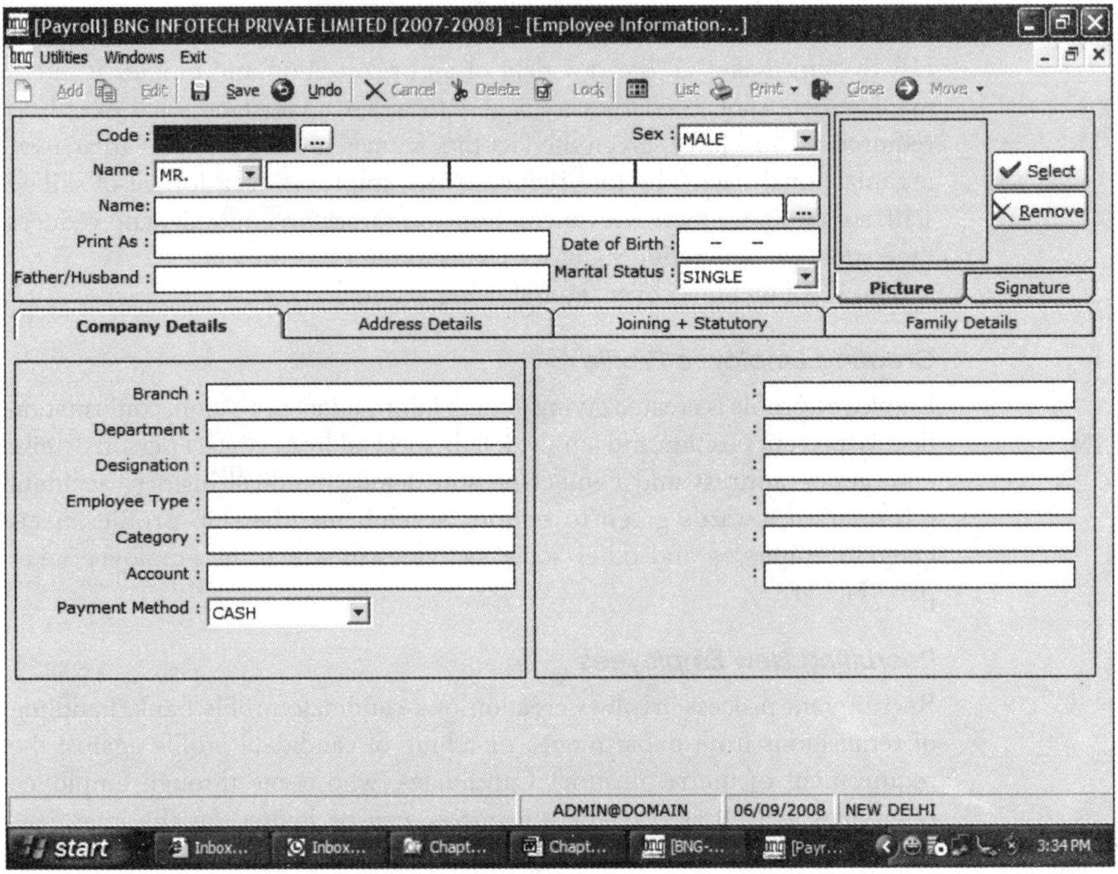

Fig. 11.15 Employee profile form in HRMS

Payroll Function

It is a subsystem of HR module. It offers user definable heads of salary, attendance, leaves, bonus, overtime, loan accounting, and tax processing facilities.

Employee Information

Creation of employees' database serves a basic purpose of primary data creation. It is like a form an employee fills up on joining a company and provides statutory details and registration numbers. The important details required by such a form are name, card number, date of birth, local address, permanent address, total experience, and previous company details (such as posts held and present designation). The form also covers statutory details and registration numbers with a number of Government agencies, such as the provident fund department, insurance department, and income tax department. Therefore, there are provisions to enter PF No, ESI No, PAN, and TIN.

Setting up salary encompasses defining salary and allowance to the employee with effect from a particular date. Any loan and advances taken by the employee are covered under 'loan' by entering the loan amount, loan date, instalment per month/year, and instalment amount. The employees' designation and qualification can also be selected from the already defined master data.

Provident Fund and Employees' State Insurance

Provident Fund (PF) and Employees' State Insurance (ESI) are two welfare measures for employees. The HRMS systems offer functionalities to manage both PF and ESI. There are periodical reports and documents that are submitted to respective regulatory bodies. These reports are generated through the HRMS packages.

Salary Processing

It involves the creation of payroll allowances and deductions, remuneration, compensation, rewards and perks. Based on the attendance data provided by time-office management software, salary is processed and desired reports are generated. Human resource and payroll modules help manage the people component of the organization. The HR management system provides salary reports, arrears and bonus details, leave encashment report, gratuity report, pension statement, PF statement, ESI statement, income tax certificates, and computation charts.

Time Office Attendance

Attendance marking system can be manual, whereby the user marks presence or absence in the computer. Alternatively, there are now good time access or attendance recording machines available. These machines are electronic devices and record in and out time of an employee, when the employee swipes his/her card across or uses the proximity card. The ERP picks the relevant data from the database thus created by the time management system.

Loan and Advances Processing

Loans and advances taken by the employees are returned by them on monthly basis. The instalments are deducted from their salary. Loan processing feature enables the company to deduct loans and maintain a loan ledger for each employee.

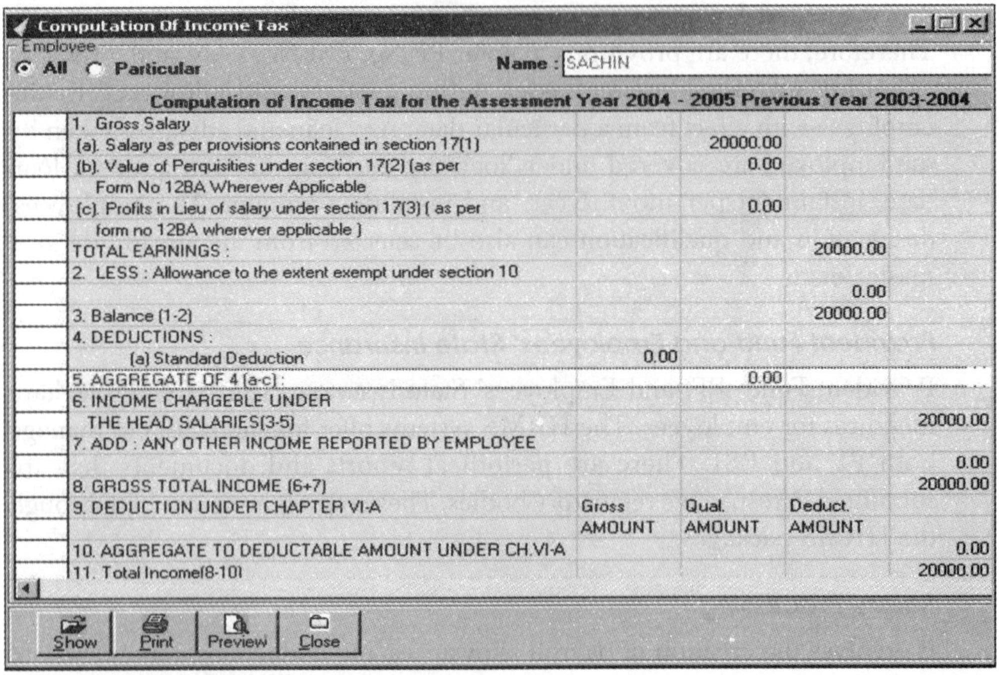

Fig. 11.16 Tax planning and computation in HRMS

Income Tax

A payroll module without income tax is incomplete. Income tax planning, deduction, and e-returns are an important part of the payroll system (Fig. 11.16). Statutory reports and income tax certificates are also provided by the system.

INFORMATION SYSTEMS MANAGEMENT AND ERP ADMINISTRATION

Information systems (IS) departments evolved from what was called electronic data processing (EDP) departments in the 1970–80. With the advent of computers for data processing, the need for independent IT departments was felt. Though IS or IT is not a function of traditional management system. The IT has now become an indispensable function to serve other functions in the modern management. The IS departments not only look after the IT management but also create support functions for need analysis, evaluation, implementation, and management of ERP software.

In the ERP parlance, IS department performs functions like defining business rules, setting preferences (Fig. 11.17), and designing document formats, while housekeeping jobs (such as taking backups, restoring data, maintaining branches, and financial periods) are managed in the administration sub-module

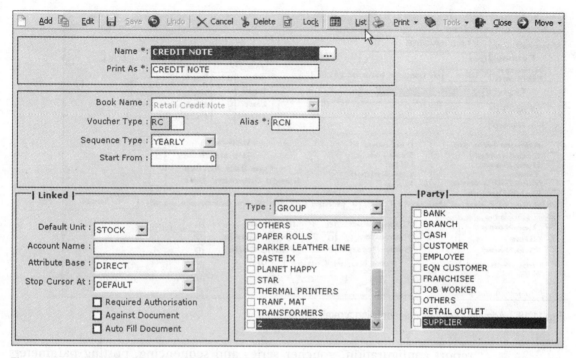

Fig. 11.17 Administrator's module: parameters setting

of the ERP systems. Let us take a quick look into the major roles of IT departments in configuring, maintaining, and managing ERP systems.

Support Functions for Other Departments

The IT departments work to serve other departments in the organization. Their task is to arrange and manage resources like hardware and software. They arrange training on new systems or for new employees introduced in the organization or schedule fresh training to old employees. The job responsibilities of the people in IT also include troubleshooting services within the organization. They are the coordinators and a bridge between the outside IT consultants/vendors and organizational management/users. They help in internal decision-making related to information technology.

Defining Business Process

The business processes of an organization are analysed and defined during the 'analysis' phase and the ERP is configured accordingly. During 'construction' phase of implementation, this involves defining organizational hierarchy, unit, and department layout, various business document layouts,

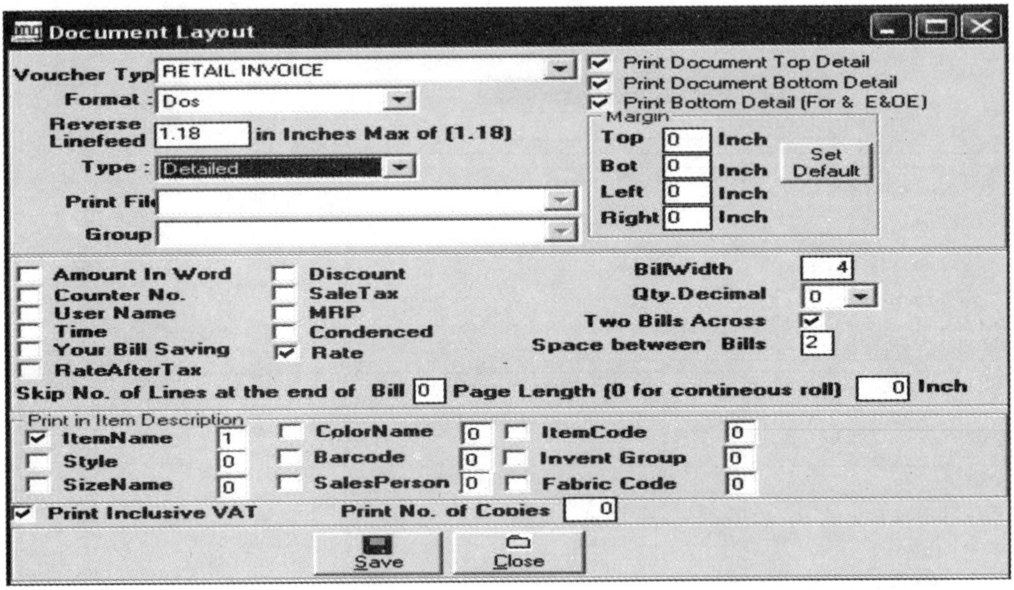

Fig. 11.18 Administrator's module: defining a retail invoice

report configuration, voucher series and sequencing, posting parameters definition, control system definition. However, in case some changes are required at a later stage, ERP administrator or functional consultant sets up the rules of business system of an organization. The system allows setting up rules for each major and subsystem within the complete information system.

Designing Documents

Documents are the legal and quasi-legal papers that are created during the conduct of business. These papers are generated as an essential proof of transaction and are a communication link between the organization and its external environment that consists of its customers, suppliers, and government agencies. Bills, invoices, purchase orders, sales orders, payment advices, material receipt notes, debit and credit notes, are examples of such documents. The ERP system gives flexibility to define and design formats of documents and reports. This job is usually done while implementing ERP, but if need arises, the authorized users can change the formats anytime in the life of ERP in the organization (see example illustrated in Fig. 11.18).

Database Administration

The day-to-day maintenance of ERP is carried out through administrative rights and privileges. The administrator is responsible for taking *database backup*

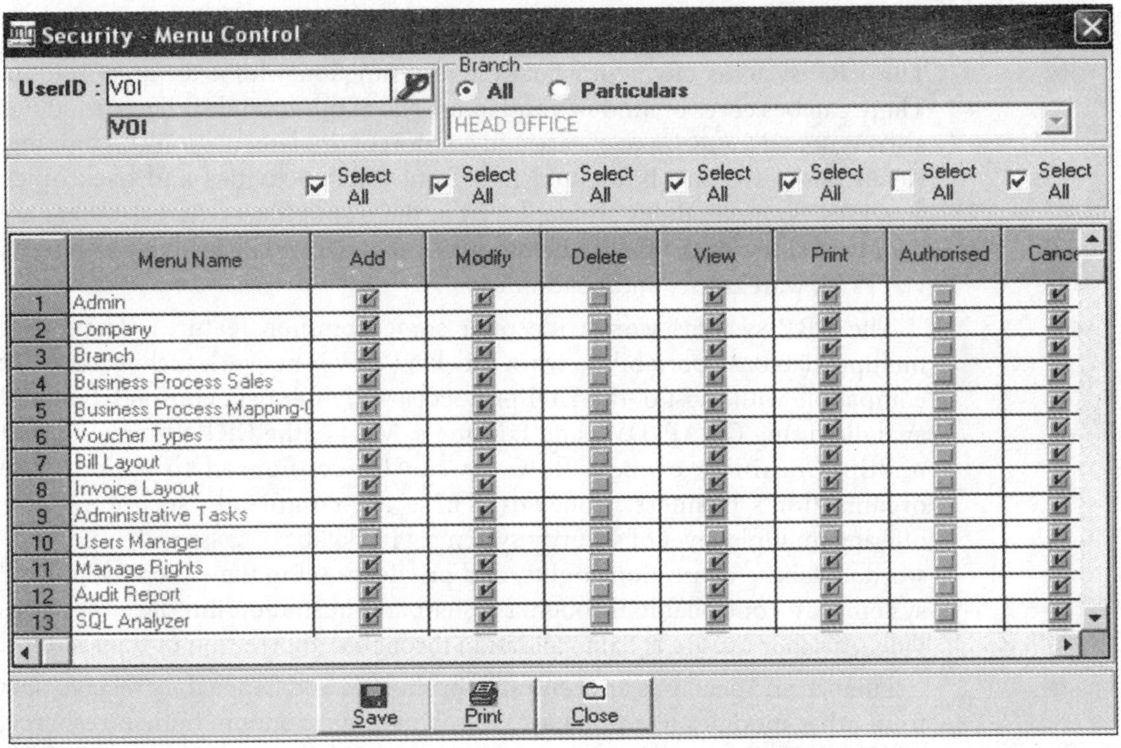

Fig. 11.19 Managing security of data

and *restoration* as and when required. Organizations implementing ERP systems hire services of a database administrator (DBA). The DBA carries out database administration functions. Database administration involves periodical tuning of database, scanning of database for redundant records, and managing unused or scarce space for data-tables besides this, DBA performs other functions as already discussed in Chapter 4, under role of a database administrator. Besides the DBA functions, he has to perform these ERP administration functions.

Managing Security and Users

Protection of data from unauthorized modification, deletions of information is the most crucial part of ERP administration. Various users are created and they are assigned rights and privileges to work on various modules, menus, and sub-menus. *Passwords* of users are managed. The administrator can *lock accounts and accounting periods* to avoid unauthorized changes in the system (Fig. 11.19).

SUMMARY

The ERP systems cover practically every function within an organization. There can be scores of modules and hundreds of sub-modules. These modules are regrouped for the sake of ease and comfort of implementation and training. Retail businesses are bifurcated into front office activities and back office activities. Some modules are deployed at the front office, whereas others are deployed at the back office. The modules are deployed in a three-tier system, viz. POS, warehouse, and head office.

The ERP systems worldwide offer some common features. They offer multiple database portability, work on client-server network architecture, are compatible with most of the EDI protocols, and offer data consolidation and analytics using OLAP, DW, and DM tools. Most of the ERP systems support multiple business process flows or can be configured to support the organization's business processes. These are completely secure systems offering multiple level of security systems, viz. database password, GUI password, database constraints, rights, and privileges set in the system. The ERP systems are controllable through a system administration interface they provide. Another feature is data validation through authorization of transactions.

Finance and accounts are central to businesses and hence they receive data from other modules like purchase, warehouse, distribution, human resource, and POS. The components of finance are general ledger, accounts receivables, accounts payables, fixed assets, budgets, and allocations. These components create transaction data as well as generate analytical reports. Taxation and ratio analysis are two modules that are purely reporting and analytical in nature, that is, they do not offer for data entry, as they use the already entered data through other functional modules. Taxation covers excise, VAT, service tax, and TDS.

Human resource management functions in an organization are classified into HR and payroll. The HR functions are non-monetary in nature and cover everything from application tracking, recruitment, training, posting, transfers, appraisals, promotions, retrenchments, and retirements. Payroll functions are related to monetary compensation, remuneration, salary, leave, wages, loan, taxes, provident funds, and employee state insurance.

The IT or EDP is an important function of a modern organization. The IT provides support functions to other departments, functions, or units. The roles of IT department become more challenging if the organization is running ERP systems. They not only provide hardware and software support to various departments but also manage and maintain ERP. These functions are defining and re-defining business processes, designing documents, performing database administrative functions, and managing security systems.

CONCEPT REVIEW QUESTIONS

1. What are various major modules of ERP systems?
2. What are the common technical features mostly available in ERP systems?
3. Explain any two major modules of ERP in the context retail.
4. What is the best way of implementing schemes in software?
5. What do you understand by consignment sales?
6. Explain salient features of finance module of ERP systems.
7. What are the salient features of an HR solution?
8. What do you understand by the concept of 'authorization' in an ERP system?
9. What are the primary functions of an ERP administrator?
10. Enumerate various ways of protecting of data.
11. Explain functions and roles of IT department.

CRITICAL THINKING QUESTION

1. 'Payroll is only a sub-module of human resource system.' Comment on this in the light of information technology.

PROJECT

1. Find out a mid-size company in your city that has implemented ERP. Analyse the roles played by the EDP/IT/IS departments in evaluating, purchasing, maintaining, and supporting the ERP. Also, do research on the hardware deployed, third-party software, size of database, modules implemented, time taken in implementation, size of the company in terms of number of people employed, number of people in each functional department, and team size of IT department.

SELECT REFERENCES

Freiberg, Kevin and Jackie Freiberg 1996, *NUTS! Southwest Airlines' Crazy Recipe for Business and Personal Success*, Broadway Books, New York.

Jaiswal, Mahadeo and Monika Mittal 2007, *Management Information Systems*, Oxford University Press, New Delhi.

CASE STUDY

Custom-built ERP for Finance, Manufacturing, and Order Processing

Company   Great Eastern Impex Pvt Ltd

Great Eastern Impex Pvt Ltd (GEIPL) was started by Mr P.C. Jain, chairperson of the company, way back in 1983 as a company providing retail support with its product marking, labelling, and bar coding items. GEIPL is the first company in India to introduce product identification through bar codes. The company imports labelling and bar code devices from leading manufacturers of the world. Some of the brands that the company is dealing with are Paxar Monarch, Toshiba TEC, Unitech, PSC, Symbol, and Argox. These brands are some of the best in the world and offer time-tested solutions. GEIPL decided to manufacture gun labels and bar code labels of its own and set up a manufacturing plant at Udyog Vihar in Gurgaon, adjacent to New Delhi.

The technology was well appreciated and accepted in India. With the increase in demands, GEIPL opened four regional offices in four cities, viz. Delhi, Mumbai, Kolkata, and Bangalore. Later, a fifth branch was created at Ludhiana. These offices made their own sales and also catered to the large dealer network.

Industry Retail support through bar code technology products distribution and labels manufacturing

Solution area Finance and Accounts Management

Problem Managing this kind of a sales network without proper management information systems is very difficult. Though, initially it was managed by writing manual books. But Mr Jain, though belonging to the older generation, is modern in his outlook and approach towards technology. In 1990, he got MIS software created with the help of two programmers using FoxPro. This program mainly catered to sales billing and debtors' management, and could well suffice the needs of the company for a decade.

But at the turn of the century, when the retail boom started to take place, the requirement increased heavily. Need for an integrated system was felt, which could provide proper management of debtors and creditors, inventories, servicing of equipment, production planning and control, and wastage control. But the main emphases were huge accounts receivables. Timely recovery of dues was necessary to strengthen the revenue and funds flow of the company. The existing system was not able to generate aging and outstanding reports in the required way and format. Moreover, the system did not have any query builder that could work on user definable parameters.

Solution In the second half of 1999, GEIPL started looking for solutions for the above requirements. A host of packages and vendors were evaluated. The international ERP packages were very costly to implement and required lot of resources in terms of time and efforts. Finally, there were two local vendors in the fray. One was with a sizable number of work force and few clients in the industrial ERP segment, but no knowledge in the label and barcode industry. The other company had a successful software package for retail, but was a relatively new entrant in the ERP segment and had hardly had any reference. But on personal interaction, the COO of the software company and Mr Jain could establish a personal rapport and generate enough confidence in each other. Mr Jain's foresightedness could see that 'he will deliver'.

Therefore, the order was given to BrainSoft Solutions Pvt Ltd for a custom-made ERP to suit GEIPL requirements.

Implementation It was a custom-built development and carried the full software development life cycle approach. The system study took three months' time and the review and approval of the same took some more time. An ERP implementation task force was created that had five members from GEIPL including the country manager and IT manager and two persons from BrainSoft.

ERP package was developed using Visual Basic-6 with Oracle RDBMS. Solutions were developed for eight key areas clubbed under eight major modules of ERP viz., purchase and supply, sales and distribution, warehouse and inventory, finance and accounts, HR and payroll, production planning and control, service management, and fixed assets management. The core module of purchase, sales, inventory, and finance were implemented first and were live in one year. Three months data was re-punched in the new system just to check the accuracy and robustness of the system. Later, production planning was implemented. Rest of the modules could be implemented, along with branch implementation, only in the third year of implementation.

Benefits   By implementing ERP, GEIPL achieved major benefits in two painful areas. The first was order processing. Now customer orders could be easily tracked, scheduled for production or dispatch. The query generator provided a list of pending orders based on multiple parameters, which was earlier difficult to do. The second painful area was the collection of outstanding dues from debtors. Now the ERP provided periodic reports on outstanding and aging of bills. Moreover, checks have been put on creation of invoice if the total outstanding dues are more than the permitted credit limits to dealers and customers.

Questions:
1. Was GEIPL's decision to build their own ERP, that too from vendors who did not command expertise in manufacturing sector, a right decision?
2. What were the pain areas that prompted GEIPL to build an ERP system?

Source: Based on interactions with Managing Director, Mr Shakti Jain, management and staff of GEIPL, personal observations during consulting and providing software solutions and information from the company's promotional material and websites.

12

Information Systems for Supply Chain Management

Learning Objectives

- To understand the concept of supply chain
- To define objectives of supply chain
- To identify factors of a successful supply chain system
- To understand supply chain framework
- To identify available tools of supply chain management from IT perspective
- To understand sub-functions of supply chain management
- To appreciate procurement functions
- To appreciate warehouse and inventory functions
- To appreciate sales and distribution functions

In Chapter 11, we have learnt functions and features of enterprise resource planning (ERP). We have learnt that various business functions are grouped under enterprise systems, namely, enterprise resource planning, supply chain management, customer relationship management, and material requirements planning. Software solutions designed to meet these specific requirements are enterprise solutions for specific area. In this chapter, we will discuss solutions available for supply chain management (SCM).

In businesses, particularly in retail one, supply chain assumes critical importance because of unpredictable demand and supply equations, more focus on customer, and improper vendor management. The procurement and ware-housing systems are as old as the business systems themselves. So, what has changed? Kuttappan (1999) answers: 'What has changed is the business dynamics. On the one hand, today's business is roughly categorized into buying, making, moving, storing, and selling—all as independent units. On the other hand, there are the fragmented market, short product life cycles, and markets that vanish as quickly as they appear to be replaced by newer ones.' Therefore, integrating information systems to create a responsive planning and execution process, which coordinates between various supply chain partners, is the key.

SUPPLY CHAIN MANAGEMENT

The total supply chain functions of an organization involve movement of goods from the supplier to the end-customer. It is often referred to as managing suppliers on the one hand

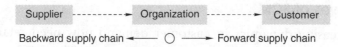

Fig. 12.1 Total supply chain

and distribution channels on the other (Fig. 12.1). The flow of goods from the supplier to the organizations and then further to the end-consumer involves the complete supply processes. Chaturvedi (2004) opines: 'Supply chain management is the strategic coordination of traditional business functions and the tactics across these business functions within the supply chain for the purpose of improving the long-term performance of individual companies and supply chain as a whole.' Thus, we can say that *supply chain management* is the process of making right goods available to the right people at the right time and right place.

Supply chain management (SCM) evolved through many phases. Whereas in 1960s, SCM referred to fragmented processes, such as demand forecasting, purchasing, and requirement planning, 80s saw inclusion of warehousing, distribution, and channel functions as the core processes of SCM. During 1990s, transportation and logistics also became part of SCM. Now in the twenty-first century, we see integration of all the functions with information technology as the enabler of the system. Evolution of SCM is illustrated in Fig. 12.2.

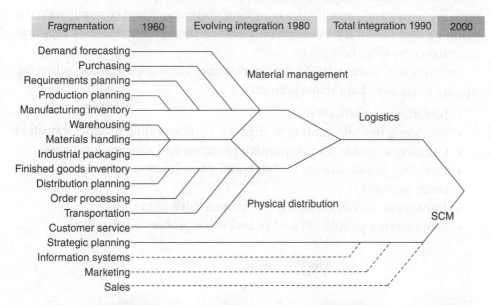

Fig. 12.2 Evolution of supply chain management

Source: Wilson and Delaney 2001

Objectives of SCM

The increasing dynamics in customer demand now need retailers to have flexible procurement, storage, and distribution. This leads to a need to optimize all resources, inventory, and capacity as well as closer customer and supplier integration. A study conducted by Harvard University reported the following objectives for SCM:

- Reduce direct and indirect cost
- Reduce capital costs
- Tax minimization
- Reduce logistic costs
- Overcome tariff barriers
- Provide better customer service
- Build alternative supply sources
- Pre-empt potential competitors
- Learn from local suppliers, foreign customers, competitors, and foreign research centres
- Attract talent globally

Factors for Successful SCM

The ultimate goal of SCM is to bring in efficiency in procurement and meet customers' demand effectively. Hence, the need is to plan, manage, and optimize inventory and capacity in a company's operations and communicate the planning and inventory information between the various levels of suppliers and customers (Fig. 12.3).

Kalambi and Bansal (1999) enumerate the following steps for achieving success in supply chain management:

- Integrating information
- Analysing this information to trigger a corresponding product transition
- Creating a nimble and responsive planning and execution process
- Enabling global process visibility and co-ordination between all supply chain partners
- Improving overall throughput and asset utilization
- Empowering people to identify and solve problems proactively

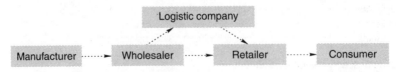

Fig. 12.3   Total supply chain partners

From IT point of view, supply chain involves efficient inventory management through a systemic approach applied across the supply chain partners. It focuses on the need to look at value delivery to the customer. In retail, the value flows from the vendor to the customer through the retailer. Some experts feel that supply chain decision are of strategic implications and taken by the top management. But, efficient management of inventory is a day-to-day business operation and should be part of middle level decision-making.

Framework of Supply Chain Management

Supply chain management tools cover the complete process of flow of goods from raw material supplier to finished product manufacturer to warehouse to end-customer through the logistic processes. These processes can be identified as buy–make–move–store–sell (Fig. 12.4).

The study of SCM in terms of information systems and available tools will be completed within these five steps in a total supply chain framework, which complete the total supply chain system. The SCM tools give people across the supply chain visibility into customer demand and the delivery of goods—helping them make faster, better business decisions and take the best course of action when adjustments are necessary. With features like automatic notification and alerts, they easily keep tabs on inventory, thus helping sustain optimal item levels without holding up funds in the warehouse. Procurement team can plan purchasing at favourable terms and in a timely manner, controlling costs and ensuring that organization meets its customer commitments.

The IT tools help people work with business partners and suppliers in such a way that everybody's business model can advance in the right direction and key business relationships deliver high value. The employees of an organization who work directly with the customers play an essential role in its business. Information technology solutions can give those employees the information, capability, and control to satisfy customers and strengthen the company's competitive advantage (Fig. 12.5).

Information technology systems provide a set of integrated applications, tools, and capabilities that give strategic insight into organizations' current processes and help replace bottlenecks and inefficiencies. The organization

Fig. 12.4   Constitution of supply chain management

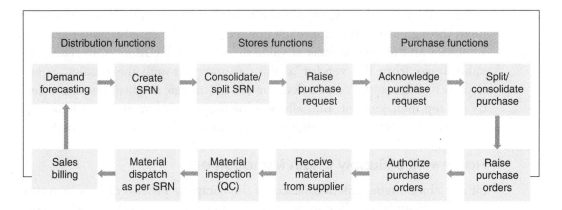

Fig. 12.5 Flowchart of supply chain divided into three organizational functions

can respond faster to customer demands and gain an important competitive advantage. Therefore, it helps keep profits high and reduce leakages by way of improvement in productivity.

IT TOOLS FOR SUPPLY CHAIN MANAGEMENT

Many people across the organization are engaged in supply chain activities—delivering sales or services to customers, shipping products, negotiating with suppliers and trading partners, managing inventory, or other critical tasks. The SCM solutions help connect information from different teams. In doing so, it can help empower people to perform with optimal productivity, maintain profitable relationships with vendors and business partners, and satisfy the customers. To achieve supply chain objectives and bring in efficiency to the organization, information technology brings in tools and processes. The new ERP solutions, which are real-time applications, address the entire supply chain through extended enterprise. (The extended enterprise encompasses suppliers and customers as well.) These solutions are capable of optimizing both material and capacity while taking into account the constraints. They involve total order management, balancing supply with demand, and support virtual enterprises. Some of these tools, such as procurement management, inventory management, and distribution management, are a part of ERP systems. The others are modelling tools used for planning and optimizing. In the context of retail, our discussion revolves around the following topics:

- Procurement management
- Warehouse and inventory management

- Distribution and logistic management
- Modelling and planning tools

Different modelling and planning tools work in synchronization with each module of ERP. Tools like advance planning and scheduling (APS) offer the promise of extending the benefits of ERP systems beyond transaction data processing. The APS tools employ constraints-based technologies that enable them to examine the constraints faced by the retailer, such as storage capacity, distribution points, and transportation modes. With this technology, companies and members of the supply chain together can streamline delivery schedules and react quickly to sudden changes in variables, such as material supply, storage capacity, transportation resources, and customer changes.

Procurement

Procurement involves evaluating and managing vendor and purchase-ordering functions (such as floating enquiries, generating comparative charts for comparing prices and terms of various suppliers, and generating purchase orders). Purchase planning is based on demand forecasting and re-order level of products, while sales estimation is a part of procurement management.

Defining Suppliers, Items, and Procurement Conditions

In the preliminary stage of implementation, the ERP systems define suppliers and product details. This also links and maps items with procurement terms and constraints, such as lead time and lot size. Individual supplier's purchase order terms and conditions are defined as shown in Fig. 12.6.

Floating Enquiries

The ERP systems facilitate creation of enquiries for purchase of goods. Also known as RFQ (request for quotation), the system creates enquiries on the set pattern and the user can fax, mail, or post it to various vendors. The auto-mailing feature enables sending automatic mails on the pre-configured addresses in the supplier database.

Supplier Quotations

Quotations received from various vendors are tabulated to create 'comparative' chart. The system calculates the least price based on quantifiable attributes of the quotation. The non-quantifiable attributes, such as good quality and the nearest location, are not considered for calculating the least price by the system. However, the purchase manager can use discretionary powers to give weights to these attributes. A supplier is approved based on the given business criteria

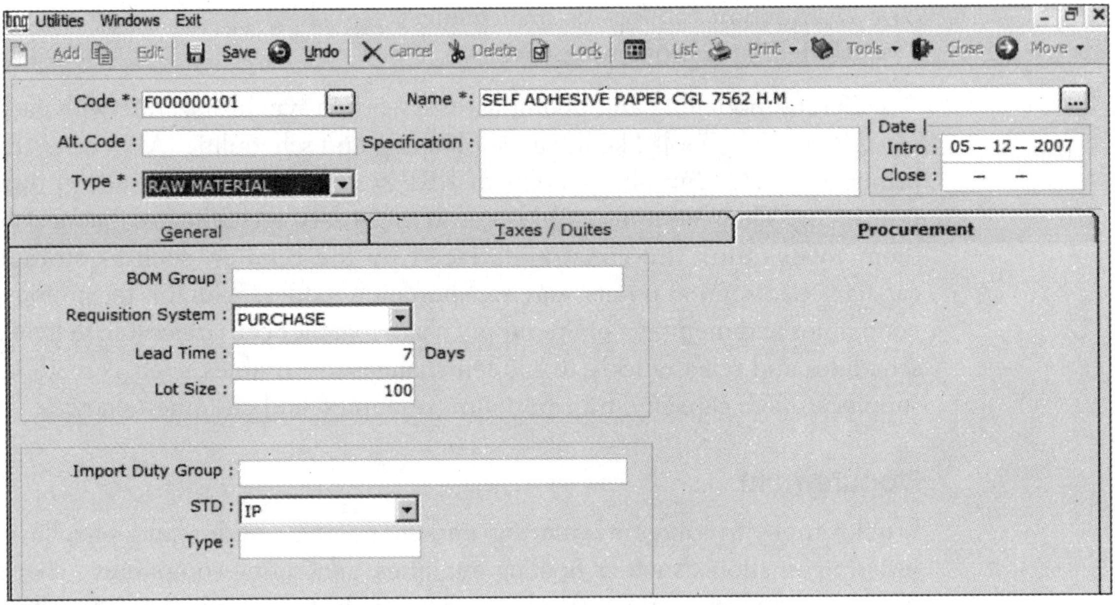

Fig. 12.6 Procurement conditions defined with an item

(like L1, with the least prices). The approved suppliers' rates become 'rate contract' for the supplier, which covers prices and other components, such as discount, sales tax, and excise duty.

Consolidation and Splitting of Purchase Request

Purchase department receives purchase request from various departments of the organization. This is known by various names, such as 'indent', 'requisition', 'purchase request', and 'demand note'. The purchase requisition raised by warehouse may be based on its re-order level, against the procurement planning for the period, based on demand from a retail store or against a sales order, i.e. against an already received order from a customer at the retail store. The purchase department further consolidates or splits the requests for processing orders for optimum quantities of goods. Purchasing optimum quantity saves on order-processing and inventory-carrying costs.

Purchase Order

Purchase orders (POs) are raised on the supplier for supply of goods. Besides details of item specifications, purchase orders cover product prices, taxes and levies, payment methods and modes, transportation and logistic details, and delivery information (Fig. 12.7). The purchase orders are based on 'purchase requests', which can be split subsequently to raise different POs to different

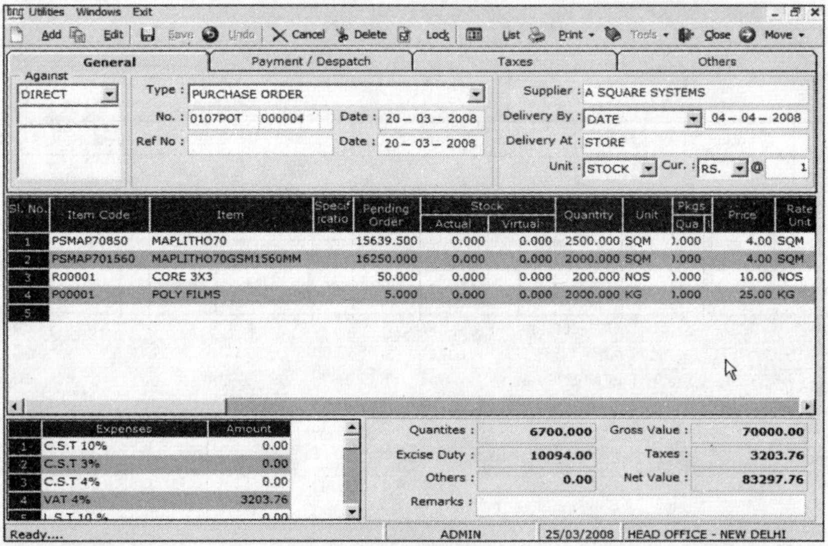

(a)

BLUES CLOTHING COMPANY PVT. LTD.

G-13, South Extension, Part I, New Delhi 49

Phone : 41828275, mail : contact@bluesclothing.com

TIN : 2323223

PURCHASE ORDER

To :	
ABC SUPPLIER X-111, GREEN BUILDING GREEN AVENUE GREEN PARK NEW DELHI DELHI 110016	**No.** HO08POF000001 **Date** 17/04/2008 **Ref. No.** **Date** 17/04/2008 **Delivery Date** 20/04/2008 **Delivery At** A-41 SECTOR 64,NOIDA UTTAR PRADESH NCR-DELHI INDIA-201301 UTTAR PRADESH

Dear Sir,

We are pleased to place our order on you for the supply of the following materials as per the terms and conditions mentioned here under: -

S.No.	Item Code	Description	Qty	Unit	Rate	Amount (RS.)
1	A047A1L17	SHIRT FULL SLEEVES COLOR : BLACK, SIZE : 42	10.00	PCS	3784.00	37840.00
2	A047A1L17	SHIRT FULL SLEEVES COLOR : BLACK, SIZE : 40	5.00	PCS	3784.00	18920.00
3	A062A1L17	SHIRT FULL SLEEVE COLOR : BLACK, SIZE : 40	6.00	PCS	3692.00	22152.00
		Total :				**78912.00**
		SALES TAX 10%				7,891.20
		Grand Total :	21.00			**86,803.20**

RS. Eighty Six Thousand Eight Hundred Three and Paise Twenty Only

Terms

1. Payment Terms CREDIT
2. Despatch Mode ROAD
3. Road Permit Form Nos.:

Other Terms And Condition

(b)

Fig. 12.7 Ordering system in ERP: (a) generation of purchase order using ERP tools (b) a sample purchase order

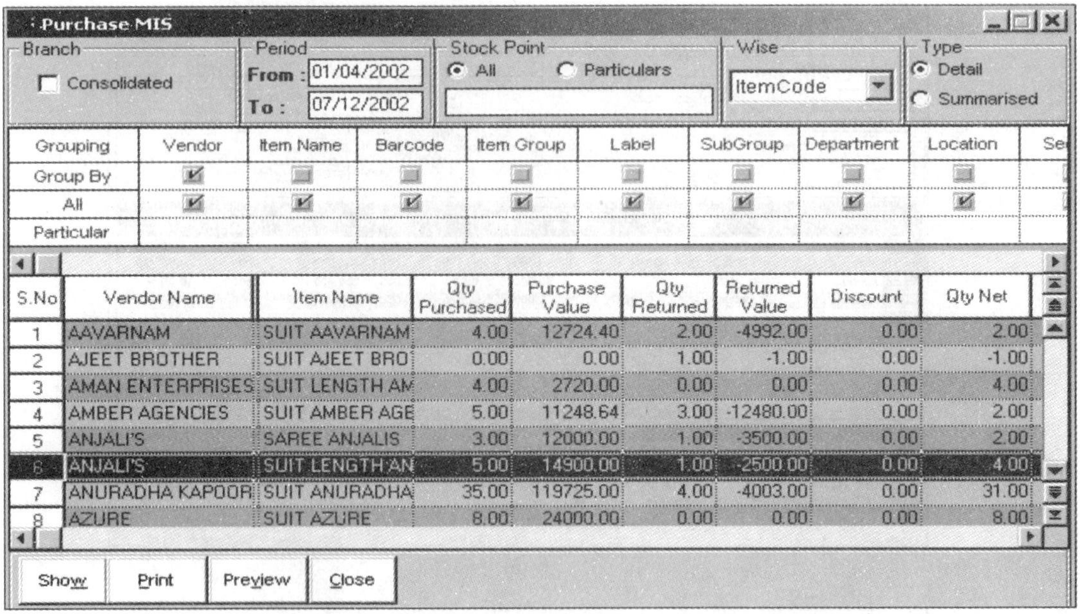

Fig. 12.8 Purchase analysis using ERP tools

suppliers (Fig. 12.8). Multiple requests can also be clubbed to raise a single PO. Purchase orders once raised and issued do not allow any changes. If there is any change to be affected, it is done through *purchase order amendment.* The in-built security system in ERP systems does not allow direct changes. As once transactions have already taken place against the document, it does not allow modification from the regular course.

Just like purchases of goods, you may need to buy services to work on your products. The jobs can be outsourced from one or more job workers in different proportion to facilitate the bulk job distribution. The same is done through *job outsourcing order.* The system works in the same way as purchase orders. Job orders are a kind of contract, which mainly covers instructions regarding how the job is to be carried out and the prices thereon.

E-Procurement

Whereas ERP systems provide tools for automated purchase ordering, supply chain systems with e-procurement give the supplier insights into the supply mechanism of the organization. The Internet provides a platform for achieving organizational efficiencies in optimum use of time, money, and labour. *Electronic procurement (E-procurement)* refers to processing of purchase order system through the Internet. It is not just about using the website for placing orders but also about involving suppliers in the purchasing network. Thus, e-procurement becomes an integral part and enabler of SCM. Information technology has changed SCM concept in a big way.

The e-procurement has many advantages over a traditional procurement system. It reduces purchase ordering cost and order cycle time. As there is no paperwork, the accuracy of data is more. Employees like to work more on the Internet-based applications and then write purchase orders by hand. This increases employees' satisfaction. Retailers make more profits by saving on purchases and then selling on high margins. The supplier relationship is improved by focusing on limited number of suppliers and making more purchases from them.

Functioning of e-procurement Establishing an e-procurement system involves the following steps:

1. The customer and the supplier's business applications (or ERP systems) run independently and severally.
2. An Internet-based middleware is developed in the form of e-portal, which works as a link between the customer and the supplier's database.
3. Suppliers are registered at the e-procurement site and given IDs, rights, and privileges to access the information.
4. The customer sends RFQ (request for quotation) to the suppliers through the e-portal. This also works like a tendering process, wherein the requirements are displayed at the web portal as tender documents.
5. The suppliers access the RFQ and respond with their quotation. The quotations are sent through the website only. Organizations may also entertain quotations through other mail and manual paper processes.
6. The customer then compares various quotations received and shortlists the suppliers based on their prices, terms, and quality of products.
7. Purchase orders are created using e-procurement with the help of Web application. The supplier accesses the PO on the site or, alternatively, the PO talks to the supplier's database and the information is sent to the supplier.
8. The supplier dispatches goods and creates a goods dispatch document through the e-commerce portal. The information is available to the customer within no time.
9. The delivery information on the Net is captured by customer's database.
10. The goods are received by the customer and an acknowledgement is sent to the supplier, which the supplier can access.

11. In many cases, the suppliers have access to customer's database and they send an advice of dispatch. This is based on certain modelling tools available with the organization.

Warehouse and Inventory (WI)

Purchase function leads to the next important part in supply chain management—warehouse and inventory management. Warehousing is one of the major components of SCM. The major functions of warehousing involves receiving goods from vendors and job workers, carrying out inspection, dispatching goods for sales, and returning defective items or excess receipts back to the vendor. Some of the inventory support functions are stock adjustments for items pilfered or unserviceable. Figure 12.9 illustrates the functions offered by warehouse and inventory.

Replenishment Management

Replenishment refers to recouping of goods to the retail store based on sales or targeted sales of the store. While replenishing stocks, the replenishment model takes into consideration the demands and available supplies. Replenishment management tools enable the creation of feasible and actionable plans. They take into account the target and constraints. Most fashion products go through a push (initial allocation)–pull (back-to-sales replenishment)–push (end of life or markdown) life cycle. Replenishment models take care of all the three phases. Replenishment plans are defined for connected supply chain—from vendor to distribution centre to store—in a single model.

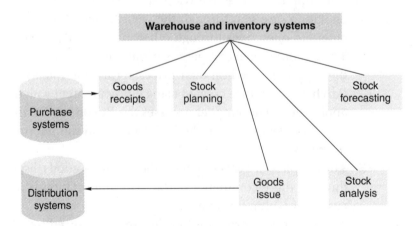

Fig. 12.9 Functions offered by warehouse module

Stock-Movement Functions

The first activity in implementation of an ERP system for inventory management is by punching the existing inventory as *opening stock* in the system. While entering opening stocks, one has to keep in mind the specifications (such as size and colour), cost price (for inventory valuation), selling prices (for further distribution), batch numbers, and expiration date (for inventory tracking of expired goods). These parameters will change depending on the type of retail product. The ERP systems provide for automatic data capturing system. The items in the warehouse can be scanned with a portable data terminal (PDT), which has already been discussed in Chapter 2, and uploaded into the database.

Stock movements in a warehouse happen through inward and outward processes. On receipt of goods from vendors, a document, called *material receipt note* (MRN) or *goods receipt note* (GRN), is created. Goods may also be received from customers as a result of sales returns. Inventory is reduced due to stock-out functions like *goods issue notes*. The stock-movement function facilitates issue of goods to selected departments, which can be done against store request or production request. It is also used to transfer goods from one warehouse to another within the branch. Inter-branch transfer of goods, which involves VAT and other taxes, is done through stock-transfer functions. Return of defective or excess receipts from a supplier is recorded through a document called *purchase return note*. It reduces stock from warehouse.

Physical Stocktaking

The warehousing functions of an ERP system facilitate physical stocktaking. This function refers to tallying physical stock with the computer-generated stock report. Every organization carries out this activity at least once in a year. Stock-tally functions for a retailer are done more frequently, e.g. quarterly. Stocktaking can also be done using data-capture units (DCUs), which have been discussed in Chapter 4. By comparing the actual and computer data, the system generates a variance report. The organization can analyse the data and can take corrective measures.

Special Inventory Functions in Retail

Retail business functions require some special treatment to inventory. Goods may be re-packaged before they are placed on the shelf for selling at the counter. Two or more products may be clubbed together to make sales easy and add more value to the goods; or a set of items may be broken if it is not saleable in a set form. These inventory activities are carried out through specialized functions available in the ERP systems. These functions are called repacking, set making, and set breaking.

The ERP system allows you to bundle a few items together for selling. It is used to define sets for specific unit of items to facilitate stocking and selling. This process have effects on the stock of item created (increased) and items used (decreased). This is only used when one finished product is bundled with another finished product. For example, the retailer may bundle a diary with a fountain pen and sell it as a single product on the New Year's Eve. The already-prepared sets can be broken down to create different stockable unit. This process is just reverse of 'set making', for example, if an item does not sell in the 'set' form, the retailer can undo the set making and sell the item individually. In the same fashion, some goods are bought in bulk but sold in smaller units of it. When the same product needs a pack change, this option is used, for example, a 100 kg bag of rice is repacked into 50 bags of 2 kg each. The 2 kg bag is more easily saleable then a 100 kg bag.

Stock Planning and Analysis

The ERP systems function as a support system for total supply chain management. The data thus created in various subsystems generates a lot of processed information. This information helps planning, decision-making, and improving business efficiency. Some of the important analyses provided are stock variance report, rate contract, supplier performance, purchase analysis,

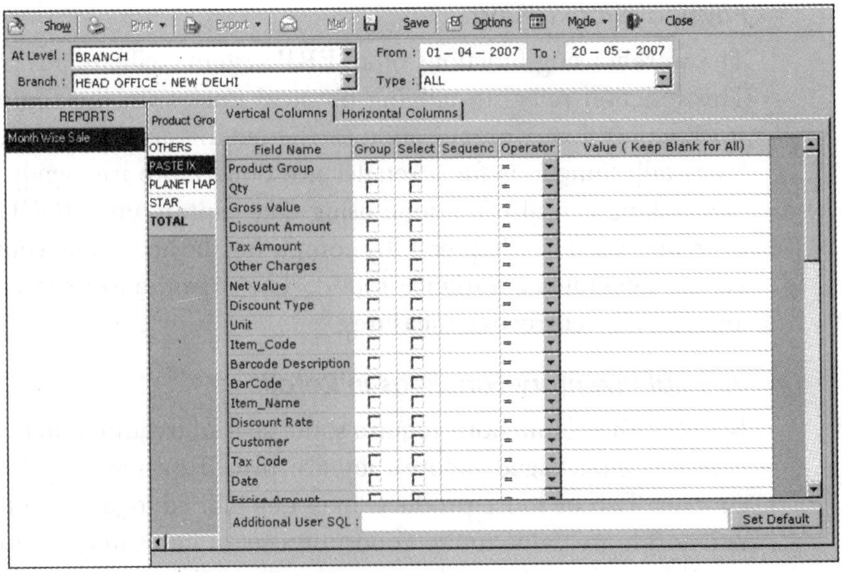

Fig. 12.10   Tools for stock analysis

stock statements, valuation, movement, and minimum, maximum and re-order level of stock (Fig. 12.10).

Distribution and Logistic Systems

In a retail chain business environment, 'retail outlets' function as customer for the head office and distribution centres. Customers' database created at the retail stores is available to the corporate office for analysis and running customer loyalty programmes. The decisions related to pricing, promotions, and schemes are taken and applied at distribution level. Besides the dispatch of goods to retail outlets, the back-office distribution system works on data generated by the point of sales and provides analytical reporting.

Pricing Decisions

The ERP systems allow single and multiple pricing for the same item. Standard prices are defined for particular item with respect to five kinds of pricing, viz. cost price, transfer price, dealer price, sale price, and maximum retail price (MRP), as commonly known. The organization may maintain two broad categories of price policy:

- Centralized pricing
- Decentralized pricing

In *centralized pricing policy*, a retail chain organization maintains uniform pricing throughout the company, whereas in *decentralized pricing system*, the organization maintains different prices at different locations for the same goods. The prices can be maintained centrally or each POS can be given authority to change prices at their location. *Re-pricing* is done to mark up or mark down prices with effect from a particular date, type of product, or just one product. The ERP systems facilitate price change based on any given parameters, attributes, or group of items, as per the requirement. This price change is reflected in databases of all stores and billing is done accordingly.

Managing Promotional Schemes

An ERP system gives flexibility to define various sales schemes and sales bill of materials (BOM). There can be hundreds of types of schemes. The user can define promotional scheme of item, such as 'buy one get one free' and 'buy two get third free', and discounts percentages or lump sum payment. Sales BOM refers to clubbing of items. What makes it critical is that these different items carry different rates of value added tax and value of products. The product should carry one description on the customer's bill but show two different

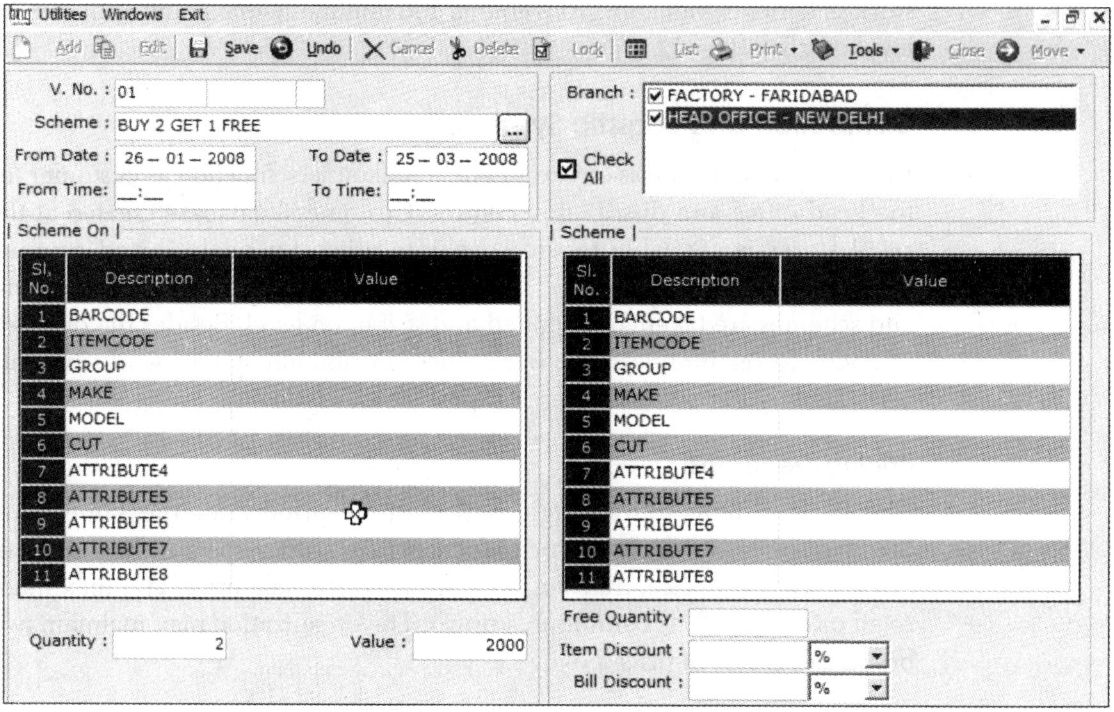

Fig. 12.11 Managing promotional schemes in retail businesses

taxes. Like promotional schemes in goods, discounts are also offered as incentives to buy. Defining and mapping discounts with products is an integral part of distribution system. The ERP system allows defining various discounts that can be mapped to a category of customer, item, or instance in billing. There can be discounts for buying in a particular day of the week or a particular hour of the day. Similarly, discount can be defined to be calculated on the bill amount in either value or percentage. Figure 12.11 shows an example of managing promotional schemes.

Dispatches

Dispatch and logistics are an important part of distribution system. The ERP systems facilitate creation of relevant documents. Dispatch system covers dispatch advice, billing, and packing notes. *Dispatch advice* is created for movement of goods to customer or retail outlet against an order or demand note sent by the store. The logistic manager creates advices for sending goods to the retail outlets, which includes quantity, payment (if any), delivery place and taxes (these are usually calculated on predefined norms in the product set-up module). This action updates order status and prepares the step for packing note. Working on the dispatch advice, the warehouse creates *packing note* for physical delivery to the retail stores. The goods are packed and are ready for dispatch. This process reduces inventory and allows 'invoicing', which takes the financial aspect of delivery into consideration. *Invoice* is made for sales to direct customers (such as franchisees, dealer, and end-consumer), whereas *stock transfer notes* are created for transfer of goods to own retail outlets (branches, as the retailers cannot sell goods to themselves). The invoice is being created against 'dispatch advice'. Stock transfer note is created to transfer stock to a branch against dispatch advice. Rest of the parameters and conditions are just same as in 'invoice'. Separate series of invoicing is maintained for transfer to own branches.

Consignment Sales

Stocking of vendors' goods in stores and franchisee systems of retailing are some modern retailing concepts. In these types of business systems, keeping track of sales and stocks at the other business premises becomes imperative. Supply chain or ERP systems provide tools to efficiently handle the consignment sales. A *consignment sale* is a system of distribution when the goods are stored at the seller's location but technically and legally, they are under the ownership of the vendor. This is used to send goods to the consignee with the arrangement for subsequent billing and payment. The ERP system takes care of this by providing a functionality by which the user makes a transfer of goods to the 'consignee'. The consignee reports daily sales to the vendor. An invoice is created for the goods already sold by the franchisee.

Sales Forecasting and Planning

Total supply chain system works on making right goods available to the right person at the right time and right place. This is possible when right tools that can analyse data and provide perfect forecasting of demand and supply are available. Based on the analysis, sales plans are made. These plans are based on historical data of each retail outlet. Sales estimation for a year can be broken down to a month and week. Target can be defined for each retail outlet or sales person within a store.

The ERP system should give a variety of analysis on sales data in the head office, which consists of distribution to retail outlets, direct sales to customers, or dealers, besides consolidation of point-of-sales data of various outlets. Analytical reports on sales data can be processed by selecting desired parameters, such as item code, name, groups, and attributes for analysing sale orders, dispatch, and other sales data.

Logistic Management

Logistic management tools synchronize critical transportation and distribution business processes in a retail chain environment. This helps in minimizing costs and optimizing service performance. Given right IT tools, it can enhance collaboration with supply chain partners. The tools can estimate demands at point of sales and deliver true, automated exception management, giving retailer replenishment analysts the ability to proactively respond to issues and opportunities. The tools help companies identify the following:

- Current and potential store stock-outs
- Stores that show inventory and an expected rate of sale but no actual sales
- Stores with current or projected excess inventory
- Forecast variance from actual sales

Demand pattern analysis enables companies to utilize store-level POS data. To get an accurate picture of demand, constraints (such as seasonal patterns, causal events, and pricing decisions) are applied. In the extended supply chain, the vendor and retailer can together manage demand and replenishment planning and decide what merchandise to put in each of the retailers' distribution centres on a weekly basis. The tool enables improved in-stock percentage at the store shelf, which leads to higher sales and increased customer satisfaction. Profitability is improved through higher sales and much lower channel inventories as well as the reduction of associated costs from price erosion.

Retailers today face numerous transportation challenges, including rising fuel costs, new regulatory mandates, and global operations with higher levels of lead-time variability. All of these factors make transportation costs a large percentage of the cost of goods sold. Customers demand better performance from transportation, higher on-time delivery performance, and reduced damages while goods are in transit. Logistic management accomplishes this by supporting processes including carrier contract negotiations, transportation network modelling, shipment order handling, freight planning, order execution, and monitoring. The transportation solution tools encompass transportation procurement, planning, execution, and monitoring.

SUMMARY

Supply chain management (SCM) involves the movement of goods from the manufacturer to the end-consumer. It refers to efficient management of inventory and making available right goods to the right people at the right time and right place. This is achieved by using right IT tools and planning systems. Supply chain partners include manufacturer, wholesaler, retailer, and consumer along with logistic companies. Supply chain evolved through a process of ordering system, inventory system, distribution, and finally information, marketing, and sales.

The objective of an efficient SCM are cost reduction, increased efficiency in product and service delivery, building alternate sources of supply, reducing lead-time, and reducing barriers. It also involves learning from various national and international partners. These objectives are achieved through systemic planning and analytical tools used. These are the factors responsible for success of SCM systems. The factors for successful SCM are integration of information, using tools for analysis of the information and generation of plans that are executable. The system is transparent throughout the supply chain network and helps increase efficiency of the assets.

The total supply chain framework involves buy–make–move–store–sell process. Information technology tools work around this framework. The retail SCM is studied covering procurement, warehousing, and distribution. Various modelling and planning tools are provided by the IT products that work alongside the business processes. This starts with purchase order processing using some legacy, ERP, or e-procurement tools. Warehouse system is storing of goods and efficient replenishment of goods to stores and optimization of inventory levels at the warehouse. The tools also include analysis on various inventory attributes. Distribution and logistics involve movement of goods from warehouse to retail stores. Distribution is done on the basis of demand analysis and sales forecasting provided by the modelling tools. Various important decisions that have effects on distribution are pricing decisions, promotional schemes, dispatch processes, consignment sales, and efficient logistic systems.

CONCEPT REVIEW QUESTIONS

1. What do you understand by supply chain management?
2. What are the objectives of supply chain management?
3. What are the key factors that determine success of SCM?
4. Which features you would look for to purchase a supply module while floating enquiries?
5. How does the IT tool help in increasing efficiency across the supply chain?
6. Discuss distribution and logistics as a component of SCM.
7. What do you understand by 'physical stocktaking'? Can you use any technology products to do the same?
8. What are different types of stock reports? Discuss their importance.
9. Explain the concept of 'auto-replenishment'.

CRITICAL THINKING QUESTION

1. 'Multiplicity of promotional schemes and taxation makes retail information system a complex task.' Critically examine this statement.

PROJECT

1. Which are the major Indian software companies providing supply chain solutions? Describe complete features and tools provide by any one of them.

SELECT REFERENCES

Chaturvedi, B.M. 2004, *Supply Chain Management: An Introduction*, IFCAI Books, New Delhi.

Kalambi, N.M. and Sam Bansal 1999, 'Why Supply Chain Management', *Data Quest*, April.

Kuttappan, Latha 1999, 'It is Not Technology but a Business Issue', *Data Quest*, Editorial Supplement, April.

Wilson, Rosalyn and Robert V. Delaney 2001, 'Managing Logistics in the Perfect Storm', *Twelfth Annual 'State of Logistics' Report*, National Press, Washington, D.C.

CASE STUDY

Making Goods Available Where They Are Needed

Company   KiD's Retail

KiD's Retail is an Indian company launched in 2006 for exclusively retailing kids' fashion. The company has its head office in Chennai and maintains a large warehouse in an adjoining industrial area, which is just five kilometres from the head office. The company procures most of the material from its Italian suppliers and distributes the products through its forty odd retail stores across the country. The retail stores are based on franchisee model. In this model of business, KiD's Retail has signed up an agreement with its franchisees to sell the products. KiD's Retail supplies products against an initial deposit (ID) by the franchisee, which is supported by minimum guarantee (MG) sales by KiD's. The goods are dispatched at maximum retail price (MRP) value. The franchisee gets a sales commission of 20 per cent on the sales value. If sales are not enough to cover the MG, a commission equal to 20 per cent of the MG is paid to the franchisee.

The store layout and interiors of the franchisee are done by the appointed designers of KiD's. The expenditure is borne by the franchisee.

The product was unique and reasonably priced. So, the sales picked up very fast. In no time, the merchandise vanished from the shelf. KiD's management was ecstatic with the booming sales.

Industry Retail

Solution Area Supply chain management

Problem The skyrocketing sales need efficient replenishment at the store. There were frantic calls from the stores managers for replenishment of goods. With most of the stuff being imported, it took a lot of time in procuring the products. Moreover, without meticulous planning, it was not possible to procure right products and deliver it to the right place.

Owned by a computer-savvy young generation, the management of KiD's was a pioneer in using modern methods and techniques in management and technologies. It recognized IT as major business driver and enabler for creating the right business infrastructure to cope with the pressures of globalization and competitions.

In keeping with the growth and diversification plans of KiD's, Rs 2.2 million was invested in state-of-the-art IT infrastructure. The outlay was planned on the latest servers, computers, operating systems, database management systems, and application software. It was felt that to service these discerning franchisees, KiD's Retail would require a world-class supply chain management system.

Solution The initial operations of KiD's were done manually. So, the management looked at a host of packages that not only supported POS, back-end ERP, but sustained an effective supply chain management. It considered world-class ERP packages that supported all global practices and conventions in supply chain management. The retailer evaluated many national, international, and locally developed packages. Since solutions offered by international vendors like SAP, Oracle, I2, Microsoft were best choices, but they fell beyond the budget of the company. Moreover, on analysis of the proposal and timelines submitted by each vendor, it was deduced that it will take more time in implementing an international product, than a domestic one.

Thus, the company zeroed in on an Indian vendor iCoM, which has a very comprehensive package and the maximum number of installations in the country. It has also incorporated the best practices in enterprise processes in its package. The iCoM also agreed to assist KiD's in addressing certain garment-specific requirements through innovative process workaround as well as in customization.

Implementation As iCoM had a segment-tested product for POS and SCM solutions, the solution provider started the implementation within no time. The KiD's core team was taken through extensive product training at the vendor's facility at Bangaluru.

Since an ERP implementation involves change management in the organization, the constant support of senior management was a key driver. A steering committee consisting of core members of both the organizations was created for monitoring and overview of the project. The team included executive director and IT manager of KiD's, technical head, consulting head, and project manager of iCoM.

The KiD's Retail provided complete IT infrastructure to its franchisees. The IT kit included a POS system with computer, scanner, printer, and retail software. The systems were tested and made ready at the HO and later shipped to the POS locations. Training to POS staff was a bit of a problem, as they were scattered all over the country. Therefore, it was decided that a team of trainers will visit each franchisee for two days training. Initial training was given to POS staff at their place of work. Later support was carried out by remote desktop sharing through a number of utilities available. The HO and warehouse were taken up for implementing ERP with a comprehensive SCM system.

Benefits Major benefit was envisaged in strengthening the SCM and franchisees order execution. Just within a few weeks of complete implementation of SCM solutions, it showed substantial improvement in the supply system of the company. The iCoM would help in standardizing business processes in various functional areas within the organization. Since POS is integrated with SCM and ERP for financial analysis, it gives online information to the senior management regarding the performance of the organization. Earlier, the franchisees used to send paper-based information of daily sales, stock, and material requirement, which required time for consolidation and compilation before a meaningful decision was taken.

The KiD's Retail saw substantial improvement in availability of goods at the retail place. Franchisees were happy that they received the right products at the right time, even without asking for them.

Questions:
1. What were the major problems faced by KiD's Retail before the suitable software was implemented to manage its supply chain?
2. How did iCoM help KiD's Retail overcome those problems?

Source: Based on interactions with the management and staff of KiD's Retail, personal observations during consulting and providing software solutions, and information from the company's promotional material and websites.

13

Customer Relationship Management (CRM) Applications

Learning Objectives

- To understand the concept of customer relationship and value chain
- To become familiar with relationship marketing strategies
- To appreciate the advantages of CRM deployment
- To understand various e-CRM tools and their applications
- To evaluate functions of marketing and sales CRM tools
- To understand functions of customer support CRM tools

In Chapter 12, we have learnt about supply chain management solution as a component of enterprise systems. Supply chain refers to efficiently managing movement of goods from the supplier to the customers. Thus, customer is an integral part of the business system and maintaining a profitable relationship with the customer is of benefit to the organization. Enhancing customer satisfaction and loyalty by understanding the customer is studied as a management function of customer relationship management (CRM). In this chapter, we will discuss various tools and applications to manage customer relationship.

Markets are fast metamorphosing from seller driven to buyer driven. Modern enterprises adopt customer-focused business approach in which customer is treated like the proverbial 'king'. As per the findings of one research, creating a new customer is sixteen times costlier than retaining an old one. The '80/20 paradox' also says that twenty per cent of the existing customers give eighty per cent of the business. Organizations pay more attention to maintaining relationships with the existing customers than investing more in creating new customers. In the highly competitive retail market, customer loyalty plays an important role in business continuity, profitability, and maintaining competitive advantage.

We are able to understand the role of technology in CRM in a better way if we mull over customer relationships and the driving forces in the context of modern marketing strategies (Fig. 13.1).

Acquisition   Enhancement   Retention

Fig. 13.1 Three phases in customer relationship

CUSTOMER RELATIONSHIP

Customer relationship refers to keeping in touch with the customers, providing them personalized services and thus cultivating loyalty. This is customer-centric approach of doing business. Customer relationship is not an event but a process of acquisition, enhancement, and retention of customer through the organizational life cycle. To do this, the organization needs to know its customers. The organization knows the customer through the various touch points where both of them come across. These touch points are the initial interactions while running promotional campaigns, during selling of goods, and finally at service delivery in the customer value chain.

A customer relationship programme takes care of the customer throughout its value chain (Fig. 13.2). This helps the organization to retain the customer and increase business and profitability with the customer, which in turn is the foundation for success of an organization. The relationship programme is looked upon from the angle of relationship value of a customer. The *relationship value* is a concept that calculates the lifetime revenue and profitability contribution by a customer. Companies look at long-term relationship and analyse costs and benefits of maintaining that relationship. Obviously, corporations aim at generating maximum revenue out of the least expenditure. As already said, the cost of maintaining a customer is much less than investing more in creating new customers.

As Sinha and Uniyal (2007) put it: 'Customer loyalty is crucial to the success of a store since the catchments area of a store is limited and the business can survive only when more value is derived out of every customer. This entails understanding the store choice and loyalty behaviour of customers.' A customer graduates to become an advocate of the brand and retail store with high level of relationship maintained by the store. The levels of relationship define the nature of association the retail store can have with the customers. Berry and Parasuraman (1991) have explained this phenomenon as depicted in Fig. 13.3.

Prospecting   Pre-sales   Sales transaction   Sales delivery   Customer support

Fig. 13.2 Customer value chain

Level	Bond	Orientation	Primary marketing element	Sustained competitive advantage
One	Financial	Customer	Price	Low
Two	Financial and social	Client	Personalized communication	Medium
Three	Financial, social, and structural	Advocate	Service delivery	High

Fig. 13.3   Levels of customer relationships

Therefore, from an IT prespective, we discuss CRM from the point of view of pricing strategy, marketing, sales process, customer interactions, and analytics.

RELATIONSHIP MARKETING STRATEGIES

The new marketing strategy represents a shift from acquisition/transaction focus to retention/relationship focus. This new philosophy of doing business focuses on keeping and improving existing customers rather than spending more on acquiring new customers. This is based on the assumption that it requires more resources to acquire a new customer than to retain an old customer. The modern marketing strategists, particularly in retail segment, appreciate this point of view. As Webster (1992) puts it: 'There has been a shift from transactions to a relationship focus in marketing. Customers become partners and the firm must make long-term commitments to maintaining those relationships with quality, service, and innovation.'

In an interview, James L. Schorr, former Executive Vice-President (Marketing) at Holiday Inn, stated that he was famous in Holiday Inn for what is called the 'bucket theory of marketing'. By this, he meant that marketing can be thought of as a big bucket—it is what the sales, advertising, and promotional programmes do that pours business into the top of the bucket. As long as these programmes are effective, the bucket stays full. 'However, there is only one problem,' he said, 'there is a hole in the bucket.' When the business is running well and the hotel is delivering on its promises, the hole is small and few customers are leaving. When the operation is weak and the customers are not satisfied with what they get, however, people start falling out of the bucket through the holes faster than they can be poured in through the top.   (Zeithaml and Bitner 2006).

So, plugging the hole in the bucket makes all the sense in customer relationship.

Thus, the modern relationship marketing, enabled by e-CRM technologies, focuses on the following areas:

- Customization, not segmentation
- Customer profitability
- Selling more to the customer
- Generating customer loyalty
- Monitoring relationships

Customization, Not Segmentation

The modern marketing approach is paying attention to individual customer as opposed to traditional marketing, which worked on segmentation. (*Segmentation* refers to targeting one group of customers sharing similar attributes, for example, marketers focused on men's formal wears.) Now, in the new philosophy of customization, each customer is treated as an individual and his/her tastes and preferences are taken care of by the marketer armoured with e-CRM tools. Earlier, the focus on individual customer was part of the Web retailing, where the portal kept records of the navigational habits and choices of the customer, but now every retailer wants to keep track of what the customers buys, wears, eats, and how much they have to spend.

Customer Profitability

For a business to be viable and in continuity, the customer should be profitable. The profits generated on the sales made to a customer must be more than the expenses made on acquiring and maintaining the customer. The profitability of a customer is called *customer value* and is the total profit or sales in the lifetime of the customer. Therefore, the segmenting is done and the price policy is decided accordingly. The price segment has to be profitable for the organization in the present and future course and attractive for the customer. Sometimes, companies invest on customers who may not be very profitable in the long run, but this is done to build the customer base. The analysis of customer data created in legacy and ERP repository indicates revenue and profit made by the company on a single customer. The customer analytics is an important part of e-CRM, which provides insights into the customer tastes and preferences.

Selling More to the Customer

At times, organizations think that they can make more profit by cross-selling to the customer. (*Cross-selling* refers to selling new products and services to the existing customers.) Analysis of customer data can reveal the likings of the customer. A customer buying formal suites can be a potential customer of neckties. A middle-aged well-settled executive may be interested in buying goods for his entire family. Similarly, organizations offer discounts and incentives on buying more of the same products. Buy two get one free and such other schemes are examples of selling efforts to the customer.

Generating Customer Loyalty

Paying more attention to the customers means more satisfied customers. Their probability of remaining with the retailer is more. The retailer can deploy various loyalty programmes to offer incentives to customers to remain with the organization. Getting a loyal customer is one thing but inculcating loyalty is another. Loyalty is developed in customers by pampering them, for example, they can be treated as special by giving them more discounts and keeping in touch with them by sending greetings on special days in their lives. All personalized communication, such as e-mails, messages, and phone calls, may be targeted to enhance loyalty of the customer.

Monitoring Relationships

Monitoring relationship over time is an important foundation of relationship marketing. Customers are surveyed to determine their level of satisfaction, perception of service, satisfaction with the organization vis-à-vis competitors. In the highly competitive retail market, customers will remain loyal only when they receive high-quality service and value. Customers' retail database is an important tool for such an analysis. The database provides insights into personal details, buying habits, demographic details, spending patterns, etc., which help the organization to target marketing communication at the right customer.

Notwithstanding the advantages, the new marketing philosophy enabled by information technology needs support from all quarters of the organization. Zeithaml and Bitner (2006) rightly opine: 'Historically, marketers have been more concerned with acquisition of customers, so a shift to a relationship strategy often represents changes in the mindset, organizational culture, and employee reward system. ... Thus, even when people see the logic of customer retention, the existing organizational systems may not support its implementation.'

ADVANTAGES OF CRM DEPLOYMENT

Deployment of customer relationship programme helps organizations in many ways. It helps organizations to delight their customers, empower the teams,

Stages

Customer research	Pre-sales transactions	Sales transactions	Routine post-sales interaction	Non-routine post-sales interaction
Customer buying behaviour Payment patterns Consumer profile	Customization of products Clarification of FAQs and specific queries	Order placing Payment Order processing Payment processing	Routine information sharing (new products/services, advisory services, etc.) Investment-specific information sharing Short-term payment redemptions	On-time/end-time settlement Claims processing in the time Claims processing in the times of eventualities
Accuracy Comprehensiveness	Decision-making Customization Scrutiny	Speed Accuracy Delivery	Speed Transparency	Accuracy Frames Speed Transparency

Expected benefits from e-CRM

Fig. 13.4   Possible benefits of CRM across the customer value chain

Source: Adapted from Jaiswal and Mital 2007

and grow their businesses. It inculcates the culture of customer-oriented business processes. Availability of customer information and database helps in improving marketing and its effectiveness. Customer behaviour is analysed through transactional data created at the retail store level. This increases customer profitability through value maximization. We can summarize the benefits offered by a customer relationship enabled by IT.

With CRM-application tools, organization can capitalize on customer insight, improve front-line efficiency and effectiveness, streamline critical business processes across customer touch points, and quickly adapt to changing business and customer needs. Figure 13.4 shows some possible benefits of CRM across the customer value chain.

Improved Access to Customer Information

The CRM systems work on data generated at various transaction levels. This provides easy access to vital sales and customer information. Organizations view and update a wealth of customer data, which covers contact details, account, sales, personal information, complaint records, service records, and history of customer interaction. (Figure 13.5 shows creation of a customer database.) Organizations then disseminate and share this information across the teams and departments. With this data, office staff knows what has been communicated to the customer, understands the precise scope of the work to be done, and helps to ensure that the company delivers on its promises. With so much information quickly available at the click of mouse to both the service workers and salespeople, it is possible to respond promptly to the concerns of the client. This boosts customer satisfaction, breeds loyalty, and ultimately leads to more revenue and profits for the organization.

Better Responsive Customer Service

A happy customer breeds employee satisfaction and hence enhances employee morale. An employee of the organization likes to serve a happy customer more than a dissatisfied customer. No longer do employees find themselves conducting hit-or-miss searches for the information they need to satisfy customers. The response time is much less and service personnel find it motivating to serve the customer. Now, such data is easy to locate. If needed, it can be put into the convenient form of a printed report (Fig. 13.5).

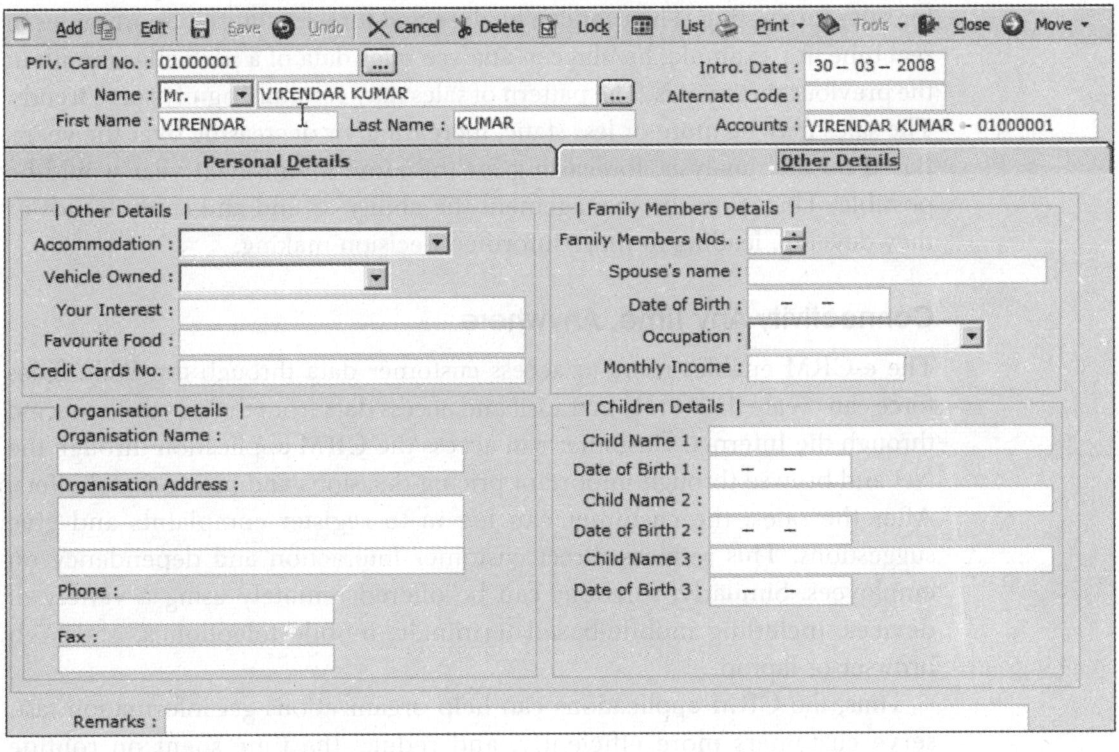

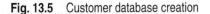

Fig. 13.5 Customer database creation

Streamlined Business Processes

The CRM applications not only centralize customer sales and service information and provide analytical reports on customer data but also provide well-structured and defined business processes to follow, for example, there are well-defined steps for complaint-handling system in a mobile service company. The employee simply follows those steps and completes the process of complaint recording, allocation, and service delivery and compliance system. Similarly, the CRM tools can be integrated with other business applications. In this way, transactions need not be entered, updated, and closed in multiple systems, which means managing every customer contact, answering every question without delay, and acting proactively. Thus, organizations are setting high standards to make it difficult for competitors to keep up.

Enhanced Forecasting Capability

Based on sales transactional data, customers' spending patterns, history of promotional effectiveness, etc., CRM applications provide important tools for sales forecasting. The user can analyse and forecast future opportunities in real time, for example, he/she can analyse sales data of a particular month in the previous three years. The pattern of sales may certainly signify some trends. The sales may be more or less static, increasing, or decreasing over the years. Based on that analysis, forecasting for the same month next year would be possible. This gives the management the ability to find and study trends as they develop, leading to more informed decision-making.

Connectivity Any Time, Anywhere

The e-CRM enables users to access customer data through the Web. Sales force can create data while in transit and access data from the server connected through the Internet. Customer can access the CRM application through the Net and browse through important pricing decisions and promotional offers. After the sales, the customer can log in to register complaints and give suggestions. This reduces direct customer interaction and dependency on employees. Similarly, solutions can be offered remotely using a variety of devices, including mobile-based terminals, mobile telephones, and Web browser or laptop.

Thus, the CRM applications can help organizations get information fast, serve customers more efficiently, and reduce the time spent on routine processes. This means that employees can spend more time focusing on the customers and service.

E-CRM TOOLS AND THEIR APPLICATIONS

The CRM applications consist of three major modules, which are built around customer-focused business processes across multiple interaction channels. Interaction channels are where the customer meets the organization. These modules are marketing, sales, and service. Most of the CRM applications provide best-in-class functionality for marketing, sales, and service. Customer-loyalty programmes are designed and executed at sales interaction with the customer. The CRM enables organizations to focus on strategies for customer-driven growth and differentiate themselves in the market by providing a superior customer experience.

The CRM gives you the capability to easily create and maintain a clear view of customers from the first contact through purchase and post-sales activities. These tools enhance the company's sales, marketing, and customer-service processes.

Each major module of CRM has the following sub-modules:

- Marketing CRM
- Sales CRM
- Customer-service CRM

Marketing CRM

It covers the following functionalities:

- Customer segmentation
- Campaign planning and execution
- Data extraction and refinement
- Analytics and reporting
- Marketing/sales collaboration tools
- Information-sharing portals

Sales CRM

It includes the following functionalities:

- Account and contact management
- Lead and opportunity management
- Quotation generation
- Customer communication
- Sales targets
- Forecasting and sales analytics
- Offline and mobile device access

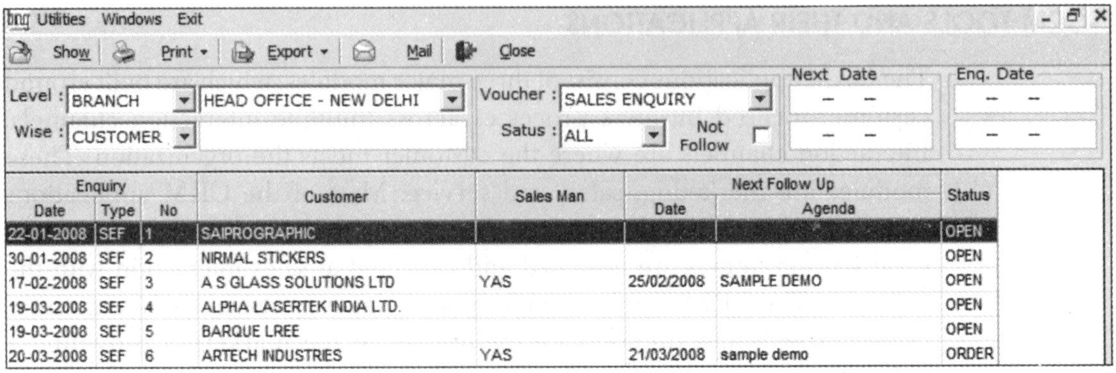

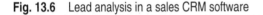

Fig. 13.6 Lead analysis in a sales CRM software

Customer-service CRM

The following functionalities are facilitated through this module:

- Account and contact management
- Customer service request
- Allocation of service request
- Performance of service and scheduling
- Service reporting and analytics

We will now discuss CRM tools in detail.

MARKETING AUTOMATION

Marketing part of CRM provides a clearer view of customers and more informed marketing investments. This module offers creating segments of customer into distinct benefit groups and then market to one or more of the identified segments using a workflow-driven model. Marketing staff members now have tools to help them identify, execute, and replicate effective marketing initiatives across the sales channels. The staff can assign, schedule, and track marketing campaign activities, and measure campaign performance. With marketing automation in place, you can integrate your sales, marketing, and service processes more effectively and present a professional company image to the customers.

Customer Segmentation

Customers can be divided into various meaningful segments based on their common traits and attributes. A simple generalized grouping in retail is segmentation based on the volume of their purchases. The segments can be A, B, or C types; or Platinum, Gold, and Silver. These segments signify the importance of customer and types of discounts offered at the retail place. Marketing strategists easily target their best customers with promotions, call downs, and e-mail communications.

Campaign Planning and Execution

Marketing campaigns are designed and run for customers. Organizations can use this tool to help them quickly and easily connect with business prospects and customers. The module permits designing promotional campaign, sending SMSs on customer mobile phone, sending an e-mail, and marketing mailers. The system can also track responses to keep connections up to date. With responsibility for several well-organized marketing campaigns each year in support of new product launches, organizations may want to automate task planning, list creation, task assignment, cost tracking, and many other tasks involved in complex campaigns. Sometimes, marketing staff plans a campaign that is executed by the sales staff at the point-of-sales location. These efforts require cross-department collaboration, execution, and tracking. Every company wants an easy way to gather a list of leads or customers, send a mass e-mailing, and track responses. The E-CRM provides functionality to send e-mails in bulk.

Data Extraction and Refinement

Marketing CRM uses basic data created during prospecting or sales data created at the retail point of sales. This makes it easy for the marketing staff to take advantage of the customer data that the organization already has. It is easy to join efforts with sales and judge the success of marketing efforts. The data created at various stages of sales and marketing can also be refined and re-segmented.

Information-sharing Portals

The e-CRM applications offer online data creation and sharing portals. Customers can log on to the portal and enter their requirements and general information. This information can later be shared by sales and marketing analysts, for example, you can log in to Airtel's portal (www.airtel.in). The customer can enter some details, which are used by Airtel in further marketing and sales campaigns.

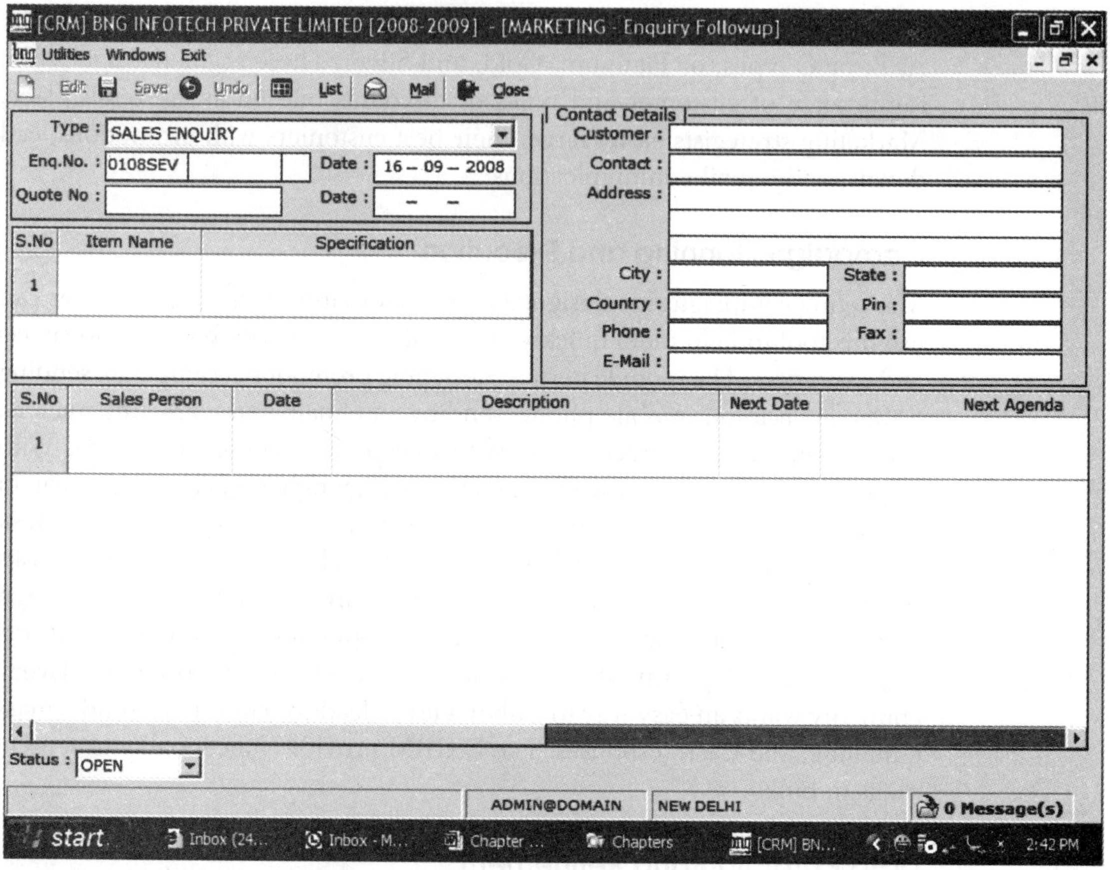

Fig. 13.7 Leads and opportunities

SALES CYCLE AUTOMATION

Sales force automation (SFA) modules of CRM help the sales staff to manage more leads and close more business. This provides access to a complete view of customer data online or offline. The SFA leverages tools that enable sales professionals to get real-time access to leads and close more deals, faster. This is mostly used for larger sales account, but is also helpful if enquiries are posted by retail prospects through the organization's touch points like web portal. The staff can capture important sales information to uncover new business opportunity and use pipeline analysis reports to create precise sales forecasts (Fig. 13.7).

The following functionalities are provided by the SFA:

- Account management
- Leads and opportunity management

- Quotation generation
- Customer communications
- Sales targets
- Sales forecasting and sales analytics
- Mobile device access

Account Management

Systems provide functionality to view past and current account activity, including contact information, communications, open quotes, pending orders, invoices, credit limits, and payment history. Preliminary account information is created at the time of receipt of enquiry, which is then updated at every stage of interaction with the customer.

Leads and Opportunity Management

Leads may be generated through the web portal of the organization, which may be available for scanning and further qualifying by the authorized staff. Leads are also generated by sales staff in the form of enquiries, which are entered in the database for further action regarding them. Systems provide functionality to track prospective customers and then convert them into qualified leads. The leads once qualified are then routed to the correct salespeople or teams for follow up.

Quotation Generation

Sales personnel create quotations against the qualified leads and send them to prospects. At this stage, they have access to all product and pricing information. Advanced features in the CRM may also give them an insight into the historical data of previous similar quotes and orders. They can also track the conversion of quotations into orders (Fig. 13.8).

Communication with the customer

All communication with the prospective customer is entered in the system at all stages of lead follow up. This is done through a suitable interface available to the user. If connected through a voice-recognition package, the verbal communication can be automatically converted into text and stored in the database (Fig. 13.9). The communication can also be sent to the customers through e-mail or any other medium of communication. Among the advanced functionalities offered by such systems is creation of print material and then sending it to prospective customers via office tools like mail merge.

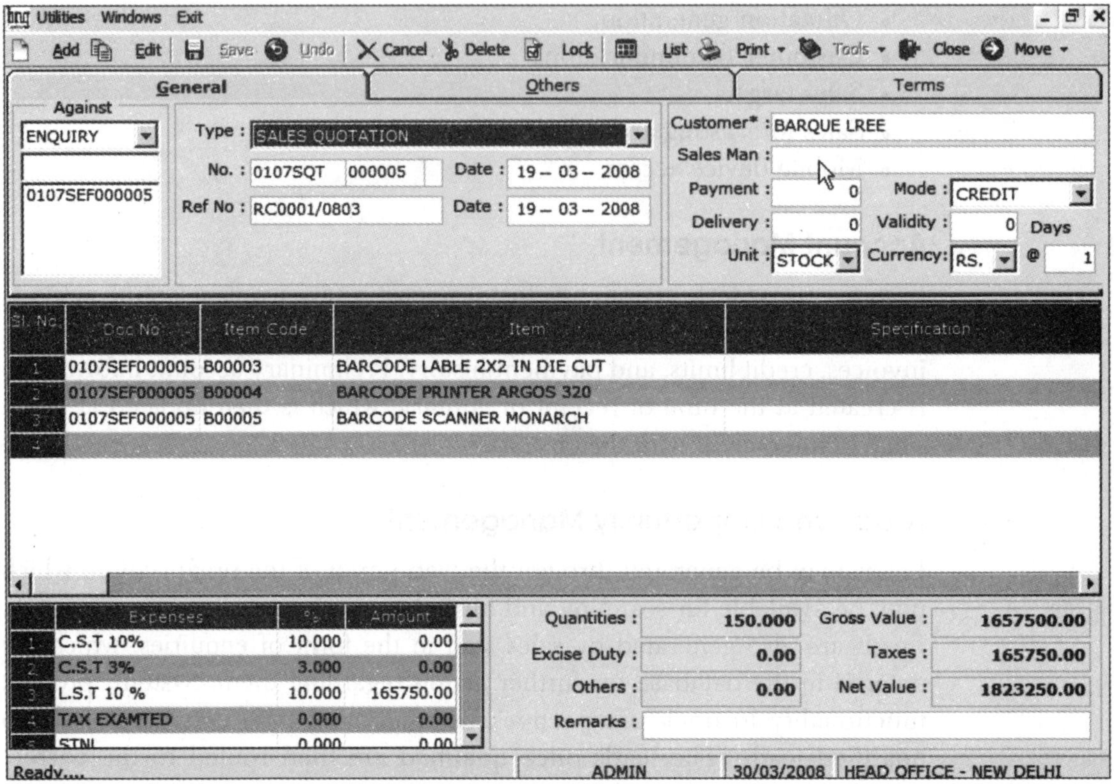

Fig. 13.8 Quotation generation in an SFA module

Sales Targets

Targets and quota management is a part of the SFA and involves setting targets for individuals or sales team. The systems provide functionality to measure employee sales performance against goals. As opportunities are closed in, they are set off against the assigned quota.

Sales Forecasting and sales analytics

Sales forecasting is done on the basis of historical data available to the sales personnel in the CRM module. It also considers the sales opportunity funnel. (*Sales opportunity funnel* is the number of sales leads in the pipeline that is closable by a certain date.) This adds to the total revenue that can be collected through sales during particular period of time. Sales analytic tools facilitate insight into customer data, i.e. customer tastes, preferences, buying patterns, and reach can be understood. This data is invaluable for any retail organization to increase customer satisfaction level and create competitive advantage.

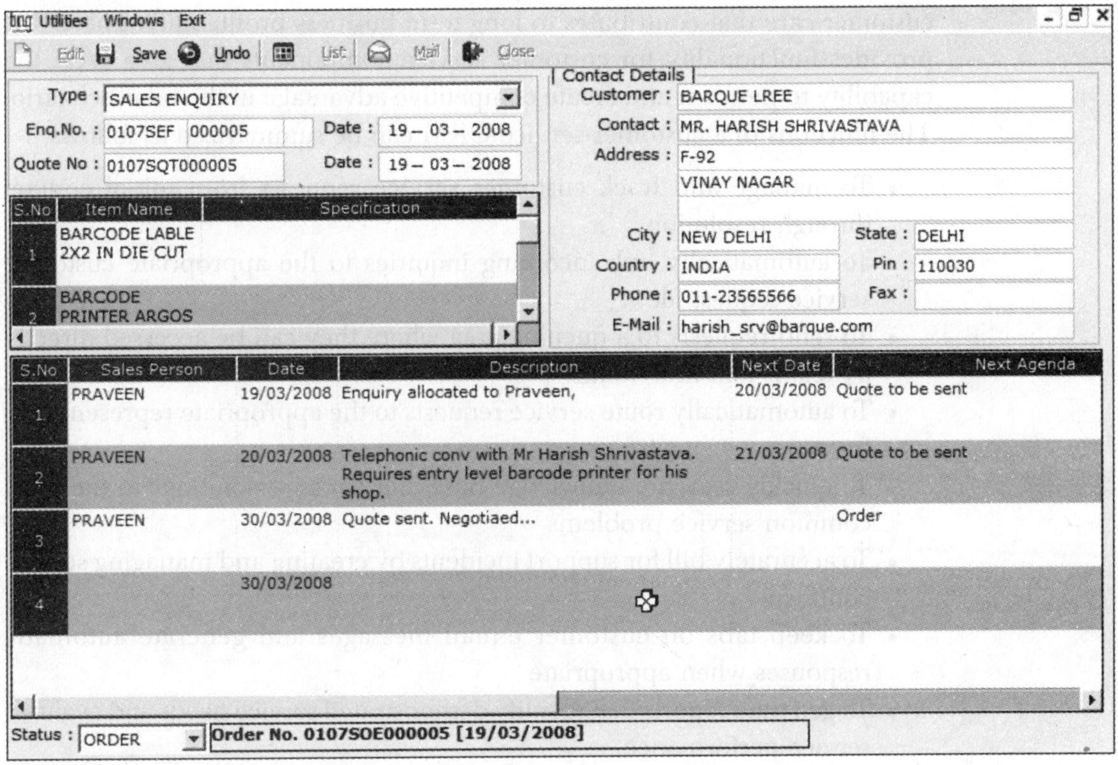

Fig. 13.9 Complete customer communication recorded and viewed

Mobile Device Access

Access, acquisition, and transmission of sales data is emerging as an important ingredient of sales force automation. Using mobile handheld devices in the distribution provides instant access to the sales personnel of availability of stocks at the distribution centre. The orders collected by the person at the retail outlet are transmitted back to distribution server within no time. Thus, the distribution system immediately knows the requirements at the retail store. This connectivity is established through GPRS system (on which mobile telephony works) or any other connectivity media.

CUSTOMER SERVICE AND SUPPORT AUTOMATION

After successful marketing and sales, the onus on the organization is to serve the customer and handle complaints. Through e-CRM, the organization can respond faster to customer-service issues and empower service organization to anticipate and address customer issues and deliver consistent, efficient customer care that contributes to long-term business profitability. The CRM provides functionality for customer service components that give users the capability to perform and create competitive advantage in the retail scenario. The functions of a customer-service CRM can be summarized as follows:

- To manage and track customer service requests from initial contact through resolution
- To automatically link incoming inquiries to the appropriate customer service request file
- To send requests to a queuing area where they can be accessed directly by teams and individuals
- To automatically route service requests to the appropriate representative for action
- To quickly search a knowledge base that contains solutions to the most common service problems
- To accurately bill for support incidents by creating and managing service contracts
- To keep tabs on customer e-mail messages and generate automatic responses when appropriate
- To generate reports that identify demonstrated service needs and evaluate service performance

Customer Service Requests

The customer service and support module of CRM works on the sales and marketing database, predefined, preconfigured, and already segmented customers. Service requests may be received by the organizations through personal interactions, e-mails, telephone calls, letters, website contacts, or chat sessions. These requests can be entered through the call-centre user interface. A call identification number 'ID' is generated irrespective of the medium of interaction. The call number or complaint number is linked with the caller ID (usually customer identification number). The entire interaction history of the contact is preserved in the suitable CRM application (Fig. 13.10).

Allocation of Service Requests

The service request or complaint is forwarded to the service personnel. The request can be scrutinized and qualified by the seniors and marked with types of action required on the call request. The system automatically stamps the request with date and time of receipt, as well as allocation.

Enquiry		Customer	Specificatio n	Enquiry	Quotation			
No.	Date			Qty	No.	Date	Value	
107SEF000001	22/01/2008	SAIPROGRAPHIC	150MMX20N	2.00	0107SQT000001	18/02/2008	4845.57	0107S(
107SEF000002	30/01/2008	NIRMAL STICKERS	50GSM H.M.	4.00	0107SQT000002	19/03/2008	9225.22	0107S(
107SEF000003	17/02/2008	A S GLASS SOLUTIONS LTD		40000.00	0107SQT000003	19/03/2008	8289160.00	0107S(
107SEF000004	19/03/2008	ALPHA LASERTEK INDIA LTD.		50.00	0107SQT000004	19/03/2008	10400.00	0107S(
107SEF000004	19/03/2008	ALPHA LASERTEK INDIA LTD.		50.00	0107SQT000004	19/03/2008	10400.00	0107S(
107SEF000005	19/03/2008	BARQUE LREE		150.00	0107SQT000005	19/03/2008	1823250.00	0107S(
107SEF000006	20/03/2008	ARTECH INDUSTRIES		19000.00	0107SQT000006	20/03/2008	5117.00	0107S(
OTAL				59256.00			10152397.79	

Fig. 13.10 Access to complete customer service history

Performance of Service Contract

On performance of the service, the service personnel enter the call performance details and generate a service performance document like service slip. The service performance is linked with the call ID.

Delivery and Billing Request of Services

On receipt of the service performance completion information by the call monitoring system, the employee updates the call as completed in the call-centre package. The monitoring system can view incomplete calls, pending calls, and call delays.

CUSTOMER LOYALTY PROGRAMMES

Sales force automation, which is already discussed, is important from distribution point of view or for business-to-business trade. In retail, it is highly unlikely that sales personnel generate leads and work on sales funnel management. Since retail signifies 'walk-in' customer, the methods of enhancing customer loyalty are altogether different. These methods are rewarding the customer for being with the retail organization. Discounts are offered based on the customer's gradation, which is again based on their purchases over a period of time.

There are tools and applications available that help design and implement customer loyalty programmes (CLPs), in which the customers are graded as

A, B, or C category. This grading is based on the volume of purchases made by the customer over a period of time, say in the last one year. Different discount structures are created as per the grading. A loyalty card is issued to the customer, which bears the customer ID. The customer can use this card on subsequent purchases. On swiping the card or entering the ID number, the system gives discount on the purchases as per the grade of the customer. Loyalty programmes offer rewards and incentives to customers for their loyalty to the organization. Retailers form buyers club and register their customers as members of the club. The identity cards issued serve the purpose of both discounts and loyalty cards.

SUMMARY

Customer relationship management refers to being in touch with the customer. As the market moves from a seller's market to a buyer's market, the business culture shifts to a customer focus approach. This paradigm shift necessitates acquisition, enhancement, and retention of customer. Retaining a customer is more cost-effective for the organization than acquiring a new one.

The relationship marketing strategy represents a shift from acquisition/transaction focus to retention/relationship focus. This new philosophy of doing business focuses on keeping and improving existing customers rather than spending more on acquiring new customers. The focus changes from segmentation of customer to customization. Now, the focus is on individual customer rather than a group of customers. The profits generated on the sales made to a customer must be more than the expenses spent on acquiring and maintaining the customer. The profitability of a customer is called *customer value* and is the total profit or sales in the lifetime of the customer. The new marketing strategy advocates selling more to the customer. Customer loyalty is cultivated through various relationship-marketing tools, rather than acquired.

To manage the customer right, CRM tools are available and its deployment offers a number of advantages, such as improved access to customer information, more responsive customer service, streamlined business processes, enhanced forecasting capabilities, and online connectivity with the customer and the organization.

The complete CRM tools work around marketing, sales, and customer service. Most of the CRM applications provide best in-class functionality for marketing, sales, and service. The CRM enables organizations to focus on strategies for customer-driven growth and to differentiate themselves in the market by providing a superior customer experience. The marketing CRM offers customer account management, promotional campaigns, communication planning and executions, and analytics on the customer data. The sales cycle CRM offers sales force automation functionalities. These functionalities are lead and opportunity management, quotations, follow up, and order confirmation. This also includes sales forecasting based on historical data and opportunity pipeline. The call centre interface of the software keeps complete communication with the customer and is available for view. The final module of CRM is customer service management. It takes care of service request recording, allocation of service request to service personnel, performance of service, and delivery and closing up.

Customer loyalty programmes are designed to breed and enhance customer loyalty in retail scenario. These programmes offer rewards and incentives to customers for their loyalty to the organization. Retailers form buyers club and register their customers as members of the club. The identity cards issued serve the purposes of both discount and loyalty cards.

CONCEPT REVIEW QUESTIONS

1. Define customer relationship management.
2. What do you understand by customer value chain? Comment on each component of value chain.
3. What is relationship marketing strategy? Which are its various components?
4. What advantages do you perceive in a suitable CRM package deployment?
5. How does CRM software increase forecasting capabilities of an organization?
6. Explain various functions offered by marketing, sales cycle, and customer-service CRM.

CRITICAL THINKING QUESTIONS

1. 'The relationship strategy focuses on existing customers.' Explain with suitable examples.
2. Explain features and advantages of any known Indian CRM software.

PROJECT

1. The biggest mobile network company in India has more than 60 million demanding customers today. It takes the customer just one call to switch over to the competitor's network. Design a blueprint for CRM software that can provide complete customer satisfaction and thus restrict him from switching over to a competitor.

SELECT REFERENCES

Berry, Leonard L. and A. Parasuraman 1991, *Marketing Services: Competing Through Quality*, Free Press, New York.

BNG Infotech, www.bng.co.in, last accessed on 02/12/2007.

Jaiswal, Mahadeo and Monika Mital 2007, *Management Information Systems*, Oxford University Press.

Laudon, Ken and Mary Laudon 2002, *Management Information System*, Pearson Education (Singapore).

Sinha, Piyush Kumar and Uniyal, Dwarika Prasad 2007, *Managing Retailing*, Oxford University Press, New Delhi.

Webster, F.E. (Jr.) 1992, 'The Changing Role of Marketing in the Corporation', *Journal of Marketing*, October.

Zeithaml, Valarie A. and Mary Jo Bitner 2006, *Services Marketing: Integrating Customer Focus Across The Firm*, Tata McGraw-Hill, New Delhi.

CASE STUDY

CRM: Let the Music Play

The Company—Vera Music Stores

Vera Music Stores is a leading entertainment store specializing in music and film CDs and DVDs, fiction and other types of books, and electronic goods. Along with the retail, the company runs its central repair service of electronic goods from its flagship store in Mumbai. Vera Music Stores was launched in 2001 as a specialty store selling Bollywood film music. But with the demand from the customers, it started selling electronic gadgets, such as iPods, digital cameras, digital watches, electronic toys, and music players. The company was launched by Lalchand group of Mumbai. Within a short period of two years, it established a large flagship store in Andheri (E), Mumbai and around 20 more stores in Mumbai to meet the ever-increasing demand from youngsters. The company has around 120 employees across all the stores including the central store.

The Problem

Retailing of consumer-durable goods requires strong after-sales service. Delivering excellent customer service is an essential part of maintaining a strong retail brand. For Vera Music Stores, one of the country's leading entertainment stores, customer service is a crucial component of success. This is particularly true in the company's repair centre, where customers expect to have their orders dealt with as quickly as possible. Sometimes, repair status of equipment was not updated and hence it was difficult to resolve online queries of customers.

To maintain its high standards, the company decided to automate customer service processes at its repair centre based at its flagship store in Andheri. Repair centre employees relied on manual, paper-based processes to check in and track customer repairs. Whenever a customer brought a machine to the centre for repair, personnel had to complete two paper forms, one for the customer and other for the store. The customer was obliged to wait at the desk during this process. Tracing the progress of repairs involved consulting large amounts of paperwork. Moreover, locating items once they had been returned to the repair centre was also time consuming and inefficient.

The Objective

Vera Music Stores wanted to reduce the time employees spent completing paperwork and provide instant information to customers about the repair status of their equipment. It also wanted to speed up the data capture process to provide an enhanced customer experience. Simple workflow was essential for the repair centre. They wanted to implement a simple, practical process that would help them manage the repair service we deliver as easily as possible. To help it maintain the highest possible levels of customer service, Vera Music Stores decided to replace its manual processes with an automated solution.

The Solution

In 2003, the company sent request for quotations to various CRM vendors in the country. A total number of ten quotes were received. After evaluating the products, implementing partners, and prices, the company zeroed in on Microsoft Dynamics CRM. CoralSoft, a Microsoft Certified Partner, was short listed for implementing the solution. With the solution in place, employees can work more efficiently, reducing the time it takes to process repairs up to 50 per cent. In addition, they can deal with larger numbers of customers. It comes handy during peak holiday periods. Employees can use their time qualitatively in engaging with customers, enhancing the overall retail experience. The company now hopes to integrate Microsoft Dynamics CRM with its existing retail solution.

Vera Music Stores was new to CRM products at its repair centre. Therefore, it decided in favour of the product only after seeing a demo. The company chose a solution based on Microsoft Dynamics CRM. According to the company's IT Manager, the product met most of the requirements of the retailer's after-sales service for electronic gadgets.

CoralSoft deployed Dynamics CRM 1.2. It created a simple workflow to log items submitted to the repair centre desk and track their progress. The workflow covers all the different stages of the repair process and makes it easy for the employees to locate up-to-date information about individual repairs. The system also provides reporting capabilities that help the company create customer lists by class and type and track dealer response times. The company also uses different tools available in the CRM package, which provides a list of all outstanding tasks and activities at a glance and helps employees search the CRM database using a variety of criteria.

Benefits

The solution was installed on five machines with a central server. Five employees at a time could use the solution for maintaining post-sales service. The solution helped reduce their workload by making it easier to deal with repairs. Initially, it took some time to implement the solution and train the employees. But after the initial teething problems, the management got a positive feedback. It became much easier for the employees to finish tasks, making them concentrate on a wider variety of activities

Automated System Reduces Repair Time by 40 per cent   The time spent on resolving customer queries and locating the product was reduced considerably. Once the correct information has been entered and the order logged, the system immediately creates a pre-defined workflow, making it easy for employees to track the order, respond to customer queries, and locate the item when it is returned to the store.

Pre-defined workflow created The workflow covers every stage of the repair process, including the following:

- Job card creation—the arrival of items at the centre
- Job assignment—delivery to the appropriate repair engineer
- Job estimation—engineer reports on the nature of faults and cost of repairs
- Estimate submission—pricing and timelines
- Estimate approval—client's acceptance and confirmation of estimates
- Receipts of goods from job work—delivery of the repaired item to the centre
- Goods delivery—customer collection schedules

Employees can access the repair history at any time to deal with customer queries or reporting requirements.

Improved Employee Efficiency and Productivity Employee morale has increased by working on a CRM package. Employees no longer have to spend time locating and completing paper forms. Instead, they simply enter repair information electronically. This process is quicker and eliminates the duplication of tasks since personnel has to enter information into the system only once. It is also easier for the personnel to deal with increased work volumes during peak holiday periods. With the right solution in place, it is much easier for the employees to deliver a rapid service using the new system because they have a single point of access for all the information. For example, just after Diwali, there is often a high demand for the repairs service and the repair centre staff is able to dispose of the papers quickly.

Increased Customer Satisfaction and Loyalty It is a win-win situation. Not just employees, customers have also benefited from the new system. Though the company has not collected any specific feedback, the fact that customers spend less time at the repair desk helps enhance the overall retail experience. Vera is now able to offer a much higher level of customer engagement and visitors have noticed the change.

Company Increases Process Efficiency and hence Profitability The company has also been able to increase its overall efficiency. The entire repair process is quicker and more transparent from start to finish. Implementation of CRM package has made things much easier for the company. The service manager maintains that they are now able to repair more equipment in a month than what they were repairing before implementation of the CRM system.

Question:
1. What were the problems faced by Vera Music Stores before implementation of Microsoft CRM? How were those problems taken care of by the CRM software?

14

E-commerce and E-tailing

Learning Objectives

- To become familiar with the basics of e-commerce
- To identify e-commerce infrastructure
- To appreciate the World Wide Web as the backbone of e-commerce activities
- To understand complexities of e-tailing and support services involved in it
- To compare a brick-n-mortar store with a virtual store
- To appreciate the business potential by looking at the current Internet retailing scenario

PayPal—Making Payments Easy Over the Net

PayPal was founded in late 1998 by an American entrepreneur, Peter Thiel, a former securities lawyer and options trader. He, along with a group of friends from Stanford University, created the company Confinity. He financed Max Levchin, a software developer who saw the need for a secure software system that allowed electronic transfer of payments. Other investors rapidly showed interest, including Nokia Ventures, which put up $3 million, and Deutsche Bank, which contributed a further $1.5 million. Following its launch in November 1999, Confinity attracted more backers, including investment bank Goldman, Sachs & Co, which invested $23 million in Confinity's PayPal.com. With the rapid expansion of the Internet, PayPal soon had 1.5 million account holders generating a throughput of $2 million per day.

This rapid success led to eBay naming PayPal.com its primary online payment service. Later, X.com, an online bank founded by Elon Musk, and PayPal merged to become the world's largest secure online payment network. The name PayPal remained although X.com was listed as the parent company.

In early 2002, PayPal was floated on the stock market for around $900 million. By July 2002, PayPal account holders numbered 16 million with 2,95,000 payment transactions taking place every day.

In October 2002, eBay acquired PayPal for around $1.5 billion.

The PayPal service enables anyone with an e-mail address to make and receive online payments quickly and securely using the existing payment infrastructure with the benefit of the latest fraud-prevention technology.

By 2004, PayPal, located in San Jose, California, had 50 million account holders with its services available in some 45 countries.

Sources: Adapted from www.internet-story.com and www.paypal.com.

Till now, we have confined our discussions to tools and applications used at retail point of sales and back-office management. The Internet brought in new business opportunities and processes. Worldwide, retailing is being done through the Internet in a big way. In this chapter, we will discuss retailing using the Internet and the tools and infrastructure required to sustain such businesses.

You will agree that the Internet is a revolution. In fact, someone rightly suggested that now dates in history should be referred to as BI and AI (Before and after the Internet) instead of BC and AC (before and after Christ). It has brought in major changes in the way business is done and customers interact with the seller or service organizations. Today, buyers would like to shop from within the comforts and confines of their homes for various reasons.

Retail has also gone through a paradigm shift in India. It has graduated from family-owned *kirana* shops before 1990s to modern retailing formats, which are more organized. These formats include department stores, hypermarkets, supermarkets, and specialty stores across a wide range of categories. Today, these retail formats have established good presence across prime locations in the metropolitan and other major cities, such as state capitals in India. In the last few years, organized retail has spread out to the second-tier cities and towns, either launched by local entrepreneurs or started on a franchisee model, which is again an acceleration initiated by multinational fast-food behemoths, such as MacDonald's, Pizza Hut, and Subway. The unhindered spread is exposing consumers to modern shopping options and experiences like never before.

The organized retail is getting its share from traditional retail. It is also playing a major role in boosting consumption levels of the people. Looking at the urban youth flocking fast-food joints, the role played by the organized retailers is justified. As per the findings of IMAGES F&R Research, the total private consumption expenditure (in direct retail sales) is estimated at INR 10,500 billion (US $233 billion) growing at 5 per cent annually; the estimated share of organized retail is only INR 350 billion (US $8 billion) in 2006, albeit growing at over 30 per cent every year.

ELECTRONIC COMMERCE

Traditionally, business activities were accomplished by involving physical channels of buying and distribution. But today, more and more organizations are using the Internet for selling and buying goods and services. Electronic commerce (e-commerce) involves transactions between two organizations or individuals over the public networks called the Internet. Buying and selling of goods and services between two organizations is called *business-to-business (B2B) commerce*. Organizational procurement systems, tendering, and e-procurement portals are some examples of B2B commerce. Most of the organizations today establish portals through which their trading partners can place orders for goods and services offered by the organization. Selling and buying of goods and services between an organization and the end-consumer is known as *business-to-consumer (B2C) commerce*. Web portals like Amazon.com are dedicated businesses selling goods through the Web. There are millions of organizations that have established e-commerce portals as an extension of their present retail businesses. There are electronic storefronts of organizations selling books, such as crossword.com, firstandsecond.com, and oup.co.in. Similarly, selling of goods and services by a consumer to another consumer is called *consumer-to-consumer (C2C) commerce*. Various Web auction sites like eBay are examples of C2C commerce, where a consumer can sell his/her new or used goods to another consumer. Commerce of any nature involves complete transaction processing, except physical movement of goods, over the Net.

Thus, e-commerce is a modern business methodology that uses the electronic media and is an effort towards cost cutting, quality improvement, and increasing speed of services.

In this chapter, we will discuss the retailer-to-consumer (B2C) part of the e-commerce.

ELECTRONIC SHOPPING

It is also known as Internet shopping, e-shopping, or virtual shopping. *Electronic shopping* refers to purchasing goods, information, and services through the Internet. It involves browsing through the electronic catalogues displayed over the web pages of the seller, placing orders, and making payment through the Net.

The Internet today has come of age and an organization cannot really ignore to set up its web interface on the Internet without losing a considerable percentage of its business and, of course, clients. In the hype of organized and mall-induced retail picture, there exists a less visible, ultra-modern and hi-tech retail channel known as online shopping. As per a research conducted by AMAI, the number of consumers (shopping online) stands at about 38.5 million and the total sales proceeds from online shopping was Rs 1180 crore in 2005–06. The number of online consumers is growing at over five million per year. The netizens are affluent and can adopt technology faster. This phenomenon is inducing retailers to set up virtual shops. Figure 14.1 shows e-shopping of gifts and toys.

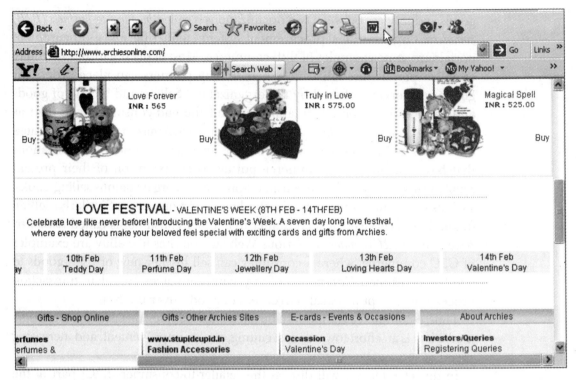

Fig. 14.1   An e-commerce portal selling gifts and toys

Worldwide, more and more people are using the Internet for carrying out shopping activities online. People are comfortable buying goods (such as books, flowers, apparels, and electronic equipment) and using services (such as travel tickets, job placements, and matrimonial). In India, the share of services in the total Internet-based trade is more than the goods.

WORLD WIDE WEB

The phenomenon of Internet-based transactions cannot be understood without understanding the World Wide Web. The World Wide Web (WWW) is the backbone of modern e-commerce. The Web began in 1989 when Tim Berners-Lee of European Laboratory for Particle Physics proposed a Web project for sharing of information among its members. The WWW is a system with universally accepted standards (protocols) for storing, retrieving, formatting, and displaying information using client-server architecture. In client-server architecture, the web servers store and retrieve information and manage data, application, and security. The client is the interface between the user and the web server and the server displays the information through a core browser or application, for example in an e-mail service, the web server hosts complete data, runs e-mail management application, and provides security to the e-mail data. The computer terminal, on which the user works and that runs Windows Internet Explorer (as browser), is a client of the web server and functions as an interface between the user and the web server (Fig. 14.2).

The Web combines text, data, hypermedia, graphics, and sound. It can handle all kinds of digital communication linking computers and networks across the world. *Hypermedia* consists of documents and links. A link or pointer in one document indicates further linkages to another document. This concept is called *hypertext.* The documents can contain text, graphs, animation, audio, video, images, or programs. The hypermedia has the ability to use several media in a single document for display through the browser and thus combines hypertext and multimedia.

The WWW works around the following important concepts:

- URL
- HTTP
- HTML

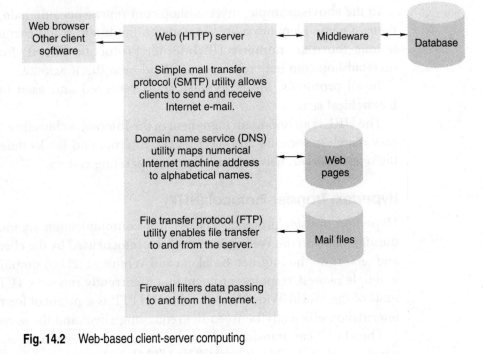

Fig. 14.2   Web-based client-server computing

Source: Adapted from Laudon and Laudon 2002

Universal Resource Locator (URL)

There are millions and trillions of computers connected to the Internet. Finding a file on the Net would be impossible if there is no structured addressing system. The addressing scheme makes the hypermedia publishing possible despite many different protocols. The documents that the browser displays are the hypertext that contains pointers to the other documents. The pointer is implemented using a concept that is central to all web browsers *uniform resource locator* (URL). A URL marks the unique location on the Internet where a file can be found. It is also known as 'web address'.

The universal resource locators use a perfectly consistent pattern. The web address consists of three parts differentiated with a dot (.). The first part gives the name of the resource, the second part the name of the server, and the third part gives full file name of the resource. For example, http//www.myretailshop.com/catalogue.html is a complete web address, also known as domain name, which has three distinct parts:

http//www	}	resource
myretailshop.com	}	server name
catalogue.html	}	file name, which has details of products

In the above example, myretailshop.com represents a domain name. The domain name identifies a unique node on the Internet and corresponds to a unique four-part numeric IP (Internet Protocol) address, for example, myretailshop.com may represent an IP address 192.168.95.22.

In all protocols, the right slash (/) is reserved and used to represent hierarchical spaces.

The URL is an important ingredient of the Internet architecture. It facilitates easy search in locating an object on the Internet and works independent of the type of server, network topology, or operating system.

Hypertext Transfer Protocol (HTTP)

Hypertext transfer protocol (HTTP) is a communication standard used to transfer pages on the Web. It is a network protocol used by the client browsers and servers on the Internet. Kalakota and Whinston (2006) simplify HTTP as a 'simple request/response protocol that is currently run over TCP and is the basis of the World Wide Web'. In short, HTTP is a protocol for transferring information efficiently between the requesting client and the server.

The HTTP can transfer multimedia data, such as text, images, or sounds, which are all in HTML formats. The HTML is discussed next.

Hypertext Mark-up Language (HTML)

We browse through or surf the Internet by clicking at links provided on web pages. These pages have been created using standards called hypertext mark-up language (HTML). The Web uses graphic user interface (GUI) for easy and aesthetic viewing and this language for creation of web pages supports GUI. The HTML is a language that every web client is required to understand. It is used for creating hypertext documents containing text, graphics, sounds, and images. It uses instructions, called tags, to specify how this data of varying nature is placed on a document. The beauty of this language lies in its ability to club every type of data in the page. It is a common basic language of interchange for hypertext that forms the basic architecture of Web. The HTML formats documents and incorporates dynamic links to other documents stored in the same or remote computers. Using these links, the user needs only to point at a highlighted keyword or graphic. On clicking over the link, the user is transported to another document, probably on another computer somewhere in this globe.

A further development of HTML is XML (extensible mark-up language). Whereas HTML only determines how text and images are displayed on a document, XML further specifies the meaning or detail of the data on the pages.

Browsers, such as MS-IE and Netscape. are programmed according to HTML standards, which are universally accepted.

E-COMMERCE INFRASTRUCTURE

Retail organizations and individuals who want to build their e-commerce businesses, need special infrastructure, and tools to construct, maintain, and manage these virtual shop fronts called e-commerce portals. The infrastructure includes the following:

- Web servers
- E-commerce portals
- Web-hosting services
- Web content-management tools

Web Servers

All the resources of an e-commerce application and data reside in a web server. Web servers are the hardware and software necessary to run websites, intranet, and extranets. The core capabilities of web server software include locating and managing stored web pages.

Web server software locates the web pages requested by the client computer by translating the URL web address into the physical file address for the requested page. The web server then sends the requested pages to the client. A web server consists of hardware like Pentium 4 desktop PC. Microsoft's Internet Information Server (IIS), Apache HTTP Server, and Netscape's Enterprise Server (NES) are currently the most popular web server software. The Apache and Netscape web servers work with most of the operating systems, whereas IIS server is designed for Microsoft operating system.

The web server can be a specialized high-end server. But the web server computer must be large and efficient enough to handle the server software and traffic of the particular site. For setting up a server, the retail organization either can buy and locate a server in specially built server farms or can rent space on large servers provided by various companies. If the requirement is small, leasing the space would be right decision. Smaller e-commerce portals can be hosted on as small a space as ten megabytes.

E-Commerce Software or Portals

The web pages through which e-commerce trading is accomplished are specialized software. These sites are also known as e-commerce portals (Fig. 14.3). Nowadays, these software applications are readily available for running e-commerce sites. The applications are installed on special servers that are connected to the Internet through a public IP address. The e-commerce sites are dynamic in nature. The websites can be classified as static or dynamic. A *static web page* is one that rarely changes the information it displays. It contains fixed information about a place, person, or thing. Usually, company profiles and product profiles are displayed through static web pages. On the other hand, a *dynamic web page* is one in which the information changes regularly as it interacts with the customer or viewer. For example, a site selling books would display availability of a book in the store and the next moment the book is sold, it would display that it is not available. The e-commerce portals fall under this category. These sites perform the following functions:

- Setting up electronic storefronts and catalogues to display product and pricing information.
- Designing shopping carts so that customers can select and buy the items.
- Making electronic payment collection system and securing the site with international authenticating agencies like VeriSign.
- Connecting with the back-office ERP servers and updating stock availability on the site.

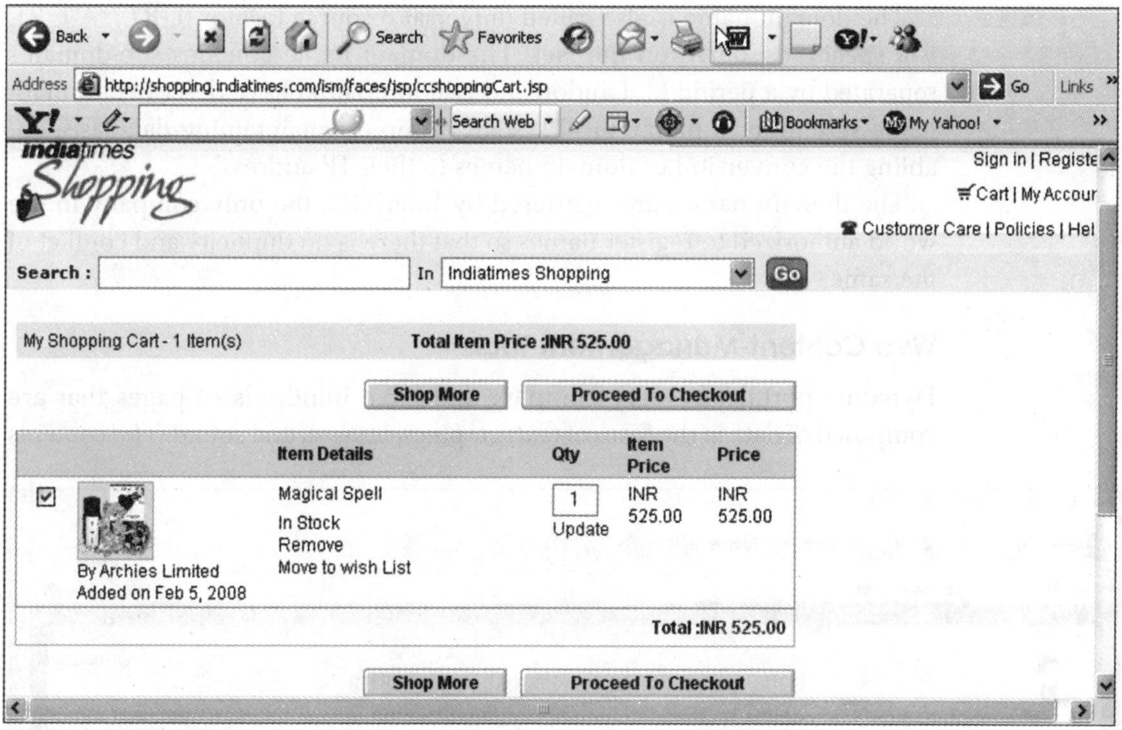

Fig. 14.3 Indiatimes portal selling Archies' goods

Web-Hosting Services

Servers involve a lot of initial and maintenance costs, technical expertise, and high Internet bandwidth for efficient functioning. The companies who do not wish to install and maintain their own servers hire web-hosting services. A web-hosting service provider maintains large web servers and rents space on these servers to a number of persons. Along with the space, the service provider also gives support related to the operating system and database. Organizations can hire third-party specialists for creating the website and designing contents. Usually, small and medium companies always like to go for a third-party server space and a portal development agency. The third-party specialists are very cost-effective and possess specialized knowledge for designing, developing, hosting, and managing such portals.

Once the retail organization has decided on hosting services, it can apply for the domain name or address. The domain name is the unique name that identifies this computer on which the site resides. The domain name is connected with the IP address. An example is given below:

www.retailsystem.com   IP address: 198.64.189.02

The domain name is also called universal resource locator (URL). A URL is a specific resource on the Net. The domain name contains sub-domains separated by a period (.). Laudon and Laudon (2002) have described domain name system as 'a hierarchical system of servers maintaining databases enabling the conversion of domain names to their IP address'.

The domain names are registered by InterNIC, the only company in the world authorized to register names so that there is no duplicity and conflict of the same.

Web Content-Management Tools

Dynamic portals are very complex and have hundreds of pages that are composed of data in the form of text, graphics, images, and sound. The contents

Fig. 14.4 IRCTC website selling e-tickets

of these pages are dynamic in nature and they change frequently depending on the environmental factors, such as type of products, customer, prices, and request of the visitor. Some of these sites maintain security and allow further navigation only to the registered customers who have been assigned passwords. These sites ask the first-time visitors to create their profile and get their passwords.

Even the static contents need updating from time to time due to changes in company profile, modification in product or contact information. These kinds of changes are carried out offline and the contents are updated frequently so that the site remains up and running. In the dynamic pages, the organization may need to change frequently the product profiles, product prices, or any other information related to the organization or the products. The content-management tool helps in making those changes. It provides a structure and easy approach to change the contents whenever needed. The company need not hire services of the experts every time a change is required.

ESSENTIALS OF E-TAILING

Electronic retailing or e-tailing, as it is generally being called now, is the direct sale of products, information, and service through virtual stores on the Web, usually designed around an electronic catalogue format and auction sites. There are thousands of storefronts or e-commerce sites on the Internet that are extensions of existing retailers or start-ups. Penetration of computers and proliferation of the Internet has given rise to many new forms of businesses, such as business process outsourcing, call centre based customer relationship management, medical transcription, remotely managed educational and medical services, and, of course, electronic retailing.

There are certain essential ingredients for an electronic retailing business to be successful. One must consider these components well in advance before setting up an electronic storefront. These essential components are:

- Attractive business-to-consumer (B2C) e-commerce portal
- Right revenue model
- Penetration of the Internet

Attractive B2C E-Commerce Portal

The business concept at both forms of retailing, brick store or virtual store, implies sales of goods or services to individual customers. As we have discussed earlier, the Internet model that sells goods to direct customers is known as B2C (business-to-consumer) e-commerce. Though there is no clear-cut distinction between B2B and B2C, as a B2C model may also sell to corporate customers or re-sellers. But, for the sake of our discussion, we assume a pure form of B2C commerce. The first priority of a retailer going electronic is to establish a B2C site of electronic storefront. We have already discussed e-commerce infrastructure and World Wide Web, the must haves for a successful e-commerce business. The World Wide Web is the backbone of modern e-commerce. The web portals work on and get their power from World Wide Web. The important ingredients of a good web portal are briefly discussed below.

Attractive web page   An aesthetically designed and attractive front page attracts good traffic. (Traffic in the Internet sense refers to the number of visitors logging on to or viewing a website.) The success of the site depends on the number of visitors it can attract. In the online channel of retail business, one does not count the footfalls. Nor do customers get the real world, touch-and-feel experience of the goods they buy. The shopping ambience, too, is only as good as the customer wants it to be, since they shop from home. This page should give the basic objective of your business. It can also display brief introduction of the electronic store.

E-catalogue   It is a database of products with prices and available stock.

Shopping cart   The customers select their goodies and fill shopping cart. Finally, as in a real store, at the time of checkout, the system calculates the price to be paid for the products.

A payment gateway   Customer makes payments through his/her credit card or e-cash. The payment mechanism must be fully secure.

Identifying Right Revenue Model

The long-term continuity of business is dependent on the revenue model. For any business (electronic or otherwise), to sustain itself in the competitive marketplace, it needs an ability to generate revenue and subsequently profit. A business model entails how the enterprise creates and delivers a product and service and how revenue is generated. The infamous 'dot-com bubble burst' of 2000–01 was because of inappropriate revenue model. The hype about making millions through the Internet businesses was based on unconvincing models. The main targeted revenue was through selling advertising on the Net. Millions of dot-com companies chased a few advertising funds. The result was that only a few companies, such as Yahoo, Google, Hotmail, Indiatimes, and Rediff, generated some revenue and the rest were sheer failures, most of them shutting up shop within a few months. But the e-stores that focused on selling goods, services, and auctions did well. The pioneers among them are ebay.com, amazon.com, archiesonline.com, and fernsnpetals.com.

Now, with the resurgence in e-commerce, millions of shoppers are flocking to these 'virtual malls'. ACNielsen, one of the world's leading market research firms, in its recent research on online shopping habits in India and across the globe found that India's online shoppers are now actively using the Internet to shop. Over one-third of online Indians buy airline tickets over the Internet. Further, online Indians register a higher number of average purchases of airline tickets per month than the global average. Credit cards and cash on delivery are the most preferred modes of payment amongst the online Indians. Other alternatives preferred by a fewer percentage of online Indians are debit cards and direct bank transfers.

The relatively higher numbers of online purchases are likely to be driven by three factors:

- The shoppers have obvious advantages of convenience in online shopping. They are able to compare various offers by providers and select the best possible deal.
- For the shoppers who 'want to be first', online shopping gives them access to the latest products that may not be accessible within close proximity. Such products are generally books, entertainment and gaming software, and video and music, which the new generation wants to buy and possess as quickly as it is released.
- Goods and services that do not require personal touch and feel but provide great value if bought through the Net (for instance travel ticketing and job sites) are in great demand the world over.

Penetration of the Internet

For any e-commerce business to be successful, penetration of computers and the Internet in that society must be very high. People should have a habit of browsing through the Net for some of their tasks or entertainment habits. They can go shopping looking for solutions, information collection, entertainment, and knowledge-enhancement activities. These habits are going to drive online shopping. Besides increasing trade and commerce, the Internet is going to be the enabler of social upgradation and justice through knowledge and information dissemination.

We see a reasonable growth of online shopping activities in India. There are four key drivers for online shopping catching up in India.

- The Internet and increased PC usage (at 48%) is aided by falling prices of computers.
- India's middle class is mushrooming, with growing purchasing power and limited time for shopping.
- There is increasing use of credit and debit cards coupled with a growing young population that spends a significant time searching the Net.

The Internet penetration will be discussed in detail in this chapter in the section on Internet Retailing Scene in India.

Thus, the success of e-commerce largely depends on the population of Internet users. The business segment that the organization chooses for e-commerce must fall within the Internet users' demographic profile.

SUPPORT SERVICES IN E-TAILING

Many purely online retailers, excluding service industries, were unable to survive the dot-com bubble burst and closed up shops between 2000 and 2002. Besides the low PC penetration and bad revenue models, organizations had problems with customer acquisition, low faith on payment mechanism, order fulfilment, demand forecasting, and logistics amongst others. There was cut-throat online competition for selling the fast-moving goods, such as books, music diskettes, and gifts, and the retailers were forced to sell at or below the costs to get rid of the stocks. Even at low prices, the distribution channels were not resourced enough to deliver.

The electronic retail business requires support services, as a prerequisite for successful operations. These services are required to support the business, online or offline, throughout the complete transaction-processing phases. The following are the essential support services:

- Communication backbone
- Payment mechanism
- Order fulfilment
- Logistics

Communication Backbone

We have just discussed how strong Internet penetration among people is important for retail e-commerce to be a successful business proposition. The e-business system needs an equally strong communication backbone to support the traffic flow. (Strong communication backbone refers to fast and wide communications channels to support the high degree of data flow.) The traditional telecommunication lines over copper wire were designed for voice transmission. The bandwidth requirement increases with complex applications and large volume of data-transmission requirements. *Bandwidth* refers to the size of data the telecommunication line transmits in one unit of time. This is the width of the pipeline that transports data or voice. Ten years back, the standard bandwidth available was 14 kbps. The bandwidth availability is now improving, that is the pipeline is getting wider. The communication network providers used to provide 32 or 64 kbps lines a few years back. Today, we talk of 4 or 8 mbps broadband lines. This is certainly going to improve uptime on the Net and would give more road space for the enterprise solutions to run.

Payment Mechanism

Banking habits and proliferation of credit and debit cards is required for e-businesses to flourish. Cash and cheques are not suitable for e-commerce applications. Payment through money orders in case of cash and mails in case of cheques both delay order processing. Companies like to ship goods once they receive the payments. On the other hand, the customer may not be sure of receiving the ordered product in good quality and shape.

The sudden rise in banking habits and use of credit cards, due to the aggressive push by major consumer banks in India, has broken down many of the earlier apprehensions about card ownership and usage. As ownership of credit cards grows, a large proportion of online shoppers are most likely to use credit cards in the future. Compared to their global counterparts, Indians also claim a relatively higher number of purchases with the use of credit cards, which is higher than the global average.

Besides good e-payment habits of the customers, establishing a reliable and secure e-payment mechanism on the e-commerce portal is crucial. People are still wary of using credit or debit cards on the Net. They still fear misuse of the card. There are systems by which the sites are secured using authentications by security agencies. The e-store site must be secured using secure sockets layer (SSL) technology by any reputed agency like VeriSign (Fig. 14.5). This authentication gives confidence to the customer and he/she is assured that his/her credit card number is not being misused. The SSL technology secures a website by encrypting information and providing authentication. An SSL certificate consists of a public key and a private key. The public key is used to encrypt information, while the private key is used to decipher it. When a browser points to a secure domain, an SSL handshake authenticates the server and the client and establishes an encryption method and a unique session key. They can begin a secure session that guarantees message privacy and integrity.

Fig. 14.5 VeriSign provides SSL security to websites

Source: www.verisign.in

Order Fulfilment

An order that has been collected on the Net is retrieved in the back office for processing and fulfilment. An efficient back-office order-processing application supports the e-commerce portal's business activities. Enterprises may have an ERP application to perform the order processing and distribution activities. In fulfilment of an order, the entire supply chain management comes into picture (we have discussed ERP and SCM in Chapters 11 and 12 respectively). The Internet order fulfilment poses greater challenges because of certain inabilities it has over the traditional business systems. E-commerce has a global reach and implications. For instance, perishable goods cannot be dispatched to a far location and there are international laws prohibiting free flow of articles. It may also involve a lot of documentation and delays. Therefore, it would require great management planning.

Logistics

E-retailers may face the problem of how to ship large quantities of goods to customers to far and wide corners of the globe. It is fine with order acknowledgement and order processing with a good Internet availability and computer penetration. But when it comes to physical distribution of goods, it poses a serious challenge for e-commerce businesses. Warehousing is also an alarming problem since storage of large quantities of goods will not be feasible for the retailer. Perishable goods are another problem of storage and logistics. Therefore, depending on the type of product, one has to find an optimum solution and trade-off between the productivity and profitability. Perhaps this is the reason why some of the goods have found favour with both e-retailers and consumers and others have not. The services like e-ticketing and classified services related to jobs and matrimonial are quite popular and making good business sense.

ADVANTAGES OF E-TAILING

E-tailing, either as an extension of the existing retail/distribution business or an altogether new start-up, has many advantages. Traditional brick-store retailers are placing more emphasis on their electronic channels and evolving into multi-channel retailers to increase their reach and support their retail channels. The new start-ups in e-tailing can be launched from a small room with one PC attached with the outside world through the Internet.

Let us summarize the advantages of e-tailing as follows:

1. The electronic channel gives the existing brick-store retailers an opportunity to reach new markets.
2. For the existing retailers, it is an extension to leverage their skills and grow revenues and profits without creating an altogether new business.
3. E-tailing overcomes some limitations of the traditional formats, for instance the customers can shop from the comfort of their homes.
4. The e-commerce software that also traces the customers' activities on the Net enables e-retailers to gain valuable insights into their customers' shopping behaviour.

5. The e-retail channels transcend all barriers of time and space. The retailers' server must be on 24×7. An order can come from any customer living at any place at any time of the day.
6. E-commerce channels are definitely efficient and retailers do not have to pay a heavy price for brick-n-mortar shops in costly shopping malls.

CHALLENGES OF E-TAILING

Although e-commerce offers a lot of new opportunities, it also presents many challenges. Besides many challenges in hosting, order delivery, and payment processing, there are some other challenges that are discussed here.

Unproven Business Models

In the formative years of dot-com era, most of the businesses on the Net were experiments in new areas and did not provide enduring sources of profit. This was the primary reason behind closing down of 90 per cent of the purely e-commerce companies in the beginning of this century. Today, dot-com businesses have matured a little. Still some of the businesses are at experimental level and do not guarantee regular revenue. Therefore, the e-business model must be proven and revenue generating, that is the products or services an organization chooses must be e-store friendly. The buyers must be comfortable in purchasing these products through the Net.

Requirement to Change Business Process

The process of procurement, storage and logistics in e-businesses is different from that in traditional brick-store businesses. The e-retail organization has to carefully redesign and integrate various processes to suit the new e-business. Traditional sections of departments and management hierarchy may pose hindrances and bottlenecks in the process of order processing and shipments, for example, the traditional business may require the goods to be present at the warehouse and inspected before being shipped to the customer, but in electronic retailing, shipping of goods from one place to another to a customer would not be possible. The retailer may appoint a local supplier at the city where the customer resides and instruct the supplier to deliver the goods. This would require bypassing certain business rules and a lot of faith on the local supplier. It would require business confidence that the supplier would follow the instructions and deliver the same product in good quantity and perfect quality. Merchandise planning and demand analysis is also difficult in e-tailing, as compared to traditional retail businesses.

Channel Conflicts

Companies selling through the Internet as well as through brick stores may find their interest conflicting at many places. In electronic storefront orders, the goods directly reach the end-consumer and so the distributors and sellers may feel the threat to their existence. Most of the time, it is seen that retailers tend to reduce price over the Net. The sale at the brick store may drop because the retailer may tend to sell more through the Internet as a result of reduction of prices. Prices are usually less on the Net because of fewer overheads in administration and inventory-carrying costs. The other reason of selling more through the Net is that retailers reduce prices in slack seasons and increase prices in peak hours. This can be managed efficiently over the Internet. For example, the prices of air tickets and hotel rooms are kept less if the booking is done through the Internet because if some seats of an airline go empty or rooms of a hotel remain vacant, there is no revenue generation. By offering the seats or rooms at a less price, the airline operators or hotel companies are going to bear the marginal costs incurred in handling of the customers in transit or in hotel room. The major costs (such as those related to the airline operations, workforce, and fuel) are already incurred in both the cases.

Legal Issues

Proper laws have not yet evolved for Internet based transactions. Validity of e-mails, digital signatures, and application of copyright laws is being checked by various government authorities. E-mail and digital signatures are now being recognized as valid for any legal purpose. Value Added Tax (VAT) is yet another area that creates problems. Taxes on goods and services are still an issue. Since the taxes are levied and shared by multiple government agencies at local, state, or federal level, there are no clear rules to guide retailers on that. In e-tailing, the place of billing, the place of dispatch of goods, and the place of delivery, all differ. If these three places fall in different jurisdictions of governments, levy and submission of taxes would be a problem.

Let us discuss an example here. A retail e-commerce owner is based in New Delhi and has his server located in California in the US. A customer places her order for a bouquet of flowers from Bangaluru. The retailer dispatches the flowers from Chennai (his logistic arrangement) and makes the delivery at Bangaluru. In such situation, it still remains unanswered that what should be the rate of VAT and which state government would be entitled to receive it.

Security and Privacy

Security is one of the major challenges in the digital world. Despite a lot of security arrangements, such as passwords and firewalls, we come across the news of website hacking and data pilferages. The Internet being on public domain is more susceptible to unauthorized peeping. People are wary of divulging information regarding their credit cards and personal details on the Net because they can be misused. Cyber criminals have exploited the Internet weaknesses and have broken into computer systems, retrieving passwords and banking information. Security of payment gateway is a major concern, which has to be taken care of by the retailer by putting up proper security layers.

Business Scenario

Some portals that have established themselves as amongst the leaders in the Indian online retail space are listed in Table 14.1.

COMPARISON OF BRICK-n-MORTAR STORES WITH VIRTUAL STORES

Different channels offer different benefits to customers. The brick-n-mortar stores offer a number of benefits to customers that they cannot get when shopping through the Internet. More people shop for social experience and entertainment value associated with the brick stores. These stores offer browsing, touch-and-feel effect, and immediate satisfaction of shopping. On the other hand, the Internet shopping offers convenience and security of shopping from home and more personalized information about products and services (Mohanty 2006). Table 14.2 compares the two modes of shopping.

INTERNET RETAILING SCENE IN INDIA

The Internet-based businesses are nowadays gaining momentum. With the surge in PC penetration, Internet awareness, and computer literacy, people are using the Internet more as an enabler and facilitator of work than mere for messaging and entertainment. We will discuss here certain findings of Internet and Mobile Association of India (IAMAI), who along with Indian Market Research Bureau (IMRB) conducted surveys across 30 cities and 65,000 users across India in the year 2007. We will compare their findings with other data available for the earlier years to get a fair picture of the e-commerce scenario in India.

In India, the relationship between the Internet and commerce has crossed the stage of nascence. According to recent estimates made by the IAMAI,

Table 14.1 Major e-tailing companies in India

Portal Name	Products/Services They Sell
shopping.indiatimes.com	Apparel, books, electronic gadgets, gifts, music CDs, movie VCDs and DVDs, cakes, chocolates and sweets, food and grocery, consumer-durable goods, flowers, home furnishing jewellery, artistic paintings and handicrafts, cameras and optics, toys, watches, computers, automobile accessories and car electronics, office stationery and office products, sports goods and gear, leather accessories, personal and beauty care products, and travel gear
shopping.rediff.com	
shopping.sify.com	
www.fabmall.com	
firstandsecond.com	Books
landmarkonthenet.com	Books
zodiaconline.com	Garments
Archiesonline.com	Gifts and greeting cards
crctc.com	Rail travel tickets
makemytrip.com	Air e-ticketing and hotel reservations
Travel.indiatimes.com	Travel services
Indiatravelportal.com	Travel services
Galileoindia.com	Travel services
Naukri.com	Largest job portal
Timesjobs.com	Job portal
Monsterindia.com	Job portal
Clickjobs.com	Job portal
Jobsforyou.com	Job portal
Jeevansathi.com	Matrimonial services
Shaadi.com	Matrimonial services
Simplymarry.com	Matrimonial services
Bharatmatrimony.com	Matrimonial services
Avenuesindia.com	E-commerce payment gateway
Baazee.com	Online auction site
Fernsnpetals.com	Flowers

online shopping crossed Rs 9000 crore in 2007–08 from Rs 7000 crore in 2006–07 and Rs 570 crore in 2004–05, representing a growth of 32 per cent over the previous year. This has surpassed the previous estimate of Rs 2300 crore for the fiscal year 2006–07.

Research Findings

Some of the findings of the research done by IAMAI on online shopping trends in India are as follows:

- Rs 9000 crore worth of e-commerce was conducted online in 2007–08 from Rs 7000 crore in 2006–07, an estimated 29 per cent plus growth.
- Fifty-five per cent of the visitors to e-commerce sites have adopted the Internet as a shopping medium.
- In the year 2000, 77 per cent users were from metros, whereas in 2007, the share of metros has fallen to 38 per cent. People from smaller cities have increased their presence.
- Twenty-on per cent of the regular online shoppers are college students in the 18–24 age group, 33 per cent are young men in the 24–35 age group,

Table 14.2   Comparison between store and Internet shopping

Shopping Through Brick-n-Mortar Stores	*Shopping Through the Internet*
Browsing Most of the time, shoppers browse through the windows and decide about the product later. Browsing, also known as window shopping, is a good pastime for the shoppers.	**Broader selection** Internet retailing offers vast number of alternatives available to consumers. For example, a person living in New Delhi can shop electronically at Mark & Spencer in New York in less time than it takes them to visit the local supermarket.
Touching and feeling products Traditional retailing allows shoppers to touch and feel the product. Perhaps the greatest benefit offered by brick stores is the opportunity for the customers to use all of their senses when examining products. While new technologies, especially in the West, can provide 3-D representations on a CRT screen, these visual improvements will not provide the same level of information.	**More information to evaluate merchandise** A shopper can easily compare different brands at their leisure. Most of the modern self-service brick stores. do not offer expert services. E-commerce sites update their database frequently and the latest information is available to the e-shopper.
Personal service Buyers may be wary of sales-persons but the salespersons at stores still have the capability of providing meaningful, personalized in-formation. For example, a salesperson can help while selecting a tie matching a suite. Customers take a lot of advice from salespersons for consumer-durable goods and technical products like computers.	**Personalization** Whereas brick stores provide personal service, virtual stores have the ability to economically personalize the information for each customer. Many of the e-commerce sites give their suggestions on products and services, such as suggesting that 'people who bought the product x, also bought the product y'. These websites keep track of the customers' personal preferences and tastes.
Entertainment and social experience Stores provide more benefits to consumers than simply having merchandise readily available and helping them buy it. Many a time, people go for shopping as a family group entertainment.	**Comfort of home** Many products and services do not require personal browsing. People are more comfortable when they buy at a click of mouse from the ease of their homes.
Cash payment Stores are the only channel that accepts cash payments. Many customers prefer to pay cash because it is easy, resolves the transaction immediately, and does not result in potential interest payments.	**Credit card payments** More and more shoppers are now comfortable with credit cards. Handling cash is a problem for them. Even we like to pay our utility bills through a online payment service like PayPal.

and 15 per cent are men in the 36–58 age group. Eleven per cent of the online shoppers are working women and just 6 per cent are house wives.

- Eighty-three per cent of the user base is educated with a bachelor or postgraduate degree, representing a well-educated audience. Fifty-four per cent of the online shoppers are at an executive level, while 24 per cent are professionals or self-employed, indicating an assured spending power.

- The Internet ownership has shown a growth of 32 per cent, whereas share of the Internet café has gone down to 38 per cent from 52 per cent in 2003. The trend shows that people want to shop from the convenience of their home.

- Eighty-one per cent of online shoppers own credit cards and 75 per cent own debit cards.

- The maximum shopping is done for travel-related purchases, the second place is captured by classifieds like job search and matrimonial, and the third place is occupied by consumer shopping or e-tailing.

- Fifty-one per cent of netizens, who use the Net for some activities, use the Internet for e-mails, 20 per cent for information search, 13 per cent for entertainment, and 11 per cent use the Net for chatting. A meagre 5 per cent use the Internet for e-commerce activities, which indicates a huge potential for e-tailing.

Across the globe, the most popular items purchased on the Internet were books (34 per cent), followed by videos/DVDs/games (22 per cent), airline tickets/reservations (21per cent), and clothing/accessories/shoes (20 per cent). But now travel ticketing is taking over all others.

In India, books followed airline reservations closely, with 35 per cent of online Indians buying them over the Internet. Apart from these, nearly one-fourth (24 per cent) of Indians have purchased electronic equipment items, such as cameras, computer peripherals and close to a fifth (20 per cent-plus) have purchased items such as apparel (21 per cent), music and electronic entertainment such as movies, DVDs (22 per cent), and games.

According to IAMAI, close to 24 per cent of the Rs 1180 crore Indian online shopping spend is for railway tickets and about half (47 per cent) of all the online rail ticket buyers are in the 26–35 age group. Toss in airline ticket bookings and travel makes up nearly 58 per cent of the Indian online shopping spends. The IAMAI estimates that the average number of transactions has increased nearly four-fold, from 2.07 lakh a month in 2003–04 to 7.95 lakh in 2005–06.

Business Potential of various segments

Based on the revenue generated, the total e-commerce activities can be grouped under four heads as follows:

- Travel (e-ticketing and reservations)—Rs 5500 crore in 2006–07 and estimated at Rs 7200 crore for 2007–08
- Classifieds (job sites, matrimonial, and dating)—Rs 540 crore in 2006–07 and estimated for 2007–08 at Rs 820 crore
- E-tailing (shopping for other consumer goods)—Rs 850 crore in 2006–07 and estimated for 2007–08 at Rs 1105 crore
- Others (miscellaneous transactions)—Rs 250 crore

Thus, the Internet audience is expected to grow to a 100 million users by 2007–08 with unlimited shelf space and is now not bound by operational timings and geographical boundaries; compulsive credit card habits and flexible banking hours, at a comparatively minuscule cost.

The AIMAI's research *Internet 2007* makes some astounding revelations regarding the Internet usage. The exposure to the Internet over the years has made people switch to it for performing even their routine tasks. Utility services (such as bill payments, ticketing, and banking), which were earlier done manually, are now preferred to be dealt with over the Internet. Continuous improvement in e-mail features has led to a bullish journey of e-mail, which was earlier on a declining trend.

Further, the popularity of entertainment activities, such as online gaming and video downloads, has increased the share of the entertainment segment in the main applications of the Net. Niche websites related to matrimony, news, and jobs have still a long way to go as content on these sites is largely in English language. The user base of these sites is expected to increase once the content becomes available in other Indian languages.

SUMMARY

E-commerce involves transactions between two organizations or individuals over the Internet. Buying and selling of goods and services between two organizations is called business-to-business (B2B) e-commerce. Sales and purchase transactions between business organizations and end-consumers is called business-to-consumer (B2C) e-commerce. Sales and purchase activities between two consumers are called C2C commerce. E-shopping involves buying goods and services over the Internet. World Wide Web is the backbone of e-commerce. The Web combines text, data, hypermedia, graphics, and sound. It can handle all kinds of digital communication linking computers and networks that are located across the world. The Web consists of website domain name or Universal Resource Locator and works on Hypertext Transfer Protocol (HTTP). Also, the websites are built with Hypertext Mark-up Language (HTML).

E-commerce infrastructure consists of web servers to store applications and data and e-commerce portal, whereby the shopper interacts with the server. The e-tailing organization has to hire services of a web-hosting provider. The portals are maintained and upgraded by using a web-content management tool. For e-tailing to be successful, an attractive portal that can fetch lot of traffic to the site is essential. E-commerce can succeed only when it is a revenue-generating system in the long run. This can be possible only when there is enough use of PC and Internet in the society. Once the e-commerce portal is launched, it has to be supported with some essential ingredients. These ingredients are a good communication backbone, secure payment mechanism, order processing and fulfilment system, and finally logistics to deliver goods.

E-tailing businesses offer a lot of advantages. They can be an extension of the brick-store with additional stream of revenue or independent businesses. They are easy to build and run with relatively smaller capital. The major challenges posed by e-tailing are that it is unproven business model, different from traditional retailing business and thus can conflict with the traditional store channels, and involves legal and taxation issues as well as security and privacy issues.

The present retailing scene in India is very encouraging. The relationship between the Internet and commerce has crossed the stage of nascence. According to recent estimates made by the IAMAI, online shopping crossed Rs 9000 crore in 2007–08 from Rs 7000 crore in 2007 and Rs 570 crore in 2004–05, representing a growth of 32 per cent over the previous year. This has surpassed the previous estimates of Rs 2300 crore for 2006–07.

CONCEPT REVIEW QUESTIONS

1. What do you understand by e-tailing?
2. What is the core infrastructure needed for successful e-commerce?
3. What do you understand by protocol? On which protocol does the Internet work?
4. What are the essentials of e-tailing?
5. What support services are needed for an e-business to flourish?
6. Can you enumerate advantages of e-tailing over a brick-n-mortar store?
7. How does a customer differentiate between services at a brick-n-mortar store and a virtual store?
8. What does the latest research on buying habits of 'netizens' indicate?
9. What are the best products to sell through e-tailing?

1. Do you think that the Indian shopper has matured enough to sustain an amazon.com-type e-tailing business? Support your reasons with valid examples.

1. Study the business practice of a retailer who has also set up an electronic storefront. Analyse the organization's order-fulfilment system.

SELECT REFERENCES

Internet and Mobile Association of India (IAMAI) 2007, 'Internet in India', www.iamai.in.

Kalakota, Ravi and Andrew B. Whinston 2006, *Frontiers of Electronic Commerce*, Pearson Education Inc.

Laudon, Ken and Mary Laudon 2002, *Management Information System*, Pearson Education (Singapore).

Mohanty, Paravahan 2006, 'Brick to Click', *Images Retail*, May, www.imagesretail.com.

CASE STUDY

Success Story of eBay: Where Complete Strangers Deal with Each Other

In 2004, there were an estimated 50 million registered users of eBay, who were supported by a team of 2500 employees of eBay. It sold over 45 million items and 250,000 items were added daily. There were 600 bids per minute for items under 1000 categories.

No one could have ever predicted the rise. Today, more than 125 million people worldwide are registered users at eBay. Those people are buying and selling more than $1000 worth of goods every second. It is an auction house that never sleeps, where anyone can be a buyer or a seller.

How did eBay get started selling over the Internet? There is a great Silicon Valley story here about a gentleman named Pierre Omidyar, who was working as a software developer in Silicon Valley. He had always been fascinated by how you can establish marketplaces to buy and sell goods and services. He had also been fascinated by how you can bring together fragmented audiences. Because of his interest in the Internet and his background in software, he developed a software program that allowed people in one spot to list items of various interests and degrees. It allowed people to be able to come to that very same site and look at what is up for sale and bid on and buy those items. He used the auction process as the method for establishing how merchandise is valued and eventually how it is exchanged between buyer and seller.

A key component that prompted him to do this was at the time his fiancée Pam Wesley, now his wife, was interested in her Pez collection. She was experiencing a frustration that many collectors have experienced, and that is often times when you are collecting a particular item or you have a passion for a particular hobby, but your ability to buy from and trade with or sell to other people of similar interests is limited by geographical considerations. Moreover, if you trade through a trade publication, which are often published by volunteers, the interval between publications can often run for several weeks, if not months.

Pierre published a website in September 1995, which he named AuctionWeb. He thought of people buying and selling goods through bids on his site. Within a year, AuctionWeb hosted thousands of auctions with over 10,000 bids. Remember, he did not charge for this service.

Challenges Faced by eBay

What unique challenges exist for companies in the online auction space?

The first challenge that always confronts an online merchant is the idea of creating trust and confidence among the users. There are still a large number of people who do not use the Internet on a regular basis, and there are, of course, a large number of people who have no interest in the Internet at all. Sometimes, they stay away from it because they are worried about confidentiality, privacy issues, and the broad area of trust and safety. Each Internet site that is going to engage in commerce must create an environment of trust and safety that will allow the users to come back over and over again.

This is one of the biggest challenges facing e-commerce sites right now, creating an environment so that a novice online shopper can come to a particular site and feel comfortable shopping there and feel satisfied that they are getting a good price and a bargain and getting the merchandise that they want.

In 1996, Pierre started charging for his service from the sellers. He was not sure of the reaction of his users. But soon cash and cheques started rolling in. By June 1996, the revenue was $10,000 a month. Thus, the first dot.com company that was profitable was born.

What has helped to make eBay as successful as it has been? The answer is that it really allows people to often connect with some very fond and special early childhood memories. It could be anything from collecting baseball cards to toy soldiers to Barbie dolls to doll houses, and so forth. It allows people to make that connection and relive a lot of those very vivid and fond memories that they have from an earlier period of time. Another factor to consider is that people really enjoy the experience of the shopping bazaar. They enjoy the hunt and looking around for merchandise. The other component is that they really enjoy the competition of the bidding process. Everybody likes to get a bargain and, in some way, shape, or form, likes to haggle a little bit over the price. The eBay auction format allows the users to do that.

The other factor behind eBay's success is that as it has grown, it has become a very practical place to buy and sell collectibles or commodities.

In 1998, the company went public as eBay. It was received well at the New York Stock Exchange. On July 10, 1998, the company's computer system crashed without any backup, which brought the company on its knees. Then millions were spent to set up a state-of-the-art technology centre.

Creating Entrepreneurs

The unique business model of eBay has thousands of stores within the 'store'. It allows the people to create their businesses. In eBay, everyone is a buyer as well as a seller. There are thousands of success stories about individual successful businesses on e-bay.

Laurie Liss and her mother, Darlene, armed with little more than a computer, a camera, and something to sell, built their own eBay business, which is now generating $30,000 to $40,000 a month. It is almost like the world's largest garage sale, even though for some people, they are selling used goods. But in fact Laurie is selling new items. The lure of a bargain, combined with the excitement of a Las Vegas gamble, is what brings in millions of Internet customers. The loyalty and enthusiasm of devoted eBay users all over the country is what has helped build eBay into the powerhouse it is today. An eBay auction works exactly the same way as an old-fashioned one—the highest bidder wins.

The eBay business model has made a phenomenal impact on the Internet usage. It is probably the best hands-on example of how the Internet has changed commerce. People have been talking about this for a good number of years. There have been many pundits and experts that have suggested that the Internet is going to change the way that business is conducted in the United States and the world. We can certainly see that in a number of ways.

But eBay might be the first example where a commerce site has actually been built around a community where people are exchanging information as well as goods, services, and merchandise. It has changed people because although we certainly have our share of hobbyists and very serious collectors, we have also learned that people who have established additional brick-n-mortar businesses are slowly moving towards eBay.

People with traditional businesses found eBay so enticing and, in many ways, profitable that they have now created a brand new business for themselves on eBay, leaving behind their professions or careers.

It is clear that eBay is going to stay focused on the personal, online trading environment. At the same time, it is also going to offer new services to its users and enhance the already available services. Still the management believes that the company is just at the very beginning of the online trading business and is using the auction process as a format to conduct commerce.

The company really sees the opportunity to expand its core business. The opportunities over the years are going to continue to expand across the globe. The regional services that started in the US within the past couple of months can be expanded to other parts of the world.

Question:

1. What were the factors responsible for eBay's meteoric growth?

Sources: Adapted from www.internet-story.com, www.ebay.com, and an interview of Kevin Pursglove by Matthew Beale that appeared in *E-Commerce Times*, April 2000.

15 Emerging Retail Technologies

In Chapter 14, we have discussed some comparatively latest paradigm shifts in the way business is being done across the globe, in the centuries-old system of trading. The Internet business is the latest phenomenon, which is just a decade-old system and became popular only in the last few years of the last century. But it is now changing very fast. In this chapter, we will discuss the emerging technological changes that have impact on the retail industry.

Information technology is an ever-changing field of study, where change is the only static phenomenon. We have studied various IT components ranging from hardware, AIDC, databases, and networking to software solutions. Still there are many technological components that are evolving day by day. Some of the technological developments in retail applications are listed below:

- Use of RFID systems for billing, inventory tracking, and anti-theft measures
- Use of information and service kiosks, automated self-checkout systems, mobile technology based marketing, and sales and distribution systems
- Use of global positioning system (GPS) and geographic information system (GIS) for store location, consignment tracking, vehicle tracking, route definitions, and logistic solutions

There are software applications like computer-aided design (CAD) available for designing store layouts. The Web has evolved into the next phase, which is being called Web 2.0, and software is being sold and used as service, popularly known as software as a service (SaaS), rather than a product. These developments in the field of IT have stressed technology providers and managers of business organizations to use and upgrade themselves in the latest technology.

In these areas, we need to learn the new technology and explore the possibility of its use in retail arena, to increase customer loyalty and satisfaction and create competitive advantage for the organization.

In this chapter, we are going to discuss emerging technologies in the computer and Web arena that are going to affect us as users and creators of applications for retail. These technologies are evolving and being used in business applications. The emerging technologies that we will discuss here are mobile computing, GPS and GIS, Web 2.0, and SaaS.

MOBILE COMPUTING AND M-COMMERCE

The growth of cellular telephony has been astounding worldwide. In India, the growth of mobile usage has been phenomenal because of sharp declining prices and easy availability of technology and reliable services. In less than 10 years, we have more than 100 million subscribers and it is increasing by 600,000 connections every month. So, what can be a better way of reaching to the masses? Corporate marketing strategists and planners find this channel highly lucrative, cost-effective, and an effective way of marketing and advertising. We will briefly discuss the technology and how it can be used for businesses, especially retail selling. Before we delve into applications of mobile technology in retail businesses, let us understand the technology behind cellular telephony.

Fig. 15.1 Cellular telephony: a mobile handheld terminal

Cellular Telephony

Cellular telephony is a radio-based system that works over a certain radio frequency (RF). Cellular telephones work by using radio waves to communicate with radio towers placed within adjacent geographical areas called *cells*. When making a call, the handset sends a message to the nearest tower for locating the phone on which the call is made (Fig. 15.1). A telephone message is transmitted to the local cell by the mobile handset. Then it is transmitted from one antenna to other antenna. So, the message moves from cell to cell, until it reaches the cell of its destination, where it is transmitted to the receiving mobile handset. The mobile office finds out the location of the receiving mobile set and sends the signal back to the tower, fitted with transceiver (for receiving and transmitting signals). As the cellular signal travels from one

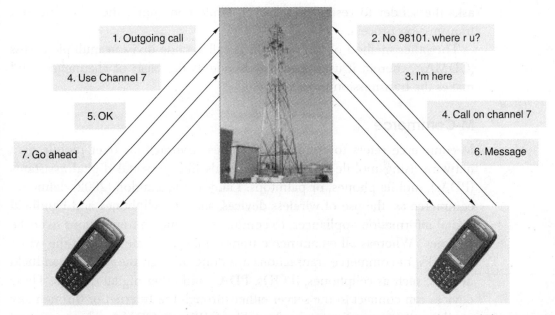

1. Outgoing call

4. Use Channel 7

5. OK

7. Go ahead

2. No 98101. where r u?

3. I'm here

4. Call on channel 7

6. Message

Fig. 15.2   Cellular call handshake between the transceiver and the handset: call begins after completing seven steps

cell to another, a computer that monitors signals from the cell switches the conversation to a radio channel assigned to the next cell.

As illustrated in Fig. 15.2, before assigning a channel for communication, there are at least seven signalled communications between the tower and the communicating mobile handsets.

Mobile Data Networks

Wireless networks explicitly designed for two-way transmission of data files are called *mobile data networks*. These radio-based networks transmit data to and from handheld computers (Fig. 15.3). Another type of mobile data networks is based on a series of radio towers constructed specifically to transmit text and data. Most wireless data schemes use 'packet' technique for transferring data. *Packet radio* is a communication method that transmits packets of data over a network via RF signals. This technology is called general packet radio service (GPRS). In this system, the transceiver, known as RF modem, breaks down the data into 128-byte packets. The data contains the addressee's information. Then these packets are released in the air. They are read by the radio towers and then transmitted to the designated addressee. Each packet is sequentially numbered. At the receiving end, they are reassembled in their proper sequence. If a packet is not received in good condition, the receiver asks the sender to resend the packet, while continuing the receiving and transmission process.

The other method of transmission is called code division multiple access (CDMA), wherein it uses specialized code as the basis of channelling and makes the transmission more efficient.

M-Commerce

M-commerce refers to conducting business transactions over mobile data network using mobile handheld terminals like personal digital assistants (PDAs), mobile phones, or palmtops. Laudon and Laudon (2002) define m-commerce as 'the use of wireless devices, such as cellphones and handheld digital information appliances, to conduct e-commerce transactions over the Internet'. Whereas all e-commerce transactions are done through the wired networks, m-commerce transactions are done through the mobile handheld devices, such as cellphones, iPODs, PDAs, and other digital devices. These devices can connect to the server either through the Internet or through any wireless communication technology like GPRS or CDMA. They can send information or receive information, as per the design of the application.

Simply put, m-commerce is sale and purchase of goods and services through use of mobile digital equipment. The sale and purchase definitely involve advertising, promotions, and marketing of goods and services.

APPLICATIONS OF MOBILE COMPUTING

The reach and power of mobile computing is enormous. The power of mobile computing will be realized when appropriate applications are available for doing business over the mobile phone. In today's competitive environment, increasing aspirations, and fast-paced lifestyle forces people to work while on the move. These circumstances demand tools that allow users to work, communicate, and even learn at their own convenience and pace. Mobile technology can basically help humankind in two ways—remote communication and remote data access.

Remote Communication

With the invention of mobile telecommunication, the physical space has vanished. For the cabled communication, people had to be at the defined places where the telephone equipment was installed. But the mobile phone has removed even that constraint. People can communicate at any place, space, or while on move, which gives flexibility, creativity, and ease.

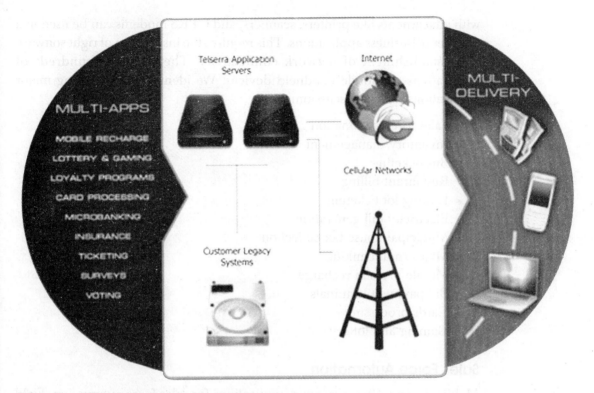

Fig. 15.3 Convergence of multimedia into mobile computing

Source: www.telserra.com

Remote Data Access

The physical space shrinks when technology allows people to log on to their computers through their mobile phones while away from the server. With the right application in place, mobile phones can give access to data and information over the enterprise network. Sales executives can transmit their orders and customer feedback into the corporate server. Retail managers can know their daily sales figures through their mobiles. We receive data of our bank balances on our mobiles. An important requirement of the mobile computing environment is to allow workers to be as effective at remote locations as they can be while on their desks and connected with the network. Connecting through mobile is as efficient and effective as connecting through local area network.

BUSINESS APPLICATIONS

The remote data access capability of mobile phone opens enormous avenues of use of mobile or handheld terminals in business. Mobile devices, loaded with attachments like printers, scanners, and GPRS modems can be used in a number of business applications. This requires the installation of right software and establishment of network connectivity. There can be hundreds of applications of mobile handheld devices. We identify the following major applications for our discussion:

- Sales force automation
- Inventory management
- Bus ticketing
- Restaurant billing
- Parking lot ticketing
- Electricity bill generation
- Municipal house tax collection
- Micro rural banking
- Mobile prepaid recharge
- Bill payment terminals
- Cards processing
- Gaming and lottery

Sales Force Automation

Mobile devices offer very good applications for sales force automation. Field sales personnel can use mobile devices for taking orders. The device works with a simple application that has the customer code, products code, salesperson's ID, and quantity ordered. Once the salesperson enters this data in the device and presses 'send' button, the data is transmitted to the server through the GPRS modem integrated in the mobile device. The order is available instantly at the distribution centre for processing. This increases efficiency and the systems can be designed to work towards implementation of new international concepts of zero- or just-in-time inventory systems.

Inventory Management

Mobile devices find great application in warehouse management. In large warehouses, it is not possible to take the computer-attached scanner to every corner of the warehouse. Thus, the use of wireless scanners is warranted. Whenever a product is removed from the warehouse, it is scanned using the scanner attached with the mobile device. The scanner captures the product bar code and stores the data in the mobile handheld device. Alternatively, if a bar code scanner is not integrated with the device, the user manually enters SKU (stock-keeping unit) number into the device through the tiny application running in it. This data is added on the server instantly and the inventory is updated online.

Bus Ticketing

Mobile devices are being used for bus ticketing in a big way. The devices are loaded with a suitable application and a receipt printer. The application has bus route number, number and names of the stations/stops falling in the route, distance between the stations, and fare chart for the entire route. The conductor enters a key that stamps the date and time on the device. The bus conductor makes a ticket for the passenger and prints it on thermal or dot matrix printer attached or integrated with the device. The data of complete route is stored in the device. If the device is GPRS enabled, this data is transmitted online to the central server. Else, the conductor can download the data on the server using a cable. The application running at the server analyses the route data and produces reports on route profitability, time taken between different routes, and passenger load on the bus. The management can take corrective actions if something goes wrong.

Restaurant Billing

Waiters in the restaurants use mobile devices for taking orders from the customers. The order is transmitted to the main restaurant server and KOT (kitchen order ticket) is printed on the kitchen printer. It saves a lot of time as the waiter does not have to take a manual order and then enter it into the computer. Once an order is placed, served, and completed, the information is transmitted to the billing server. The bill is created against the KOT and settled. The bill is printed with the normal printer and computer, thus completing the transaction.

Parking Lot Ticketing

Mobile handheld terminals have become very popular in parking time management. With these digital terminals, one can enter the in time, out-time of a vehicle, and print a parking ticket. With a suitable application in the terminal and price database, it calculates the amount one has to pay for the parking usage. These terminals invariably come with integrated thermal printers. A parking lot ticket generator terminal is shown in Fig. 15.4.

Fig. 15.4 An HCL handheld device with fast 32-bit ARM processor with 8 MB SDRAM and 16 MB flash RAM, 19 key keypad, and thermal graphic printer

Electricity Bill Generation

The process of electricity billing is a very complex and time-consuming process. The meter reader personally visits houses, notes down the meter reading, submits the reading to the data processing department, which is then entered into the system, and bills are generated. These bills then are delivered to the house owners who then make the payment to the electricity distribution company. This process takes up to two months time. If mobile computing devices are used, this process can be brought down to two minutes for each household. With the suitable application in place, the customers' previous reading can be downloaded into the handheld terminals for a particular route, from the server at the electricity distributor's company office. The meter reader can visit the house with this device in hand and enter the current meter reading into it. The device calculates bill value and prints the bill on an integrated printer. The reader can collect cash or cheque from the consumer there and then and print a receipt for the same. Back in the office, the data can be uploaded on to the server. Just in one visit, the entire process is completed, which saves a lot of time and makes a lot of revenue for the electricity distribution company.

Municipal House Tax Collection

Similar to an electricity billing system, municipalities can set up servers and mobile applications. The data of each route, residential block, and houses can be downloaded on the mobile terminal. A rich application in the device can also calculate the house tax based on certain inputs like location, property usage, area of the land, built up area, and number of floors. If the municipality server already has all the information related to houses, it can be simply downloaded in the terminal. On visiting the household, the officials can collect taxes and generate a receipt. This saves a lot of time of the consumer and there is much more tax compliance.

Micro Rural Banking

Cash collection is an issue for the banks from far-flung rural areas, where setting up of a branch is not viable. Small traders, labourers, hawkers, and people operating kiosks do not have enough time to go to a bank and deposit their daily savings. If banks designate collection centres in each city corners and authorize them to collect cash through these terminals, much of the problem is solved. These terminals can connect with the bank server through GPRS or CDMA technology or plan a wired telecommunication line (as done in case of credit card authentication). The mobile device generates a receipt for each depositor and the bank server accounts for the money, online. In the same way, these centres can be authorized to disburse cash. Any retailer, PCO operator, and mobile services operator can provide this service as an add-on to their regular business, which is going to be a great revenue earner for them. The technology not only provides ease and comfort in banking transactions but also generates new areas of businesses, thus increasing employment and inducing banking habits in the people living in remote areas.

Mobile Prepaid Recharge

Mobile handheld devices can be used for recharging prepaid cellular phones. Some organizations are already offering their products and services for recharging public call offices (PCOs) with handheld devices. The modus operandi is similar to gaming operations. With the connectivity-enabled terminal, the operator dials the telephone company's server. On connecting with the server, the operator enters the required value of recharge. The server generates a PIN number and communicates back to the handheld device. This code number is dialled from the mobile or fixed phone line and the server increases prepaid value for that particular telephone number at the PCO booth or mobile phone.

Bill Payment Terminals

Perhaps bill payment utility is the most used utility and has a wide presence today. Most of us must have seen these terminals working at a number of retail outlets that collect payments for utility bills, such as electricity, water, and telephones. Bill payment terminals use both land telecommunication lines as well as wireless technology available in mobile handheld terminals. 'Easy Bill' by Hero Services is the most widely used service in this arena and more companies are coming up to give stiff competition. Bill payment services have reduced a lot of burden from the customers and increased the business potential for such companies.

Cards Processing

The oldest utility of handheld terminals with dial-up modems is for credit card processing at a retail outlet. We are aware that on offering a credit card for making payments at retail, the vendor swipes the card through this handheld device (that is still now connected with the bank's server through the wired telecommunication lines). The bank server authenticates the card and generates a transaction PIN, which is printed on the slip. The amount entered by the vendor is added in the payment list of the cardholder (customer). This amount appears in the next credit card statement of the holder.

Gaming and Lottery

People use mobile devices for online games and lotteries. In online lotteries, there are no pre-printed tickets. When the mobile device connects with the server with a request to game, a random number is generated by the server, which is at a remote place. The number is transmitted back to the mobile device within seconds. If the mobile device has a receipt printer attached with it, it prints the ticket. In such types of online lotteries, the draw is done every half an hour or hour. The winning numbers are also communicated to the device. Thus, the winner claims the reward from the game operator.

GLOBAL POSITIONING SYSTEM AND GEOGRAPHIC INFORMATION SYSTEM

Global positioning system (GPS) and geographic information system (GIS) are modern technologies to locate and track objects on the earth with the help of computers and satellite links. These technologies are emerging as the next important technological breakthrough for managing modern businesses.

Global Positioning System

Global Positioning System (GPS) is a technology that can give an accurate position of an object anywhere on the earth based on latitude and longitude. The GPS receiver fitted on the object is designed to receive signals from the satellites (Fig. 15.5).

The GPS is owned and operated by the United States Department of Defense and is the only fully functional Global Navigation Satellite System (GNSS). The system uses at least 24 medium earth-orbiting satellites that transmit precise microwave signals. The GPS receiver determines its location, speed, direction, and time.

This system is available to anyone in the world for use. One has to bear the receiver's cost only. Other countries are also developing similar satellite

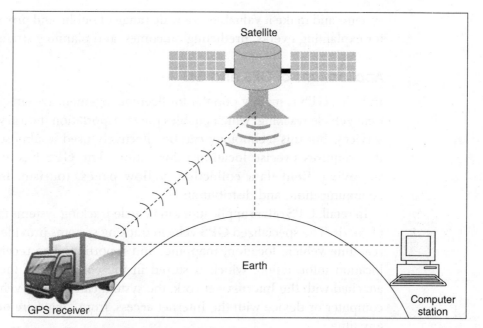

Fig. 15.5 Functioning of a global positioning system

navigation systems of their own, for example India is developing a system called Indian Regional Navigational Satellite System (IRNSS), European Union is developing a system called Galileo, and Russia has an operational system called GLONASS. Most modern receivers are capable of using signals from all these systems.

The GPS can seamlessly integrate with GIS data and provide quality information.

Geographic Information System

Geographic information system (GIS) is a computer-based information system used to digitally represent and analyse the geographic features present on the earth's surface. The GIS is also defined as an information system designed to work with the data referenced by spatial/geographical coordinates. It is a digital map that relates to a database system with specific capabilities for space-referenced data. Thus, we can say that GIS is any system for capturing, storing, analysing, and managing data and associated attributes that are spatially referenced to the earth.

The GIS technology integrates common database operations such as query and statistical analysis with the unique visualization and geographic analysis benefits offered by maps. These abilities distinguish GIS from other information systems and make it valuable to a wide range of public and private enterprises for explaining events, predicting outcomes, and planning strategies.

Applications of GPS and GIS

In India, GPS is mainly popular for fleet management systems. It allows real-time vehicle tracking, which enables the transportation industry and delivery services. But this technology can be effectively used in almost any business that requires precise location information. The GPS has applications in surveying, field data collection, yellow pages, tourism, infrastructure, communication, and distribution.

In retail, GPS offers applications in vehicle-tracking systems for distribution of goods. The specialized GPS vehicle-tracking systems provide cost-effective real-time vehicle location, mapping, and reporting. The receiver sends the location information, which is stored in the computer. If the computer is attached with the Internet network, the system can locate a vehicle from any computer or device with the Internet access, from anywhere on the globe at any time.

WEB 2.0

From a mere sharing of data, website, free e-mail, and bulletin board chat concepts to the modern-day e-commerce, blogs, social networking, and collective intelligence, the Web has come a long way. Web 2.0 refers to next generation of the Web though people have been talking about Web 2.0 since 2005 when Tim O'Reilly coined this word. In an article, Tim himself clarifies his concept of Web 2.0, which was published on his site in September 2005.

The term *Web 2.0* refers to second-generation Internet applications and services, which are generally rich in user experience and allow the users to become contributors to the development of the contents. For example, Wikipedia, a free Web-based encyclopaedia allows the users to add and/or edit information on the site. In various e-commerce sites, review sites, and blogs, people can actively participate. Most of the tools are collaborative, socially oriented, and are perceived to be personally enjoyable and beneficial. Examples are social network sites, such as Facebook, Orkut, Lovehappens, Tagged, and dating.Indiatimes.

Web 2.0 offers interlinked computing platforms that function like locally available software in the perception of the user. It also includes a social element where users generate and distribute content, often with freedom to share and reuse.

Table 15.1 Comparison of Web 1.0 and Web 2.0

Web 1.0	Web 2.0
Double click	Google Ad Sense
Mp3.com	Napster
Britannica online	Wikipedia
Personal websites	Blogging
Domain name speculation	Search engine optimization
Page views	Cost per click
Screen scraping	Web services
Publishing	Participation
Content-management systems	Wikis
Directories (taxonomy)	Tagging ('folksonomy')
Stickiness	Syndication

Source: O'Reilly 2005

Web 1.0 and Web 2.0 are compared in Table 15.1. Services at Web 2.0 are certainly upgradations of the first, but they are not altogether a new phenomenon. They have evolved as a more focused, intense, and personalized services from the earlier version.

As per Tim, 'There is a huge amount of disagreement about just what Web 2.0 means, with some people decrying it as a meaningless marketing buzzword, and others accepting it as the new conventional wisdom'. Tim further maintains, 'You can visualize Web 2.0 as a set of principles and practices that tie together a veritable solar system of sites that demonstrate some or all of those principles, at a varying distance from that core'.

There is a comparison between the product-centric approach in the earlier phase and service-centric approach in this phase (Web 2.0) of the Internet. For instance, Google began its life as a native Web application, never sold or packaged, but delivered as a service, with customers paying, directly or indirectly, for the use of that service. None of the trappings of the old software industry is present. There was no scheduled software releases but just continuous improvement. No licensing or sale, just usage. No porting to different platforms so that the customers can run the software on their own equipment, just a massively scalable collection of commodity PCs running open source operating systems plus home-grown applications and utilities that no one outside the company ever gets to see.

Characteristics of Web 2.0

The following are the core characteristics that make Web 2.0 different from the earlier version:

- Services, not packaged software, with cost-effective scalability
- Harnessing collective intelligence and creating data sources that get richer as more people use them
- Collaborative production by trusting users as co-developers of contents
- Social networking as one of the key driver of WebNext
- Ever-increasing data source and data transformation
- Software applications built for multiple devices

Services, Not Packaged Software

With Web 2.0, the packaged software migrated to services. Now, software as a service concept is getting acceptance and popularity. This concept evolved with market economics and technological breakthroughs. As Tim opines, 'Web 2.0 does not have a hard boundary, but rather, has a gravitational core. You can visualize Web 2.0 as a set of principles and practices that tie together a veritable solar system of sites that demonstrate some or all of those principles, at a varying distance from that core.' The earlier approach was 'application' approach while this approach is 'platform' approach. If Netscape was the standard bearer for Web 1.0, Google is most certainly the standard bearer for Web 2.0.

The comparison goes beyond application and service. Even in the same platform, there are two different business models. On the one side, there is a single software provider, whose massive installed base and tightly integrated operating system and application programming interfaces give control over the programming paradigm. On the other hand, there is a system without an owner, tied together by a set of protocols, open standards, and agreements for cooperation.

Collaborative Intelligence

The Web companies that survived the notorious Internet shake-up of Y2K aftermath were those who have embraced the power of the Web to harness 'collective intelligence'. Now everybody contributes to the making and collection of information on the web. Look at Wikipedia, an online free encyclopaedia, which is based on the unlikely notion that an entry can be added by any web user, and edited by any other. It is an unbelievable radical experiment that is founded on trust. This is a revolution in content creation techniques. Wikipedia is already in the top 100 websites, and many think it will be in the top ten before long. This is a profound change in the dynamics of content creation.

Similarly, 'tagging' is a style of collaborative categorization of sites using freely chosen keywords, often referred to as tags. Tagging allows for the kind of multiple and overlapping associations. Websites are being tagged and enhancing human knowledge with collaborative intelligence.

Collaborative Production

Collaborative production refers to a situation in which people from diverse fields work on a project and upgrade and share the results of the project, especially applications. The Web of today flourishes on a lot of freeware and open source like the Linux, Apache, MySQL, Perl, PHP, or Python. The code involved in most web servers relies on the 'peer-production' methods of open source, which is an instance of collective, Net-enabled intelligence. There are millions of freeware available and posted on the Web and there are more than 100,000 open-source software projects listed on SourceForge.net. Anyone can add a project and can download and use the code. As a result of usage and refinement, new projects become important and take centre stage. This is unique style of software-adoption process, which is not a result of any active marketing.

In open-source development practices, users are treated as co-developers. Software is being developed in collaboration, even if the software in question may not be released under an open-source license. The open-source dictum says, 'release early and release often'. In fact, this has changed into an even more radical position of perpetual 'beta release', in which the product is developed in the open, with new features coming up every day or week.

Social Networking

One of the most highly admired and criticized features of the Web 2.0 era is the rise of blogging. A blog is an advanced form of diary on the Web, which one can update and keep open for his/her peer group to see. There have been bulletin boards and social group interactions on chat sites. Personal home pages have been around since the early days of the Web, and the personal diary and daily opinion column have always been there. The personal home pages have given way to blogs (Fig. 15.6). At its most basic form, a blog is just a personal home page in a diary format. But it drives an entirely different delivery, advertising, and value chain.

Web 2.0 proliferates the live Web. We have already discussed static and dynamic web pages. Dynamic websites are database-backed sites with

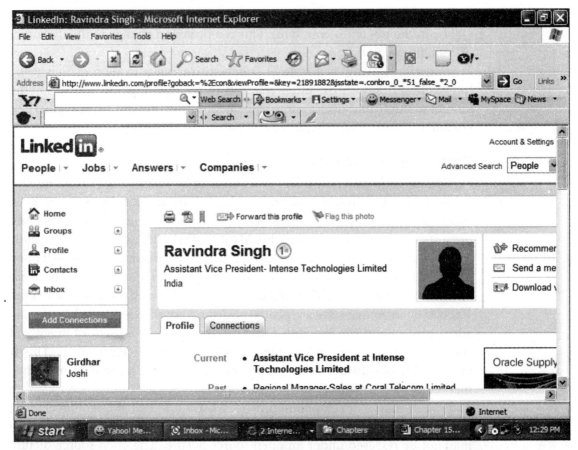

Fig. 15.6 Blogs present a door for social networking where one can post messages

dynamically generated content, i.e. whose contents keep on changing. So, the dynamics about the live Web are not just the pages but also the links. With a lot of dynamism in construction, collaboration, and open source in place, the links change every now and then.

Data Repository

The Web has transformed itself into a large repository of databases scattered over millions of servers across the globe. Database management has emerged as a core competency of Web 2.0 companies. Any significant Internet application to date has been backed by a specialized database, such as Google's Webcrawl, Yahoo!'s Directory Services and Webcrawl, Amazon's database of products, eBay's database of products and sellers, MapQuest's map database, and Napster's music database.

Large IT companies are Web companies providing data services. Only the companies owning and managing large chunks of data will make it big. The companies are vying for owning and managing certain classes of their core data of their own. As Tim O'Reilly forecasts: 'In many cases, where there is a significant cost to create the data, there may be an opportunity for an Intel Inside style play, with a single source for the data. In others, the winner will be the company that first reaches critical mass via user aggregation, and turns that aggregated data into a system service'.

Application for Multiple Devices

One other feature of Web 2.0 that deserves mention is the fact that it is no longer limited to the PC platform. Many handheld mobile devices, PDA, and iPod can be integrated with the Web. They can download information from and upload queries, searches into the Web. Thus, the application has to support multiple hardware devices. The next-generation Web applications are built with multiple connectivity in mind.

One of the best examples of this principle is iTunes. This application seamlessly reaches from the handheld device to a massive Web back-end, with the PC acting as a local cache and control station. There have been many previous attempts to bring Web content to portable devices, but the iPod–iTunes combination is one of the first such applications that can work on multiple devices. The application of iTunes also demonstrates many of the other core principles of Web 2.0. Basically it is not Web application but leverages the power of the Web platform, making it a seamless, almost invisible part of its infrastructure. Data management is most clearly the heart of their offering.

SOFTWARE AS A SERVICE

We have studied in Chapter 11 on ERP implementation that how difficult it is to build, implement, and maintain enterprise solutions. Therefore, organizations evaluated another option of a third-party creating, implementing, and maintaining enterprise solutions, usually Web-enabled and on rental basis. Application service providers (ASPs) came into existence to provide solutions to various organizations on these issues. Therefore, the new concept is not buying software as a product but renting it as a service. Thus, the concept of SaaS (software as a service) came about (Fig. 15.7).

Evolution of SaaS

The disadvantages of piecemeal legacy software (already discussed in Chapter 7) led to invention of integrated, single-platform solutions called

Fig. 15.7   Saas.com: a solution provider's web front page

enterprise solutions. Enterprise solutions under the intriguing name of ERP started coming into market in the mid of 1980s. They are surviving and flourishing. Their longevity is testimony to the fact that ERP applications are far more efficient, versatile, and integrated. Before ERP, organizations built software clubbing some business functions to plan and compute material requirements. These solutions were called material requirement planning (MRP). These were the initial form of planning software, which were basically programmed as per the requirement and functionality of business divisions. For instance, the production system, inventory system, or the delivery schedules, had different MRP modules to manage its tasks.

The ERP applications are potent enough to handle multitasking large-size business enterprises and are designed as per the businesses of clients and its unique needs make it a highly customizable and configurable program. But these customized features have made it an expensive piece of software, keeping it out of the reach of business enterprises and firms concerned about affordability. Furthermore, most business enterprises are reducing their workforce but want high productivity matched by profits.

Hosted Solutions

The ERP solutions are indispensable for organizations and at the same time, they require fortunes. Fortunately, the technology providers have addressed the cost issue with an innovative method of hosting. In fact, this hosting method has bypassed one of the intermediaries in ERP application deployment, which has helped in cutting costs. Here, these companies directly cater to business enterprises overlooking the vendors that are required for ERP deployment process.

Under a pay-as-you-go model, the customers gain access to desired applications developed and managed by application service provider (ASP) company. All necessary application and database-management software and connectivity are provided by the service provider company, in addition to implementation and maintenance support. Under this method, the ERP applications are not deployed on site in business firms. Instead, all the data related to processing and resource management is hosted on the data servers or data centres of the ERP software companies. This enables the business firms to access the ERP software round the clock as per their requirements, using the Internet connectivity via a browser.

One of the defining characteristics of the Internet era software is that it is delivered as a service, not as a product. This fact leads to a number of fundamental changes in the business model of such service provider and the user company. Software as a service (SaaS) is a pure subscription model, where the service company (vendor) provides the delivery platform, ongoing software updates, and the server infrastructure. This is in contrast to the traditional software licence model, wherein the user company buys licences of application software and database software, setting up a server and workstation infrastructure.

This new form of ERP applications as hosted services has given birth to software as a service (SaaS) module. Presently, major ERP software companies are offering SaaS modules for enterprises keeping in view the cost factor. The ERP applications as a hosted service or in the form of SaaS module have helped businesses in cutting the overall cost of an ERP program deployment, without compromising on ERP utility.

This latest form in ERP applications is available in the market on timely and pay-per-use mode basis. The companies charge business firms either on the number of its employees that access the ERP program software or pay either monthly or annually for the subscription of ERP programs.

Advantages of SaaS

SaaS is a relatively new phenomenon and is going to emerge as a futuristic technology with the advancement in Web technologies and Internet usage. We enumerate here certain advantages of using a SaaS model:

1. Through this feature, enterprises are free from setting up a large dedicated IT department and technical staff. It immensely cuts down the partial cost in ERP applications deployment.
2. The SaaS provider companies extend their support in the field of data security and management, technical faults, and other technical services, thus helping the firms to focus on their core business strengths.
3. The initial set-up costs are low, as SaaS is used on the basis of 'pay-as-you-use'.
4. Organizations can use SaaS as an upgrade on existing client-server applications.
5. For the companies having multiple locations and those that are into business or services that would be delivered more effectively over the Internet, SaaS is a better model to work on.
6. The SaaS solutions offer mature and rich functionalities as they understand the complexities of delivering SaaS in a multi-customer environment.
7. The user organization carries minimum risks on two accounts. One, the initial set-up costs are low in comparison with client-server ERP systems. Two, if the user organization thinks that the solution does not fit its requirements, the services can be discontinued anytime.

SUMMARY

M-commerce refers to conducting business transactions over mobile data network using mobile handheld terminals, such as personal digital assistants (PDAs), mobile phones, and palmtops. Cellular telephony has changed the communication style of the world. It refers to communication over mobile network using radio frequency. Wireless networks explicitly designed for two-way transmission of data files are called mobile data networks. These radio-based networks transmit data to and from handheld computers. Another type of mobile data network is based on a series of radio towers constructed specifically to transmit text and data. These devices can connect to the server through either Internet or any wireless communication technology like GPRS or CDMA. They can send or receive information, as the application is designed to work. Besides telecommunication and advertising on mobile, there are hundreds of applications. Some of the applications are sales force automation, inventory management, gaming and lotteries, bus ticketing, electricity billing, municipality tax collections, mobile recharge, rural micro banking, and restaurant billing, to name a few.

The GPS and GIS are latest technologies used for locating and tracking objects on earth. Global positioning system (GPS) is a technology that can give accurate position of an object anywhere on earth based on its latitude and longitude. The GPS receiver fitted on an object is designed to receive signals from the satellites. GPS and GIS can be used in retail as an application for distribution and delivery van tracking.

The term 'Web 2.0' refers to second-generation Internet applications. The second generation applications and services are generally rich in user experience and allow the users to also become contributors to the development of the contents. Web 2.0 can be distinguished by its collective intelligence and content creation, collaborative production of software packages and open source, remarkable data management and data transformation, social networking through dating and blogging, software as a service concept and availability of applications for multiple devices.

Software as a service (SaaS) refers to the hosted applications over the Net and is available to the users on rental basis. Presently, major ERP software companies are offering SaaS modules for enterprises keeping in view the cost factor. The ERP applications as hosted services or in form of SaaS module have helped businesses in cutting the overall cost of an ERP program deployment without compromising on ERP utility. The SaaS model helps an organization to concentrate on its core business, while the service provider takes care of all technical requirements of the organization.

CONCEPT REVIEW QUESTIONS

1. What is mobile computing?
2. How can you categorize various applications of mobile computing?
3. What are the various business applications of mobile handheld terminals?
4. Define m-commerce.
5. How does GPS work?
6. Explain the applications of GIS and GPS in retail businesses.
7. What is Web 2.0?
8. What are important characteristics of Web 2.0?
9. What do you understand by SaaS? Explain in detail.
10. What are the advantages and challenges of SaaS?

CRITICAL THINKING QUESTIONS

1. 'After e-commerce, m-commerce is the next happening thing.' Comment on this statement.
2. 'SaaS is just a new abbreviation for ASP.' Explain this statement in the light of new developments in this area.
3. 'Web 2.0 is a misnomer for the same technology and a marketing gimmick of some overzealous technocrats.' Do you agree with this statement? Why or why not?

PROJECTS

1. Visit a restaurant and make a business case for mobile terminals to be used for taking orders by the waiters.
2. Assume that you are manager of a retail chain organization having one corporate office, three warehouses, and thirty retail outlets. You want to implement global positioning system across the organization. Draw a blueprint covering technological requirements, commercial budgets, and time-frame estimates.

SELECT REFERENCES

Images Retail, www.imagesretail.com, last accessed in January 2008.

Internet and Mobile Association of India (IAMAI) 2007, 'Internet in India', www.iamai.in.

Kalakota, Ravi and Andrew B. Whinston 2006, *Frontiers of Electronic Commerce,* Pearson Education Inc (Licencee: Dorling Kindersley, New Delhi).

Laudon, Ken and Mary Laudon 2002, *Management Information System,* Pearson Education (Singapore).

O'Reilly, Tim 2005, 'What Is Web 2.0: Design Patterns and Business Models for the Next Generation of Software', www.oreilly.com, September.

www.gisdevelopment.net, last accessed in March 2008.

www.saas.com, last accessed in February 2008.

www.technologyevaluation.com, last accessed in January 2008.

CASE STUDY

Harsh Express Couriers Implements Wireless Devices

Company   Harsh Express Couriers

Harsh Express is a purely domestic company promoted by two friends Ravi and Roshan in the year 1992 to delivery fast couriers across cities. It has operations in the major cities in the country. The company rolled out wireless devices for its courier field force agents. The wireless devices keep them posted with real-time information on pick-ups and delivery of shipments. India is one of the first countries in the DHL international network to adopt this new technology, which was rolled out at an investment of Rs 1,000,000. The devices have been deployed across 15 cities—Ahmedabad, Bangaluru, Bhopal, Coimbatore, Chennai, Cochin, Delhi, Hyderabad, Indore, Jaipur, Kolkata, Mumbai, Pune, Tirupur, Raipur, and Hyderabad.

The Pain Area in Traditional Processes

In the traditional process of booking of a courier, giving receipt for the consignment was difficult, as every field staff had to carry a blank consignment book. The booking was made through a pager receipt, which the field staff carried to office. In the office, it was punched into the system late at night. It was a big problem for a field staff employee delivering hundreds of shipments a day, literally writing the shipment details at the customer's door and again posting the same data after reaching the office. Initially, all the data about pick-up and delivery was only getting recorded once the agent reached the base office.

The Solution

To solve this problem, the company decided to take help of technology by implementing wireless mobile devices. The wireless scanner considerably helps reduce the interval time between posting and recording the information from the field to the shipment record database, which is usually the consumer service centre. The scanner has GPRS as the prime mode of connectivity with GSM in the backup, which is connected to Harsh's servers placed at various locations.

The wireless scanner considerably helps reduce the interval time between posting and recording the information from the field to the shipment record database, which is usually the consumer service centre. The data gets updated online by the mobile device. The device when attached with a printer can print an acknowledgement receipt. The same number can work as consignment number for the courier document.

The Challenge

Buying the right mobile devices and getting the telecommunication networks was really a big challenge. Being one of its kind of service, the challenge during the implementation was negotiating with the telecom companies about integrating the technology and deciding on the tariffs accordingly. The GPRS connectivity was to be provided by the telecom companies. The telecom companies did not want to take any chances and were little reluctant to provide the service. However, finally a major telecom player in India agreed to offer its services for the wireless scanner.

Benefits after Implementation of Wireless Scanner

After the introduction of wireless devices, the field agents were able to post real-time data about pickups and delivery. Unlike earlier times, when the agents were unable to accept the pickup once they had passed the customer checkpoint, the devices now enable the customer service agents to post the pickup request to a field employee who is nearest to the respective customer checkpoint.

The information gets posted on the global website through the servers within thirty minutes after it is posted on the scanner through GPRS. In case the GPRS is down, the GSM network is configured to check for data every three minutes. The GSM backup comes handy as every city has some pockets with weak connectivity.

Once the data is on the national server, even customers could check their consignment status. The courier company got indirect and direct benefits from the introduction of handheld devices. This saved a lot of money to the courier company.

Questions:

1. What were the major problems faced by Harsh Express Couriers before implementation of handheld mobile devices?
2. Devise a similar case for use of handheld mobile devices in retail businesses.

16

Retail IT Products and Vendors

Learning Objectives

- To learn purchase steps for technology products and vendor selection
- To design questionnaire for product evaluation with the help of an example
- To help students and managers with ready references of various IT products and vendors

By now, we have analysed and understood various components of retail information systems and technology used in running retail businesses. In this chapter, we will discuss steps for buying technology products, vendor selection, and preparing for implementation of technology in the organization. We examine some of the popular brands in EPOS hardware, software, and auto-identification systems. The objective is to equip the students and managers with knowledge of available products and technology in the market, and not to compare the functionalities and features offered by them. The task of comparison is left to the knowledgeable managers, who need to evaluate each system in the light of individual requirement, infrastructure, and financial budget of their organizations.

PURCHASING RETAIL IT PRODUCTS

In previous chapters, we have studied various IT products and solutions along with their applications, limitations, and challenges in adopting them. In short, the following sequence of steps must be adopted while planning for technology implementation.

Understand the Need

You must know in advance what you want to achieve by implementing a solution. The decision-maker must identify the problems or challenges. So, greater the clarity in defining the targets, better it will be for implementing solutions in terms of qualitative and quantitative objectives.

Fix Budgets

The types of products and solutions to buy are defined by budgetary constraints. An organization's budget for IT solutions defines the range of products that it can shortlist for evaluation. A tight shoestring budget would not allow much elbow space to go for large customized software or expensive hardware, for example, if the organization has a good budget, one can go for good POS solutions with high-end back-office international ERP systems. If the budgets are average, one can settle for a low-cost best-of-breed solution.

Choose a Product for your Business

There are various products and solutions available in the market. Select a product for evaluation that offers a solution close to your business model, for example if you are in a business of hospitality (own a restaurant or fast-food outlet), an EPOS system that supports touch screen would be an ideal choice. But, even restaurant solutions can be mouse driven and run on normal CRT monitors.

Learn by Others' Mistakes

An organization can do research on what its competitors are using in terms of various brands and categories of machines and solutions. It can try to find out the disadvantages of the product and limitations of the technology. It can then choose a product that would have high acceptance in the organization. It should also consider availability of a skilled and trained workforce.

Select an Established Vendor

Information technology products are easy to find but difficult to implement. There are enumerable examples where the same product, particularly software solutions, is highly successful in one organization but a disaster in another. In software implementation, there are a number of technology partners involved. Since an organization is dependant on the implementing team provided by the vendor, it should take utmost care while assigning the task of implementation. The vendors must be established and should have industry reference, i.e. they should have ample experience in implementing such solutions in retail industry.

Strong Will to Implement

Last but not least, an organization should be strong willed to implement solutions. There will be occasional resistance from employees, suppliers, or customers because technology implementation involves process changes, additional documentation, and, many times, vested interests. All stakeholders are taken into confidence. Also, there are no short cuts. There is a normal human tendency to resist change. In such situations, the driver of the project must be 'strong willed' and must force the implementation.

Preparing Questionnaire for Product Evaluation

A set of well-defined and well-structured questions helps an organization judge the vendor and the product's strengths and weaknesses. For different kinds of products, the shape and contents of questionnaire will change. A company can make its own evaluation questionnaire for evaluating products and vendors. However, Fig. 16.1 shows some standard questions that will help an organization design its own questionnaire. This questionnaire has been designed keeping in mind the retail software. The questionnaire will be entirely different if a company is evaluating bar code or RFID products.

---

1. Vendor's name and address _____

2. Head office and branches, in India or abroad _____

3. Date of establishment _____

4. Directors' and CEO's name _____

5. Approximate numbers of employees _____
   (a) Engineers _____
   (b) Support staff _____

6. Turnover of the last three years _____

7. Technical specifications _____
   (a) Hardware _____
   (b) Software _____
   (c) Operating system _____
   (d) Front-end _____
   (e) Back-end/database _____

8. Current version of the software _____

9. Upgrade policy (whether free upgrades available) _____

10. Future plans of upgradations and enhancements _____

11. Is local support available? The number of persons locally deployed _____

12. Types of support available _____
    (a) Online/Web support _____
    (b) Engineer visits _____

Contd

13. Telephonic support _____

14. List of current installations/customers _____

15. If implemented in the same industry, name and contact number of the customer _____

16. List of current known bugs/errors in the software _____
    (a) _____
    (b) _____

17. Free support/warranty period _____

18. Customization policy–is the software customizable? _____

19. Data migration policy (Would you convert the existing data in the new system?) _____

20. If yes, is it priced? What is the price? _____

21. Per person-day price _____

22. Does the software support LAN/WAN/RF? _____

23. Preferred connectivity medium _____

24. Minimum bandwidth required to run the program _____

25. Does it support off-line data transmission and consolidation? _____

26. What are the third-party software licences required? _____

27. Does it support bar code interface? _____

28. Can this software run on multiple operating systems? What is the preferred operating system required? _____

29. Is the system secure and protected with system, application, and database passwords? _____

30. Are database consistency and recovery tools available? _____

31. Can this software connect to any other ERP systems? If yes, which one? _____

32. Price of the product _____

33. VAT, excise duty, inclusive or extra? If extra, how much? _____

34. Implementation price, if extra _____

35. Support price after warranty _____

36. What is the response time in case of troubleshooting? _____

37. Training charges, if not included _____

38. Any other hidden costs involved? _____

39. Remarks _____

Fig. 16.1 A sample questionnaire for POS software

Now, we will discuss various retail IT products and their vendors. This is only for reference and does not cover the entire range of products available in the market. These products and vendors are not recommended by the author or the publisher, but being given for the students and managers of retail to explore further and choose the best that suits their requirements. The readers may refer to the websites for further information.

ELECTRONIC CASH REGISTERS

There are only a few vendors of electronic cash registers (ECRs). Some of them are listed below:

- Bradma (www.bradmaindia.com)
- Samsung (www.samsung.in)
- Trucount (www.trucountindia.com)
- ABS (absbharat.com)

The machines supplied by various vendors come with the standard configurations. The add-ons are separately supplied and priced by the vendors. These add-ons on the machines are customer display unit, cash drawer, and bar code scanner.

ELECTRONIC POINT OF SALES (EPOS)

Some major vendors supplying EPOS are discussed below.

IBM SureStore (www.ibm.in)

IBM is one of the few major companies in the world that offer end-to-end solutions, which cover hardware, software, services, and consulting. Since its inception in 1992 in India, it has been working with its agenda of 'on-demand business' providing for changes in mode of business, reducing costs, enhancing customer satisfaction, and increasing efficiency.

IBM is a leader in POS machines. Some of the POS machines it offers are SureStore, IBM Mobile Tablet, and IBM Self-checkout system. The IBM touch-screen computer, equipped with a bar code scanner, mounts directly on the cart. The sophisticated location-tracking system consists of ceiling-mounted beacons from IBM.

The IBM Store Integration Framework provides a platform that connects all shopping activities, point-of-sales systems, product description, and customer ordering capabilities in a single solution.

HCL BeePOS (www.hclpos.co.in, www.hcl.in)

HCL Infosystems deals in the domestic IT products, solutions, and related services. The stable of products provided by HCL includes PCs, servers, office automation, networking products, imaging, broadcasting, communication, peripherals, POS, and handheld mobile terminals. HCL introduced its POS division in 2003 and now its POS range comprises HCL POS Elegance, HCL POS Ambience, HCL POS kiosks, and other POS peripherals. HCL is national distributor for bar code printers and scanners from Argos and thermal bill printers from Star. The company deals in POS hardware, software, and mobile POS terminals.

NCR POS (www.ncr.com)

NCR is an Ohio-based US company established in 1884. At NCR, the technology has evolved from the world's first cash registers to the retail systems, ATMs, and IT services in over 124 years. NCR provides ATM technology and continues to produce advanced products for retail. The following products from the stable of NCR are given below:

- NCR FastLane—self-checkout system for delivering faster and more convenient service by speeding up the checkout process
- NCR EasyPoint—self-service kiosk
- NCR RealPOS—POS workstation
- NCR RealScan—POS scanner
- NCR RealPOS peripheral—designed for the harsh retail environment for use with NCR RealPOS workstations
- NCR RealSolutions software—for helping the retailers build stronger customer relationships

RETAIL SOFTWARE SOLUTIONS

RetailPro by RetailPro, Inc (www.retailpro.com)

RetailPro is provided by Retail Technologies International, a US-based company headquartered in La Jolla, California. RetailPro is one of the world's most renowned providers of merchandising software for retailers. Originally developed in the mid 1980s, it has emerged as one of the premier store operations solution providers around the world. RetailPro is a cost-effective, scalable solution available to small and mid-tier retailers who wish to grow their businesses beyond the constraints of ordinary software limitations. Whether a business has only one store or has thousands, RetailPro is always the solution of choice because of its scalability, ease of use, and affordability.

Over more than two decades, RetailPro has developed a reputation for delivering high-quality software to the retail industry. Its software solutions manage billions of transactions annually in more than 35,000 store locations worldwide. Besides the US, the company has its offices in the UK, China, and Australia. RetailPro is represented by business partners in over 40 countries. It is the pre-eminent international business management software solution for retailers. Widely known for its impressive scalability and adaptability, RetailPro's application suite consists of POS and store operations, merchandising, payment solutions, planning, and business intelligence.

Shoper by Tally Solutions India (www.tallysolutions.com/www.retailbusiness.com)

Shoper is available from Tally India, a Bangaluru-based company. Tally acquired Vedas Software a few years back and strengthened its offering. Since its inception in 1986, Tally accounting software claims to have more than two million satisfied customers in more than 103 countries, which has made Tally a premier software product company in India. Tally's retail solutions suite comprises Shoper POS for retail outlets and Shoper HO for retail chains that require central control for all the connected outlets. These comprehensive solutions cater to every aspect of managing a retail business, with features that cover billing, CRM, inventory management, pricing, bar code generation, and printing among several others.

In addition, Shoper POS can work in conjunction with the Tally business accounting and inventory management software, to offer a comprehensive business solution. The features are billing, cash account, item classification and analysis, merchandising and inventory management, tag and bar code printing, CRM, promotional schemes, reports, decision support systems, and security control.

Tally Solutions FZ LLC, incorporated in the UAE, is the registered office of Tally Solutions and is the head office for West Asia and for North African operations. In South Asia, the arm is Tally (India) Private Limited.

BNGpro Retail by BNG Infotech (www.bng.co.in)

BNG Infotech is a New Delhi based firm creating software solutions suite for retail chain companies. BNG-Retail ERP is one of the well-appreciated retailing solutions in India. Built around the latest development tools and multiple RDBMS compatibility, it offers complete security and is highly user-friendly. The system has evolved through a decade of research, development, and testing at the marketplace. The BNGpro POS module is integrated with BNG-Retail

ERP at the back office. The ERP is a complete solution for procurement, distribution, inventory control, and accounting management.

The BNGpro and BNG-Retail-ERP come with different variants for large retail chains, supermarkets, and stand-alone shops. The solutions also cover different types of retailers, such as apparels, footwear retailing, FMCG, restaurant, food courts, fabric retailers, service retailers like beauty parlours, and pharmacy retailing. It has been designed to suit multiple RDBMS. It supports ORACLE®, SQL SERVER®, and MSDE. The new versions come with built-in report writers and user-definable document. The solution provides high security with each module and sub module and menus are protected by passwords and authorizations. BNGpro works on all modern retail devices like POS System, card readers, customer display, cash drawer, magnetic card stripe reader, receipt printer, bar code scanners, and data capturing units and are also bar code printer compatible.

BNG-Business suite is offered to manufacturing companies. Retailers who are also into manufacturing can integrate this with the retail ERP and POS solutions from BNG Infotech.

Retail Excel by Polaris Retail (www.polarisretail.com)

Polaris Retail is a Polaris Group company, based in Chennai, which started its retail operations from the Middle East. Polaris is a specialist provider of IT services and enterprise software for organizations across the world. Some of the world's leading firms have partnership with Polaris, optimizing their IT investments.

PRIL Retail Excel is a robust and comprehensive application suite that embodies the mandatory functionality of a typical business while providing ample scope for configuration and customization to each retailer's business needs. The features are drawn from the best retail practices from around the world and are set atop a state-of-the-art technology development framework that understands the art of merging business and technology together to achieve maximum results.

PRIL Retail Excel offers the following modules: Retail Excel Merchandise, Retail Excel Inventory, Retail Excel Replenishment, Retail Excel Procurement, Retail Excel Club and Campaign, Retail Excel Sales, Retail Excel PoS, Retail Excel Accounting, Retail Excel Reports and Analysis.

GinSys Retail by Ginni Systems (www.gsl.in)

Ginni Systems Ltd (GSL) is headquartered in Kolkata. This is an enterprise software company focused on developing and delivering cutting-edge solutions for the retail industry. GSL claims to have implemented retail and ERP applications at more than 800 retail stores (6000 points of sales) and 28 manufacturing units in India and abroad. Ginsys offers three product suites to cater to different market segments.

GinSys POS (Point-of-Sales Solution)

It is a comprehensive POS solution ideally suited for independent single-store retailers as well as franchisee or captive outlets of a multi-store retail chain. It covers a vast area of functionalities, such as billing, store management, procurement, and inventory and customer relationship management.

GinSys Retail (Retail Solution)

As the retail business starts to grow beyond a single store, it becomes increasingly difficult to manage the business effectively without a solution that gives an analytical understanding of critical business parameters. Back-office operations gain more importance for successful running of the business. With all features of GinSys POS and additional features to handle the added complexities, GinSys Retail is best suited for a growing retail business. GinSys Retail has two variants—GinSys Retail Standard and GinSys Retail Enterprise. The variants are designed to meet the needs of small-to mid-sized retailers.

GinSys Business

It is a fusion of both retail and manufacturing solutions and caters effectively to the requirements of both. GinSys Business has two variants, GinSys Business Standard and GinSys Business Enterprise, which are designed to meet the needs of small-to mid-sized retailers and manufacturers at an optimal cost.

Wings Retail by Wings Infonet (http://www.wings2000.com)

Wings Infonet Ltd, an IT solutions company, is based in Hyderabad. Started in 1988, Wings software has evolved through 16 major versions, innumerable upgrades, and expansions. Software products from the house of Wings are rigorously field-tested and have proved to be extremely stable and robust. Wings has evolved beyond accounting over the years. Today, it offers a suite of the most powerful and comprehensive business-management solutions designed to meet the needs of a large spectrum of businesses and professions. The company launched Wings e-Biz suite and plans to expand business overseas. Addressing a press conference here, a director of the company, Ajay Gandhi, said that the e-Biz suite had features such as ability to work in any major world language, MS Office integration, and mobile device enablement.

Wings Retail

A complete POS system right for all kinds of retail businesses, Wings Retail can take care of POS, accounting, and inventory management requirements.

Wings Central

A multi-store consolidation software, Wings Central works tightly with Wings Retail to enable company-wide consolidation without the weight of an ERP system.

Wings Retail Enterprise

It is a Web-based ERP software that takes care of all requirements of the company. It is suitable for retailers having multiple retail outlets and those who wish to deploy an ERP system across entire enterprise, including the retail outlets. This system not only automates the retail operations but also automates all functions of the company, end to end.

WinApp by SoftInfo Systems (http://www.softinfosystems.com)

SoftInfo is a New Delhi based company and provides low-cost retail software solutions. The software provided by it caters to various kinds of retailers and is particularly popular among garment traders. Some of the salient features of this version are as follows:

- Client server architecture for better performance, stability, security, and scalability
- Article-based approach and user-definable attributes for various items and photographs thereof
- Counter/floor-wise stock maintenance
- Hold bill facility in retail sales
- Audit trail, scheduled auto-backup facility, smart card compatibility for CRM, data transfers to and from FTP site with auto-zipping that leads to WAN connectivity of stores
- Provides stock-level specifications for all business locations (Min-Max-Reorder)
- Cashier module for daily cash counter cash tallying.
- Gives exclusive MIS reports, such as key performance indicators (KPIs) report, stock/sale ratio, and open-to-buy (OTB) report

FlexiPos and FlexiWare (www.eretailtech.in)

FlexiPos and FlexiWare are the products offered by eRetail Technologies, a company based in Secunderabad. These products can be implemented across different segments of the retail industry, such as super markets, apparels, food and beverage, bookstores, jewellery, and automobile industry. The company is committed to establish long-term relationships with each of its clients and come out with better solutions specific to the retail industry.

In addition, the company offers professional services focusing on technical implementation, process improvement, and change management. It is using all possible time-and money-saving tools in order to remain competitive in this aggressive industry. The company has good installation base in the country.

Logic by Logic Software (www.logicsoftwareindia.com)

Logic Software operates from Chandigarh. In 1993, Gurbir Singh and Swarandeep Singh started the Logic Group with a team of IT professionals. Logic started by offering a pharma product for medicine wholesales and slowly switched over to other retail segments. The company is now offering Logic Apparel for garment retailers and Logic Enterprise for back-office operations. Logic is better suited for apparel manufacturing, trading, and retail segments.

Sify Forum (http://www.sifycorp.com/scripts/ps_forum.asp)

Sify Forum, is a retail and supply chain management software from Sify Technologies Ltd, Chennai. Sify Forum equips businesses with a simple and cost-effective tool for managing the forward supply chain. Forum works as a two-way street where data and information is accessible to the suppliers. This helps greatly in logistic planning, inventory management, sharing crucial market information, and speeding up service.

Forum collates stock and sales information from distributors and exclusive retail outlets. It enables two-way communication between the organization and the supply chain partners including distributors. For instance, product or scheme masters can be delivered to the distributors through the Internet, or additionally, the distributor's claims can be uploaded to the company's ERP and invoices can be delivered online to the distributors impacting on the collection timelines. Companies can implement a continuous replenishment mechanism, reduce inventory levels, cut operation costs, and make channel members more efficient, thereby increasing profits. It can directly integrate the distributor data to the customer's ERP, such as SAP, JD Edwards, and MfgPro. Forum, therefore, aids in integration of supply chains with minimum disruption to pre-existing IT infrastructure. By integrating and connecting handheld applications to the main system, it extends the supply chain and enables unprecedented reach. Forum has multiple versions, such as regular micro-ERP to manage any finished goods distributor business, service version to manage products and servicing, and serial number version to manage products like mobile phones.

ShawMan POS by ShawMan Software (www.shawmansoftware.com)

ShawMan is a Mumbai-based software company and has a dozen full-blown products. Besides catering not just to the hospitality and retail market segment, with products like HRIS, CRM, CFS, KM, DM, and Tests, it has a long list of major corporate clients that use these solutions. ShawMan has an ever-growing installed base in major cities in India like Mumbai, Delhi, Bangalore, and Pune, the Middle East, and Asia.

The hospitality suite is a combination of various solutions required in the hospitality vertical. This supports small fast-food outlets to coffee shops, fine dining operations, and large malls to large leisure and spa resorts. It is currently being use by leading hotel chains, restaurants, fast-food chains, malls, entertainment centres, and corporate.

ShawMan's retail suite is a solution for the retailing segment. Retailers like supermarkets, garment shops, pharmacies, music stores, and others are currently using this solution. ShawMan has focused on the entire gamut of CRM. It is foundation software that handles customers effectively through a host of offerings, not forgetting the loyalty engine.

ETP VX by ETP International (www.etpgroup.com)

ETP International, with its headquarter in Singapore and R&D lab in Mumbai, is a software company that focuses on developing and delivering cutting-edge solutions for the retail segment. ETP helps its customers through a comprehensive range of services, which include ETP implementation services, ETP customer support, and enterprise consulting and technology services. The company claims to have presence in Hong Kong, Taiwan, Malaysia, Singapore, India, UAE, Saudi Arabia, Bahrain, and Qatar.

ETP VX integrates with point of sales, online sales, and call centre sales. It covers functional modules, such as warehousing, distribution, and procurement, and incorporates advance merchandise planning, promotional planning, and retail merchandise planning. It provides retail-analysis tools to help business managers in decision-making.

INTERNATIONAL ERP, SCM, AND CRM SYSTEMS

JDA (www.jda.com)

JDA has global presence in large retail vertical. The company claims to provide services to more than 5500 organizations worldwide. It provides sophisticated software solutions meant for retail businesses. The company offers the following solutions:

- Strategic demand and supply solution, which reduces operational costs and increases revenues.
- Transportation management, which helps in planning and executing the strategic, operational, and tactical components that support the distribution of goods.
- Merchandise operation, which manages inventory and the movement of goods through the customer-driven value chain.
- Store systems, which help in providing multi-channel chain and enterprise visibility and empowers operational teams to speed up transactions.
- Contract manufacturing, which provides solutions for manufacturing and production companies.

With new go-to-market strategy, JDA has already added the resources in sale and development by opening its first support centre in India in Hyderabad.

SAP (www.sap.com)

SAP Ag, the topmost ERP solution provider in the world, has its headquarter in Germany. With its SAP R/3, it has complete business modules, such as manufacturing, SCM, sales and distribution, inventory, warehousing, finance and control, human resources, and CRM. Spanning across 107 countries, the solutions are available in twenty-four major languages and cater to and comply with international accounting standards and procedures.

To cater to the needs of medium and small-scale industries and retailers, SAP has come up with MySAP and SAP Business One solutions, which are cost-effective and less complex to implement. SAP vendors also offer IS Retail, a fully integrated retail solution. SAP for retail users, one integrated database to ensure one version of the truth and to support the company-wide adoption of standard best practices.

The SAP customer relationship management (SAP CRM) application provides best-in-class functionality for marketing, sales, and service. By supporting customer facing business processes across multiple interaction channels, SAP CRM enables organizations to focus on strategies for customer-driven growth and to differentiate themselves in the market by providing a superior customer experience. With SAP CRM, the client company gets the help it needs to delight its customers, empower the teams, and grow the business.

ORACLE (www.oracle.com)

Oracle Corporation, a California-based company established in 1977, is primarily known for its robust database management systems. Oracle offers ERP systems for manufacturing, financial transactions, supply chain, CRM, and retail, covering around 45 modules. Though a late entrant in retail, it has robust solutions for the industry. Oracle Retail is a comprehensive set of solutions and provides multifaceted and cross-channel information at all points of service, enabling retailers to make precise decisions and focus on what matters most—the customers. Oracle Retail modules cover the merchandising systems, point of service, store inventory management, retail sales audit, invoice matching, data warehouse, and business intelligence.

Oracle has supported retail organizations worldwide. The Oracle Retail Centre of Excellence in Bangaluru is playing a pivotal role in supporting customers in India.

PeopleSoft (www.peoplesoft.com)

PeopleSoft, a US-based global company, was established in 1987. The first software it released was human resource management system, PeopleSoftHRMS, which today commands big chunk of world's market share. PeopleSoft offers ERP and e-business solutions for various domains, industry verticals, and functional areas. The solutions offered by it include financials, distribution, human resource management, and supply chain management.

Vantive is a CRM suite by PeopleSoft, which offers front-office customer service, interaction management, and field support. It offers both best-of-breed back-office and front-office management. Vantive is the second most popular CRM after Siebel and is well integrated with PeopleSoft ERP solutions.

Oracle acquired PeopleSoft in January 2005. Oracle and PeopleSoft bring together the best and brightest talent in the enterprise software industry. They plan to accelerate innovation and offer customers a superior solution at a lower price. Both the companies together represent more applications and database customers than any other company in the world.

Microsoft Dynamics (www.microsoft.com/dynamics)

Microsoft was a pioneer in recognizing the potential of IT as a driver of economic growth in India. Microsoft Dynamics NAV (Microsoft takeover of

Navision) is an integrated solution that brings together disparate business processes to increase productivity and drive business growth.

Microsoft has dozens of ERP, SCM, and CRM solutions to offer, as a result of Microsoft's penchant for buying successful product companies worldwide. Some of the solutions are MS-Navision, MS-Axapta, Microsoft-GP, Microsoft-SL, Attain, and LS Retail. All these products are offered under the aegis of Microsoft Dynamics. Besides focusing on retail and hospitality industry, Microsoft has now developed segment-specific solutions, with the intention that retailers can pick and choose the elements required by them, such as inventory optimizer, theft control, business intelligence, and measurement of footfalls in the store.

Microsoft Dynamics solutions can provide the customers with a multitude of ways to plan, coordinate, and execute delivery of goods and services productively. One can realize a strong return on investment as a result of better individual and team productivity, streamlined operations, and more effective collaboration.

Microsoft Dynamics offers Attain CRM, a fully integrated CRM system. Microsoft Dynamics CRM gives the capability to easily create and maintain a clear view of customers from the first contact through purchase and after sales. With tools to enhance the company's sales, marketing, and customer service processes—along with native Microsoft Office Outlook integration—Microsoft Dynamics CRM delivers a fast, flexible, and affordable solution.

JD Edwards (http://www.oracle.com)

JD Edwards, a PeopleSoft product, was acquired by Oracle on June 1, 2005. All PeopleSoft.com content is now available at Oracle.com.

JD Edwards EnterpriseOne is an integrated applications suite of comprehensive ERP software, which combines business value, standards-based technology, and deep industry experience into a business solution with a low total cost of ownership (TCO). Oracle's JD Edwards EnterpriseOne offers a choice of databases, operating systems, and hardware to build and expand IT solution to meet business requirements. Oracle offers seventy JD Edwards EnterpriseOne application modules to support a diverse set of business operations.

i2 (www.i2.com)

Founded in 1990, i2 Ltd is a total supply chain management company, providing solutions across the world. The i2 suite of supply chain management software helps to manage the supply risk inherent in today's global supply chains. The i2 total supply management drives toward perfect parts availability, thus ensuring a maximum facility throughput. The resulting benefits can be measured in various areas, such as reduced direct material spending, increased compliance, reduced inbound supply chain and logistic costs, improved user productivity, decreased inventory, increased revenue potential, and shorter cash-to-cash cycles. The SCM offered by i2 has the following modules.

The i2 Total Plan Management

It appropriately identifies, analyses, and resolves plan deviations using a closed loop, plan-synchronize-control-review-publish cycle in a repeatable manner.

The i2 Total Logistic Management

It creates value by synchronizing critical transportation and distribution business processes, resulting in optimal cost and service performance. Companies can minimize IT complexity and, through more accurate data, can enhance collaboration with supply chain partners.

The i2 Total Supply Management

It combines supplier relationship management (SRM) processes with supplier collaboration and procurement processes that cut across time horizon and functional and geographical boundaries.

The i2 Total Channel Management

It provides the framework to drive results. It is a comprehensive methodology comprising i2's domain expertise, solutions, and service offerings that enable companies to create, evaluate, synchronize, review, and publish all plans across the enterprise.

The i2 Total Merchandise Management

It helps retailers confront the challenges of the highly competitive contemporary retailing environment with advanced planning and supply chain software solutions that enable a superior, differentiated customer shopping experience, supply chain efficiency, and revenue growth.

The i2 Total Inventory Management

It provides a comprehensive range of supply chain technology and services that deliver quick results and lay the framework for ongoing incremental value.

Siebel (www.siebel.com)

Siebel is one of the leading CRM solution providers in the world. Siebel launched its sales enterprise in 1995 for the sales force automation. Till now, it has come up with many versions of e-CRM suites. The company offers its solutions for various industries, such as automobile, consumer goods, communication, finance, insurance, and retail. The CRM software is configurable and integrates with most of the ERP. Whereas ERP systems create data through various transaction processes, Siebel CRM helps analyse the data and provides insights into customer habits.

In January 2006, Oracle took over Siebel. Siebel CRM, Oracle ERP, Oracle Fusion Middleware, and Oracle 10g Database combine to form a complete, world-class set of customer-centric, information age applications. Together they are a stronger, more strategic partner, with complementary resources and maximum deployment flexibility.

Besides the above, the major ERP systems provided by Siebel are BaaN, MFGPro, SSA, IFS, RAMCO, and ACCPAC. But these ERP systems are mainly for manufacturing segment and finance segment, so we are not covering any discussion on them. There are thousands of others that have just local presence and gathering data about them is not a simple task. A simple search on the Net can give information on them.

AUTOMATIC IDENTIFICATION AND DATA-CAPTURE PRODUCTS

Bar Code Products and Data-Capture Units

There are a number of international brands that are available in India through their distributors. Each brand has created a niche market for itself. It will not be possible to cover all brands and their vendors. However, some of them are given below:

Paxar Monarch (USA), Intermec (USA), Argox (Taiwan), Sato (Japan), Toshiba Tec (Japan), Gedox (Japan), Symbol (USA), PSC (USA), Epson (Japan), Star(China), Metrologic (USA), Automix (Japan)

Some of the vendors dealing in the above brands are discussed below.

Great Eastern Impex (www.geipl.com)

Great Eastern Impex (GEIPL) is a New Delhi based vendor founded in 1983 as a company providing retail support with its product marking, labelling, and bar coding items. It is the first company in India to introduce product identification through bar codes. The company imports labelling and bar code devices from leading manufacturers across the world. Some of the brands that the company is dealing in are Paxar Monarch, Toshiba TEC, Unitech, PSC, Symbol, and Argox. These brands are some of the best in the world and offer time-tested solutions. GEIPL manufactures gun labels and bar code labels at its own manufacturing plant in Gurgaon. The company has a countrywide presence through its offices and dealer network.

Protocol Solutions (www.protocolsol.in)

Headquartered in Bangaluru, Protocol Solutions has extended its operational territory to other major cities of India, viz. Chennai, Hyderabad, Mumbai, Delhi, Kolkata, Cochin, and Coimbatore. Protocol's forte lies in providing IT solutions in retail sector. The company offers total solution for material tracking in the supply chain, warehouse management packing and dispatch automation, work in progress, inventory management, time attendence, touch screen for information kiosks, flow management, and other spheres. It deals in Posiflex, POS machines from Posiflex (Taiwan), bar code printers from Autonix (Japan), and scanners and data-capture units from Metrologic (USA).

Rachna Overseas (www.rachnasystems.com)

Rachna Overseas Pvt Ltd (ROPL) is a Delhi based bar code solutions company. It was established as a privately held Indian Company in June 1988. The company has been promoted by Mr Prem Khanna along with Mr A.S. Shekhawat.

The company has pan-India presence with its offices and dealer network. It deals in bar code printers, bar code scanners, portable data terminals and data capture units, tags, labels, thermal transfer ribbons, and bar code generation labels. The company is a distributor for Godex, Toshiba Tec, Avery Dennison textile printers, Opticon bar code data collectors with in-built laser scanners, and fit applications requiring bar code data capture with time stamp.

Prakash Labels (www.prakashlabels.com)

Prakash Labels, a privately held Indian company founded in 1993, caters to the growing needs for product identification systems. The company began its operations by manufacturing self-adhesive labels, viz. price marking and EDP labels, both plain and pre-printed. The company introduced BLITZ and OPEN brands of hand labellers in 1998. During the same time the company introduced BLITZ SEQUENTIAL labellers for the garment industry. The company claims of having around a 95 per cent market share in India.

Prakash Labels diversified in 2000 into bar code systems and solutions while representing ARGOX bar code printers and scanners from Taiwan, Avery Dennison bar code printers, Germany, Sony thermal transfer ribbons (Singapore), Blitz handheld labellers (Italy), Symbol bar code scanners/portable data terminals (USA), Zebra bar code printers (USA), and Fujicopian Co Ltd (Japan).

Intercode Solutions (www.intercodesolutions.com)

Intercode Solutions is a division of Interlabels Industries, a Mumbai-based leading label manufacturer. Interlabels specializes in providing innovative and customized labelling solutions in automatic identification and data capturing (AIDC) using bar coding, RF-ID and biometric-based technology. The company sells AIDC products in the retail, manufacturing, automobile, healthcare, hospitality, sales force, routing accounting, field sales, logistics, utility, and warehousing segments as well as in government agencies. It has partnerships with leading organizations like Symbol Technologies, SATO, Access Inc, Hunno, Georgia Softworks, Ipico, and Ekahu amongst others.

Bar Code India (www.bar codeindia.com)

Bar Code India is a system-integration service provider in the field of AIDC (bar coding, RFID, wireless, and mobile computing) technologies for more than a decade. It develops customer-specific solutions for warehouse and inventory management, point of sales, work-in-process tracking, shipping and distribution, sales force automation, and transportation. These solutions address market verticals of manufacturing, retail, logistics, aviation, healthcare, and hospitality. Bar Code India represents Symbol (now Motorola), Zebra, Intermec, and Microscan for their complete range of bar code scanners and printers, RFID readers and tags, handheld terminals, RF and mobile systems, and wireless infrastructure.

Bartronics (www.bartronics.com)

Established in 1990, Bartronics is a Hyderabad-based company that started with providing solutions in bar coding, one of the oldest AIDC technologies and RFID, POS, and smart cards. It caters to the requirements of the industry and specific applications within an industry with respect to the AIDC/RFID/retail/smart cards related initiatives. The company deals in Intermec 700 series colour mobile computers and other PDTs and DCUs.

EAS AND RFID PRODUCTS

Sensormatic Solutions by ADT Security Systems Inc (www.sensormatic.com)

Sensormatic solutions are delivered through ADT Security Systems Inc in most areas of the world as well as through a global network of distributors and partners of ADT and Tyco. Its products are used to safeguard firefighters, prevent fires, deter thieves, and protect people and property.

Sensormatic solutions provide vital loss prevention and support for the retail industry. Backed by more than 1,500 patents for innovative, market-leading technologies, Today, nearly 80 per cent of the world's top 200 retailers using EAS rely on EAS anti-theft visible and concealed systems as well as tough-to-defeat hard tags, labels, deactivators, and detachers.

Checkpoint Systems, Inc (http://www.checkpointsystems.com)

Established in 1969 in the US, Checkpoint Systems, Inc, today provides radio frequency (RF) based loss-prevention systems to the retail industry. The company manufactures anti-theft devices for retailers worried over retail shrinkage. Product innovation and subsequent introduction in market is the forte of the company. Such products help the retailers in keeping shoplifters at bay. Checkpoint has come up with the latest RF technology, Evolve, which includes increased system performance, enhanced system integrity, enriched data connectivity, investment protection design, efficient cost of ownership, full system connectivity, and aesthetically pleasing designs through Slimline.

Checkpoint sensors offer advanced system features integrated transmitter and receiver electronics. As retail needs evolve, the company designs new systems to be compatible with the existing tag styles and deactivation equipment as well as to enhance performance.

Checkpoint Systems, Inc is a US $834.2 million multinational manufacturer and marketer of technology-driven integrated solutions to protect people and assets and to facilitate the merchandising, tracking, and securing of consumer goods at key checkpoints in the supply chain.

MOBILE COMPUTING DEVICES

VISIONTEK (http://visiontek.co.in)

VISIONTEK e-POS is launched by Linkwell Telesystems (P) Ltd in close cooperation with Visa and Master International, the largest payment system worldwide. VISIONTEK e-POS terminal is the first indigenously developed point-of-sales (POS) terminal in India. It is built on ARM processor based technology with thermal printer and RTC powered by in-built battery backup.

Telserra (www.telserra.com)

Telserra Global Inc, a US-based company, having a research and development arm in India is into solutions based on mobile handheld terminals. The company has developed mobile handheld terminals around GPRS and Bluetooth technology. The terminals are also fitted with tiny dot matrix or thermal printers. The applications running in terminals are customizable with Java-based software development kit.

The application areas identified by the company are POS billing, mobile recharge, gaming and lottery, bus ticketing, parking lot systems, and sales force automation.

SUMMARY

In this chapter, we have discussed various technological products used at retail point of sales. As a manager or future manager of retail businesses, one needs to know the buying processes. The first and foremost task is to understand the need of the organization. Cost estimation and fixing of budgets for the product comes next. The manager must choose a right product by checking references, thus avoiding a mistake by learning from others' mistakes. It has been seen that established manufacturers and vendors always give quality products and provide good service. Everything done, still there is no surety of success. Therefore, the management has to be strong willed to implement solutions, whether hardware or software. Strong will power is needed to thwart off resistance from various quarters in the organization.

Information is collected from various vendors through questionnaires. The questionnaires seek information in standard and homogenous formats so that various vendors can be compared easily. Students and managers can design their own formats, which are as per the products and organization's needs.

There are a number of products and their vendors for each type of retail technology products. The chapter covers only a few well-known products and vendors. The students can explore further.

CONCEPT REVIEW QUESTIONS

1. What are the various steps in making a purchase decision for technology products?
2. What type of questionnaire will you give to various vendors implementing RFID solutions at retail stores?

CRITICAL THINKING QUESTION

1. Design a hypothetical questionnaire for evaluating self-checkout products and their vendors.

PROJECTS

1. Log on to various sites of retail IT solutions and product suppliers. Explore more products, features, and functionalities offered by them.
2. Compare three retail ERP products based on their features, installation base, and pricing structure.

Glossary

Application server — Software that handles all applications between user client and back-end application or databases.

Application software — A program created to perform certain task for the end-users.

Arithmetic logic unit (ALU) — A segment of the CPU that performs all arithmetical and logical calculations in the computer.

ASP — Application service provider (ASP) is a vendor providing software on pay-per-use basis, usually over the Net or private network; a third-party specialist who owns and manages applications and application servers.

Automation — Using computers to bring in efficiency in the work.

B2B commerce — Buying and selling of goods and services between two organizations.

B2C commerce — Selling and buying of goods and services between an organization and the end-consumer.

Back office — A physical space like head office and warehouse of the company; covers functional modules, such as merchandise management, vendor management, price management, distribution, human resource, and finance.

Backbone — A part of a network handling the major traffic and providing the primary path for traffic flow.

Bar code — A type of optical character-recognition technology used for identification, in which the data is coded into series of bars.

BASIC — *Acronym for* beginners' all-purpose symbolic instruction code.

Bespoke development — Development of a software solution from scratch; also known as custom-built development.

Best-of-breed software — A POS software system that runs independently at the retail outlet and have all the basic functions of sales, purchase, stocks, and reporting.

Big bang approach — An ERP system implementation approach in which all modules of the ERP software are implemented in one go across all functional departments and business units of the company.

Bill hold — The process of suspending a billing exercise temporarily to allow the retail customer to pick some more articles.

Bill sundries	Levies and incidentals required in billing, such as discounts, taxes, freight, and delivery charges.
Biometrics	Automated methods of recognizing a person based on a physiological or behavioural characteristic.
Bit	A binary digit representing the smallest unit of data; represented by either 0 or 1.
Bridge	A unit used to connect two networks using the same protocol.
Broadband	A high-speed transmission technology.
Business model approach	A system of implementation in which a global prototype is developed, followed by a geographical roll-out across all business units.
Business process re-engineering	Radical changes in the process of carrying out businesses by eliminating repetitive tasks, reducing wastages, and, improving quality.
Byte	A string of eight bit; used as a unit of measurement of memory.
C2C commerce	Selling of goods and services by a consumer to another consumer.
CDMA	Code division multiple access (CDMA) is a method of digital wireless transmission wherein a specialized code is used as the basis of channelling.
Cellular telephony	A radio-based system that works over a certain radio frequency (RF).
Centralized processing	A kind of processing that is done by a large centralized computer system.
Change agent	A system that works as a catalyst to re-engineer the work processes within an organization.
Client	A computer with a user that receives data and resources from the server.
Clint-server computing	A computing system in which the processing is distributed between the clients and the servers on a network.
Clock speed	The internal speed of a computer, measured in megahertz (MHz). (A computer of 1 MHz speed can perform 1 million cycles per second.)
Coaxial cable	A cable made of two cables, a central solid wire, usually made of copper, covered by a mesh or foil of metal; used for connecting computers in a network.
COBOL	*Acronym for* common business-oriented language.

Communication backbone	A fast and wide communication channel to support high degree of data flow.
Communication technology	Physical devices and software products that link various computer hardware products; used to transfer data from one location to another.
Compiler	Special system software written to translate high-level language into machine language.
Construction	Customization within the scope of the gap analysis in ERP implementation.
Control unit	Control and coordination between various parts and components of a computer.
Convergence of ICT	Coming together of computers and telephones—information and communication technologies (ICT).
CPU	Central processing unit (CPU) is the main unit of a computer, which controls other parts of the computer system and performs processing of data and instructions.
Credit cards	Electronic payment cards that help in payment transactions with the help of banks.
Credit note	A physical voucher issued to a customer against his/her returns value, which is sealed and signed by the retailer and honoured for future purchases.
CRM	Customer relationship management (CRM) comprises the business processes that relate with the customers.
Cryptography	A data-encoding method involving a pair of numeric keys that are very large integers.
Customer insights	Understanding the customers and knowing their tastes and preferences by analysing sales data.
Customization	Making changes in software involving changes in the source code to meet the requirements of individual customer.
Data	Raw facts and figures about organization and objects before they are processed to convert into information.
Data dictionary	A tool that maintains information about data stored in a database.
Data element	A field name or header of data.
Data mining	The process of extracting data from data warehouses.
Data normalization	The process of removing all duplicate data that has crept in because of variety of data sources.
Data redundancy	The presence of duplicate data in various data files.

Data warehousing	Maintaining a single, centralized, and unified repository of data that works across the enterprise.
Database privileges	The assigned rights and privileges to work on various modules, menus, and sub-menus.
Day registration	The system of logging in to the EPOS for keeping record of individual logins and logouts for security reasons and shift change.
DBA	Database administration (DBA) refers to the technical and operational aspect of managing data, designing physical database, and maintenance.
DBMS	Database management system (DBMS) is used for creating, storing, and retrieving data and information from the structured file system.
Decision support systems	The information systems that support the management at the top level with analytical reports combining internal and external data.
Dedicate lines	Telecommunication lines available for continuous transmission to the lessee organization.
Digital signature	A cryptographic system for verification and authentication of electronic documents.
Distributed computing	The distribution of computer processing work among multiple computers linked by a network.
Distributed processing	Use of multiple computers linked by communications networks for processing.
Documentation	Creation of documents that describe the system from technical or user's point of view.
Domain name	The unique name of a node on the Internet.
Dynamic web page	A web page in which the information changes regularly as the organization maintaining the page interacts with the customer or viewer and changes its content in response to visitors' queries.
EAN bar codes	European article number (EAN) bar codes are universally applicable bar codes.
E-cash	Currency represented in electronic form.
E-commerce	Sales and purchase of goods and services and related transactions carried out through the Internet and related digital technologies.
EDI	Electronic data interchange (EDI) is the direct computer-to-computer exchange of standard documents between two or more partner organizations.

EDP	Electronic data processing (EDP) refers to entering, sorting, grouping, and retrieving data using computers.
Electronic fund transfer	Transfer of funds initiated through an electronic terminal, a telephonic instrument, or a computer.
E-mail	Computer-to-computer exchange of messages.
Enterprise systems	The information systems that cover the entire organization and integrate key business processes and enable unhindered flow of information across the organization.
EPOS	Electronic point of sales (EPOS) refers to billing system on a computer equipped with software, bar code scanner, etc.
E-procurement	The processing of purchase order system through the Internet.
E-R diagram	Entity-relationship (E-R) diagram illustrates the relationship between various entities in a database.
ERP	Enterprise resource planning (ERP) is an integrated information system that is built on a single platform, using unified database, and covers the entire organization's key business processes.
E-tailing	Retailing through the Web, i.e. direct sale of products, information, and service through virtual stores on the Web.
Exchange of goods	The situation wherein a customer wants to return an item she has purchased earlier and takes a new product in lieu of the old.
Feasibility study	The preliminary study to ascertain if the proposed solution is achievable within the resource constraints.
Fibre optic cables	The cables that carry signals in the form of light.
FORTRAN	*Acronym for* formula translation.
Front office	A retail outlet that covers functions related to the product sales and customer management.
Gateways	The communication processors that connect dissimilar networks and are entrance points for another network in the network path.
GIS	Geographic information system (GIS) is a computer-based information system used to digitally represent and analyse the geographic features present on the earth's surface.
GPS	Global positioning system (GPS) is a technology that can give accurate position of an object anywhere on the earth based on the latitude and longitude.
Goods-on-approval sale	A system in which local retailers deliver goods to 'known' customers without making a bill. The bills are made once the product is approved by the customer.

GPRS	General packet radio service (GPRS) is a communication method that transmits packets of data over a network via RF signals.
GUI	Graphic user interface (GUI) is the user interface that offers icons for executing a command by clicking the mouse instead of writing commands in the computer.
Hardware	The physical equipment used for input, processing, and output activities in an information system.
Home page	The introductory page that opens on the World Wide Web and contains text and graphics.
Hosted solutions	Setting up enterprise solutions over the Internet that enables the business firms to access the ERP software round the clock as per its requirements using the Internet connectivity via a browser.
HTML	Hypertext mark-up language (HTML) is a standard language used to write web pages, using the instructions called tags to specify how a data of varying nature is placed on a document.
HTTP	Hypertext transfer protocol (HTTP) is a communication standard used to transfer pages on the Web.
Hubs and switches	The devices that provide a junction for data transmission from one direction to another.
Images	Pictures downloaded from the servers by clients.
Implementation	Installation of application and training to end-users.
Implementation methodology	A road map of project implementation.
Implementation strategies	Preparing the organization to take up the task, ascertain the budget, start resource development, and set objectives and benchmarks.
Information	The data that have been processed to become meaningful and useful to humans.
Information systems	The interrelated components working to collect, process, store, and distribute information to support decision-making.
Input	Raw data collected and entered in the computer through a device or system.
Interactive kiosks	Computers, preferably with touch-screen monitors, that provide information about the store, products, and services.
Internet	The network of networks connecting computers worldwide through telecommunication channels.

Internet browser	The software that works as an interface between the user and the computer and downloads text, pictures, and images from the server to the client computer.
Interpreter	A special utility that executes a program without compiling it. A compiler translates the source code in (English language) into machine-level language.
Intranet	A private network owned and managed by a single person or organization.
IP address	Internet protocol (IP) address is a four-part numeric address that indicates the location of a computer on the Internet.
KPIs	Key performance indicators (KPIs) are the defining benchmarks for testing success of ERP once the solution has been implemented and stabilized in the organization.
Knowledge level	The information system that supports knowledge workers in the organization.
Knowledge management systems	The systems that help in creation, storage, and dissemination of knowledge.
KOT	Kitchen order ticket (KOT) is a customer's order to waiters.
LAN	Local area network (LAN) is networking among computers located at a limited distance, usually one floor or close floors on the same building.
Legacy systems	The in-house developed solutions or those developed by third-party consultants for the specific needs of the organizations.
Localization	Changes in the software to suit the requirements of a particular place or country.
Machine language	A program code written in binary digits of 1 and 0.
Mainframes	The first-generation computers, which were very large in size and used for large business data processing.
Management level	The system that supports managerial functions of decision-making, monitoring, and controlling of business activities.
Manual billing	Writing bills with hands in case of computer failure.
M-commerce	Conducting business transactions over mobile data network using mobile handheld terminals, such as personal digital assistants (PDAs), mobile phones, and palmtops.
MHz	A unit of measurement of cycle speed. (One MHz is equal to one million cycles per second.)

Microprocessor	The integrated circuit technology that integrates the computer's memory, logic, and control on a single chip.
Microwave communication	A mode of communication that requires line-of-sight transmission and reception equipment.
Middleware	A piece of software that connects two diverse applications and allows them to communicate and exchange data.
Mini computers	The second generation of computers used for large data processing.
MIS	Management information systems (MIS) are the systems that focus on the use of information in management of business and supports the business with basic summary and exception reports.
Mobile computing	Computing through mobile handheld terminals, such as personal digital assistants (PDAs), mobile phones, and palmtops.
Mobile data networks	Wireless networks explicitly designed for two-way transmission of data files.
Modem	Modulator and demodulator (modem) is a device that translates digital signals into analogue signals and vice versa.
MRN	Material receipt note (MRN) is a document generated while receiving goods from a supplier.
Multimedia	The integration of two or more types of media, such as text, graphics, sound, and moving pictures.
Multiple database portability	Ability of an ERP system to run on multiple database management systems.
Multiplexer	A device that enables a single communications channel to carry data from multiple sources simultaneously.
Multitasking	The capability to perform more than one task at a time.
Network operating system (NOS)	The system software that manages the communication on the network and manages the resources.
Networks	The linking of two or more computers to share data and resources.
OLAP	Online analytical processing (OLAP) is a capability of manipulating and analysing a large volume of data from various data tables.
Open source	A concept that propagates non-proprietary rights on the product and allows developments, changes, and improvement in the software by any user, mentor, or developer.

Operating systems	The systems managing and controlling various activities of the computer and providing utilities for file and peripherals management.
Operational level	The system where basic transactions of a business are carried out.
Output	The distribution of processed information to the end-user through a device like monitor or printer in computer.
Outsourcing	The practice of contracting operations and software development activities.
P2P payment	People-to-people (P2P) payment system allows a person to pay on behalf of the other. Both the payer and payee must be registered with the middle person or service provider.
Payment modes	Settlement of bills through various payment types, such as cash, credit card, cheque, and coupon.
Personal computer	The modern-day computer that an individual can own and operate.
Phased approach	An implementation approach wherein the implementation is done in phases.
Pilot approach	A strategy to introduce a new system to a limited area of the organization. Once successful, it is replicated to other areas.
Primary storage	A part of computer that temporarily stores program instructions and data; also known as memory of the computer system.
Programming language	An instruction code to the computer that gets translated into the binary numbers.
Protocol	A set of rules and procedures that govern communication between two devices or components on a network.
Prototype	The preliminary working version of an information system.
Proximity technology	A contact-less payment system built on a device that reads information from a distance.
Query language	A high-level computer language used to retrieve specific information from databases.
RF	Radio frequencies (RF) are radio waves carrying data over a network.
RAM	Random-access memory is a temporary memory that can be accessed randomly.

RDBMS	Relational database management system (RDBMS) is a database management system that establishes relationship between two tables of the database as long as they share a common data element.
Remote data access	Accessing data into computer through a mobile device while away from the server.
Repeater	A device that regenerates a weakening signal on a network path.
Replenishment	The process of filling up stocks again at the retail outlet usually against the sales made during a particular time period.
Return of goods	Return is used if a customer returns an item and does not buy a new product in lieu of the old one.
RFID	Radio frequency identification device (RFID) is used for product tracking and anti-theft measure in retail.
ROM	Read-only memory (ROM) is a memory chip that contains program instructions. It is a permanent memory and the retrieval is sequential in nature.
Router	A hardware device or software product that acts like a station on the network.
SaaS	Software as a service (SaaS) is a concept of renting out software as a service instead of buying it as a product.
Satellite communication	Communication through the satellites orbiting the earth; the satellite functions as a very large antenna and repeater.
Scalability	The ability of a computer or software system to expand with requirement without breaking down.
SCM	Supply chain management (SCM) comprises business and technology processes involving buying, storing, and moving the product.
SDLC	Software development life cycle (SDLC) involves various stages and phases in development of a software product.
Server	A system comprising specialized computers designed to serve data and resources to other computers over a network.
Servicescape	Physical surrounding on the customers and employees at a service delivery point.
SKU	Stock-keeping unit (SKU) refers to products. Each product in its stockable identity is called SKU.
Smart card	A plastic card capable of storing digital information in the embedded chip, which is also used as electronic payment system.

Social networking sites The websites where people can participate in a collaborative, socially-oriented way and create their personal web profiles; and the interactions are perceived to be personally enjoyable and beneficial.

Software A set of instructions given to a computer to perform a certain task. It controls and coordinates various hardware components.

Source code Program instructions written in high-level language that is compiled and converted into machine language before execution.

Source labelling A system of bar code labeling in which the barcode labels are put on the product at the vendor/manufacturing stage.

SQL Structured query language (SQL) is a system of extracting data from the database using commands.

SSL Secure sockets layer (SSL) technology secures websites by encrypting information and providing authentication.

Static web page A web page that rarely changes the information it displays.

Stock transfers The movement of goods between the own branches/retail outlets of the organization.

Strategic level The system that supports top-level decisions pertaining to long-term planning.

Strategies The plans (*in the context of ERP implementation*) that involve preparing an organization to take up the task of planning and implementing ERP.

System analysis One of the steps in development of software in which a problem is analysed to enable the organization to design a suitable solution.

System design Defining organization structure for ERP implementation. (ERP package is later configured through parameter setting to accommodate this organization structure and gaps or 'to-be-built' findings.)

System software The software that controls and coordinates between various hardware functions in a computer; manages computer resources, file system, other hardware peripherals, and communication links.

TCP/IP Transmission control protocol/Internet protocol (TCP/IP) comprises standardized rules of linking different types of computer networks in the Internet.

Telecommunications The transfer of information by electronic means and telephone lines over some distance.

Topology The shape and configuration of a computer network.

Touch-screen system　An electronic point-of-sales system with touch-screen monitor, in which the user has to touch large icons with finger instead of clicking the mouse.

Transaction processing systems　Computerized systems that perform and record day-to-day transactions related to basic business activities.

Twisted pair cables　A set of two or more insulated copper cables used for connecting computers in a network.

URL　Universal resource locator (URL) is the address of a specific resource on the Internet.

User interface　The part of a computer system through which the user interacts with the system.

VPN　Virtual private network (VPN) is a secure private network over the Internet for transmission and sharing of corporate data.

WAN　Wide area network (WAN) is a computer network that is scattered over a large geographical distance.

Blog　An advanced form of diary on the Web, which one can update and keep open for his/her peer-group to see; a personal home page.

Web browser　A software tool that accesses the World Wide Web and Internet.

Web content management tools　Software tools and utilities that help manage and manipulate text and graphics on a website.

Web-hosting services　Maintaining large web servers and renting out space on those servers to a number of people.

Web portal　Web pages through which e-commerce trading is accomplished.

Web server　Hardware and software that manage user requests for Web page and display it on his/her computer.

Wireless networks　Wireless transmission that sends signals through air, water, or space without any physical cable.

WWW　The Word Wide Web (WWW) is a system with universally accepted standards (protocols) for storing, retrieving, formatting, and displaying information using client-server architecture.

Word length　The number of bits one computer processes at a time.

XML　Extensible mark-up language (XML) is a further development over HTML. While HTML only determines how text and images are displayed on a document, XML further specifies the meaning or detail of the data on the pages.

Index